"This pastoral guide by a director
munity hospital...offers a comt
poetic advice for those who mu
that's all of us."

"Chaplain Meyer obviously possesses the credentials to illuminate the experiences of dying and assisting others to die. It is clear that he has, as a hospital chaplain, listened carefully and sensitively to many hundreds of persons who are dying themselves or who grieve for the the death of others. He has no patience with cliches, slogans, or myths, least of all from those in roles of religious leadership for some of whom these glib answers are their stock in trade.

"This is a sensible, thoughtful, balanced, and deeply biblical treatment in fresh and incisive terms."

(The Rt. Rev.) John M. Krumm
Retired Episcopal Bishop

"Chaplain Meyer begins with the premise that 'we are all dying.' By the time the reader reaches the end, it is clear that the book is unsurpassed in its concrete, step-by-step instructions on everything from walking into a patient's room, to talking with dying and bereaved individuals, and coping with the full range of emotions and behavioral demands that survivors face.

"There are many books on death and dying for professional and lay readers, but this primer will certainly surface to the top of recommended reading both for helpers and also for the dying and bereaved themselves."

Karl A. Slaikeu, Ph.D.
author of *Up From the Ashes*

"...an excellent book for terminal patients and their families, pastors (who may get needed pushing around), hospital personnel, ethicists, and families on the journey through grief....Very basic, offered in a caring, organized, refreshing way....The material on post-death grief, as well as ethics, offers important new insights that will stir up considerable discussion and reflection."

Chaplain Richard B. Gilbert
The Bereavement Support Group

|||||||||||||||||||||||||||||||||||||||||||||||||||||||||||||||||||||||||||||||||||||||||||||||||||||||||||||||||||||||||||||||||||||||||||

"A sensitive, helpful guide to a subject we need to think about. Charles Meyer opens new attitudes and offers specific steps to make death the natural part of life that it is."

Liz Carpenter
author, *Getting Better All the Time*

|||||||||||||||||||||||||||||||||||||||||||||||||||||||||||||||||||||||||||||||||||||||||||||||||||||||||||||||||||||||||||||||||||||||||||

"Out of a rich experience as a hospital chaplain, Charles Meyer has written a sensitive work that will help everyone concerned with death and dying: medical practitioners, nurses, caregivers, relatives, friends, and bereaved. This work will help us to avoid the common mistakes and to cope with confidence with what most of us dread."

Reginald H. Fuller
Professor Emeritus of New Testament
Virginia Theological Seminary

Surviving Death

•

A PRACTICAL GUIDE TO CARING FOR THE DYING & BEREAVED

CHARLES MEYER

TWENTY-THIRD PUBLICATIONS
Mystic, Connecticut

Second printing   1988

Twenty-Third Publications
185 Willow Street
P.O. Box 180
Mystic, CT 06355
(203) 536-2611

ISBN 0-89622-364-7
Library of Congress Catalog Card Number 88-72011

For Parents, Mentors, and Friends

CONTENTS

APPENDICES

Introduction

There are many books on "death and dying." This is a book on survival. It developed out of my experience with dying patients and their families over the last nine years at St. David's Community Hospital in Austin, Texas. In the course of that work I was asked by community organizations for help in dealing with the practical and emotional difficulties experienced by those involved with dying persons.

As I talked with these groups it quickly became clear to me that the only preparation for handling these issues came from individual family traditions. People learned how to cope with death by watching how their parents and relatives coped. There was no formal training, no open explanation of what to do or how to do it, no educational program designed to deal with personal and societal options for death, funerals, and bereavement. Indeed, my own training in college, seminary, and post-graduate school contained few or no options for the exploration of these inevitable concerns.

Because of the fear and denial associated with death, our cultural and religious institutions have relegated the responsibility for dealing with the issues surrounding death and dying to hospitals and funeral homes. But these two organizations, themselves cloaked in clinical and social mystique, have no particular monopoly on appropriate responses to dying patients, much less to bereavement. It is strange that religious institutions particularly have capitulated this responsibility to the medical establishment, which often behaves as though no one should ever die, and to the funeral home industry which, knowing everyone will, seeks to turn a profit from it.

This book addresses death and dying from many viewpoints. Dealing first with the dying process, it offers specific suggestions for what to do (and not do) with the patient and family. In exploring how we make decisions about refusing, withdrawing or withholding life support measures, we will discuss first those ethical issues which have been brought about by the increasingly technological environment in which dying occurs. The failure of the church to deal directly with these issues is examined next, along with theological misconceptions used to describe the dying process. Finally, we will assess the tasks of bereavement, including sexual interactions after the death of a loved one, and offer practical options for grieving persons as well as for those who wish to be of help to them.

This book focuses upon the caregiver; thus I hope the information and suggestions will be used by and useful to family members, nurses, physicians, Hospice and other home health workers and volunteers, as well as to high school, college and, in particular, medical school and seminary students.

I am indebted to many persons for the information presented here. Dana Joslin, R.N. and the staff of the 4 West Oncology Unit at St. David's Community Hospital welcomed me into their network of team care and educated me about the appropriate way to be around dying people. Phoebe Kelly, R.N., and her Intensive Care Nursery staff taught me how to respond to dying infants and their parents, as did Wanda Lary, R.N., and the Labor and Delivery nurses. Physicians John Sandbach, Dennis Welch, Harold Cain, Ruth Bain, and Don Spencer are among the many who offered varying models of bedside care with dying patients. The staff of St. David's Community Hospital, with their incredible ability to go out of their way to be caring and helpful, taught me about the value of the healing team—whether from housekeeping, dietary, business office, or security—in meeting the whole array of needs of the persons in our charge.

With regard to this manuscript, I am grateful to Julia Hamilton and Dana Joslin for their careful reading, thoughtful suggestions and gentle editing. Their time and effort provided clarity and encouragement, and resulted in a more complete presentation of the material.

The piece entitled "Hospice Volunteer" is included with the permission of Jean Loving, who served faithfully as a volunteer with St. David's Hospital and Hospice/Austin for many years. Her insights empathically summarize much of the didactic content of the rest of the book, and I am grateful for her viewpoint.

The three poems are by Kathyrn Morfey, a practicing Episcopalian and attorney in Southampton, England. Written in response to her eldest son's sudden accidental death (leaving a surviving daughter), the poems balance the perspective of the rest of the material. They are sensitive, thoughtful, and healing. I very much appreciate her permission to offer them here.

Most importantly, I am indebted to the patients and families themselves who have taught me about the incredible resilience of the human spirit. In the midst of coping with horrible debilities, excruciating pain, tortuous treatments, and embarrassing side effects, they lived and died with dignity, humor, defiance, sadness, and faith. These patients, along with the families who struggled with, and sometimes against, them in that process grieved loudly and softly with anger and acceptance, pain and relief. It is they who taught me the following lessons as we journeyed together on the road to surviving death.

I

BEING WITH THE DYING

1

How to Be With Dying Persons

We all are dying. There will come a time when each person reading these pages will not be alive. But there are some people who know they are dying before us. They have been diagnosed with a terminal illness, injured in an accident, or born with a congenital condition that guarantees a short lifespan. It is interesting that we treat these people differently than we treat each other. We treat them as though *they* are dying and *we* are not, as though death is a secret that must be guarded or a taboo that must be avoided at all costs.

Still, a part of us feels obligated to tell the secret and approach the taboo. We want to show our affection without being sad and teary. We want to ask what the person thinks and feels about dying without appearing to be intrusive or impolite. We want to share our own fears and hopes without sounding morose or unrealistic. We want to be of help but we don't know how.

There is no "right" way to behave toward a dying person. There are, however, some general principles to remember that will enhance your effectiveness and make your time together more meaningful. Because each person is different, the information presented here can offer only general guidelines. Each person can then incorporate the suggestions into his or her own particular style and method of interacting with the dying person.

Contrary to popular literature and belief, there are no "stages" of dying. The Kübler-Ross categories are helpful for observing the different behaviors likely to be seen in people who are dying. But the denial, anger, bargaining, depression, and acceptance are not always in the sequence she describes. For instance, the patient's first reaction might be anger, but it might also be bargaining or acceptance, depending on a whole list of psychological and sociological variables affecting that person. Likewise, it is not unusual for a dying patient to show depression, denial, and acceptance—all in the course of a few days, or even hours.

Thus, to simplify matters, and to avoid the already overused "stages," we will divide the time frame of dealing with a dying person into three parts: *Before, During, and After,* and will explore separately what to do—and not do—during each time.

Before. In the time preceding the death of the patient, the most important thing to remember is *be there.*

Be there consistently, as often as the patient wants you there and as frequently as your own time schedule permits. When the person is initially diagnosed, or is initially hospitalized, friends flock around for the first two weeks. They bring flowers, they offer to run errands, they stop by the hospital room with somber expressions on their faces. Wondering what to say, they try to be cheerful, offering assurances that the sick person will be just fine, and avoiding any talk of death. Then they vanish.

Naturally, people do go on with their lives when a friend or family member is initially diagnosed. Babies need to be fed, kids taken to ballet class, spouses looked after, and personal needs met. But, for the patient, a sudden change has occurred that has radically rearranged his or her outlook on life. Things that were extremely important before hearing the words "incurable," "comfort measures," or "attempt to slow the process down," are now of minor interest. Things that were taken for granted—personal projects, family relationships, friendships—are now of the highest value. The patient's life continues to go on, but with a very different perspective, and she or he may wish to share it with the very people who have suddenly disappeared.

The most common complaints, and the most poignant ones, from terminally ill patients involve isolation.

"The worst thing about this is the loneliness."

"Nobody will talk to me anymore. I feel like I've done something wrong."

"Where are my friends? Where did they all go?"

"Why won't anyone listen to me talk about death?"

But being there consistently does not mean devoting every waking minute to the needs of the patient. It means continuing to go on with your own life just as everyone else does. However, unlike most everyone else, it also means continuing to maintain regular contact with the person. Whether the contact is in the form of a personal visit, a periodic phone call or letter or card, or a weekly game time or night out together (depending on the acuity of the illness), what is important is the certainty of a consistent, continuing relationship.

Most people, for whatever reason, will abandon the dying patient at some point. But to continue to stay in touch consistently with that patient reinforces the value of his or her life and indicates that you are not being scared off by the dying process. Maintaining contact on a regular basis will also, over a period of time, build the kind of relationship that will allow the patient to share with you thoughts, feelings, fears, wishes, dreams, and hopes that begin to surface as she or he comes to terms with dying. As that reality sets in, you, based on your regular contact, may be the person the patient feels most comfortable with to share ideas and opinions, or to make final plans.

It is important to remember, however, that you and your family still have obligations and duties to be maintained. You can, without feeling guilty, set limits on your involvement with the dying patient just as you would with anyone else. Everyone has realistic boundaries that preclude being at someone's beck and call every minute. Dying patients (just like the rest of us dying living folks) can understand that and appreciate the honesty. The object is to continue to go on with your life *and also* to maintain a consistent relationship of care, assistance and support with the patient throughout the entire course of the illness.

As you begin to spend time with the dying patient, from the initial diagnosis through the final breaths, be sure to *listen more than talk*. If you notice during the course of the conversation that all the words are coming from your mouth, something is wrong. Either you're not listening to what the patient is trying to say, you really don't want to hear about the pain and the death, or you're trying to cheer the patient up and avoid "unpleasant" topics, topics like the reality of dying.

It is important to *follow the patient's agenda* as you spend time in that room. Listen carefully for the clues dropped for you to follow: feelings of uncertainty as to the outcome of the illness ("I'm not sure I should bother with further treatment"); fear or apprehension about getting better ("I hope I live to see my hair grow back"); concerns about caring for the family now and later ("I wish I could be home to cook dinner tonight").

Most patients will let you know what they are willing to talk about and what they are not. It is not *required* that dying patients talk about their illness and death. Some will and some won't. What *is* required is that their friends listen to their agenda and follow it wherever it leads—from weather to whether or not they'll survive, from sports to life supports, from daily news to the latest news of their test results.

If, for whatever reason, dialogue is difficult, look around the room for clues about the person's family or friends or support system:

• Are there photographs? Who are the people? What are the relationships? Are there books lying near the bed? Ask about them.

• Are there religious materials in the room? Inquire about the person's religious background. How does he or she see God in this illness? What religious resources can be brought into the situation? Would the patient appreciate a visit from the clergy, Bible study or prayer group, or a bedside service of prayer, communion, sacrament of the sick, or baptism? Does the person wish to go to church "one last time?"

• Is the room fairly vacant and bare? What does that mean? Does it mean the patient has no friends, does not want money wasted on flowers, or does not want to be reminded that she or he is ill?

Never say to the patient: "I know how you feel." The truth is, even if you have been through a similar illness or hospitalization, neither you nor anyone else *knows* how the patient feels. Likewise, do not bring in pamphlets or articles describing miracle cures or suggesting how to deal with pain and death. Such information is extremely unhelpful, angering, and depressing for the patient.

Whatever ideas come to mind as you talk with the dying patient/family always *ask* rather than *assume*. Something that might be extremely helpful for you in the situation might not be helpful at all for the patient. Your presumption about the meaning of something the patient has said, an object you see in the room, or about what you think the patient "should" be thinking or doing may be totally inaccurate. Check out any hunches you may have directly with the patient. When in doubt, *ask*.

As you listen to the patient, help him or her to clarify whether it is "death" or "dying" that is most problematic or fearful. Since, at some level of our being, we all know that death is inevitable, most people fear the process of dying much more than death. Concerns range from uncertainty regarding pain control and loss of physical and mental functions to the effect of the patient's disability on family members, both emotionally and financially.

"Will I die with tubes running in and out of every orifice I've got and some I didn't start out with?"

"Will I die with loss of bowel and bladder control and be infantilized?"

"Will I die with brain cancer causing loss of control of my words and making me say things that are terrible to my loved ones?"

"Will I die in excruciating pain?"

"Will I die knowing I am dying, yet unable to do anything about it?"

"Will I die not knowing my loving spouse of many years, but knowing the nurse who has taken care of me only a few days?"

Some patients, however, will be worried about the afterlife and will want to talk with someone about religious beliefs and practices.

"What will happen to me after I'm dead?"

"Where will I go?"

"Will I see my family again? My children? My wife? My parents?"

"What happens if I don't get into heaven?"

Thus, an extremely helpful resource to the patient and family can be their relationship to a religious congregation or member of the clergy. (This can also be disastrous, as will be discussed later.) Does the patient have a religious affiliation? Is that group willing to be of help? In some cases the congregation will supply money to help through difficult times. People from different church groups may volunteer to provide food, transportation, child-sitting service, or help with homework. They may even provide persons to stay a few hours during the day (or overnight) in the hospital room with the patient to give the family members a break from the intensity of the hospitalization and allow them to take care of the normal business details that inevitably pile up when someone is ill.

You will quickly find, however, that most people have no church, synagogue or clergy affiliation whatsoever. A recent Gallup poll found that fewer than 40 percent of Americans had any current such affiliation. In this case, many service organizations (for example, Lions, Kiwanis, Rotary, Eastern Star, Hospital Auxiliary) will provide the same service. Again, ask the patient or family about these suggestions before acting on them. It may be that they want no outside involvement at all.

Another organization that can be incredibly helpful throughout the course of the illness, the death of the patient, and the following period of bereavement with the family is Hospice. If there is a Hospice of some kind in your vicinity, check with the family or physician (most hospices require a physician's order) to see about their involvement. Sometimes the Hospice is a building, or a place patients go to die. Often, it is a program, using a variety of community resources to enable the patient to die at home. Usually a trained volunteer is assigned to the patient to be a friendly support, a listener, a companion on the final journey. It is the job of the Hospice team to help patients live those final days as fully as they are able.

Medicare patients now have the option of signing in to the Medicare Hospice program. While normal Medicare reimburses 80 percent of reasonable costs, the Medicare Hospice program reimburses at 100 percent of such costs. But the focus of care becomes *palliative only*. This means that, once the determination is made that the patient is dying, care will be aimed at comfort only, not at aggressive treatment. Usually no more CAT scans or surgery will be done, no more blood or chemotherapy will be given, tubes may be withheld or withdrawn, and antibiotics will probably not be administered in case of infection. And, of course, the patient's "code status" (resuscitative status) will switch to DNR (Do Not Resuscitate.)

Many patients and families are likely to choose this option as a reasonable alternative to aggressive, high-tech, high-cost dying. In any case, they will need caring, competent people around to help with these and other decisions.

At an appropriate time it is important to raise the issue of *death planning*. This need not be done with a morose tone or a sense of foreboding. Usually the patient will make a direct or indirect statement concerning "what will happen." At this or any other timely point, you can simply ask matter-of-factly, "Well, have you thought about any funeral plans?" Most patients are not shocked at this inquiry and, in fact, welcome the opportunity to talk about what arrangements they want and do not want.

In addition it is a good idea to check out other related areas:

• Do they have a legal, binding will?

• Do they have a durable power of attorney in case they become incapacitated?

• Have they talked with a funeral director (and, even more importantly, with their family) and decided on the arrangements, casket of choice, type of service, hymns, and readings?

• Have they chosen someone to do the service?

• Do they want to be embalmed, viewed, cremated, buried? (All of these?)

• Have they made a decision regarding organ donations? Are they registered with The Living Bank or an Organ Procurement Agency so those wishes will be honored?

• Have they made a decision regarding extraordinary life support? Do they have a Living Will so that decision might be honored?

• Have they filled out a "Death Planning Record" indicating all of these decisions?

Finally, it is much easier for you to ask these questions of others if you have made your own plans for yourself. If you have not faced these issues, you are probably not going to feel comfortable talking about them with the patient. In fact, you may not even *hear* the patient raise the issue due to your own hesitation or fear about it. If you really want to be helpful to dying persons, take the time to make your own plans, in writing, and to discuss them with your family. Then, as issues arise, you will be much better able—and willing—to face them with the patient.

During. During the actual time of the patient's dying, the most important thing you can do is, once again, *be there.* Be there as much as the patient and family want you there. A disinterested or less involved third party can often take care of the many small tasks that need to be done, such as making phone calls, cancelling or making arrangements, and organizing meals and relatives. You can also provide small comforts to ease the pain of being at the bedside, both for the patient and the family: cold cloths for the forehead of the patient, wet washcloths gently passed over the mouth or tongue to provide moisture to the dry wheezing breath, pillows carefully placed, blankets or bright quilts to maintain warmth, fans to circulate air and ease breathing, favorite music gently playing in the background.

It is hard to overstate the indelible impression made on family members in this trying time. To be there with them, providing comfort for them and their loved one is both a privilege and a gift. Your presence will be remembered always, the small tasks you performed never forgotten. But being there also means knowing what to do while there, even modeling the appropriate behavior so the other persons present will learn from you what to do.

Most people have no idea what to do around dying persons. Although many courses in death and dying deal extensively with psychological reactions, seldom do they give concrete suggestions for being at the bedside. Simply put, the most helpful things to remember are to *touch and talk.*

Tactility (the sense of touch) and hearing are the last two senses to diminish as one dies. In fact, the more the other senses fade due to coma or medication, the more sensitive and acute touch and hearing become. Contrary to the opinion of some physicians and other healthcare practitioners, it is clear that even comatose or highly sedated patients can hear and feel touch. Many times, those persons working daily with dying patients have seen responses to particular voices, individual touches and special persons entering the room. Reactions range from a sense of panic to obvious relaxation, depending on which person arrives.

In addition, the comatose or sedated person loses a sense of body boundaries, forgetting or not being able to tell where the body ends and the bed begins. Thus it is extremely important to keep touching the patient. Stroke, caress, hold, pat, or do whatever feels natural to you. You will not only help establish those body boundaries internally but also will be adding comfort and security to a very uncomfortable and insecure situation.

Talking, at first, may be more difficult. We are used to talking *with* someone, sharing information back and forth, holding a conversation. With a comatose or sedated patient who is dying, this type of interaction is obviously not possible. More desirable in this situation is to give information to the dying patient. Often this will help to orient the patient to time, place, and date. It also helps to relieve some of the fear caused by hearing voices in the room but not knowing whose they are.

Caregivers are often the worst offenders in this area. They turn patients, give baths, take temperatures and blood pressures, change i.v.'s, and give medication (even through i.v. lines) without *telling* the comatose, dying patient what they are doing. It is important to remember that these patients can hear and feel touch, may experience an internal change due to the drug or bed positioning, and may be quite fearful of that change. Thus, it is extremely important for caregivers, visitors, family, clergy, housekeeping staff, and others to explain to the patient what is being done and by whom. From fluffing a pillow to changing the sheets, dying patients must be treated as though they were fully cognizant of their surroundings on the strong possibility that they very well are.

Let the patient know who is in the room. Encourage visitors to go to the bedside (and not stay plastered against the wall, gawking) and speak to the patient. Do not *ask* the patient questions since the patient can't respond. *Tell* him or her who is touching an arm or patting a shoulder. Remind the patient of the time and date. (Dates are often important to a dying patient in terms of birthdays, anniversaries, special times of the year.) Reminisce with dying persons, telling pleasant stories or funny incidents that occurred in their lives. (It really is okay to laugh around a deathbed.) Give information about who might be coming to visit and at what time. If a beloved brother or grandchild is arriving at three in the afternoon, the dying patient may wait to die until after that arrival. If it is a less than beloved family member, the patient may decide to die sooner. Caregivers working with dying patients have witnessed both occurrences.

While in the room do not talk about the patient in the past tense, as though already deceased, or in the third person, as though not present or nonexistent. This can be very upsetting for the patient who can hear but not respond to the conversation. The dying patient may think the visitors believe that he or she is already dead and thus disregarded. Continue, instead, to treat him or her as a whole, complete, sentient person deserving of respect and acknowledgment all the way up to the time of death.

A common occurrence, and one promoted by the daytime t.v. soap operas, is demanding that dying patients do tricks for their family and visitors. The scenario usually involves the tearful son or daughter coming in at the last minute from out of town, frantically rushing up to the bedside of the comatose patient and demanding in loud, sobbing tones: "Momma! If you can *hear* me, *squeeze* my hand!" Or ..."*blink* an eye!" Or "...*wiggle* a toe!" Or "...*nod* your head!"

Remember that the patient is using every ounce of energy just to force air in and out of gurgling lungs and so cannot begin to perform these acts to please and reassure the visitor. Imagine yourself in the patient's position: you can hear the request and you very much want somehow to let this loved one know that you do hear, and understand that you are still alive and listening to their words. And yet it is all you can do to breathe or to remember to breathe, to gasp at times for air, to muster your strength to suck in one more shallow breath. You want desperately to "squeeze...blink...wiggle

...or nod" and you just *can't* do it. Imagine how frustrating that would be for you and how disappointed you would feel that you had failed your loved one's last request.

Dying patients have enough to worry about and plenty of hard work to do without being asked to perform and respond in their final moments. Give them information, treat them with the dignity they deserve, and comfort them with touch and talk.

Throughout the length of the illness, and especially during the hours or minutes immediately preceding death, arrangements need to be made for the patient and family member, friend, spouse, or significant other to have *time alone*. Friends and family members frequently forget that a couple has spent twenty, thirty, or fifty years together and might like some personal, or even intimate moments to hold, to touch, to say things one last time before they part. The same need is often present for younger patients and their friends, as well as for infants and parents. Be sensitive to this need for time alone and offer to arrange for it.

Depending upon the religious belief system of the patient, *prayer* can be a meaningful way to comfort and support someone during the dying process. If the patient is lucid and responsive, first *ask* what she or he would like to pray about. Do not assume that you know what's important to the patient at that time.

A woman going in for a Hickman Catheter placement was asked if she wanted to have a prayer. When asked what she wanted to pray about, she replied, "my divorce," a subject she had not mentioned in the entire interview up to that time. Asking patients what they want to pray about is a powerful way to get at the most pressing concerns on their mind at that time.

Next, pay close attention to what is said, as you may be asked to offer it up in prayer. Then ask if the person would like to start or would prefer for you to begin. Gather others in the room around the bedside, touch the patient, tell the patient (if comatose) what you are doing together, and invite his or her participation with you. Keep it relatively short and also invite the persons gathered around the bed to offer their prayers or comments silently or aloud.

Many things may happen at the time of death. (See Appendix.) Usually the patient will wind down slowly, breathing ever more shallowly until the breath finally ceases. Facial contortions, muscle jerks, and skin color changes are not uncommon. Occasionally the contents of the lungs or stomach may be aspirated or vomited up, and loss of bladder and bowel control will result in urine and feces being excreted. Most of the time the death will be quiet and peaceful, aided and supported by all of the things you and others have done by being present there.

After. Following the death, whether immediately or long term, again the most important thing to remember is *be there.* Be attentive without being obtrusive. Be available to hold the survivors as they express their sorrow in the room. Escort them to a waiting area while the nurses remove tubes and prepare the body to be picked up. Help them make the phone call to the funeral home and to begin to make funeral and other arrangements for the coming few days of organized confusion. Offer to help pack up the room for or with them and help them remember to check the bedside table, closet, window sill, and under the bed for personal belongings.

While waiting for the funeral home, ask if you can help with phone calls or food arrangements, gently reminding survivors that they will need to eat to keep up their own strength in the coming days. Ask what they are tentatively planning to do for the next twenty-four hours. This question begins the process of thinking about the future and moving slowly beyond the painful present.

When the funeral home attendant arrives and people have said their goodbyes, there is frequently a reluctance on the part of the family to leave the hospital. It is very difficult, sad, and lonely to leave carrying the remnants of the illness and of the relationship in plastic bags.

Support the family in whatever makes them feel best. There is no need for them to hurry to leave the hospital. They can leave when they feel comfortable or when they gather the strength to do so. Be sure to escort them from the room to the car. The longest walk in the world is from the empty hospital room where a loved one has died to the car that is now filled only with fading flowers and plastic bags of memories.

Because many survivors become disoriented following a death, it is wise to assess their ability to drive. Offer to call a cab, to drive them home, or to follow them in your car if a family member or friend is not available to do so. Walk the survivor(s) into the empty house for the first time, or arrange for someone to be there when they arrive, to help them deal with the feeling and thoughts that will, inevitably, surface.

While the information here has focused primarily on hospitalized patients, the same suggestions apply when the patient is dying at home. The involvement of Hospice, the rising cost of (and lower reimbursement for) inpatient care, and the increasing availability of supportive home care services have combined to enable more and more persons to be at home for the final days of their lives.

Patients frequently want to die amidst the familiar surroundings of their own bedroom or den, maintaining closer contact with neighbors and friends, and having favorite pets at their side. Families, fearing they will be unable to adequately care for their loved one, or thinking they will always see the person dead in that room, usually want the patient to die in the emotionally neutral territory of the hospital. Thus, when the decision is made to die at home, both patient and family will need the constant support and encouragement of friends.

When the patient does die in the home, care must be taken to avoid the extremely unpleasant, though frequent, occurrence of having the EMS (Emergency Medical Services) arrive with lights, sirens, police cars, and fire trucks. In addition, EMS personnel will usually feel obligated to attempt to resuscitate the person, even though the person has been dead for some time.

Proper arrangements often can be made by first calling the physician and then notifying the funeral home. Since laws and practices vary widely from state to state, it is important for the family to check with the physician or Hospice program ahead of time to know how to avoid this potentially traumatizing scene for the family at the moment of death.

Whether the death occurs at home or in the hospital, as time goes by remember to *be there* by periodically checking in with the survivor. Friends, neighbors, and other family members will flock around (just as they did during the initial diagnosis) for about two weeks following the funeral. Then, as is to be expected, they leave and go on with their lives. You may be the *only* person who calls one month, three months, six months, or a year later *on the date of the death* to express your concern and to offer to stop by for coffee, take the person to lunch, and be available to listen. You may be the *only* person who is not afraid to call on holidays, birthdays, anniversaries, or other special times to show your support and risk having the person cry with you. You may be the *only* person who checks in periodically and is willing to hear the pain told and re-lived again and again.

As you maintain contact and continue to hear the survivor's strug-gle with grief, *do not demand* that the survivor hurry up and "get over it." Many persons, due to their own discomfort with death and sad feelings, will push the survivor to "get on with life" and "stop thinking about the past." They will say and do insensitive things, encouraging the grieving person to get rid of personal mementos of the deceased and to take on new commitments, relationships, and obligations so as to ignore the grief and accept the future.

Once again, you may be the *only* person who is not pushing the survivor to change, to date, to go out with people, to throw out clothes or take down pictures, to move and change jobs. You may be the *only* person who is willing to listen to the tears and loneliness, and even encourage their expression, two or three years after the event, with the same empathy you offered on the day of the death.

NEONATAL DEATH

Death of an infant at birth or shortly thereafter is thought by many people to be the most difficult of losses to handle. In addi-tion to the helplessness and innocence that make the death seem unfair, the abrupt ending of a life not yet begun is, for some people, more tragic than death at the conclusion of years of relationships. It is the death of a dream, rather than the death of a memory.

But others express relief that the infant did not live or survive very long. They find it easier to handle the death now than months or even years later. In any case, neonatal death involves some special procedures in addition to the general care of the pa-tient and family described above.

Care relating to the infant and parents follows the same guidelines as with adults: be there, touch and talk, ask rather than assume, listen more than you talk, and offer to be available for other family members. In addition, a hospital staff member (nurse, chaplain, social worker) will offer some options to the parents that will require discussion and support.

If possible, shortly before the time of death, in the Intensive Care Nursery where the infant is attached to artificial support, or in the delivery room where the stillborn is about to be delivered, the parents will be prepared by a staff member for some of the decisions facing them after the death has occurred. They will need to begin thinking about funeral arrangements, religious services, and cremation or burial, depending on the size and weight of the infant or fetus. (Many states set the gestational limit at 20 weeks; if below that number the fetus may be disposed of as tissue, above 20 weeks it must have some legal disposition.) Even if the fetus is under the weight or gestational limit legally requiring such services, the family can still have a funeral and burial if they wish.

Though it may sound macabre to those who have never witnessed such an occasion, the couple also will be offered the opportunity to see and hold the dead infant. After the woman recovers from the anesthesia, or rests from the birthing process, she and the father will be asked, and even encouraged, to see the baby. Although the choice is up to the parents, it is helpful to explain that "...though this is a tragic, difficult time for you, I can tell you that people have come back six months later to say how meaningful the time was."

A staff member (frequently from Pastoral Care) will bring the infant into the room, wrapped in a blanket, and place it in the mothers's arms. The parents (and whomever else they want in the room—grandparents, children, friends) are encouraged to touch and hold the baby for as long as they wish. One couple with premature twins expressed the meaning of spending time with the dead babies in this way: "I just wanted to get to know them before I had to give them up."

In the case of an anomalous baby with some physiological defect, the healthy, fully formed parts of the child will be pointed out in contrast to the deformity. Even with a deformed baby, the reality of touching and looking is almost never as bad as it is in the mind and imagination of the parents.

Sometimes the physician or family will request an autopsy to attempt to determine the cause of the anomaly. While many families recoil at the thought of "cutting on our child," others will permit the procedure to relieve their concern about future children. A common guideline is the "six month rule:" "If you can project yourself six months into the future and think you will be satisfied with understanding the cause of the child's death, then you probably do not need to do the autopsy. If you can imagine that in six months you will look back and wonder what happened, then you probably do need to have it done."

Usually the couple also will be asked if they want the baby baptized. For persons with a sacramental religious tradition (Roman Catholic, Episcopalian, Lutheran, Methodist) this event may be very important. It symbolizes the welcoming of the baby into the religious community and, by its performance, recognizes the baby as a fully human member of the church and of that particular family. In situations where the fetus is under the gestational age or weight limit and is stillborn, no birth or death certificate is issued to the parents and the baptismal certificate may be the only document that indicates they actually had a baby. Such a remembrance is very important to help fill some of the emptiness that results in the loss of a child at birth.

Unfortunately, many clergy will not baptize a dead baby. They cite theological arguments against the practice for the child and ignore the extremely positive *pastoral* support it provides for the family. Theological arguments can also be made that baptism is the welcoming initiation of the infant into the *larger church*, the whole *Communion of Saints*, consisting of the entire "cloud of witnesses," past and present, those living and dead. Most hospital chaplains, therefore, will perform this service for the family, having had experience with the relief, acceptance, and healing it provides for parents at the time of the death as well as months later.

Naming the child is a very powerful and tender event. It can be done in the context of baptism or in a secular manner for persons not of those religious traditions, by simply giving the child a name and referring to him or her by that name. In either case, the procedure gives the family someone to mourn and remember.

In addition to the above options, most Intensive Care Nurseries or Labor and Delivery Units will take pictures of the infant for the parents. Usually these will be held by Pastoral Care or Social Services and given to the parents when and if they want them. Once again, the pictures, time spent with the dead infant, and perhaps a baptism or naming ceremony, all reinforce for the grieving couple the reality of the birth and death, and help to fill the emptiness they feel at this time, and in the future.

Often, parents, relatives, or well-meaning friends of the couple will want to rush to the house and dismantle the nursery, making sure the room is returned to its former state, with the baby clothes carefully packed away, before the mother comes home. This mistake, however, will only lead to a feeling of even greater emptiness and disappointment. While it is extremely painful for the couple to return to the room they had set up to receive the newborn, it is a realistic and meaningful part of the grieving process for them to take things down and put them away together.

Finally, just as with adult deaths, *be there* after the event to support and listen to the pain as the days, months, and even years pass. One of the major common occurrences following the death of an infant is marital difficulty between the parents, frequently leading to separation or divorce. You may be the *one* person who is willing to hear and acknowledge the pain of both parents, separately expressed, support both in their loss, and possibly recommend counseling to work out the anger, resentment or disappointment stirred up by the death.

The death of an infant is indeed a tragic and difficult loss. It can be made more tolerable with the help of those persons who are willing to accept and encourage the distraught and often disbelieving parents in their grief.

Reading and following the above guidelines for *Before, During*, and *After* death will be helpful in dealing with dying patients and their families. But there is another factor which, if not taken seriously, will prohibit you from approaching the bedside with a willingness to listen, to hear and to discuss the issues of death and dying. That factor is your own fear or comfort with your *own* death.

Larry Bugen, Ph.D., a therapist and educator in private practice in Austin, Texas, has written and lectured extensively on loss and grief and has carefully observed reactions to death in himself and others. During a class on "Death and Dying" he had arranged to have as a guest speaker a woman who was terminally ill. Before she came into the room, he pre-tested the class, asking the students a list of questions that would indicate their comfort level with their own deaths. The woman then joined the class, spoke of her illness and impending death, and her feelings about dying. After she left, Dr. Bugen post-tested the class, asking questions that would elicit how well the students thought the woman was coping with her situation.

Not surprisingly, after comparing the two sets of responses, Dr. Bugen found that the students who saw themselves as having a very difficult time talking or thinking about their own deaths saw the woman as coping very poorly with her death. The students who reported a level of relative comfort in discussing or planning for their own deaths thought the woman was handling her death quite appropriately and with courage.

The implication here is obvious. If you *seriously* want to be of help to dying patients and their families, take the time to come to terms with your *own* death. Ask yourself the same series of questions listed in the *Before* section; then carry them out. Make a will. Plan your funeral arrangements. Compose a durable power of attorney and sign a Living Will. Talk with your family or significant others about your plans and wishes.

If you do *not* do these things yourself, you are very likely to avoid the subject with dying patients and possibly not even *hear* them cautiously bring up their concerns. When you have made your plans, faced the fearful issue of your own demise, and explored with someone close to you the feelings of anger, disappointment, hope or surprise about your own death, you will be more comfortable, open, and effective in being with others who are dying. And you also will have begun your own process of surviving the inevitable deaths of people you love.

II
ETHICS
AND
DEATH

2

Death Myths

As everyone knows, medical decision making in the area of withholding, refusing, or withdrawing life support has become increasingly complex and difficult. New technology has had the most obvious impact on these dilemmas as patients, families, and physicians are offered more and ever newer diagnostic and life prolonging equipment.

• CAT scanners, until recently thought to be state of the art in radiology, are being rapidly supplanted by Magnetic Resonance Imagery machines which use no radioactive materials and produce incredibly clear (computer assisted) pictures.

• New neonatal respirators push air into the undeveloped lungs of infants with greater impact, forcing more oxygen exchange and enabling even more and smaller premature babies to stay alive longer.

• Laser technology will soon be used in cardiology to replace the current "balloon" technique of destroying plaque inside clogged arteries, virtually opening them entirely.

While technology has increased our options for treatment (or non-treatment) in both crisis and long term illnesses, it is usually not the determining factor in making such decisions. Rather, there exists a set of subtle and extremely powerful internal presuppositions which inform and direct our choices regarding withdrawing, withholding, or refusing life support. It is necessary to examine these deep seated, culturally reinforced death myths in order to more openly and realistically evaluate the appropriate options for and with dying patients and their families.

Whether based on medical tradition, social obligation, or religious teaching, the death myths influencing which treatment decisions we make are indelibly embedded within our collective psyche. They flash through our minds when the doctor tells us the patient's condition is poor. They are the screens through which we hear the diagnosis of serious illness. They are the standards against which we weigh our response to the terminal prognosis. They are not "myths" in the traditional sense of beliefs which represent symbolic truth, but are myths in the usual, popular sense of ideas which obscure the truth, or even serve to perpetuate falsehoods.

The death myths most prominent in our culture are as follows:

1. *"Only old people die."* Conversely stated this means that "Young people should not die." Neither assumption is true. The mortality information from most hospitals shows that nearly equal (and, as AIDS patients become more prominent, increasingly greater) numbers of people under age 65 die, especially in the 0 to 10 category.

It is agism at its worst to think that an old person has "lived his or her life" and therefore is more accepting or more deserving of death than a younger, 20- to 40-year-old counterpart. In fact, it is entirely possible for the situation to be quite the reverse; the aged person may be more vital and have more to live for than the youth.

Belief in this myth can result in young persons undergoing extraordinary efforts from chemotherapy to intubation *just because* they are young, or old persons prematurely denying further treatment *just because* they are old. The myth also serves to reinforce our own wish for a long life, and to defend against our fear of our own death coming "prematurely."

The truth is, whether we like it or not, people of all ages die. Death is no respecter of age. There is no guarantee of lifespan given with conception. Each death is sad, tragic, acceptable or a relief based on the life of the person, the quality of that life, and the kinds of relationships that person has had. Each dying situation, therefore, where a decision must be made to withhold or withdraw artificial intervention, needs to be evaluated on those criteria, not on a myth about age that presumes that it is "okay" for old (but not young) persons to die, perhaps intimating that the elderly want to die or even ought to die.

2. *"Medicine can cure everything."* Even in the face of long term illness when the patient is finally about to die, panicked family members frequently ask "Can't you *do* something?" The panic and the request (or demand) reflect a strong belief in this country that medicine can find and cure all illness and physicians are or should be omniscient.

The media to the contrary, most physicians, and other health care professionals, do not act to reinforce this image. (They know better.) Rather, the myth persists because it is what people very much want to believe. As another denial of the inevitability of illness or death it is we ourselves who want to believe that drugs, medical technology, and their physician purveyors can prevent or cure the effects of disease, self inflicted injury (smoking, diet, lifestyle), and aging.

But it is also true that the medical community has frequently oversold the efficacy or advisability of a particular technical or therapeutic breakthrough." The current promotion of the artificial heart is the latest example of such a media event. Heedless of the availability, advisability, and ruinous financial cost of such a device, the heart is proffered as another example of technology's ability to cheat death, and the myth is reinforced.

It is more honest to be straight with patients and ourselves about the limits of tests, treatments, medications, and tentative prognoses. Not to do so is to embrace this myth of medicine and to end up feeling angry, disappointed, guilty, and resentful.

Medicine cannot cure everything. Death is a normal bodily function. It is not optional for the human race.

3. *"Life is always the highest value."* The initial presumption in nearly any accident or illness is always in favor of preserving life. But once the patient is stabilized and the prognosis is clear, considerations other than the priority of "life" come into effect. It is at this point that the meaning and quality of life *as the patient experiences them* are of the highest value in making the hard decisions of treatment and life support.

The easy temptation is to presume the patient either believes or ought to believe this myth, especially if the physician does. To presume that life is of the highest value supports our own refusal to see death as an acceptable outcome for the patient, and for ourselves. Fortunately, however, families and patients are increasingly moving toward the "meaning and quality" standard of judgment for discontinuing treatment. They seem to understand that life is more than breathing, living is more than subsisting, and presence with us means more than physically being there.

4. *"Money should not be a consideration."* This myth is supported by those who believe it is crass and insensitive to give the cost of treatment any weight in medical decision making. In our "bottom line" oriented culture we see the consideration of money to somehow diminish the image of the person. We rightly reject placing a monetary value on a person's life. We emotionally recoil at the prospect of finances determining treatment, preferring to spend "whatever is necessary" to save the life of our loved one.

But what of the young couple whose baby is dying yet can be kept alive a few more hours or days in our technologically equipped Intensive Care Nurseries? Or the elderly woman maintained by a respirator in ICU whose husband is barely subsisting on Social Security? And what of the use of resources devoted to these dying patients (not just for comfort but for continuing active treatment that is much more than palliative) that could be used for taking care of other, curable patients, for research, or for reducing hospital costs for everyone?

The honest, if uncomfortable, truth is that money is *already* a consideration in medical decision making and it will continue to play an even greater role as healthcare rationing becomes a reality in the United States. Given a limited amount of resources and a virtually unlimited demand, it is reasonable to conclude that financial concerns are and will be a part of the process of deciding to withhold or withdraw treatment.

As many European countries have done, the United States has begun to experiment with healthcare rationing. In Great Britain, if a person over the age of 55 comes to a hospital with cardiac arrest, she or he can be treated and kept comfortable, but open heart surgery will not be done; neither will renal dialysis. In Sweden the age cut off is 50.

Similarly, as mentioned earlier, if patients are on Medicare (where hospital bills are reimbursed at 80 percent of reasonable cost) and have less than six months to live, they can switch into the Medicare/Hospice track. Bills will then be reimbursed at 100 percent of reasonable cost, but the patient agrees to go ahead and die.

And it is not unreasonable, in the case of dying patients, to suggest that the focus of care switch from curative (an unrealistic goal) to palliative. Concentrating on pain control, dignity, safety, comfort, and quality of remaining life, the patient will usually no longer receive further chemotherapy, blood transfusions, CAT scans, or antibiotics for infections. Pain is palliated, patient comfort is the highest goal, and costs of expensive and extraordinary technology and treatments are dramatically reduced.

As our entire healthcare system undergoes more changes in the coming years, more areas of rationing will inevitably appear. In the meantime, it can be argued that, sensitively done, consideration of the family's or patient's financial situation is a *very* caring gesture, as is weighing the effect of treatment on the cost of healthcare to the entire community, indeed to the nation. As the percent of GNP spent on healthcare jumps from the current 11 percent to as much as 15 percent by 1995, financial considerations will become even more important as patients weigh their treatment options.

5. *"Death is evil. Death means failure."* While the church is largely responsible for promoting the first of these, the medical/ healthcare profession is responsible for the persistence of the second.

Many people, desperately attempting to make some kind of logical sense out of their illness, have been told by their religious community that good is always rewarded and evil is always punished. They then extrapolate that good is always a reward and evil is always a punishment. They are sick or dying, therefore they must have done something bad and incurred the punishment of a wrathful God.

In fact death is not evil; neither is it intrinsically good. Sickness and death are *amoral* occurrences. They have nothing to do with good/bad, right/wrong, punishment/reward. We get sick. We die. As one doctor said: Welcome to Earth; the death rate here is 100%. One out of one dies."

The only thing "good" or "bad" about death is the manner in which one responds to it. Death, like any other amoral occurrence (birth, accident, marriage, divorce, trauma) is merely an occasion for good or evil to become manifest. That manifestation is shown in our response to the event, not in the event itself.

Likewise death has nothing to do with failure. Assuming one has done everything necessary (not possible, but necessary) and the patient's condition is said to be "incompatible with life," it is understandable that the person dies. The death has nothing to do with the ability of the physician or nursing staff. "Success" and "failure" are value judgments that reveal the bias of the training of healthcare staff (using military terminology—triage, fight, battle, win/lose, bravery).

Such judgments have no meaning when applied to the event of the death, which is *amoral*. In fact, it seems the height of arrogance to assume that we (patient, family or physician) have "failed" when a natural process (death) has followed its normal route. To support this myth is the same as saying hurricane or earthquake victims "failed" to stop the hurricane or earthquake.

All this is not to imply that death is not often sad, angering, relieving, unfair, or crushing. It is all this and more in feeling terms. The problem arises in treating death as though it should not happen, denying it as a logical, acceptable, and sometimes desirable possibility for the outcome of the patient's illness.

Death might more easily be tolerated by all of us if we saw it as a form of *healing*. Death as healing transposes its symbolic meaning from that of evil enemy to that of an acceptable, and at times even welcomed, alternative.

6. *"Where there's life there's hope."* This myth, though frequently cited when making treatment decisions, is patently untrue. Where there's life there is quite often the opposite of hope: There is agony, fear, excruciating pain, anger, frustration, loneliness, and despair. The sentiment really expressed here is that where there is biological activity (whether mechanically assisted or other-

wise), there is reason for optimism that the person may recover, even against all odds.

The questions to be asked of this myth are: "What is life?" and "What is hope?" Is life merely the activity of air being forced into stiffening lungs, or blood being pumped inside a human cavity? Is it biological activity mechanically produced or substantially supported? Again the quality of life standard (as judged by the patient if competent or by the patient's significant others if incompetent) comes into consideration. Increasing numbers of people believe that life is not life if there is no quality of relating, quality of experiencing and enjoying, quality of being. Life, for them, means much more than the rather shallow definition of longevity.

"Hope," also, is quite different from "optimism." Optimism demands the patient get well (not just better) and return to the former state of health. Nothing less is desirable or acceptable. The meaning of hope, on the other hand, was expressed by a cancer patient who commented: "It's okay with me if I live and it's okay with me if I die. Because either place I'm loved." Hope implies that death is as acceptable an outcome to one's condition as life. Hope embraces and affirms both life and death as parts of a greater whole of existence. Hope sees life not as a problem to be solved but as a mystery to be lived, and death as a part of that mystery.

7. *"Suffering is redemptive."* Believe it or not, some people, (patients, families, physicians and nurses), will refuse pain medication, withhold palliative measures to increase comfort, or deny the obvious existence of pain because they see the suffering as cleansing, deserved, or redemptive. Followers of this myth, based on a conservative theological or philosophical tradition, conquer their own helplessness in the face of illness and death by assuming that discomfort and pain are spiritually or psychologically helpful to the patient.

Of course it is sometimes true that suffering can be an occasion for redemption, for the healing of memories, relationships, hurts, fears, or guilts. Pain and illness often are the precipitators of change in behavior or perspective on the person's lifestyle. But suffering is also quite often the occasion for unquenchable bitterness, debilitating despair, collapse of faith and disintegration of personhood.

Once again, in our attempts to make sense of an illness we want to believe there is some purpose, some plan, some reason for the horrible suffering we or our loved ones are enduring. Once again, the truth is that suffering is as amoral as the virus, bacteria, or systemic condition that is its cause.

But redemption or collapse are *responses* to the pain and discomfort. These individual and varied responses depend largely on the personality and belief system of the patient, and the quality of interactions between the patient and loved ones, not on the condition or amount of suffering the patient experiences.

8. *"Pulling the plug is suicide or murder."* Many people refuse to make a decision to withdraw hydration, nutrition, or respiratory maintenance because they believe such an act constitutes murder. Likewise, to designate a personal directive such as a Living Will may seem tantamount to suicide. The underlying presupposition is that it is improper to take any control over one's own death. To do so is seen to usurp the power and prerogative of an all-controlling God.

In fact, not to decide is to decide. Not to make a Living Will, designate a surrogate decision maker, or withdraw artificial intervention systems is to decide to abdicate responsibility. It is to relegate the burden of decision making to someone (physician, hospital, committee, court) far less qualified to make it, and refuse to accept our ability and responsibility as "co-creators with God" to share in the rational determination of our destiny.

One could just as easily argue that not to pull the plug or make a Living Will designation is to stand in the way of Nature, God, and the normal procession of life to death.

A major theological task for the church is to re-examine its beliefs regarding suicide, assisted suicide, active and passive euthanasia, to adjust to modern technological developments, and to enable individuals to exercise options that, heretofore, were unacceptable.

9. *"To die of dehydration or starvation in a healthcare setting is inhumane, cruel, and immoral."* When many people think of food and drink, they imagine sitting down at a table with steaming dishes and good friends. But that image of wholesome food staring invitingly at us (and we, hungrily, back at it) is vastly different from the reality of the dying patient, or even the veget-

ative non-dying patient, who is maintained by artificial nutrition and artificial hydration.

Instead, picture blue humming boxes sucking high calorie pastel liquid from bags and bottles and forcing it through clear plastic tubing into the patient's nose or directly into the stomach or intestine. This artificial intervention is ethically parallel to the use of a respirator that artificially pumps air in and out of failing lungs.

In addition, it is important to realize that the natural process of death is totally subverted by our demand that loved ones die in the midst of high-tech drama. In fact, before the technological armamentarium included such things as respirators, i.v. pumps, or the Thumper (mechanically-conducted CPR) patients usually went home to die, assisted only by drugs to relieve the pain. Anorexia (lack or loss of appetite) first set in, followed closely by dehydration and malnutrition.

> Dehydration and malnutrition cause azotemia, (a condition in which) the body's waste nitrogen products become elevated in the blood, and these products, acting as a natural sedative, diminish a patient's awareness and elevate the pain threshold. Appetite decreases, alertness diminishes, and the obtunded patient (one whose senses are dulled) dies; the stuporous state suffices to free the patient of pain.
>
> The technological imperative to have patients die in electrolyte balance and well-hydrated is a grave disservice. It serves onlyto ward off the sedative effect of the azotemia. The result not only increases pain perception, but also adds to the mental agony of the patient who is kept alert enough to appreciate his or her situation. (Abrams, "Withholding Treatment When Death Is Not Imminent," 42 *Geriatrics* 77, 84, No. 5, May 1987)

For increasing numbers of people, to die of dehydration or starvation while being kept comfortable with the large array of palliative drugs available is far preferable and much more humane than the prolonged dying by incessant medical intervention that is demanded of patients by misinformed relatives and practitioners, acting on outdated and ineffectual death myths.

It is clear that these death myths at one time served a proper and meaningful role in medical decision making. It is equally clear that they can no longer serve that same role. As a part of the standard cultural presuppositions about life, death, and medicine, these myths stood to call all the available medical resources to the service of life at any cost. But current technology has changed the perspective about and meaning of the concepts of life, death, and medicine. As these concepts are revised in light of even newer treatment options, we will need to develop a different, more flexible set of "death myths" to guide our treatment decisions. (Some of these guidelines are presented in the next chapter.)

It is important to examine and acknowledge how much we rely on these outdated presuppositions. Only then will they not become impediments to caring, meaningful decision making regarding the treatment and life support choices offered to our loved ones—and to ourselves.

3

Pulling the Plug: How Do We Decide?

The Lone Ranger and Tonto were out in the middle of the prairie surrounded by thousands of Indians. From their hiding place behind the rocks they could see Apaches to the North, Sioux to the South, Cherokee to the East, and Kiowa to the West. The supply of silver bullets was dwindling. It was clear that the end was near. The Lone Ranger turned to Tonto and said: "Well, old faithful companion, old Kemosabe, old friend, we've been down a lot of dusty trails together. But it looks like we won't make it out of this one alive." Tonto then looked over at The Lone Ranger and replied with a smile, "What you mean, 'we,' White Man?"

In considering the withdrawal or withholding of life support, it is well to remember that the patient is usually in the Lone Ranger's position, while we are in the rather enviable position of being Tonto. It is also well to remember that we Tontos will one day be in the Masked Man's situation ourselves, so our decisions must be carefully made, for future reference.

The answer to the question "How do we decide?" and the perspective from which it is approached can vary with who *"we"* are. On the one hand "we" are the caregivers, the family, close friends, physicians, nurses, clergy, social workers, attorneys, and other healthcare professionals involved with the dying patient. But it is equally important to realize that (with Tonto) "we" are also the dying, and to use that realization to empathize more closely with the person lying before us. Had Tonto understood this fact, he would not have smiled so broadly as he withdrew the Lone Ranger's life support.

Life support decisions are made in two basic contexts:

1. crisis situations
2. non-crisis, longer term spans of time

While some of the considerations and guidelines for decision making in both situations overlap, it is important to deal with the contexts separately, as different dynamics are present in each.

CRISIS SITUATIONS

• Your spouse of twenty-eight years has been brought into the Emergency Department with a stroke and is paralyzed on the left side. He never wanted to be on a respirator but requires one now to keep breathing. His blood pressure is falling but can be maintained with drugs.

• Your newborn infant has severe congenital anomalies. She can be kept alive for days or even a few weeks in the Intensive Care Nursery at $1200 per day. Then she will eventually die.

• Your 86-year-old father has had a massive heart attack. He is on a respirator in the Intensive Care Unit, and his physician recommends immediate open heart surgery before he arrests again.

Deciding what to do and how to do it in crisis situations such as these can be extremely problematic. The pressures of time, emotionalism, and uncertainty of outcome weigh heavily on those who must sign consent forms and act in the patient's stead. To provide some order to this chaos, the following guidelines may be helpful.

1. Get the best information available. It is important to know how many Indians are *really* out there and how many silver bullets are *really* left. Talk to the physician, and listen when he or she answers you. Many families complain that their physician did not tell them everything, when in fact they themselves did not want to hear and so did not listen.

Ask as many questions as you need to ask. Write your questions down while waiting for test results and don't let the physician go until you get answers. Remember that the physician (like any other consultant you might hire) works for you, and you have a right to know all of the information gathered. You are also free to get a second opinion, or even a third given the constraints of time. Many physicians will request or encourage another opinion anyway. Having heard their best experienced conclusions as to diagnosis and prognosis, the decision regarding treatment and life support is up to you.

2. *Aim for a balance.* If the patient is competent (awake and able to converse), consider first what she or he wants done. If the patient is incompetent it will be up to you (individually or in consultation with other family and friends) to determine what you think he or she would want done. In nearly every situation the wishes of the patient should be given priority and honored wherever possible.

Next, balance off the wants and needs of the patient with those of the family. It is vital that no unilateral decisions be made. Both the desires of the patient and the desires of the family or significant other need to be considered and a consensus carefully reached. Sometimes it is appropriate to consider the needs of the larger community as well: for example, Will this expenditure of healthcare (respirator, neonatal or ICU bed space, dialysis, heart surgery) limit the available resources for less catastrophically ill patients? What is our ethical consensus, if any, on the provision of lifetime care for severely disabled persons?

Consider the emotional issues of the past, present and future. How has this person dealt with decisions in the past? What is this person feeling about the present dilemma? What will be the emotional fallout for the patient (assuming treatment and survival) or for the family (assuming withdrawal of treatment and death) in the future? Imagine yourself six months from now. How will you feel about this decision then?

3. *Seek disinterest and clarity.* People in crisis need someone to help who is disinterested but not uninterested, someone who will

help seek clarity about the issues without the distortion of personal involvement. If you are the person in crisis, seek out someone (pastoral care, social services, patient representative) who will assist in this way. If you are the helper to someone else, know when to make a referral if the issue hits too close to home for you.

Remember that time is not always of the essence. Usually you need not feel pressured into instant decision making (unlike the dramas portrayed on the soaps). Take the time you need to defuse the "crisis orientation" of the decision and get some help either from friends or from professionals at the hospital.

4. *Ethic of love, Ethic of need.*Two major guidelines that are helpful in crisis decision making are the those of "love" and "need." Jesus' suggestion that we love our neighbor as we love ourselves implies putting ourselves in the position of the person from whom life support is about to be withdrawn. Ask, with all the honesty you can muster: "What is the most loving thing to do (for the patient, family, community) in this situation?" The same approach is echoed in Augustine's "Love God and do what you will."

Second, in nearly every crisis decision, the Old and New Testaments come down on the side of the needy, dispossessed, and helpless. Determining who is most needy may be difficult. Is it the dying infant, the grieving family, the respirator bound adult, or the anguishing spouse? Along with the love ethic, the presumption in favor of the helpless is indeed a powerful decision-making premise.

This guideline does not imply a bias in favor of maintaining the comatose, incompetent, or dying patient. Indeed, the most loving thing to do may often be to remove the respirator, i.v. or feeding tube and allow the natural healing of death to proceed

5. *Continuity and support.* Whether you are the caregiver or the significant other, don't just make the decision and leave. Often families decide to withdraw treatment and then quickly absent themselves from the scene. Likewise caregivers participate as helpers in the high drama of the decision making and then find other things to do.

While the decision is itself important, it is of equal import to back up that decision behaviorally with continuity, contact, and constant support for the patient who is dying as well as for the family or significant other. Be by the bedside of the dying patient or the family who has made a withdrawal or withholding of treatment decision. Agonize with them, cry with them, remember with them as they lie dying. Of course it is difficult to be present as the wishes of the patient or family are carried out, respirators removed, i.v.'s withdrawn, dialysis stopped. But for all involved—patient, family and staff—it is important to support the decision with the dignity with which it was made.

The second major area of critical decision making involves longer term illnesses or disabilities. Situations such as the following require responses slightly different from those listed above.

NON-CRISIS, LONG-TERM SITUATIONS

• Your mother, who has had asthma for thirty years, has been on a respirator for eight weeks. She is alert and conscious, though in end-stage lung disease. She will be discharged to a skilled nursing facility where she will remain until she dies, however long it takes.

• Your 15-week-old fetus has been diagnosed through amniocentesis with a fatal hypoplastic left ventricle. There is a chance you will need a Caesarean section if the fetus develops full term and goes into cardiac distress.

• An employee with whom you work has been confirmed with AIDS. Having no immunity to ordinary disease, he will die within the next two years. You both know the dying will be a long and probably painful process.

• Your best friend has just been diagnosed with liver cancer which has metastasized to the brain. She probably has less than six months to live and is refusing any but palliative treatment.

Life support decisions in the context of long-term illnesses have both the luxury and disadvantage of time. While not exerting the pressure that it does in a crisis, time can seem a fearful burden to those faced with the daily chores and demands for decisions it brings.

The recommendations listed for crises (get accurate information, balance needs and wishes, act with disinterest and clarity, act in love/protect the helpless, provide continuity and support) obviously still apply over the long term. The issues are the same, only the time frame in which they are considered has changed. But the longer term nature of the process means that some additional guidelines are necessary.

1. *Plan while you can.* Whether you are the person who is dying or the helper, consider the options and make the decisions *now*, while still lucid and relatively rational. Even though they have had the time, many patients and their families deny the obvious and avoid making plans or decisions until they are in a crisis.

Business and personal affairs can be put in order, wills and Living Wills filed, treatment decisions made and even funeral arrangements designated before illness (or sudden accident) precludes those choices.

Eighty percent of deaths occur in healthcare institutions in this country. That means that we stand an *80 percent chance* that our death will be *decisional*, rather than natural or accidental. (It is very difficult to die naturally these days.) Someone will have to decide, in 80 percent of the cases, when to discontinue artificial intervention, when to stop treatment, which treatments to begin withdrawing, and when to end a "code" (or not even initiate one.) Rather than leaving those decisions up to significant others, or next of kin, who at best may be uncertain of your wishes, and at worst may do the opposite of what you want, make some tentative decisions now by signing a Living Will. At the very least, *talk* with your significant other or whoever is likely to be in the position of making those decisions, including your physician, about what you do and do not want done.

The twofold effect of such discussion and planning is that, once again, the more you have faced these decisions for yourself, the more effective you will be in assisting others to make them.

2. *Know the stance of your tradition.* If you have a religious tradition that is meaningful to you, find out its stand on the issues of abortion and withholding/withdrawing/refusing life support. Are there any impediments to organ donation or to Living Wills? While you may not necessarily agree with the position of the organization, the information may provide a starting place for discussion and decision making.

3. Loneliness and grief. Long-term serious illness is frequently accompanied by an insidious partner—silence. As one patient said: "The worst thing about all this is the loneliness." Dying persons usually want and need to talk about their dying, but not in any special or unduly morose manner; yet few people seem to be around who will really listen.

Share the loneliness just as you would share their happiness. Be realistic with patients and families; listen to their stories about the complexities of their lives whether they talk about the bills, the weather, the treatment, the hospital bed, or dying. Listening and spending "normal" time with patients will alleviate the sense of isolation and loneliness that inevitably and repeatedly occurs.

Especially in the long term, be sensitive to and aware of *anticipatory grieving.* Patients may wish themselves dead to unburden their families and avoid pain or a slow death of increasing debilitation. Family members may wish the same and feel guilty about their secret thoughts. Each may begin grieving the loss of the other long before the final stages of death take place.

Be supportive and accepting of the sense of loss, whenever it is felt. Do not discount or reject the feelings by telling the patient or family they shouldn't feel that way" or by reminding them of "all the time they've had" or have left. You cannot fix or alleviate the feelings of loss, fear, or guilt. You *can* allow persons to express their feelings in your presence without fear of judgment or rejection. And you can express yours with them as well.

4. Promote educational programs. As you become more sensitive to the issues faced by dying persons and their caregivers, plan some consciousness-raising activities in your religious organization or through your business or club affiliations. Organize a death planning workshop with speakers from the community on the topics of wills, funeral plans and service options, Living Will legality, and organ donations. Present varying points of view through a series of speakers on ethical issues such as as withdrawing/withholding life support, informed consent, artificial organs, and the rationing of health care. The more information people have about an issue or dilemma ahead of time (removing respirators, making funeral plans), the less confused and more clear they will feel about decision making under the pressure of the moment.

Finally, in both crisis and non-crisis decision making there are identical considerations to keep in mind:

1. *Good ethics begin with good facts.* As mentioned earlier, regardless of the time factor, make sure you have the most accurate medical, legal, philosophical, and spiritual information possible. Several opinions are valuable and each perspective will be helpful in making your own personal choice. Listen carefully and caringly to what you are told. Seek clarification and get assistance from friends or other hospital personnel.

2. *What is medically or legally right may not be ethically right.* Just because a procedure is medically "indicated" or legally "propitious" does not mean it is the procedure or action of ethical choice. Decisions have frequently been relegated to the medical and legal communities on the assumption that these groups have some expertise in determining the appropriateness of an action.

Patients and families, especially in a crisis, may turn first to external guidelines from physicians or attorneys hoping to find some solid ground on which to base their opinion of what is "right." Often it is only after some confusing, disappointing or conflicting medico-legal advice that they begin to ask what is "right" for *this* person, given who the person is and what the person wanted.

It seems clear that the basis for moral decision making must be primarily other than legal and medical, though those disciplines may offer helpful information that will affect that decision. The place to start is with the desires of the patient.

3. *Can does not imply ought.* This clearly revolutionary maxim is nearly un-American. Our country was built on the principle that "can implies ought." If we can built a railroad across the country, we ought to do so. If we can put a person on the moon, in a space station, on another planet, we ought to do it. Our new medical technology, however, is permitting us the ability to do things that in many cases we ought not to do.

Prolongation of life and the prolongation of dying, animal

transplants, some reproductive technologies, and other bioethical procedures currently being discussed that will one day be realities will have a profound impact on our societal structure and ways of living and dying. Boundaries will have to be clearly drawn using the above statement as a guide, particularly in the realm of life support decision making.

4. *The Bible is not a model for morality, it is a mirror for identity.* There is not much information about respirators in Genesis or even Leviticus, much less Revelation. Thus it is inappropriate to look to the Bible to tell us specifically what to *do*. It is, however, important for those involved in a religious tradition to view the Bible as a mirror, reflecting commentary and stories to describe who we *are*, what kind of covenant people we are with our peculiar God, and how we interact with God and one another. Using that information will then make our treatment and life support decisions more aligned with the reality of our faith and tradition.

5. *All conclusions are provisional.* Whatever decision is made has to be considered a provisional one. You may get new test information tomorrow that impacts directly on your choice. (The cancer has not metastasized as was first thought. The infant's abnormality *can* be repaired by a new microsurgical technique.) Likewise, you may get information that opens up (or closes down) a previous avenue of choice. (The surgery is not healing as it should. The chemotherapy is not working. The cobalt is relieving the pain. His appetite is getting better.)

No decision is written in cement. Be open to new information of whatever kind. Convey to patients that you are willing to follow their wishes and keep them informed of progress or the lack of it. Keep updating and asking what their decision is *today*.

The issues we have discussed here are not theoretical or rhetorical ones. The question is not "if" you will have to make these decisions, especially about life support, but "when?" Preparation through education, dialogue, and decision making now will enable you to put those considerations into action when it is your turn to be The Lone Ranger.

III
THE
CHURCH
AND
DEATH

A YEAR'S GRIEF

No red clods now
Ungainly thrown to cover a new grave;
No new grave now —
A year's weathering has worn the soil away,
A year's decay
To coffin and to corpse.

Smooth grass spreads
Where shovel dug to wound and scar the earth.
A standing stone
Tells all that shall be known about this plot
Where rain and rot
Work steadily together.

There can be peace:
Why spurn what makes you fit to fight again?
There can be power:
Give up what was and is, hope and desire,
Kneel at the fire
For this is holy ground.

The mark of death,
Scored on this stone and on our sight, is cross-shaped.
A year ago
The boy we buried here received its grace.
Anoint my face,
Redeem me, Holy One.

K.M.V. Morfey

4

Death Planning— Church Denial

She stands by the bed watching her husband breathe and listening to the gurgling in his lungs. Hanging onto life is such work. She holds his hand and gently strokes what remains of his once beautiful, thick white hair. The chemotherapy has reduced it to strands; but she lovingly pats him, kisses him, tells him she loves him as she has always done.

The interval between gasps for breath lengthens. Ten seconds, 15 seconds, 30 seconds—forever. She calls for the nurse who searches for and cannot find a heartbeat. The nurse leaves to summon a doctor to make the medical pronouncement. The dead man's wife breaks down and sobs.

Then the questions begin.

What plans have you made for the body? Do you have a funeral home in mind? Do you want cremation? What kind of service do you prefer? How much do you want to pay for the funeral service? What about embalming? Have you talked with your clergy about the plans? Will you sign this form to release the body, please?

And the answers are usually the same.

"I don't know. We never talked about it. Does our church allow cremation? I wonder what his wishes were. My church never taught me about funerals. Do I need to call my clergy? What do I do next?"

The scenario portrayed here is familiar to anyone working with dying patients and their families. People come into the hospital either in the final stages of disease or in the midst of a medical crisis and die quickly or unexpectedly. Family members are then at a total loss as to what ought to be done. Their religious affiliation has not prepared them for this moment.

Often, conflicting wishes or beliefs lead to serious arguments at a time when closeness, consolation, and mutual support are needed. Sometimes decisions are made in the rush of the moment that are later regretted. Such issues as embalming, the use of make up, closed or open casket, and cremation are very emotionally laden. If not handled carefully, they can provide the basis for years of resentment and separation.

Frequently, no one has ever talked to the deceased about specific wishes concerning funeral arrangements even though the person has been sick for some time. The conspiracy of silence regarding the family member's illness and dying then results in the availability of far fewer options which are now chosen under less than rational circumstances.

There are, of course, many cultural biases in favor of denying the inevitability of death and the obvious need for plans to be made (regardless of age or situation) to prepare for that certainty. There is, however, another source of reluctance to deal with death planning. The church (meaning here the entire religious community in this country, regardless of denomination or sect) has consistently been a willing partner in this cultural avoidance in two ways.

1. *Non-affiliation.* The clear majority of patients, families and staff in the hospital have no church or clergy affiliation. A recent Gallup poll revealed that only about 40 percent of Americans claimed any such relationship with church or clergy, although most people state a religious *preference* on their hospital admission

data sheet. Often the hospital's Pastoral Care personnel are the first contact with religion the patient or family has had in years.

Most people do report religious training of some kind, usually with anecdotal stories of church meetings, Bible school teachers, and religious authority figures, most of which come across as alternately stern, overwhelming, or ludicrous. It is clear that religious education, as the child's first impression of what spirituality is about, leaves much to be desired.

Even if the early exposure was meaningful, the current experiences they have had in churches (particularly regarding illness and death) have been unfavorable or, worse, irrelevant. From the feelings expressed by hospitalized patients, it seems that the real spiritual needs of individuals and families are frequently not being met in the parish church.

For those who are involved in local churches, this serious indictment of the meaning and efficacy of parish programs may come as a surprise and even may be greeted with some anger. But it is hard to discount the feelings of patients who, at a time when they desperately need some internal and external spiritual resources, find that they have none. For this lack of support, education, and spiritual training, the church must bear some culpability.

2. Church-supported Denial. It would be easy to assume that unaffiliated persons having no church contact would be less knowledgeable about rituals, procedures, and appropriate behavior before, during and after the death. It is interesting, however, that even those persons who are weekly attenders, devout Christians and Jews, and whose clergy come to visit regularly in the hospital are often equally frustrated, uninformed, and unprepared for the onslaught of questions to be answered and decisions to be made.

Clearly the church has, both overtly and covertly, participated in and reinforced its parishioners' denial of death. Furthermore, by failing to deal effectively with the issues of death planning and dying, through education, preaching, worship and witness, the church has downplayed and discounted its own very powerful message about how to *live*. This denial by the church has taken three forms: *Practical, Theological, and Sacramental.*

1. Practical Denial. Few persons have been taught by their local parish the practical details of what to do when they or someone they love is about to die. As a result, people seldom know their particular church's rituals or liturgies surrounding dying, including what prayers might be appropriate at the time of death. Whether and how to call for clergy, which funeral home to use, whether or not to embalm or to consider cremation, and whether to have the service (if there is to be one) in the church or funeral home are practical matters that have largely been ignored by the church.

Organ and body donations, extraordinary means of life support, and decisions about withholding, withdrawing, or refusing medical treatment are issues that could be addressed by informed clergy and laity *before* the need for definitive action arises.

Although local physicians, memorial societies, and funeral directors would welcome the chance to provide such information along with clergy, they are seldom asked to do so by the church. Thus the practical matters surrounding death remain a mystery to most parishioners until such time as they are forced to discover them.

2. *Theological Denial.* This kind of denial by the church is perhaps more regrettable than the reluctance to deal with practicalities of dying. It is primarily due to poor or nonexistent theological teaching that most people (churched and unchurched) believe that "good is always rewarded and evil always punished." If that is true, it is easy to see how people might conclude that those who are prosperous and healthy must therefore be living good lives, while those who are sick or deteriorating must have done something wrong.

Hospital staff are frequently asked the question "If good is rewarded and evil punished, why is my good, kind, Christian husband lying here dying in excruciating pain?" Of the many usual responses to that question, none is satisfactory. There are some theological approaches to the problem that are helpful in dealing with what appears to be illogical tragedy. Unfortunately, because illness and death are seldom wrestled with in the pulpit or church classroom, parishioners are left to face these crises with the usual meaningless cultural platitudes that leave them feeling empty and unresolved.

Mixing together the issues of good/evil with sickness/punishment, many people assume that their sickness is a punishment for something they have done or not done. An unfortunate result of this largely unexamined theological assumption is a cycle of anger and guilt. They feel frustrated and angry at God because of the pain, shock, or unfairness of their illness but are prevented from expressing those feelings due to poor theologizing by the church ("It's not permitted to be angry at God.") These persons then end up feeling guilty about feeling angry about feeling punished.

The daughter of a dying patient experienced just this emotional cycle. After much discussion she was relieved to have her angry feelings affirmed without risking alienation or punishment. It was helpful to her to acknowledge that she could feel angry and frustrated at God while still trusting God.

There is indeed a wealth of theological literature available on the subjects of illness and death. The church, however, has almost universally ignored it, to the detriment of patients and their families who are or will be in times of crisis.

3. *Sacramental Denial.* The church's refusal to teach its people to deal with death sacramentally is a direct result of the expropriation of power and authority from religion to medicine. In the overwhelming popular presence of "miracle drugs," microsurgery, and biomedical technology, the church has increasingly discounted the efficaciousness of its own sacraments.

Holy Communion, anointing, and laying on of hands, intercessory prayer, confession, absolution, and baptism into the covenant community are, or could be, powerful resources for patients and families to confront the reality of dying. The church's witness to the presence of God in whatever form healing may take, including death, could be a valuable tool in the treatment of illness and in sustaining and nourishing those who are dying.

Unfortunately, the religious community does not take its sacraments seriously enough to offer them with the confidence and assertiveness that the medical community offers theirs. Confession and communion are not believed to be as powerful as cobalt and chemotherapy. Anointing and absolution are seen as less effective than medication and surgery.

By taking an extremely narrow view of "healing," limiting it to visible, physiological change, the church has allowed the mystique of medicine to supplant its own holy mysteries and to become the treatment of choice, often to the exclusion of religious ministrations to the ill and dying.

The medical community, on the other hand, usually treats religious and sacramental resources with more respect than the church itself. Physicians, nurses, and other healthcare personnel regularly refer patients and families to Pastoral Care staff and parish clergy to offer the kind of healing resources which medicine cannot provide. It is as though the medical community, far from being competitive or critical, is calling on the church to *be* the church, to exercise its proper, historical function and to do what mere medicine cannot—to support, sustain, transcend, and offer healing to the *whole* person in body, mind, and spirit.

The reasons leading up to the church's threefold denial in death planning are also threefold:

- Clergy and lay conspiracy
- Resurrection theology
- Cultural capitulation

1. *Clergy and lay conspiracy.* Clergy are no different from anyone else when it comes to death. They have the same fears, hopes, apprehensions, and fantasies as the lay persons with whom they minister. Often, therefore, an unwritten agreement develops between the two not to talk about illness and death until the need arises.

As has been stated earlier, in order to offer programs, seminars, workshops, or sermons about death and dying, clergy (like others) must be somewhat comfortable with their own finitude. To talk about the death of others raises the issue of our own. To get into the specifics of funeral planning for others raises the spectre of our own demise.

Frequently clergy are reluctant to offer practical, theological, and sacramental perspectives on death and dying due to their own discomfort about dealing with their own mortality. Supported and reinforced in this behavior by an equally fearful laity, the conspiracy leads to the problems noted above in time of medical crisis.

2. *Resurrection theology.* To focus on resurrection theology is to talk of new life here and now, and of an afterlife where "we will all meet up yonder." It can be uplifting, hopeful, positive and en-

couraging. It can also be a way to discount and deny the sadness, brokenness, and finality of the end we all must face.

This theological orientation has its basis in the usual Good Friday sermons. On a day appropriate for mourning, anger, sadness, and grief, clergy and laity alike quickly skip over, ignore, or treat shallowly the painful, agonizing transition of Christ Jesus' death on Good Friday in their hurry to get to the positive feelings associated with Easter.

Practically, this resurrection theology takes the form of denying death, demanding cheerfulness and strength in the face of helpless deterioration, and covering sadness with a veneer of forced happiness. The unreality of this approach is so painfully clear to most people going through bereavement that they reject out of hand the source (the church and its teachings) from which it comes.

Congregations which follow this belief system are unlikely to deal with the issues of illness and death in ways that encourage the expression of pain, doubt, depression, or sadness. Until such groups deal with their own fear of death, they are also unlikely to understand the fullest meaning of the Crucifixion and the balance and depth it brings to the experience of Resurrection.

3. *Cultural capitulation.* Due to the church's own discounting of the value and efficacy of its sacraments and theology, a gradual change in allegiance has occurred. Instead of following the tenets of the church, which now have fallen into disfashion, both clergy and laity have begun following popular social methods of dealing with illness, dying, and death. The church has quietly acquiesced to cultural norms, such as preferring that death occur in sterile hospitals and that final religious services be held in equally sterile funeral homes. The docile acceptance of these practices has meant a capitulation of responsibility for death planning to cultural caretakers and a virtual exclusion of church presence at two important times of impact, the death and the funeral. Physicians and healthcare workers manage the death. Funeral directors orchestrate the burial.

Two recent trends may wrest these events away from the grip of the cultural caretakers, and provide the opportunity for the church to regain its position of priority and responsibility in affecting the place and the rituals of death. The recent growing interest in Hospice care for the terminally ill could refocus death in a more personal setting, with opportunity for church and family ministrations. And the new concern for "simple burial" and/or cremation may result in greater involvement on the part of clergy and others indetermining appropriate rituals (and the sacramental place of those rituals) surrounding such desires.

The importance of death planning, especially for the community of the church, is clear. It is a logical outgrowth of the church's religious commitment and belief. It is the natural result of a fair balance of both resurrection and crucifixion theology. It is the necessary topic of practical, theological, and sacramental involvement in the life and death of the community.

Both clergy and laity alike have a number of options available to enable them to explore the meaning of their own death and the manner in which they would prefer to plan for it. Some of those options are: *Read, Discuss, Decide, Encourage,* and *Live.*

Read. Read about illness, death, and dying. Read about how others have grappled and coped with it. Experience with those writers the confusion, the whole range of feelings from anger to resignation to protest to fear, and the resolution, if any, they or their loved ones found in that process.

Read about the various options for death planning, including burial, cremation, simple funeral, and the scattering of ashes. Read about the ethics of dying, of euthanasia, of suicide, of discontinuing, withholding, or refusing all but palliative care. Read about Hospice and how it helps those who are dying to live every day of their lives as much as they are able. Read whatever interests you on the subject and as you read...

Discuss. Discuss with friends and family what you've read. Share the feelings raised in you as you read and contemplate your own death. Talk with your physician about how medical decisions are made and with your clergy about the church's position on abortion, life support, dying at home, and funeral practices such as embalming, cremation, scattering of ashes and burial. Discuss the meaning of your own denomination's funeral service, the sacraments and their meaning in life and death, the theology of guilt, forgiveness, sickness, punishment, healing, and death.

Perhaps most importantly, discuss with your loved ones their and your wishes concerning your death and as you talk.

Decide. Decide on your own funeral plans. Make determinations about a Living Will, a durable power of attorney, a last will and testament, and body organ donations. Pick out the hymns, readings, and other service items you want included at your funeral. Make a visit with your family or clergy to a funeral home to make prearrangements.

As you make these decisions, write down your wishes and go over them with your family members so they will know what to do when the time comes. After you decide, or as you are deciding...

Encourage. Encourage others in the church to do likewise. You will find that many people share your concern and have been equally reluctant to discuss their own death with anyone. You may find they are relieved to have someone to talk to who is willing to listen and take them seriously. Encourage the formation of a study group whose goal would be to have members plan their own funerals.

Encourage and take the lead in setting up a conference or workshop on options for dying to raise the consciousness of other parishioners. Encourage and support your clergy to preach, teach, and witness to the practical, theological, and sacramental aspects of illness and death.

Finally, in the midst of all the experiences of death:

Live. Live one day at a time. Live hopefully, rather than optimistically. The Judeo-Christian tradition is not *optimistic* about life and death; it is *hopeful*—hopeful that death is an end but not *the* end, a last word but not *the* last word, the end of one life and beginning of another. Optimism denies death and discounts disease; hope affirms death and transcends disease.

In the Episcopal tradition there is a prayer for the funeral liturgy that sums up the meaning of integrating the issues of illness and death into our everyday experience. The prayer encourages us to "live as those expecting to die and to die as those expecting to live." Such an attitude, contrary to the current popular practice of the church, will result in a realistic appraisal and action orientation regarding the issue of death planning.

JUNE 18, 1983

Who killed you,
You who lie dying by the twisted metal
Stretched on the pavement that smashed your skull
Twitching in your senseless agony?
Surrounded by your courtiers—that passing crowd
Who knew you, saw your danger
(But not how it was caused, if that would comfort me),
Ran at the insane screech of brakes and tires,
Beheld you graceful in the air before so great a fall,
And now wait murmuring—
Prince of your life
I must deny a crown for you in mine.

Who killed you, you or the man in the car
Who stayed awhile but fled from questioning?
Would that I had, that I might blame myself and know
    searing forgiveness;
Yet I must plead not guilty to killing you—
Guilty only of smothering and crowning you in retro-
    spect
By asking insistently to know
By requiring of God to answer me
Who killed you.

You must be free from me and from my question.
You needed me to stroke your hand and speak to you
When you were dying;
You needed me to pray with you and stay with you
So you might find the good and easy way
To that far country;
But not this question, it was not needed then.
I never thought to ask until
Grieving how you were gone from me
And goaded by others' curiosity and by their needs

I started to immure you in my life
And make a puppet-ruler of you there
(An ancient tendency, against which you and I had of-
   ten fought together)
By requiring obsessively an answer to this unanswera-
   ble question.

I must give all; it is required of me not to know.
(You tell me so and fight in me again the possessive
   craving.)
It lies between you and Him Who judges all
Into whose mercy you have already moved;
The case is shut and I am turned away.
How else could be you free to be
Undefeated as the young David was
Triumphant over Goliath's head
Glorious in victory?

                                        K.M.V. Morfey

5

Theology
By Slogan

Emma Hawley lies dying in room 423. Her family stands around her bed, watching and waiting. She is no longer responsive, but they all keep talking to her, holding her hand, loving her.

Symbols of her life surround them; her Bible, religious tapes, crosses hung by safety pins on the faded hospital curtains, many cards from her long stay there, religious tracts, flowers from church, and notes from prayer groups.

Throughout her illness her family and friends have encouraged the belief that God would surely cure her because she was such a devoutly religious woman—despite her physician's statements to the contrary. Thus, the air around her deathbed is charged with anger, tension, fear, and growing disbelief.

With her family silently watching, the patient breathes one last shallow breath and—it is finished. Her husband looks up at his daughter and says: "This wasn't supposed to happen." As Emma Hawley died a large part of her family's faith and belief died with her.

This scene is repeated with alarming regularity, not only in situations of serious illness and death but also in the lesser traumas of minor surgery and recoverable illness. It is clear from these and other comments made by patients, visitors, and healthcare workers that contemporary church teaching about death is either grossly misinterpreted or theologically bankrupt.

Perhaps practical matters such as heating the building, paying inflated maintenance costs, or dealing with drugs, divorce, and alcoholism have demanded a higher priority in the church's agenda. Perhaps clergy and others have been poorly prepared to accurately interpret the particular denomination's understanding of these issues. Perhaps in our haste to deny our mortality we gloss over the frightening and painful issues of death and dying, and in doing so have developed a theologically shallow and ultimately dysfunctional system of beliefs to protect and insulate ourselves from the inevitable.

Whatever the reason, contemporary Christian belief about illness and death has been ultimately reduced to a number of trendy slogans. All of us, clergy and laity alike, have used these stock phrases with ourselves and others. Mostly the words have seemed harmless social niceties spoken because we have heard them said before, because they seem to have something to do with church, and because we don't know what else to say. Seldom, however, have we examined the implications of the content of the phrases, much less their effect on the patients and families hearing them from the perspective of the sickbed.

When closely examined, the slogans are seen to be both demanding and disturbing. Each phrase *demands* something on the part of the patient, the family, and God. The person must conform to a certain set of criteria for healing, accept a particular explanation for the event, or behave in a specified manner.

Furthermore, while many persons say that they are trying to console the ill or dying patient or family member, the phrases result only in further *disturbing* everyone involved. Rather than being helpful, these slogans are a way of shutting down the conversation by glibly presenting a banal answer or solution to understanding the illness. To use them is to convey that the visitor really does not want to talk about what is meaningful to the patient but rather wants to avoid any mention of the fearful issues of uncertainty or death.

The following pronouncements are the most common examples of current American "theology by slogan."

1. *God will cure him (her). (Expect a miracle.)* Although many people would argue otherwise, this statement has nothing to do with faith. It is, rather, another method of denial and protectiveness. It denies the reality of the patient's pain, illness, discomfort, and dying and so protects the visitor from sharing any of those uncomfortable experiences. Instead of listening to the medical information that is given and making the most of the time left, people offer this theological slogan which serves to insulate and further isolate the patient and family.

The words also demand that the patient make a choice between medicine and faith. Imagine the patient whose doctor has just said he has less than six months to live and is then confronted with his prayer group demanding a cure from God and the patient and the physician. This unnecessary dilemma only increases the sense of confusion and helplessness. It also results in anger and resentment when the members of the family who had expected a miracle are faced with a death for which they were not at all prepared.

In fact, medicine and faith need not be viewed as opposites working toward contrary goals. The first tribal shamans were both priests *and* physicians. The two roles have only recently been separated as disagreements have arisen between science and religion. For the good of the patient and family, it is possible to accept and combine the unique offerings of each perspective into a realistic, prayerful, scientific *and* sacramental approach to illness and death.

2. *If you have enough faith, you'll be healed.* This often stated slogan assumes that the patient's worsening condition is directly proportional to a lack of faith. Demanding that the patient "try harder" with some internal spiritual resource, the phrase suggests healing is merely the result of extra effort. In fact, the result of such a comment is the creation of a deepening cycle of depression and despair. The patient, dying or in pain, feels responsible for having too little faith to overcome the situation, then feels guilty for that lack, and depressed or angry at the unreasonable demand.

The Gospel information concerning healing is quite different from the popular expression embodied in this statement. Healing in the New Testament has a vastly broader meaning than usually given it, and it happens in a much different manner.

Clergy and physicians are the worst offenders at seeing healing in an extremely narrow context. Usually "healing" when used by either group means physiological change has taken place: the tu· mor vanishes, the blood pressure returns to normal, the intestinal blockage breaks up In fact, to hear clergy and physicians talk the only *acceptable* form of "healing" is this kind of obvious physiological change.

But "healing" is much broader than this myopic, demanding definition. In fact, many things can be healed. Memories can be healed, dreams, disappointments and broken relationships can be healed; anger, resentment, and guilt of a lifetime can be healed; fear of pain, rejection, and judgment can be healed.

And all of this *healing* takes place *during the course of the dying*, so that death and healing, again, are not opposites. Quite the contrary: Death, viewed from this perspective, is a part of that ongoing process of healing which ultimately results in being in "God's nearer presence," where perfect wholeness has occurred.

Sometimes, and only sometimes, bodies are healed also, but that ought to be the *last* goal and understanding of healing, not the first. To see the whole person, as Jesus did, is to view healing in the context of that whole person and not just myopically focus on a required change in the physiological disease process.

It is interesting that this slogan focuses on and demands action on the part of the sick person, when the Biblical evidence is quite the opposite. In nearly every instance of healing, the event has nothing to do with the faith of the sick person. When the Centurion comes to Jesus, his servant is not even in sight. When the man's friends lower him down through the roof tiles, we are told that "when Jesus saw *their* faith" the man was healed.

Thus, the healing of sick or dying patients has *nothing* to do with *their own* faith (or lack of it). Biblical evidence points out that healing occurs in the context of the faith of the believing, caring, nurturing *community* surrounding that patient. It is within the context of *these* relationships—the servant's Centurion master, the man's concerned friends, the visitors who come to hospitals, whether family or otherwise—that faith and healing interact, not in the individual faith of the sick person. Healing takes place in the context of the community of believers, and that healing may be of past, present or future occurrences. Sometimes it may also be physiological. Often, the form that healing takes is death.

3. *It is God's will.* This covers everything from birth defects to hemorrhoids. It is often alleged to be the faithful person's answer to "Why me?"

Assuming that disease, congenital abnormalities, or self inflicted abuse are somehow the mysterious "will of God" implies that God is responsible for purposely planning these occurrences, usually to further some vague cosmic plan which the sick person is not allowed to question. If this belief is true, then God is as capricious, vindictive, and reprehensible as the diseases and disorders are insidious.

It is theologically inconsistent with the Biblical evidence of the Gospels to believe that God wills or wants people to have disease and sickness. Yet most people would prefer to think that God is the purveyor of pain and disability than to recognize the two major components of illness: personal responsibility and randomness.

We all know that there are certain things we can eat, smoke, drink, and do with our bodies (or not do, such as exercise) to increase the probability that we will be physical and emotional wrecks in 20 to 30 years. And yet, after 20 years of smoking, ingesting the usual American high calorie, high fat, high sugar and cholesterol diet, persons with cardiovascular difficulties suddenly blame their condition on *God's will.* The same argument is used for other stress related, or even genetically related illnesses. In fact, most people would like to relieve themselves of the responsibility for their health and wellness, relegating that chore to expensive, high technology "miracle medicine," and to a God who they hope will rescue them from their own imprudent lifestyles. Thus, when major illness strikes, they drag out God as the culprit.

Similarly, many people would prefer to believe that God plans out illness, distributes it like door prizes at birthday parties, and generally is in control of everyone's destiny. While this rather rigid understanding of God may be comforting for some, it completely ignores the element of randomness in disease. It also ignores free will. Imputing meaning and even intention to illness is a way of refusing to see that, as in many natural occurrences, some people get it and some people don't. Viruses and bacteria and whatever else may be precursors to disease seem to have as much free will to exist at random as the rest of us. Not knowing "why" people get disease (even when they have attempted to stack the odds in their favor through exercise, diet, etc.), many would rather rush to the mysterious will of a dictator-God than to embrace the lifetime of uncertainty that free will implies.

Personal responsibility and free will provide a particular image of God that will be examined in depth later. For further exploration of this complex issue, see the treatise by Leslie Weatherhead entitled, appropriately enough, *The Will of God* where the intentional, circumstantial, and ultimate wills of God are described.

4. *There's a reason for everything. The Lord works in strange ways.* A corollary of the previous slogan, this one has a slightly different nuance. In addition to assuming God is still playing Trivial Pursuit with your life and inflicting illness to make an unknown and probably unknowable point, there is also an emotional undertone of retribution. It assumes God is out to get you and finally did. It also implies you probably deserved it, and that somewhere, deep down inside, you know what you did to bring about the vindictive disease process with which you are now rightfully plagued.

Although sometimes stated as a message of comfort, the slogan is taken by patients as an affront, and rightly so. Rather than comforting someone who has just had a full-term stillborn, been given the news of an inoperable cancer, or told his arthritis will eventually be crippling, this theological anomaly results in anger, defensiveness, and disbelief.

Once again, Biblical evidence, personal responsibility, and randomness of disease are disavowed in favor of belief in a God who exercises a flawless memory with unmerciful vindictiveness.

5. *You have to be strong.* A theological injunction particularly common to men, this slogan confuses Jesus with John Wayne. If one is faithful, so the logic goes, one has nothing to fear, nothing about which to be sad, no reason to cry or be depressed or enraged. Patients tell themselves to be strong for their families, and families are strong for the patients.

What this slogan obscures is a conspiracy of denial. It is a denial of feelings, a denial of medical facts, and a denial of Christ Jesus' message of support and suffering with us. Hiding behind the model of Christian "strength," patients and families are able to deny their fear, sadness, and anger. They can ignore the advice of the physician and nurses to talk about the situation. They can totally miss the intent of Jesus' presence until it is too late to feel, talk, and be nurtured.

Contrary to this much practiced bit of popular wisdom, it is not only "okay" but *recommended* to be "weak" in the face of serious illness. It is desirable to cry, rage, to sink into the depths of depression, to reject, demand, bargain and wish. All these emotions are a natural part of us, and their expression can be used to increase or open up communication with God and one another and thus to strengthen, not diminish, faith.

To repress and deny our thoughts and feelings, even the unthinkable ones, is to forget that Christ Jesus exhibited all of these and more in the Garden of Gethsemane, where he tried to renegotiate his future three times.

6. *You don't die until your number comes up.* This often-heard remark reduces God to the clerk in the deli section of the supermarket. One can imagine God in a white deli apron standing behind the counter pulling the chain and announcing "Number 103," while people in hospital beds all over the universe painfully wait, their ticket stubs clenched in painful, clammy hands.

The function of the slogan is to attempt to understand unexpected recoveries, spontaneous remissions, and long term "lingering." The implication is that God personally decides the time of death for each individual, based on an unknown formula having something vaguely to do with guilt, suffering, reward, retribution, and, only occasionally, with mercy.

The experience of caregivers who frequently observe deaths is quite the opposite. Very often, in fact, people decide their own time of death. It is not at all uncommon to hear hospital stories of persons who physiologically could have lived for months but one day decided to quit—and died. Often the death decision relates to a particular date: birthday, wedding anniversary, holiday, or special day of remembrance for that couple or family.

Sometimes the comatose or seriously ill person will wait for the arrival of a particular relative, grandchild, or friend. Thus it is important to keep people informed of what persons are in the room, and who is arriving from out of town.

In the situation of a long, lingering process of dying, the patient may be waiting for "permission" to die. Once the family has verbally expressed to the person that they (the family) will be all right, that they will look after the survivor, and that it is okay to let go, the patient takes a deep sighing breath (of relief?) and dies, sometimes in a matter of minutes.

Especially in the case of close friends or family, people may tend to feel extremely guilty if they are not present at the very moment of death. And yet it is important to remember that patients frequently wait to die until their loved ones are *out of the room*.

Perhaps death is so intimately personal that one wants to do it alone; perhaps separation is so painful that the patient wishes to spare the loved one further anguish; or perhaps they fear the survivor will have to live with the memory of the death scene forever. In any case, from newborn infants to the elderly, one need not be surprised (or feel guilty for not being there) if the patient dies when loved ones are absent.

7. *God took him (her).* More direct than the previous line, but still presupposing an all-controlling God who capriciously determines our fate, this slogan makes God into a celestial body snatcher, or as one person said, "the great Hoover in the sky," randomly vacuuming people up off the earth. If true, it is no wonder survivors feel frustrated and angry at God. Rather than providing comfort, this statement often results in blame and resentment for God's alleged theft by appropriation.

But the New Testament has no place for a God who randomly and inexplicably "takes" people away from the ones they love. We see there instead a very different picture of trust and nurturing. Rather than "taking" the seriously ill person in some mysterious way we are not to question, the God of the Gospels is presented as one who welcomes and *accepts us with open arms when our bodies quit working*. God, then, is not the killer of infants, the murderer of the elderly, the destroyer of lives. God, to the contrary, is the welcomer of spent bodies, the comforter of mourners, the lover of all souls.

Whether survivors follow the image of an accepting, welcoming God or a controlling, taking God makes a great deal of difference in how they will grieve and how much they will continue to turn to God for support in the future.

8. Time heals all wounds. While purporting to express sympathetic understanding, this statement actually implies that sickness is abnormal and self indulgent; it subtly demands that patients hurry up and get well, or that families "deal with" the illness or loss quickly, as though the mere passage of time guaranteed healing. To be told "time heals all wounds" is to be judged guilty of psychological malingering and urged to move on and be over the death, since an adequate amount of time has presumably passed.

The truth is that time itself does *not heal anything.* In fact, time makes it worse—always. Especially during the first year (and often into the second and third) following the death of a loved one, the passage of time will exacerbate the pain and loneliness by daily verifying the reality of the loss. With the passage of birthdays, anniversaries, holidays, special days for the couple, and the anniversary of the death and the funeral, the feelings of loss and grief are made *worse,* not easier. Indeed there are some losses over which we may grieve our entire lives, and that process is perfectly normal.

It is also true that people will handle grieving (whether anticipatory grieving by the patient and family at the time of diagnosis and during the illness, or on the part of the survivors following the death) the same way they handle other major problems in their lives—at their *own* pace and following their *own* style of managing and coping. To be urged to comply with another person's manner and time schedule is both insensitive and unrealistic. Such a demand has more to do with the discomfort of the onlooker than it does with real concern for the person experiencing the loss.

Christian theology never equates time with healing. Rather, the stories and parables throughout the New Testament indicate that *repentance, faith, love, forgiveness, relationships,* and *trust* heal, not time. It is far more helpful to support these experiences than to demand a change in sad or grieving behavior in order to alleviate our own discomfort.

It is important to remember that all of these slogans are attempts to use ideas thought to be based on Christian theology to come to terms with the realities of sickness, healing, and death. They are not, in fact, examples of Christian theology, but rather are statements of an American civil religion which presupposes an all-controlling, all-responsible, capricious, and punitive God. As such they function to reinforce an optimistic worldview of a national God who rewards good (our country) and punishes evil (our enemies) and who sees illness either as a logical punishment for real or imagined wrongdoing or as part of a plan of an individual Manifest Destiny.

A major issue raised by the examination of these slogans is the nature of good and evil. The church also has taught for centuries that good is rewarded and evil punished. Yet anyone old enough to read the headlines of their local newspaper knows that is untrue. What, then, is the value in being "good?" What ought we to be teaching our children about the real nature of good and evil? How will we understand these ideas ourselves and how will we relate them to illness and death? It is clear that much more study and education need to be done at the local church level in order to relieve the confusion and disruption caused by the poor theologizing characterized in the slogans listed above.

One of the ways to approach this discussion is through the two major (and opposing) views of God. The first posits an *active God in a responsive universe.* This belief system sees God as omniscient, omnipresent, all-powerful and in total control, while the rest of the universe (including illness and death) merely responds to God's command.

The second view assumes a *responsive God in an active universe.* This system sees the universe actively, freely going about its natural business of building up and breaking down, living and dying, while God, supporting the free will of natural and human law, seeks to respond to that activity. This belief structure finds God not sending or controlling disease, but rather supporting and upholding those afflicted with illness—*suffering with them,* and grieving with them and their survivors.

In their need to combat the feelings of helplessness and loss of control, it is understandable that many people choose to believe in an active God who is totally in charge. But, as Weatherhead says in *The Will of God:* "There is ultimately no comfort in a lie." The slogans, therefore, and the God they presuppose, will ultimately prove shallow and unfulfilling. They are also inconsistent with the image presented in the New Testament of a loving, forgiving, merciful God who sees humankind as co-creators. It is this God who, as shown in Christ Jesus, suffers *with* us, feels helpless *with* us, *shares with us* our sense of being out of control. It is only this God who can affirm *both* our living *and* our dying.

FREEDOM

They made a coffin for me
Then they put me in a box
They laid me on silk pillows
To keep me from all shocks.
They told me to rest quietly
And not disturb their peace:
If I was a good girl
One day I'd get release.

They nailed the lid upon me,
Put a hammer in my hands
And I hit the final nail in
As propriety demands.

Then, Lord, you came and broke in,
Wrenched the lid from off the box,
Gave bread to my enfeebled frame,
Blood to revive my stock.

You grasped my hands in your hands,
Threw the pillows far away,
Said, "Kathryn, dare you follow
Into the light of day?

Your eyes will be no use to you,
The radiance is so bright;
But if you follow close to me
You need not fear the light."

I left the box behind me,
Forgot propriety's demands,
Stumbled gladly into freedom
Holding you with both my hands.

Then today I was fainthearted,
I wanted to see ahead.
I took my hands from you, my Lord,
Looked out of the light instead.

I saw a wasted desert,
No water anywhere,
Corpses, coffins with silk pillows—
That's all was growing there.

That graveyard's where I could be
But it's what I've left behind.
Accept these hands again, my Lord,
Let your light make me blind.

K.M.V. Morfey

6

Death and
Spirituality

The previous two chapters have
indicated that we who say we are Christians are quite reluctant
to make death planning decisions for ourselves or others. Though
we claim to know something of dying as the central core of our belief, our slogan approach to theology reveals a death-denying orientation based more on civil religion than on traditional Biblical
thought. Following directly from these situations is the formation
of a spirituality that also denies, fears and avoids acknowledgment of finitude and death.

One of the ways that spiritual system begins to develop is by the
use in our culture of carefully chosen euphemisms to insulate ourselves from the reality of death. Phrases like *passed away, gone,
lost, going down the tubes, cashed in his chips,* or *bit the dust* are
common expressions for death. A favorite healthcare euphemism is
expired. Library cards and parking meters expire. *People* die.

Sometimes just before death we say the person is: *on his last
leg, ready to go, hanging on by a thread, circling the drain, preparing for the celestial discharge,* or *packing it in.* Even the Roman Catholic church has changed its theology, naming "the sacrament of the sick" what used to be known as "last rites" or
"extreme unction."

We also portray our relationship with death in *military* language and metaphors. We describe patients as having *fought the
good fight, lost the battle, gave up the ship/ghost* or *surrendered*

to their fate. We bring in the troops, *combat* illness and disease, *triage* patients, *allocate* resources. Patients are seen and described as *victims* of heart attacks, cancer and stroke. Germs *invade* the body; physicians and nurses *feel defeated* when they do not *successfully overcome* a disease. This military imagery sets up yet another good/bad dichotomy where death is never an acceptable outcome.

In an attempt to lessen the fear of death and further deny its reality, we tell some wonderful jokes about the afterlife. To illustrate just how many are in our common memory, it is necessary only to list a few of the punch lines: *Oh, that's just God, he likes to pretend he's a doctor; Be quiet, they think they're the only ones up here; Oh, that's just God, he likes to pretend he's Tom Landry; The good news is there's baseball in heaven, the bad news is you're scheduled to pitch tomorrow.*

Our language describing illness, dying, and afterlife accurately reflects a mirror image of our spiritual belief about death. And the image is that death is bad, the evil enemy, wrong, unacceptable, and unjust.

As we have seen, the church seems to have exacerbated and supported this denial by consistently offering an inadequately defined theology, resulting in the previously presented cliches. The euphemisms, military language, jokes, and theological slogans are further evidence of the shallowness, misunderstanding, and fear surrounding death and dying. And those characteristics show themselves in contemporary Christian spirituality.

How might we, then, approach death so as to better integrate it into our spiritual journeys? The following ideas may be helpful as guidelines.

Death as daily process. That we each die a little bit every day is not only metaphorically true, it is indeed *physiologically* true. Each day we destroy millions of cells, most of which are replenished in our systems with new ones. In addition, the natural, normal aging process accelerates as our bodies expand, grow, and work their way toward atrophy, deterioration, and death. Because we are looking from the inside out we usually do not see this daily process; it only becomes evident after the passage of time, or when seeing our photographs compared with those of a few years ago. Daily physiological death is necessary in order for new cells to generate and take over. It is likewise ultimately necessary for us (as whole bodies, collections of cells) to die so that our children and grandchildren can take over what we have left behind.

It is also true that we die a little each day *psychologically*. As we take in new data about who we are, about the way we see ourselves and others, about our past, our parents and growing up, it is necessary, if we are to allow ourselves to mature, to let the old images of ourselves die. Likewise, old images of our parents, our families, and our children must also die and be replaced by new ones if we are to see these people as who they are now. This psychological death is largely out of our immediate awareness although we get glimpses of it through new dreams and new relationships.

We also die *spiritually* every day. Just as psychological and physiological processes continue to evolve within us, so spiritual growth can only take place if we allow our images of God to die daily, along with imagesof ourselves in relationship to God. If we do *not* let them die, rigor mortis sets in. We find ourselves defending rigid spiritual beliefs, unchangeable ideas of God and the world, with an unwillingness to let God's new words break into us because we are so comfortably surrounded by ancient beliefs and images.

The biblical witness of Jesus is clear on the fact that God does not wish us to live forever under the same beliefs, rituals, and images of ourselves and God. As God dies daily—changes, renews, heals, overturns—so we must also as made in God's image. To accept our task of dying daily is to begin to see death as a normal part of daily living.

Hospital and other institutional caregivers who are present at the bedsides of hundreds of dying patients know from experience (often contrary to their own belief at first) that death is normal, natural, expected, and often welcomed at any age. As they see people die, watching the lines drop from their faces, watching them relax, be calm and at peace for the first time in months, death loses its horror and fearsomeness and becomes as natural and acceptable as any other part of our life's journey.

Death as daily process—physiologically, psychologically,

and spiritually—is the first step toward realistic Christian spirituality.

Death as letting go. Jesus was constantly telling people to die, to be reborn, and to let go of things. He indicated that they indeed could not be reborn, know the kingdom of heaven, or have peace until they *did* let go.

It's as though Jesus knew the stress and energy we use, or that consumes us, in our desperate attempts to control, to hold on, and to understand. He understood that that same energy could be used for other, more significant endeavors in the building of the kingdom. And he understood from his own experience that it was in the letting go that the death and new life were able to occur, and *only* in that experience.

It was only after the tables were overturned that that the temple could be a place of healing. The image is the same for us: unless we are willing to have our carefully placed, comfortable tables that are secure and known overturned, healing cannot and will not occur in our lives.

It was only after letting go in the Garden of Gethsemane that Jesus was able to feel peaceful and face his death realistically. The image is the same for us: unless we are willing to desperately argue, to wrestle and grapple with our God and then to let go, we will never know the peace that "passes all understanding."

It was only after crying out in anguish and despair, and questioning on the cross that Jesus again let go and *risked* resurrection. The image is the same for us: unless we are willing to question, cry out, and, once again, let go and die, we will never know the present meaning of resurrection in our lives.

The images are clear: We are called by God to let go. Some of the things we are encouraged to let go of are:

Parents. Jesus was speaking plainly and psychologically when he said "Unless you forsake father, mother, sister, brother for my sake you will not know the kingdom of heaven." It is indeed true that unless we let go of images of our parents and the family we grew up in, unless we relinquish them and stop blaming that environment and those people for our present day difficulties, we will never be free to grow in the here and now.

We will never be free to know the kingdom of heaven because we are too (literally) damned busy hanging on to the past, hanging on to grudges, to unfinished business that can never be done, to mistakes we made, to things we said or didn't say or that were said and done to us. Unless we literally let go of the image of parents and/or family in our heads, we will not know the kingdom of heaven. It is crucial to our spirituality and our spiritual journey that we relinquish those images and allow those feelings to die.

Children. The same statement is equally true concerning our children. We do not own them and they do not own us. If we would allow ourselves to see them as separate people rather than as "the children," some incredible changes would immediately occur in our relationships, in our expectations, in our demands, and in our exchange of feelings with each other. If we were willing to drop the bonds, the expectations, the assumptions about their and our behavior regarding wishes for love and attention, then each of us would be free to give and get those things if we so chose, not because they were demanded. When Jesus said "Let the little children come to me," he meant yours and mine. If they belong to God (which they do, as do we all) then we exist in new relationships. It is important to our spirituality that we also let go of our children from birth.

The World. Jesus said "Be not conformed to this world." As Christians we are daily confronted with advertising messages on how to be, who to be, how much to spend. We are told repeatedly how much popularity, power, and prestige our money and influence can buy us. We are warned in contrast by Jesus to be careful with these powerful objects.

We are also told the world is not a forbidden or foreboding place, that there are pleasures abounding here and we are to enjoy them as much as possible, smelling the flowers along the way, loving and being loved, hugging, being sexual, sensual, sensitive and caring, wallowing in the simple luxuries God has provided for us in this world.

It is no wonder then that we get so attached to our existence here and to the people with us. Hospice and hospital caregivers daily witness dying patients fearing leaving this world, who are angry at leaving these pleasures and pains behind and leaving behind the ones they love and have loved for many, many years. Such attachment is deep and painful to break off.

And yet the message is clear: "Be not conformed to this world." We are clearly told that the world is larger than we see it now; that there is more to life than the physicalness we experience here and now. Death is a passage from life to life, as are childhood, adolescence, adulthood, and old age.

Letting go of the world is the beginning of coming to terms with our unrealistic images of power and control. Letting go of the world, detaching ourselves from it ultimately while working in it penultimately, is a crucial part of developing a daily spiritual life.

God. This is perhaps the most difficult death of all. And yet, if we are to find God we must let go of him/her/it or however we see and use God. It is not only true that "They who save their lives will lose them and they who lose their lives for my sake will save them." It is also true that whoever hangs on to God will never find God and whoever lets go of God, who dies to God and lets God die to him or her, only that person will ever know God as God is.

Death as letting go of God means letting go of God as always in control; God as ultimate punisher and demander; God as made in the image of our father or mother, or God as the anthropomorphic image of ourselves. It is to let go of God as the cosmic vending machine into whom we put our fifty cent prayers and out of whom come the candy answers and solutions. It is to let go of God as the cosmic insurance policy guaranteeing that life is ultimately fair and will turn out all right; God as the defender of whatever our current cause happens to be and vanquisher of national and international foes. Indeed, letting go of God means letting go of God as the ultimate denier of death and accepting the fact that God is as helpless as we are.

Dietrich Bonhoeffer in his *Ethics* describes this image of death as the letting go of God:

> The God who makes us live in this world without using him as a working hypothesis is the God before whom we are ever standing. Before God and with him we live without God. God allows himself to be edged out of the world and on to the

cross. God is weak and powerless in the world, and that is exactly the way, the only way, in which he can be with us and help us. It is not by his omnipotence that Christ helps us, but by his weakness and suffering.

This is the decisive difference between Christianity and all religions. Man's religiosity makes him look in his distress to the power of God in the world; he uses God as a Deus ex machina. The Bible however directs him to the powerlessness and suffering of God; only a suffering God can help.

Death as letting go means letting go of the God we currently know and allowing God to witness to us out of weakness in the world with us, by us and for us.

Death is a powerful paradigm for our spirituality. Until we come to terms with our own death we will not have come to terms with our life, alone, and alone with God.

IV
SURVIVING DEATH

7

Grief Tasks

Just as there are no "stages" of dying, so there are no such easily identifiable categories of grieving. Elisabeth Kübler-Ross did provide assistance in understanding the behaviors that a dying patient is likely to exhibit with five phases: denial, anger, bargaining, depression and acceptance. But it does a severe disservice to a dying patient and family to label their reactions merely for the purpose of pigeonholing them, demanding they fit into these neat boxes and move through them sequentially.

The phases are, in fact, seldom seen in a regular sequential order. The patient may feel angry one day, depressed the next, and denying the next. Or the time frame for these reactions may be a matter of hours or minutes. The categories, therefore, are better understood as "tasks" to be performed in no particular time or pattern, with no moral judgment determining which phases are "good" and which are "bad."

These same guidelines can be applied to the process of grieving. While many persons have described "stages" of grief, it is important both to survivors and the people interacting with them not to categorize or demand that they move through these phases in a particular sequence. Rather, these reactions, too, must be seen as "tasks" to be performed or behaviors that are likely to be evidenced as the survivor responds to the death.

One of the best models for describing grief reactions is that of Colin Murray Parkes. In his book, *Bereavement—A Study of Grief in Adult Life,* Parkes, borrowing somewhat from Kübler-Ross, sets forth five "stages" of grieving, complete with suggested time frames. With the disclaimers mentioned above about sequence and stages, the Parkes model is a useful way to understand the tasks of grieving.

1. *Alarm/Shock.* The initial reaction to the death, whether sudden or expected is the same. As one emotionally distraught family member said when her mother had taken a last breath: "You get prepared but you never get ready." Even when funeral plans have been made, the will is in order, and a Living Will has enabled the patient's wishes to be honored, there is something about the finality of the actual death that is always disturbing at a deep level for the survivors. The tears, the wailing, and the stoicism reflected by different cultures all indicate both the shock of the loss of the patient, and the alarm of the realization that the survivor will also one day die.

A common occurrence during this period is sleep disturbance. The survivor may sleep constantly or not at all. Especially after a long illness, the person may be so physically exhausted that extra sleep time is needed to recuperate. Feelings of "weariness" and "numbness" are pervasive. As the person begins to work through the events surrounding the death, time is needed for the body to process those events and make them part of the present understanding and mind set. This "processing" often takes the form of lying in bed for hours on end, thinking, staring at the ceiling, remembering, and feeling. Survivors for whom the normal routine was early rising followed by a regimen of work or caretaking or hospital visits may think they are "cracking up," "falling apart," or "going crazy" because of their weariness or inordinate need for rest.

Likewise, people who were once sound sleepers now find themselves unable to make it through the night without waking every couple or three hours, only to have difficulty getting back to sleep. Dreams, flashbacks to the scene of the death and the funeral, concerns about the future (financial, social, health), as well as the physical difference of not having the person in the house or in the bed all combine to prevent sleep and rest.

While Parkes believes that this reaction occurs mainly in the first two weeks after the death, it is entirely possible for the survivor to awaken on a birthday, anniversary, or holiday many months hence and have the same feelings of alarm and shock. The important thing is to know that these feelings, along with the sleep disturbances, are common to persons who have experienced a death.

2. *Searching.* After the initial shock has passed somewhat, a period of searching ensues. This is a time of pining, of intense yearning for the dead person, and of continuing to act as if that person were still alive. There is a part of the survivor that will not believe the death has happened, protesting the event by still going through the old behavior patterns as though the loved one was there.

The survivor may think of something to tell the person, pick up the phone and dial the first few digits of the number, then put the receiver down, realizing that there will be no one there. The survivor may start to write the person a note, barely getting through the name before the paper is wadded up and thrown away. Pulling into the driveway after a busy day at work, the survivor may look forward to telling the loved one some particular incident of importance, imagining the person to be fixing dinner in the kitchen, then suddenly remember that there will be no one there to tell. This part of the search is the expectation that the person will continue to be present in the old patterns of relating.

Another part of this task is the search around town for the missing person. As the survivor continues on with his or her life, frequenting the same places for shopping, religious services, entertainment, study, and relaxation, she or he keeps one eye open to spot the loved one, imagining the person will be physically or spiritually present there. It is not unusual during this time for survivors to report hearing, seeing, or smelling the scent of the loved one.

Frequently the survivor will return to the hospital or nursing unit for a brief visit. While ostensibly this visit is to thank the nurses or staff for their good care and to bring them some gift of flowers, fruit, or candy, the survivor invariably wants to stop by the room where the loved one died. There is something very therapeutic or completing about the experience, painful as it usually is. It is as though the survivor is searching, but at the same time validating that the loved one really is no longer there. Friends or staff members can help by understanding this need, and by offering to accompany the survivor on this painful journey.

Again, although Parkes places this period at four to six weeks after the first, the search continues off and on for many people for years and years to come.

3. *Mitigation.* This task, according to Parkes, occurs about the third or fourth month, when the searching begins to come to an end. The pain starts to ease and the protest lessens somewhat. No longer does the survivor think of what to say to the person while driving home. No notes are begun. The phone is not dialed. The results of the search are becoming more obvious and reluctantly acceptable.

Understandably, this is a time of depression and deep despair. Coming to terms with the emptiness is a painful and difficult task. As Parkes quite beautifully describes it, this period is the one in which "presence changes to memory." The survivor begins to have an image of the loved one no longer as present, but as past. The expectation that the person will be nearby diminishes and is replaced by the resignation to find that person only in memories.

This task frequently involves the processing of grieving dreams. Often the following sequence of dreams has been reported:

A. The survivor sees the loved one as dead, in a casket, on a slab, lying down, with no affect, no movement, no color in the lifeless body. There is no interaction between the two in this set of dreams.

B. The survivor sees the loved one as dead, but the loved one is sitting up and talking with the survivor. There is still no affect, no color or life in the body, but there is interaction. Often the talk is purely factual, rather than emotional.

C. The survivor is home alone in a room in the house (or elsewhere) and suddenly becomes aware that someone has entered the room. Turning around, the survivor is shocked to see it is the dead loved one. This time, the loved one is clearly alive, color and affect are seen in the body, and conversation takes place as though it picked up where they left off before the death. The survivor feels stunned, confused, and often worried about explaining events that have taken place since the loved one's death.

D. The survivor goes to visit the loved one in another place (house, apartment, city, etc.) The survivor is usually happy, smiling, pleasant and the scene is sunny and attractive. This scenario usually signals the end of the sequence. Dreams from here out may be sporadic, relating to specific instances in the growth or experience of the survivor.

Frequently (especially in the third set of dreams) these experiences are so real and powerful that the survivor will awaken feeling confused about whether or not the loved one is really there.

Keeping a journal can be an important method for working through the task of mitigation. Recording the dreams, the survivor will begin to see a pattern of progression from images of death to images of health, both for the survivor and the loved one. Writing a dialogue with the dead person can be very helpful in working out whatever unfinished business there might be to complete. Composing a letter, saying the unsaid things, stating unstated feelings and thoughts can be useful. Sometimes, going to the grave (if there is one) and talking to the person can help to work through the depression and despair.

Whatever methods are chosen, friends are an indispensable part of this task. They need to be there to listen, support, and hold the survivor as the pain and presence move toward mitigation and memory.

4. *Anger/Guilt.* The fifth and sixth month, following the Parkes model, are filled with emotional turmoil. This is a period of the "what ifs:"

"What if we'd have caught it earlier?"

"What if he'd gone to the doctor like I asked him to six months ago?"

"What if she'd had one more chemotherapy treatment?"

"What if I'd have spent more time with him?"

"What if a different doctor had seen her?"

The survivor is torn with guilt about things that were done and things that were not done, things that were and were not said, or thought, or imagined. Feelings of anger surface from deep within the grieving person and are aimed at the caregivers, the family, friends, God, the survivor—and frequently at the dead person. Then the survivor feels guilty for feeling angry at those persons, especially the loved one. Such feelings need to be affirmed as acceptable, understandable, and necessary.

Anger and guilt are overwhelming as the person goes on with life without the dead person. There is anger about socializing alone, guilt about seeing other people; anger at others who get to go on together, guilt about resenting their happiness, or at least their companionship. There is anger at being in the situation of having sustained a loss that will never be retrieved, and guilt about coming to terms with it.

Once again, knowing that the feelings are to be expected can help obviate the fear that the survivor is the only person who ever experienced them. Talking to others in a bereavement group or having coffee with the hospital chaplain, social worker, or Hospice volunteer can allow the survivor to ventilate with someone who is not going to give advice, but rather listen with understanding and confidence.

5. *Identity/Recovery.* Eventually (Parkes says during the last six months of the first year), the survivor begins to move back into social events, religious and community activities, and work or other daily routines. New patterns are formed, new relationships developed, and a new identity begins to emerge based on parts of the old and parts of the new self.

This is a very difficult, tender, and vulnerable time. The survivor is testing out new behaviors, or rather using old ones and updating them with new experiences. He or she, therefore, may feel extremely tentative during this period, and may need sustaining without pushing, understanding without judgment.

The survivor may seek out different kinds of persons entirely, or may jump too quickly into a relationship for which she or he seems unready. (See Chapters 8 and 9.) Going to a movie, out to dinner, or to a social gathering may seem like a good idea at the time, but turn out to be too overwhelming once there. Friends can allow grieving persons the freedom to change their mind at the last minute, or to leave when they feel the need, regardless of the hour or circumstance.

With good friends supporting and affirming the survivor during this time, a new identity will develop that will integrate the dead loved one into the pattern of the person's past. Strengthening that identity and developing it further will very likely take the rest of life to complete.

It is important to reiterate that these tasks are not necessarily sequential. They may be performed and felt in any order and at any time. The original in-depth grief studies conducted following the Cocoanut Grove fire in the 1950's concluded that if survivors were still having grief reactions after *six weeks*, then their response was dysfunctional and they needed psychiatric support. Later studies in the 1960's found that *six months* were needed to *complete* the grieving process. The Parkes model, written in the mid 1970's, suggests a *one year* time frame in which to have all the problems neatly wrapped up and finished. At a recent Hospice symposium, psychologists proposed *two to three years* as a more reasonable period for resolution of grief.

The truth is that people handle grief the same way they handle every other major difficulty in their lives. There is no designated time frame within which survivors *must* resolve their grieving. Whether assertive or passive, with emotions or stoicism, resignation or remorse, they will grieve according to who they are and what works best for them—and they will do it *at their own speed*.

Furthermore, it may be that twenty years from now the survivor is in a particular place, hears a song on the radio, or remembers a special day of the month and becomes teary, depressed, or melancholy. This perfectly normal occurrence underlines the fact that there are some deaths over which we may grieve our entire lives in varying degrees of intensity.

Many people want to know how to identify "abnormal" grieving. Obviously bizarre behavior that is out of character for the survivor is relatively easy to recognize. But less blatantly, if it seems clear that the emotional intensity of the survivor is consistently getting in the way of regular patterns of functioning (shopping, eating, work, health), then additional support in the form of counseling or medication could well be in order.

In any case, understanding the framework of grieving is useful both to survivors and their support system. It is only as these two work together that resolution and healing may occur.

8

Sex After Death

Your lover has died. The person you dreamed with, for however long a time, is no longer there to dream with you. The person you shared space with, no matter how big or small, is no longer there to rattle around the house, bother you with tasks or questions, play and laugh with and share secrets and argue and talk with anymore. The person you crawled into bed with late at night and held close and stroked gently and wanted to touch and hold you is gone. The one you snuggled with deep under blankets in the cold sheets of winter and wrestled with in the sweat of summer under ceiling fans and nibbled and kissed and explored, sometimes with passion, sometimes with duty, has suddenly vanished.

The bed, whether double, queen or king, is gigantically vacant. It is as empty as the rest of your life without the one you loved.

Death of a lover is one of those things that is not supposed to happen. It happens in *Love Story* and it happens in the daytime soaps, but it is not part of the script we write for ourselves. It is, indeed, so far from our consciousness that when it does occur we are shocked, devastated, and indelibly changed for the rest of our lives.

While many books and articles are written on grief and bereavement, they seldom deal with the delicate and intensely personal issue of the survivor's need for sexuality and intimacy after death. People who consider themselves friends may jokingly ask

"How's your love life?" but, as with grief in general, few seriously approach the subject due to their own discomfort. Survivors are then left with a plethora of questions, feelings, demands, and needs that go unanswered in a society content to focus itself on life and youth; a society where death is consistently denied, as are the needs of those who have experienced it.

The following examination of sex after death is, first of all, meant to provide information for survivors. By discussing common experiences reported by persons who have had a lover die, a picture of usual responses and normally expected tasks will gradually emerge to offer guidelines for this most singular kind of bereavement.

This information may be helpful not only to those who have experienced the loss of a lover. Those who are friends of the bereaved also may gain insight into how they can be more supportive to the survivor and be better prepared when their own lover dies. The guidelines will also be useful to persons who have experienced the death of *anyone* close to them. With the death of a child, parent, close friend, or even co-worker, many of the responses are identical in terms of sexual needs, feelings, and behavior on the part of the survivor.

Although a direction may be seen in the pattern of the descriptions, they are *not* meant to be sequential. For example, while one might assume that "recovery" from the death would begin with loss of libido and end with acceptance of nurturing, the truth is that loss of libido may occur repeatedly and in no particular "order" in the coping process. Similarly, acceptance of nurturing may begin the day after the death and ebb and flow as the survivor accomplishes the other tasks of mourning.

There may be some raised eyebrows at the use of the word "lover." It is an emotionally loaded term because it implies strong, usually sexual, feelings, and is not as definitive or exclusive as the word "spouse." But "lover" is purposely meant here to be *in*clusive. It can (depending on the reader) mean "spouse," "love," "partner," "friend," or "lover" in the usual sense.

Likewise, in the pages that follow, the term "sexuality" is used because it is the most obvious form of interaction. But one could also read "intimacy" for "sexuality," and be even more inclusive in understanding the dilemmas of vulnerability, openness, and closeness faced by those surviving death.

Feelings of intimacy do not die with the spouse or lover's death, though (as we will see) some temporary abatement will occur. Survivors will continue to be sexually active or intimate in some manner. Initially, and often permanently, this behavior will occur outside of marriage. (Often there are quite reasonable legal, insurance, property, medical, or emotional reasons for this.) The worst that may be said, morally, about this is that it is unfortu nate. While marriage may be the desired goal, it is grossly unrealistic to demand it as a requirement for survivors. To do so is to be rigidly legalistic, unforgiving, and unmercifully critical.

The issues discussed are behaviors and episodes that usually occur in the journey following the loss of a love. As with the discussion of death and grieving above, they are to be seen as tasks to be experienced rather than an orderly plan to "overcome" the loss. Likewise, they are not meant to be construed as right or wrong ways to feel, think, or behave. There is no proper or correct way to react to such an experience. There are only the ways that we *do* react, and the following are descriptions of those behaviors.

As survivors slowly make their way through the days following the death, they can expect these events to occur:

1. *Loss of libido.* While most people are prepared for the emotional turmoil and exhaustion of grief, they are never told that grief is incredibly physically draining as well. The combination of both the physical and emotional elements logically leads to a diminishment of sexual interest and ability.

Lying in bed for hours at a time, gazing at the ceiling, remembering, sorting out thoughts and plans, all one thinks about is rest from the tasks ahead. Sex is not a high priority when there are so many other things to be done: bills to be corrected and paid, clothes to be donated, business affairs to be settled, children to be tended, employment to be continued or found. Often sex is seen as one more time consuming thing that, fortunately, can be put off a while longer while one uses the available energy to solve the other problems at hand.

People frequently report feeling "numb from the neck down" as depression and sadness drain sensitivity from the skin, and desire is replaced with disinterest. Even sexual dreams end without a climax, accentuating the sense of emptiness, the loss of self worth and desirability.

Often one behaves sexually and otherwise as though the lover is still around, even long after the lover's death. Whether the issue is spending money on a new outfit or observing a potential sex partner, the resulting feeling is one of overwhelming guilt for "cheating" on the loved one or "disrespecting" his or her memory. It is easier not to have sexual stirrings than to have them crushed by the weight of self doubt and guilt.

Early post-death sexual experiences are often reported to be physically or emotionally painful and confusing, fraught with diametrically opposed feelings, and a sense of panic or fear. After one or two such experiences, loss of libido seems a welcome relief.

An underlying issue here is powerlessness. The death of a lover leaves the survivor stranded, alone, powerless to change the situation or to bring the person back. The survivor is overwhelmed, not only with physical tasks to perform, but also with an emotional reshuffling of expectations, plans, and feelings. The result is a sense of helplessness and powerlessness with obvious sexual ramifications.

Eventually, as plans get changed, business is put in order, and immediate decisions are accomplished, the gradual sense of reorganization and control will begin to result in the return of sexual desires, at least temporarily.

2. *Sex as searching.* "Starting over" is a misnomer. Nobody starts over; rather, they continue from where they left off. No one can undo the experiences of the relationship leading up to the time of the lover's death. But an interesting psychological phenomenon commonly reported by survivors is a kind of regression back to the time before sex began with the former partner.

If, for instance, the relationship dates back to one's early twenties, one may suddenly feel as if one is in one's late teens again sexually: uncertain, untried, unsure. It is as though the death somehow wipes out the sexual maturity and experience that occurred during the time of the relationship with the lover and the person is "back to square one again." It is natural, then, to imagine the survivor would search for another partner to renew and continue that lost experience.

However, as one almost "shops" for a replacement during the initial time following the death, the search encounters major impediments. Loss of libido and severe mood swings, from passionate to disinterested, often leave the survivor confused, frustrated, and angry about sexual experiences, with a similar effect on new partners. Sex becomes a perfunctory chore in the search to take up the lonely space that seems never able to be filled.

In fact, many people report that sex makes the loss worse. Flashbacks are commonplace occurrences. In the midst of intimacy or intercourse with a new partner, one's mind races to comparisons with or memories of the dead lover. Lying together afterwards engenders tender feelings of previously happy moments. Whether the sexual experience with the former partner was good or bad, sex now is a constant reminder of that loss, of the lack of what one had, of the pain of the death.

Often this searching is a time of mechanical difficulties during sex: impotence, lack of lubrication, vaginismus, premature (or no) ejaculation. Such experiences only exacerbate the absence of the lover and leave the survivor feeling more despair. It is important to remember that this time, like the time of libido loss, is temporary. With further experiences and the rebuilding of one's sense of self worth, the mechanical and emotional impediments begin to dissipate, even though memories may still blindside the survivor from time to time.

3. *Sex as distraction.* The grieving process is intensely time-consuming. The survivor dwells for moments, hours, even days on the memory of the dead lover, reviewing experiences, wondering about the death and what he or she might have done to prevent or alter it, still hoping for a sign of communication. To help assuage these thoughts, sexual activity is often a strong distraction. It takes one's mind off the past and demands attention powerfully to the present. It helps pass the time, even if one is merely "going through the motions" with a new partner.

With the body feeling generally numb and unresponsive to any outside stimuli, one's sexuality seems to be in neutral. Severe depression and grieving dreams (sometimes sexual ones) further decrease the desire for sexual intimacy with anyone. But even a few sexual contacts may also re-awaken the survivor to the powerful potential of this most distracting and potentially healing pastime.

Recreational sex is frequently a sign of some forward progress on the part of the survivor. If indiscriminate, it can be an indication of the searching process or a behavioral expression of anger. But if sex is pursued for its playfulness and distracting quality, it can be a sign of the beginning of recovery. As the survivor deals more realistically with the loss, he or she is better able to reach out and do what is pleasurable, even if it is only momentarily distracting. The distraction may also develop into new bonding relationships, though this is unlikely in the early months of grieving a lover.

4. *Sex as anger.* As most people know, anger is a perfectly normal, even healthy, response to death. One has angry feelings at oneself for things done and not done; at the caregivers (physicians, hospital staff, family members) who looked after the loved one; at the pressure from others to be over the grieving; even at the lover for dying and leaving. Often this anger will be expressed sexually.

Indiscriminate sex with multiple partners (as mentioned above) can be a way of striking back at men or women for the loss, or a way to defiantly prove one is still "okay." It can be an angry form of flailing about with no direction, recoiling from the devastation of the death, putting oneself at high risk for disease and even one's own death. Many people report "having sex with a vengeance" as though the kind and number of partners provides a means for getting back at the dead person, or for punishing oneself for guilt about things done or not done, said or not said concerning that death.

Sometimes the anger is directed at the new partner when the survivor realigns too quickly or seeks a replacement for the dead lover. The otherwise normal anger is turned inward to become self punishing or outward to physical or emotional harm to others. Hurtful or violent sexual interactions are expressions of this hostile response to the loss.

Possibly the most difficult kind of anger to experience or express is anger about the situation. The lover's death was not in the scenario the two had written. Where once there existed a relatively comfortable arrangement of some sexual and emotional security, now the survivor is thrown unwillingly into the incredibly disruptive and time-consuming maelstrom of dating, sexual gaming, and social insecurity at a time when defenses and self image are at their lowest ebb. Anger at this unchosen situation is often made worse by sexual or intimate encounters as one is again reminded both of what is desired and what is missing.

5. *Sex as a substitute for closeness*. Frequently sex is seen as the requirement (price paid) for what is *really* wanted: closeness and intimacy. Many people report simply wanting literally just to "sleep with somebody."

As one person described it: "The bed is empty. There is no one to throw a leg over, snuggle in with, bump butts with in the middle of the night, hear breathing beside you, kiss on the forehead when you come back from the 3 a.m. bathroom call, and hug when the mutually dreaded alarm goes off."

All the little signs of warmth, acceptance, and sharing are gone, and their absence is shattering. It is often the search for these things that leads one to sex, rather than the reverse, and sex becomes the ticket to getting them. In fact, sex is sometimes "endured" to get to the closeness of sleeping in someone's arms.

In an attempt to recapture the sense of well being, security, or comfort, the survivor frequently repeats (almost ritualistically) the sexual behavior patterns shared with the former lover. But instead of recapturing the desired feelings of intimacy, the result is a sense of vacuousness, an incredible emptiness made even more severe by current sexual interactions that are leading nowhere.

Unfortunately, sex, usually narrowly defined as intercourse, is the only expression of intimacy and closeness many people know how to show or to receive; it is indeed the nearest thing to nurturing they have experienced. Thus they give and receive it, wondering why they still feel empty when the morning finds them staring at the ceiling wondering what they are doing there.

6. *Sex as fear*. Strange as it may sound, sex is often found to be an

expression of fear. Getting lost in sex with someone is a powerfully distracting way to relieve one's fear of the present and future. Fear of commitment is the most common experience reported by those whose lovers have died. Having felt badly hurt by the loss of the relationship and the investment in the person, the survivor is at best skeptical and at worst terrified to begin another commitment of any depth. Even partners with whom one develops a fairly exclusive sexual understanding are constantly evaluated as to their involvement and their potential for leaving or being left.

It is as though the survivor, having lost the lover of choice, always reserves or holds back a part that will never be that committed again. The pain is experienced as too great ever to risk another loss of that kind; the hurt is too deep ever again to be that vulnerable; the loss too overwhelming to be recovered and lost again. Sex as fear is here expressed in physical interaction with no concomitant emotional involvement.

Once a new sexual relationship has begun, another fear may involve the lack of parameters on the relationship. The survivor immediately wants to set the limits, make clear the recreational nature of the sex, deny the involvement (whether real or imagined), assure himself or herself of the freedom to leave at any moment without question, or get a commitment of non-commitment from the new partner. Boundaries are quickly established either by much talking, or none at all.

The underlying dynamic in this expression of sex as a component of fear is the apprehension that the new lover will die and leave as the former one did. Some people report that, in the midst of a new relationship, they will suddenly back off and retreat for no apparent reason. Upon reflection they come to understand that the motivation for their withdrawal has to do with the frightening realization that, sooner or later, the new lover will also die or leave. Rather than face yet another loss, they choose to disengage emotionally, often maintaining some semblance of a sexual involvement that soon ends. At least, when the *survivor* breaks off the relationship, she or he feels a sense of control that is not present when the new partner leaves or dies.

Sex as fear is seen in those persons who practice serial monogamy, never quite allowing themselves to get close enough to commit, but enjoying the sexual interactions, knowing all along those interactions will be ended before they are permitted to grow into involvement.

7. *Sex as nurturing*. When one reaches this experience of post-death sexuality, real clarity and health are just around the corner. One may see attempts at nurturing in relationships early on, but it is usually not until the previous six tasks have been completed (in no particular sequence) that this component of sexuality is allowed to be risked.

In the months following the death of the lover, survivors consistently report a sometimes desperate sense of wanting to be nurtured; they seek sex and intimacy, carefully or indiscriminately, as a means to that end. It is only as they begin to feel more secure and able to offer themselves as valuable and worthwhile that they begin to seek out others to both *give* and receive sex as a form of nurturing.

Sex as play is a part of this nurturing. It is a sign that the survivor has begun to let go of the old self and to begin rebuilding a new identity, incorporating the death of the former lover into current life experience. The playfulness of sex only begins to occur when the survivor decides to go on with life and to risk involvement to that end. This may occur periodically throughout the early days after the death, but is only most evident after several new partners have helped the survivor move through the earlier reactions to the death.

As a new identity begins to develop without the former partner, the survivor's sexual experience is described less often as "having sex" and more frequently as "making love" with the new partner. It is at this point that the survivor may begin purposefully to seek out a new, longer term (even permanent) relationship.

Sex as giving and receiving nurturing is an important signpost for the one who has had a lover die; it is an indication that some significant bridges have been crossed and that it is time to renew a commitment to further and deeper relating.

We have here examined some of the initial reactions to the death of a lover. We will, in the next chapter, look at some guidelines for survivors to follow as they actively pursue sex after death.

9

Guidelines for Sex After Death

People handle death the same way they handle any other difficulty in their lives. If the person is an aggressive problem solver, he or she will take on grief (and sexual, intimate relationships as a part of that grief) in the same way. A person who passively reacts to other life events will more passively respond to the death of a lover, hoping that some resolution eventually will present itself.

Of course, there are variations on these two extremes. The point is that we are consistent in our handling of life's circumstances and will follow our own style of grieving as well as our own pattern of involvement with new sexual partners.

Thus the following guidelines are meant to be general suggestions that may be fitted to each person's particular style of coping. Like the ideas in the previous chapter, they have been gleaned from interactions with many survivors who have been and are still working through the death of a lover and have found the ideas to be helpful. (Also, as in the previous section, "lover" may be read "friend," "love," "partner," or "spouse"; and "sex" may be read "intimacy.")

1. "Give sorrow words..." Shakespeare's Macbeth says: "Give sorrow words; the grief that does not speak whispers the o'er-fraught heart and bids it break." It is important to talk about the loss, talk about the feelings, the hurt, the anger, the disappoint-ment, the sadness, the relief from the pain of a long and agonizing illness or a short, traumatic one. Survivors need to find someone to talk with who will not give advice or tell them not to feel that way.

They also need to talk with the new sexual partner, especially when experiencing any of the mechanical or emotional difficulties noted in Chapter 8. Survivors need to tell the partner about these difficulties, not to seek sympathy, but to be honest in asking for understanding. If the partner does not or will not understand, that will indicate something about the choice of partners.

To put thoughts into words, and to do self appraisal, survivors often keep a journal or buy a small notebook to jot down feelings about everything, especially intimacy and sex, every few days or so. Such a journal can be a way to keep track of dream life as well as other events that are important to remember such as dating, new sex partners, and time alone. Looking back over a few months (years, eventually) it will be helpful to see progress and change, as well as which ideas and behaviors have remained the same.

It is possible that short term counseling may be in order if problems persist, or if some objective insight is needed into thoughts, actions, and feelings. There are many excellent counselors listed in the Yellow Pages of the phone book, but it is hard to tell the duds from the pros just by their ads. Rather, encourage the survivor to ask someone who has been through a similar experience for a recommendation, or call a hospital chaplain or someone in a Hospice setting for a referral. Make it clear to the therapist that short term counseling is the goal. A good counselor will accept stated boundaries and offer appropriate help, while at the same time gently urging the survivor to look beyond current difficulties to old life patterns that may be informing the choice of new sex partners.

Above all, it is important to talk. Grief, especially the deep grief experienced around the loss of a lover and the sexual ramifications of it, is like gas on the stomach that needs to be relieved—there's more room on the outside than there is inside. The more survivors talk, the more likely it is that their sex life after a lover's death will be satisfying.

2. *Slow down.* Often when a lover dies, survivors feel pressure (both internal and external) to hurry up and get their lives back to "normal" again. They will need help from friends to ignore the

pressure and slow down. The meter is not ticking; there is no time limit or required deadline to obey.

Internally, the death leaves one empty and disoriented, missing the stability or at least relative predictability of life with the other. Of course, there is internal pressure (even panic) to recapture that lifestyle, and that is part of the search and replacement syndrome mentioned earlier. But it is important to allow space to heal and, perhaps even more importantly, time to establish a new (or at least separate) identity apart from the dead lover.

External pressure comes from supposedly well-meaning friends who want the survivor to please hurry and get re-coupled so *they* (the friends) will feel better. If possible, these people are to be summarily ignored. They will only increase the sense of panic and provide occasions for further depression and anger. Real friends will understand and support survivors in their journey to renegotiate who they are sexually and otherwise at their own speed. Friends will help to acknowledge the panic, face it head on, and, in doing so, ease the pressure to re-couple.

As a part of slowing down, reevaluating the future, and examining life as a sexual being, survivors need to keep in mind that grief is intensely physical. Remembering to eat, exercise, and rest are as important to recovering libido as they are to overcoming the depression and lethargy that keep one from enjoying (or even wanting) sexual interactions.

Finally, when feeling pressured to get a date or to find a table for one in a restaurant, survivors need to be reminded that *alone* and *lonely* are not synonymous. Contrary to the image presented in telephone and diamond commercials, it is possible to spend time, even enjoyable time, alone. Time alone without sex is called celibacy, and many people are choosing it over the risk of disease or too hasty involvement. For some people, celibacy is a serious decision for a permanent lifestyle. Others alternate between periods of celibacy and periods of sexual involvement. Survivors will follow whatever variation on that theme fits. They need to be supported, however, in the belief that, regardless of internal or external pressure for sex, it is as acceptable to say "no" as it is to say "yes."

3. *Date friends first.* A major difficulty following the death of

a lover is where and how to meet safe, single persons. One way to gently ease back into the social scene is to date people known a long time as friends. Good, close friends will provide nurturing and companionship without demanding sex as the price to pay for it. They are also frequently the source of other "referrals" for dating.

Survivors need to beware of most singles groups and meat market bars or parties. Both can be gathering places for persons who are desperate for relationships. As they search for closeness, some people may be willing to go through the gaming and the disease risk of recreational sex with someone they know little about. Though most people report that such experiences lead to feeling even emptier, such activity appears to take the edge off the loneliness for a while.

Where business is involved, it is usually considered wise for survivors not to date employees or subordinates. The relationship is immediately changed, making supervision and evaluations awkward at best. Some people even recommend not dating coworkers, though this may unnecessarily restrict the number of social opportunities. In any case, it is recommended that coworkers or subordinates be approached with extreme caution for anything but casual dating. They are almost always poor choices for sexual or intimate partners.

Probably the best way for survivors to meet people is by slowly continuing to follow their own interests and interacting with the people naturally found there. If they take a course in the local community school, play golf once a week, work out at the fitness club, socialize at church, travel, attend a special interest group, or work for a candidate, they are likely to come into contact with persons who have similar interests and compatibilities.

As survivors work through the tasks described in Chapter 8, their social interactions will change somewhat. They will be attracted to different kinds of persons to provide different things at different times. However those interactions progress, the place to start is with friends.

4. *Just because someone is dead doesn't make them right.* In the course of grieving the death of a lover, people frequently believe they are in some manner still obligated to do things or maintain

activities and behaviors consistent with what the lover "would have wanted me to do." While in some instances this can simply be a way of reaffirming a decision, it can also be a method of coercing oneself into doing something against one's better judgment, and resenting it later.

Just because the lover died doesn't mean that *his or her* wishes are always and forever to be followed for the rest of *the survivor's* life, especially since the survivor probably did not always do what the person wanted when the lover was alive. Survivors need to know it is all right to continue to disagree and to follow the course of best self interest, regardless of what the lover "would have wanted."

This is especially true in new sexual interactions. It may be fairly clear, for instance, that the lover would not have wanted the survivor to see other people, much less to have sex with them. Whether this expectation is meant for the short or long term, if survivors feel obligated to "respect those wishes" they will feel guilty and eventually angry at themselves, the dead lover, and the new partner.

It is important to remember that obligations to the former lover ended at death. Of course the dead lover will be respected and remembered for the rest of the survivor's life; but to arrange the new life in accordance with the dead person's wishes is to die with them and maintain an existence as a shrine to the memory of the loved one. It is vital to keep in mind that death does not confer posthumous infallibility on anyone, particularly regarding sexual activities, where the survivor's vulnerability and intimacy are potentially at greatest risk.

5. Be honest. No matter how difficult it is at first, survivors must be encouraged to tell the truth, to say what they want and don't want, when they want or don't want it. They need to make it clear with a new partner that the goal of the relationship is nurturing, physical contact, or companionship without the pressure of sex (at least for the present). Or they can talk about wanting the enjoyment of physically being together without commitment. If commitment is desired, they need to say so directly and check out the other person's wants and needs as openly as both persons are able.

There will be times, as noted earlier, when survivors will have flashbacks (sexual and otherwise). If these are overwhelming and cause for withdrawing for a while, partners must be told what is occurring. Likewise with feelings of fear, anger, joy, and playfulness. It is always better to know than to guess.

A commonly held guideline is: Talk rather than assume. If survivors don't say what they want, both in terms of sex and the entire relationship, they are likely to end up frustrated and disappointed. Though difficult, it is important to talk about the limits of the relationship, going out with other people, sex with others, how to handle issues of disease and birth control. The more people talk, the less anxious they will feel and the more certain they are about what is and is not going on in sexual interactions.

Finally, it is important to remember to temper honesty with a sense of humor. Many relationships die from "terminal seriosity." Survivors can learn to appreciate their imperfection and the awkwardness of the situation. It is okay not to be perfect; in fact, it's the imperfection that makes us interesting. Survivors need to be able to laugh at their own groping, and be prepared to forgive themselves and their partners when the inevitable mistakes are made.

6. *Be open.* Rather than repeating choices regarding sexual partners, types of personalities, or dating behaviors, it is important to be open to new relationships. This openness usually comes only after the searching, distraction and anger tasks have been worked through. It may only develop after short term counseling with someone who can point up the repetition in the survivor's behavior, thereby allowing them to choose new ways of relating.

Openness to new sexual behavior happens as one becomes more playful with a new partner, having let go of some of the attachment to the past. Such behavior may include an increase or decrease in sexual activity or even different sexual activities than one has practiced before.

The attitude of openness means also broadening the definition of sex beyond that of intercourse only. Sex can mean varying types of physical interaction, with varying degrees of eroticism or with none at all. One who is grieving the death of a lover quickly learns what people with chronic diseases such as arthritis, diabetes, cancer, or heart disease have had to learn: Sex is possible in many different positions, at different tempos, and with different levels of intensity. Sexual intimacy means whatever the couple decides it means, from cuddling to intercourse to massage to sleep.

Finally, survivors need to be encouraged to be open to love resurfacing from within. Although they feel as if that ability has been permanently damaged, the truth is it is only temporarily out of order. It will surface periodically, as if coming up for air, and then only very cautiously for fear of being damaged once again. Hurt, pain, anger, and fear all serve to protect that love from too quickly rushing to the surface in its need for expression and encouragement. Survivors need to allow these feelings enough time to interact with the love, then gradually allow it to come forth.

As has been said before, it is simply not true that "time heals all wounds." What people *do* with that time will determine whether and how much healing occurs. Grieving does not automatically mean growing. The above guidelines are meant to provide some suggestions for dealing with the time in such a way as to expand the possibilities for growth and change.

Part of the survivor's grieving time is certain to be spent in intimate, sexual activity. The sex may be perceived and felt as anger, distraction, nurturing, recreation or as a part of an overall relationship with a new partner. It may be depressing at some times and invigorating at others.

There is indeed sex after death. It is important to allow that sex to be an active and supportive part of the healing process.

10

Surviving
Death

The young woman, weak and
dying, reaches out from her hospital bed for her sobbing husband. He bends over her, wrapping his arms around her thin
frame as she cries: "I'm so sorry. I'm so sorry. I didn't mean to
leave you like this." He answers: "I know. I love you. It's
okay. I love you."

Three hours later, having lapsed into a coma, she takes
her final breath and dies. For her it is over. For her husband
a new task has just begun. The task is survival.

There are no courses in how to survive deep losses. Most of the
literature on grief and bereavement is either coldly clinical, un-
realistically emotional, or piously religious. Grieving persons
are described either in terms of aberrant behavior or with such
faith as to make the rest of us appear hopeless. Cultural guidelines are unclear or nonexistent, and advice from friends is frequently contradictory.

It is possible, however, to get some clarity about the task of survival from those who are going through it. You will note that we
did not say "have gone through it." Surviving deep loss is always
a *present* task. One does not "get over it," "recover from it," or "go
on" in the usual decisive sense of those phrases, as if one were
dealing with a broken arm, a scab that will come off, a bruise that
will go away, or even a long term illness from which gradual return to health is possible. Once a deep loss has been sustained, the

experience of it will continue to recur periodically, calling on the best coping resources the person has available.

Some of the people who are facing the task of surviving the death of a spouse, child, parent, or friend meet together monthly to share their reactions and experiences in local bereavement groups sponsored by hospitals and hospices. The following suggestions, comments and observations from those groups help shed light on a largely uncharted path, and provide relief in the affirmation that we are not alone in the sometimes bizarre feelings and behaviors that accompany the daily struggle to survive death.

1. *"Give sorrow words."* This advice from *Macbeth*, discussed in Chapter 9, relates to surviving more than just sexual encounters. It is an important (perhaps the most important) strategy for gradually coming to terms with the loss.

Whether the survivor talks to a friend, family member or professional (psychologist, pastoral counselor, psychiatrist), it would be well to choose one or two persons with whom to "check in" periodically. Meeting weekly (eventually monthly) at a regular time allows space for ventilation, support, affirmation, and feedback. The person chosen must be one who will not give advice, tell the survivor how to feel, or be upset by the frequent expression of gut wrenching tears and sorrow. An honest listener will ask questions and point out possible dangers the survivor may not see due to the emotional obfuscation of grieving.

Often it is difficult for the survivor to continue to talk after many months have passed. Feeling as though he or she should be "over it" or coping better" by now, the person may be reluctant to keep going over the same (old) themes. It is necessary to reassure the survivor at these times that the listener is not bored with the inconclusive repetition of painful events or angry that the survivor has not totally come to terms with a particular feeling or issue.

Talking with someone who will really listen, even when they don't understand or agree, is a way to relieve the stress, share the fear, and bear the loneliness. Talking and listening are gifts that enrich both givers and receivers immeasurably.

2. *Grief is physical.* Most people expect bereavement to be a time of deep emotional exhaustion, and indeed this is true. They

are, therefore, usually ready for the emotional roller coaster of highs and lows, the fragility of their feelings, and the emotional emptiness inside. What they don't expect is the constant tiredness, lethargy, and lack of initiative. The body seems to require inordinate hours of sleep (and at odd times) to physically process all the emotional turmoil. Even persons who sleep well may complain of lying in bed for long periods of time just staring into space, resting and thinking.

Grief is hard work both emotionally *and* physically. This is especially true after a lengthy illness during which time people may not have realized the stress under which they functioned. The survivor needs to allow time for rest and, if possible, to let sleep come whenever it will.

Occasionally, survivors will experience the same symptoms of the disease from which their loved one died. They may even think that they are coming down with the same thing and will soon, therefore, die themselves. Friends and supporters can tell the survivor that this occurrence is not unusual, but it is also important to recommend seeing a physician for complete verification. It is helpful, in addition, to allow the survivor to talk about the symptoms and their meaning in relationship to the dead loved one (identification, the wish to be dead and be with him or her).

If what comes *out* of the survivor's mouth (talk) is the most important strategy for the tasks of grieving, then what goes *into* it runs a close second. A major problem most survivors report regarding food is remembering to eat. Initially following the death, of course, the person often feels too upset or weary to ingest any but small portions at odd intervals. A cultural understanding of this fact is shown by the way friends bring food to the mourner's house, often to be frozen for later. During this time friends may encourage (not insist) and remind the survivor to eat, and, as a way to facilitate that, eat *with* the survivor.

As days and weeks pass, the reason for not eating changes from lack of interest to the dislike of cooking for one. Underlying the reality of going to the trouble of meal preparation for one person is the symbolic nature of food and its association with the loved one.

Food is seen as a form of nurturing. It is often a symbolic reward for accomplishments or a way of celebrating a particular event. The survivor often does not want to be nurtured, feels no desire for reward, and certainly has nothing to celebrate. Thus, in addition to avoiding single meal preparation, the survivor may also feel reluctant to go out to dinner. Likewise, the thought of sitting down at a table for one, whether out or at home, revives pleasant (now painful) associations of occasions with the loved one. It is no wonder that the survivor avoids, forgets, or refuses meals.

And yet, because grief is so physical it is important not only to maintain a healthy diet but also to exercise regularly. These two factors (diet and exercise) can reduce the stress associated with grieving and maintain a healthy enzyme, hormone, and chemical balance that will have a positive effect on both the experiencing and handling of emotions. Prudent diet and exercise routines should always be confirmed by the survivor's physician.

3. *Just because someone is dead doesn't make them right.* Although discussed in Chapter 9 regarding sexual behavior, this notion quite obviously has much broader connotations for the survivor. Not only related to socializing, the idea impacts the investment of money, work and living arrangements, purchase of clothes or other items, and travel and leisure plans. Again, the fact that your loved one died does not mean that *his or her* wishes need be followed the rest of *your* life.

Many people conjure up this aphorism as a means of providing some safe boundaries for their behavior immediately following the death. Frequently, survivors fear they will behave foolishly without the counterbalance of the former loved one. They keep old rules and guidelines intact by constantly asking what the dead person would have wanted them to do.

The fact is that seldom do survivors use the loss of boundaries that occurs with the death as an excuse for aberrant or highly unusual behavior. Most people remain consistently within their own behavioral limits regardless of outside circumstances. While in some instances the nature of the death or the relationship may result in a temporary extension beyond the usual limits, these occurrences are rare. Most people stay who they are, though they may now have the time and opportunity to expand upon parts of themselves (art, travel, spirituality, study) they never felt able or willing to explore before. It is, therefore, important that this phrase not be used to stifle this exploration.

Usually, as some old boundaries are reinforced and others, by testing out new ideas or relationships, are expanded, the real or imagined wishes of the dead person become less and less of an issue in decision making.

Many survivors use the "one year rule" as an initial guideline, based on the experience of those who have preceded them in the grieving process. This rule suggests making *no major decisions for one year* following a significant loss or death. Because that first year is so incredibly emotional, physically draining, and a time when identity and psychological balance are being reexamined and reevaluated, the survivor is thought to need the protection of the full year's time and space before major decisions are considered. As one person said: "I was so emotionally unstable and mentally disconnected that year I could barely decide what clothes to wear to work. I can see that now, but I couldn't then. I'm glad I knew to wait."

Of course some major decisions may not be able to be delayed. Good friends who either are or know competent attorneys, financial planners, and counselors may need to be consulted and trusted to help. Usually, however, decisions about moving, investments, whether and where to work, and especially romantic relationships, can be postponed until one year has elapsed and some of the turmoil and confusion have cleared.

4. *It is possible to feel opposite emotions simultaneously.* Unfortunately most people in this culture have been taught to believe that their feelings exist in an either-or dichotomy. Thus if they feel extreme sadness about the death, they wonder how they can feel extreme relief at the same time. If they feel love for the person who has died, how can they also feel anger? The fact is that people do feel both sadness and relief, love and anger, hope and despair all at once as they react and respond to the different parts of themselves working to make sense out of what has happened.

As they yo-yo from elation to depression and back again their emotions are usually right on the surface, sensitive and volatile. Sometimes it feels good to feel bad and often it feels bad to feel good. It is important that the survivor have permission and support to feel many things at once. It is then useful to take the time to sort those feelings out by talking with someone or through some creative expression such as keeping a journal, drawing or painting the feelings, or working them out in clay.

5. *Releasing pain is not erasing memory.* Strange as it may sound, most people are apprehensive about giving up intense grieving. They believe that their grief, however publicly or privately portrayed, is a sign of their caring for the dead loved one. To give it up or even lessen it might be seen by themselves and others as diminishing that caring. Likewise there is the fear that to release the pain will mean relinquishing the person's memory.

The physical pain of grieving, especially crying, may indeed be the only sense of sustained contact the survivor still feels with the person who died. To experience sadness, tears, depression, emptiness, and despair is to maintain a powerful connection of presence with the loved one. It is feared that to lessen the pain is to diminish that connection and lose contact forever. To the survivor of a deep loss, the pain and depression are far preferable to the anticipated sense of increased emptiness that might come with a decision to let go of these feelings.

In fact the exact opposite is true. Releasing pain gradually allows time and space for more pleasant and vivid memories to surface. The loved one's memory becomes more a realistic part of daily living and less a chore to be remembered. The sense of continued contact with and caring about the memory of the loved one also becomes more realistic and there is less panic about feeling bad in order to "safeguard" the relationship, lest it somehow slip away.

A commonly related experience of survivors seems to occur at the three year mark following the death of the loved one. (It may occur earlier or later, depending on the particular style of grieving of the individual.) Moving into the fourth year, survivors report that they are doing quite well, feeling better, adjusting, handling the day to day affairs of life with some good ability now, perhaps even getting into a meaningful, long term relationship with someone, and then suddenly find themselves deep in the midst of another devastating depression.

They think they are going crazy, that they have had a severe relapse, or have somehow been psychologically tricked into thinking they were recovering when, obviously, they are back to square one again after all this time. Friends and supporters need to assure the survivor that *none* of these things is true. What they are experiencing is *grieving the loss of the grieving.*

It is as though the grief has become, if not a friend, at least a known, familiar companion on the journey for this long period of time. The feelings, behaviors, depressions, and difficult times of the year have become known, anticipated, and expected. To begin moving beyond those feelings, to begin letting them go, replacing them with new ways of relating and feeling, is to experience the loss of that "companion" which has been intimately present on a daily basis for the three years. And that involves some grieving for this, another, loss.

6. *It's okay to feel suicidal.* Just because survivors *feel* suicidal doesn't mean they *are* suicidal. Feelings are *not* facts. To want to die is a normal response to deep loss. Along with maintaining painful feelings, death seems the only certain way to be back with the loved one again.

Often the desire to die, as paradoxical as it sounds, is also a statement of strength. It can be a sign of wanting to regain control over a life that has felt uncontrollable. A common phrase used to describe suicide is: "He took his life into his own hands." When contemplating dying, that is exactly what the survivor is expressing. Thus, rather than quickly admonishing the survivor for talking about suicide, friends need to listen openly to this expression of desire for an end to grief and encourage the person to talk openly about it. Care should be taken, of course, to insure that the survivor does not *act* on such an impulse. Frequently, simply sharing the desire diminishes the possibility of seriously carrying it out. In any case, referral to a competent professional counselor must be offered and encouraged.

For the same reason it is okay to "wallow." Having sustained a deep loss, it is perfectly normal to feel despairing, depressed, and incredibly sad. Instead of denying or discounting the feelings, it is important to let them surface a while, and to spend some time talking about them with someone who understands that the person is not crazy, just grieving. A good wallow will help the survivor feel better later.

7. *Time doesn't heal—it merely passes.* As has been mentioned before in discussing recovery from death, the old truism that "time heals all wounds" is untrue. In fact, at least for the first year or two, time makes it worse. The passage of days and weeks filled with anniversaries, holidays, special remembrances, and things that were planned to have been done together only makes the death more vivid and the loss more real.

There are certain variables that can provide guidelines for anticipating, very generally, the kind of grieving experience the survivor may have. Such things as the length of the relationship, the depth and intensity of the relationship, the cause and type of death, and the length of the period of dying will all interact with the problem-solving style of the individual to produce different grieving experiences in different people.

The most important variable, however, is that of communication. How well did the dying person communicate with the survivor in their normal lives together? What did they talk about as the dying process occurred? Did they talk about what the survivor was to do without the loved one? Was there talk of going on without one another? Or were these issues avoided, due to the sadness and pain they would surely evoke?

Survivors seem to do better if there has been some clear communication, of whatever depth, during the dying, about surviving, what that may be like and what the wishes of the dying person are. Even if those wishes are highly restrictive, at least they are known and can be openly discussed with a friend or counselor.

Many people describe deep loss "as though someone cut something out of me and left a gaping, bleeding hole." Such wounds will not passively heal themselves with the mere passage of time. They need active attention and mending. Forgiveness, love, creativity, sharing, relationships: These are the threads that will suture the wound and mend it, so that healing can begin. Time will pass. How the survivor actively fills that time will determine whether and how healing occurs.

8. Expect to be "blindsided." One of the most embarrassing and frightening experiences of deep loss is to be perfectly normal one minute and, for no apparent reason, emotionally dissolved the next. It is as though a part of the survivor is always on the lookout for tender or painful remembrances. The survivor may be in a restaurant or in the car when a song comes on the radio, doing dishes or other housework alone, visiting friends, hearing the phone ring or watching t.v., when suddenly some part of the person makes a connection and the person becomes teary or sad, usually without knowing why.

Depending on the situation and the memory, the feeling can be fleeting or longer lasting. In either case, the survivor needs to allow it to run its course, preferably by telling the incident to someone. It is important to know that it is okay, that it is normal, that it will pass and that it will happen with less and less frequency.

One of the most important ways friends can help is to offer the "2 A.M. Insurance Policy." They can tell the survivor: "Here is my phone number. It is okay to call me if you're having a difficult time—even at 2 A.M. I can't change it and I can't fix it, but I can listen to you and that's even more important, regardless of the hour." This simple action has helped many survivors make it through otherwise unbearable times. Chances are they will never actually call, but it makes a great deal of difference to know that they can do so if necessary.

9. Laughing is not disrespectful. Even though someone has died, funny things will continue to happen at work, at home, to others, and even to the survivor. It is okay to laugh at these things without feeling guilty or disrespectful to the person for not spending twenty-four hours a day grieving. Humor is a great stress reducer; it is another of the active sutures necessary to help close the wound and heal. Besides, glumness is boring; but suture self.

10. Not less pain, only less frequent. As discussed in Chapter 9, there is no "normal" time for the "completion" of grieving. Different people with different kinds of losses and relationships will grieve for different periods of time.

It is extremely important for the survivor to know and remember that, while the loss may not become any less painful, the occasions of experiencing that pain become less frequent. Especially during times of deep despair, friends may remind the survivor that he or she will feel different a year from now—not necessarily "better," but certainly different. The depth of the pain never decreases; when the person gets in touch with the loss from time to time, the depth of feeling is the same. The only change is that the times she or he gets in touch with it will be spaced further and further apart.

And there is some comfort in this fact. A part of the survivor will always remember the relationship with the loved one as it was at the time of the death. Another part moves on, not forgetting or denying the pain and grief, but rather incorporating and integrating it into the whole of life's experience.

11. *Life is too short not to.* This phrase is a helpful one for survivors to remember when faced with spontaneous, perhaps even fun, decisions, especially when they have the opportunity to do something they've been reluctant to do before, or when a new idea or experience is presented for their consideration. Because something doesn't fit with one's former image or would not have been done when the loved one was alive is no reason to reject it now. Gradually the survivors will find themselves actually beginning to enjoy some (not all, of course) of these people and experiences. They will also have fewer regrets regardless of how long or short their own lives turn out to be.

12. *Remember, only you will remember.* As days turn into months and years, survivors need not be surprised or disappointed when they are the only ones who remember the date of the loved one's birthday, the wedding anniversary, the time of the year they took that special vacation together, and the date of the death.

Special friends will still be there to talk with about these dates when they occur year after year. But the dates were important only to the survivor and the other person, and they generally will be remembered only by the survivor, just as the survivor alone will remember the silly, funny, tender, and sad things about the person who died. It is not that other people don't care; they simply don't care the way the survivor did.

As the above statements indicate, there are commonalities in responding to deep loss and there is some comfort for grieving persons in that knowledge. It is important to remember, however, that each person will experience loss in his or her own individual way, with nuances, feelings and memories that arespecial to their particular situation.

11

The End

I could think of no more appropriate title for the final chapter of a book on death. It is hoped, however, that this ending will instead be a beginning for you; a beginning of further study, of insight and decision making regarding your own death planning, of consciousness raising in churches and community groups, of the intentional living of life until death.

But before ending, I want to briefly (and admittedly with only a surface rendering) acknowledge three other issues that need much further explication by others in the field. They are *Children, AIDS, and Long-Term Reactions.*

1. *Children.* The focus of this book has been primarily upon the reaction of adults to death, dying, and surviving the death of a loved one. But readers will undoubtedly ask what to tell their children about death, whether or not to take them to the hospital to visit dying people, or to the funeral home to see the dead body.

Although I am not an expert on children, my experience working with them at the hospital indicates three guidelines regarding their involvement in this process:

A. Ask the child what she or he believes about the event.

B. When in doubt, tell the truth.

C. Listen for feelings of guilt.

Children will make up their own explanation of the events surrounding the death of a loved one, and the reaction of adults to that death. Thus it is important to *ask* the child what the child thinks happened. The answer might be more accurate or at least more satisfying than your own. Feel free to confess that your best guess at an explanation is still confusing for you, thus teaching the child that there are such things as inexplicable mysteries in our universe.

Also, tell the truth. Do not say "going to sleep," "passing away," called Home," "gone to live with Jesus," or "gone to take care of other little boys and girls in heaven." These phrases, and others like them, can be very unsettling and even threatening to the child, who usually takes them literally. Instead, tell the truth about death. The sooner the child realizes death is a normal, natural part of our life together, the sooner he or she will begin to seek accurate, realistic information about it and come to terms with it.

Do not shield the child from the events, as it will usually make things seem worse, given what the child is imagining about them. Often the reason children are frightened and apprehensive about death is because they are reflecting the views and feelings of the adults around them. If adults are shielding themselves from the death or dying process, due to their own discomfort or confusion, the child will follow that model; if the adult model shows comfort as well as emotional upset, the child will follow that model. In either case, ask and talk about it. It will be good for both.

Part of that coming to terms will involve participation in our particular cultural/religious activities surrounding dying and death. It is important, again, to *ask* children what their wishes are regarding hospital visitation, viewing dead bodies, or attending funerals, once an accurate explanation is made of what is happening.

An infant died and was in the Intensive Care Nursery. The mother was still in recovery and the father stood outside the door of the ICN with their four-year-old daughter, wondering what to do. The head nurse suggested we ask the child what she wanted to do, with some explanation as to what she would be seeing. We took her in with her father, she looked at the baby, touched it, looked at us, and said, "Okay." Later discussion proved the image from that experience was far less traumatic than what she thought was in there.

Finally, be careful to listen for feelings of guilt from the child. Children think they are omnipotent. When a loved one dies (or a cat, dog, or goldfish) the children may think they had something to do with it. Phrases like: "If I had been better, then Gramps would not have died," or, "If I had visited him that last day...If I had minded Dad before he left..." and the like, indicate a sense of culpability for the death.

Straightforwardly telling the child that that thought is untrue, and explaining the medical or accidental cause of the death may save the child years of self punishing behavior and diminished self worth.

2. *AIDS.* When this book was begun, the AIDS epidemic had not yet begun to appear; by the time it is published, the number of persons with AIDS will have doubled. As the manuscript goes to press, three million people worldwide have AIDS, 150,000 have died from it, and hundreds of thousands more are predicted to succumb in coming years.

Nearly everyone reading this book either knows or knows of someone who has AIDS and who will die with it. Thus it is extremely important to relate the concepts in this book to the predictable results of the AIDS epidemic. While entire volumes have been written on the peculiar details of dealing with AIDS patients, it is possible to walk through the chapters of this book with that particular disease group in mind.

The same steps and suggestions apply in Section I, *Being With The Dying.* But, in addition to the usual loneliness expressed by dying patients, AIDS patients have an additional *social* isolation caused by the negative stereotypes accompanying its transmissal, and *physical* isolation inflicted by blood and body fluid precautions necessary to protect patients and caregivers from increased exposure to infection. As friends and family members flee from, reject or agonize with their relatives and loved ones, they will need significantly more support in dealing with this particularly insidious method of dying.

Section II, *Ethics and Death,* equally relates to patients dying from AIDS or ARC (AIDS-Related Complex.) We are quickly learning that it is simply not true that "only old people die," as we see scores of young persons in their twenties and thirties gradually waste away and die.

Withdrawal of artificial interventions will have to be considered as the influx of AIDS patients increases. Lack of funding, along with the current certainty of death will probably result in more and more deaths at home A complicating problem of AIDS patients, however, is that they frequently have no home to which to go to die. Often they are abandoned by friends, unwanted by family, and medically indigent. Church groups, nursing homes, hospices, and state and federal insurance pools will have to combine resources to meet the coming needs in this difficult area.

It will be necessary to extend the current Medicare Hospice regulations to Medicaid in order to lower costs of terminal, palliative only care for AIDS patients. In doing so, *managed, limited* medical care may well become the norm, and set the stage for such managed care of other terminally ill patients as well. The church will have to diligently monitor the ethical implications of such care, as the slippery slope may be impossible to reclimb when it comes to determining who dies and how.

The church is already examining its own stand on AIDS. Both evangelical and liberal denominations are attempting to deal with the social and religious implications of the disease. Variations on the slogans in Section III have developed, such as: "The AIDS epidemic is God's judgment on homosexuals and drug abusers"; and "God-fearing Christians need have no fear of AIDS." As the percentage of heterosexual AIDS patients increases, these slogans will take their place beside the equally erroneous ones listed in Chapter 6.

Probably the greatest impact of the AIDS dilemma is to be reflected in Section IV. *Sex After Death* takes on whole new fears and anxieties. The survivor seeking intimacy must now realize that having sex with a partner is not just having sex with *that* partner, it is having sex with *all* of the people *both* partners have ever had sex with. Proper precautions are, of course, in order, including medical testing (though one would have to be retested nearly every six weeks to maintain certainty) and a new interest in celibacy.

The *Guidelines…* chapter must also now take AIDS into consideration by encouraging "safe sex," and warning of the extreme dangers of promiscuity or even serial monogamy. In every case there are no easy answers, and survivors must deal with the threat of their own death in seeking intimacy and sexual behavior after their loved one has died.

Finally, the suggestions in the "Surviving Death" chapter still apply. But, in addition, special care and consideration must be afforded those families and loved ones surviving AIDS deaths. Their increased social isolation, fed by unwarranted myths about AIDS and how it is and is not contracted and spread, is an additional dimension which will only serve to exacerbate their grief responses.

It is interesting that the AIDS crisis, for all its horror and danger, may be the precipitating factor in demanding that our culture—and our church—come to terms with the reality of death. It may, in addition, alter our sexual mores, entirely restructure our system of healthcare delivery, and force us to examine our theology of illness, death, judgment, and reconciliation.

3. *Long-Term Response.* A final item that needs exploration is that of the long term response to death. What is it like to have had a loved one die twenty years ago? How does one think of that person twenty hears hence? What feelings arise as long distances of time pass? Since most of my experience is with immediate death and bereavement, I have little information about the effects of death many years later.

Several possibilities, however, come to mind. The survivor may choose never to work through the tasks of grieving, deciding to continue life with the loved one always present in mind and thought, never reengaging in social activities to any significant level and never allowing for deep personal joy again.

It is also possible for the tasks of grieving to be adequately "worked through." The survivor may indeed go on with life with the loved one as a more and more distant and pleasant memory. Current activities could take the place of the former relationship and, from time to time, bittersweet remembrances would occur.

But it is most likely that survivors will handle bereavement the same way they handled other long term losses—childhood, adolescence, major illness, divorce, separation from family, or job change—bringing to bear the same coping skills that were helpful in other situations. Other options are possible, I am sure; I just don't yet have the data to describe them. I would be glad to hear from readers who can offer their experience about this matter.

If you have read this far, you have begun the most difficult part of the process. You have begun to face your own feelings and thoughts about death in general, and about your own personal death. You will now be better able to be of real help to others who are dying. You will also be more willing to talk with your family and loved ones about your own plans and wishes.

Indeed, like the patients and families who provided the material for this book, you have begun your own journey toward surviving death.

APPENDICES

Directive to Physicians

(The following Directive to Physicians is legal in Texas. It is meant only as a sample illustration for interested readers. For the specific format required for a particular state, check with the State Medical Association, or see the "Handbook of Living Wills; 1987 Edition" available from The Society For The Right To Die, 250 West 57th Street, New York, New York 10107.)

Directive made this _____ day _____ (month, year). I_____, being of sound mind, willfully, and voluntarily make known my desire that my life shall not be artificially prolonged under the circumstances set forth below, and do hereby declare:

1. If at any time I should have an incurable condition caused by injury, disease, or illness certified to be a terminal condition by two physicians, and where the application of life-sustaining procedures would serve only to artificially prolong the moment of my death and where my attending physician determines that my death is imminent whether or not life-sustaining procedures are utilized, I direct that such procedures be withheld or withdrawn, and that I be permitted to die naturally.

2. In the absence of my ability to give directions regarding the use of such life-sustaining procedures, it is my intention that this directive shall be honored by my family and physicians as the final expression of my legal right to refuse medical or surgical treatment and accept the consequences from such refusal.

3. If I have been diagnosed as pregnant and that diagnosis is known to my physician, this directive shall have no force or effect during the course of my pregnancy.

4. This directive shall be in effect until it is revoked.

5. I understand the full import of this directive and I am emotionally and mentally competent to make this directive.

6. I understand that I may revoke this directive at any time.

7. I understand that Texas law allows me to designate another

person to make a treatment decision for me if I should become co-matose, incompetent, or otherwise mentally or physically incapa-ble of communication. I hereby designate _____ ,
who resides at _____ to make such a treatment decision for me if I should become incapable of communicating with my physician.

If the person I have named above is unable to act on my behalf, I authorize the following person to do so:

Name _____

Address _____

I have discussed my wishes with these persons and trust their judgment.

8. I understand that if I become incapable of communication, my physician will comply with this directive unless I have designat-ed another person to make a treatment decision for me, or unless my physician believes this directive no longer reflects my wishes.

Signed_____

City, County and State of Residence

(Two witnesses must sign the directive in the spaces provided below.

The declarant has been personally known to me and I believe him/her to be of sound mind. I am not related to the declarant by blood or marriage, nor would I be entitled to any portion of the declarant's estate on his/her decease, nor am I the attending phy-sician of declarant or an employee of the attending physician or a health facility in which declarant is a patient, or a patient in the health care facility in which the declarant is a patient, or any person who has a claim against any portion of the estate of the declarant upon his/her decease.

Witness:_____
Witness:_____

Power of Attorney

(This durable Power of Attorney is legal in Texas. It is mainly for decision making. A regular Power of Attorney may also be executed for financial, banking, and other personal matters. Check with your state for the legal requirements for this document.)

POWER OF ATTORNEY

THE STATE OF TEXAS
COUNTY OF TRAVIS

KNOW ALL PERSONS BY THESE PRESENTS:

That I, _____, of Travis County, Texas, have made, constituted, and appointed, and by these presents do make, constitute, and appoint _____, of Travis County, Texas, my true and lawful attorneys, for me and in my name, place, and stead, in the event of my inability or mental incapacity to make any and every decision regarding my medical care and treatment; and I agree with and represent to those dealing with my said attorneys in fact that this power of attorney regarding my medical care and treatment may be voluntarily revoked only by a revocation filed of record in the office of the County Clerk of Travis County, Texas; and further, that this power of attorney shall not terminate on account of any disability on the part of the undersigned.

Witness my hand _____ day of _____ 19__.

STATE OF TEXAS
COUNTY OF TRAVIS

Before me, the undersigned authority, on this day personally apppeared _____ , known to me to be the person whose name is subscribed to the foregoing instrument, and acknowledged to me that he executed the same for the purposes and considerations therein expressed.

Given under my hand and seal of office, this ___ _____ day of _____ , 19 _ .

_____

Notary Public in and for
The State of Texas.

My Commission Expires:_____

Home Death

(The following information has been prepared for patients and families by The St. David's Community Hospital Oncology Center.)

Death at home rather than in the hospital is an option that more patients and their families are beginning to consider. Because of familiar surroundings, the easier accessibility of friends, and the comfort of home rather than hospital sounds, smells, and tastes, many persons wish to die in that setting.

Although not always possible, given the extent of physical disability, the need for full time care, or the problem of severe pain control, often the same things offered in the hospital can quite easily be provided at home.

Hospital beds, bedside commodes, tray tables, and other items can be supplied by the local branch of the American Cancer Society (or other community organization), usually at no charge. Families can learn to give medications and injections; they can be taught to give bed baths and flush catheters. Special medications or appliances, i.v.'s and physical therapy all can be handled through the hospital or local home health agency.

Nurses, with a physician order, can visit several times a week as needed at home and sitters can be hired through these same agencies. If you are interested in exploring this option, the hospital or Hospice staff will work with you and your physician to make whatever arrangements are necessary.

Once home, family members often want to know what to expect when the patient is nearing death. The usual indications are:
1. *Changing breathing patterns*
   - apnea (periods of forgetting to breathe)
   - secretions accumulating in throat or lungs
   - loud bubbling sounds in lungs ("Death Rattle")
   - like snoring, these breathing sounds may be alarming to visitors, but are seldom painful to the patient

2. *Change in temperature and color*
   - bluish discoloration in feet and hands
   - extremities begin to cool, moving up legs to upper body
3. *Change in pulse*
   - increased pulse rate
   - decreased blood pressure
4. *Loss of bowel and bladder control*
5. *Decreased urinary output*
6. *Decreased responsiveness*
   - gradual withdrawal
   - difficulty swallowing
   - unable to talk, move muscles, follow with eyes
7. *Possible uncontrolled movements*
   - twitching
   - tossing and turning
   - picking at bedclothes

At the time of death you may expect the following:
1. *No breathing.*
2. *No pulse.*
3. *Change in color, usually to a dusky blue color.*
4. *Body becomes cool or cold.*
5. *May have "carbon dioxide" breathing and tighten jaw or gasp for breath a few times following loss of pulse and cessation of breathing.*
6. *Loss of facial muscle control (jaws sag, eyes may remain open).*
7. *Loss of bowel and bladder control (not always).*
8. *Possible muscle twitches.*

If you have questions or concerns about any of these issues, call the hospital oncology unit nurse, the Hospice office, your Hospice volunteer, or the Home Health after hours number for assistance at any time.

Resources

Becker, Ernest. *The Denial of Death*. New York: The Free Press, 1973.

Bugen, Lawrence. *Death and Dying: Theory, Research and Practice*. Dubuque, Iowa: William C. Brown Publishers, 1979.

Kopp, Sheldon, and Claire Flanders. *What Took You So Long?* Science and Behavior Books, 1979.

Morgan, Ernest. *A Manual of Death Education and Simple Burial*. Burnsville, North Carolina: Celo Press, 1980. (A practical manual for inexpensive burial.)

Parkes, Colin Murray. *Studies of Grief in Adult Life*. Tavistock Publications, 1972.

Shelp, Earl E., and Ronald H. Sunderland. *AIDS and the Church*. Philadelphia: The Westminister Press, 1987.

Slaikeu, Karl. *Crisis Intervention: A Handbook for Practice and Research*. Boston: Allyn and Bacon, 1983.

Slaikeu, Karl, and Steve Lawhead. *Up From The Ashes: How to Survive and Grow Through Personal Crisis*. Grand Rapids, Michigan: Zondervan Publishing House, 1987.

Timmerman, Joan. *The Mardi Gras Syndrome: Rethinking Christian Sexuality*. New York: The Crossroad Publishing Company, 1984.

Weatherhead, Leslie.*The Will of God*. Nashville: Abingdon-Cokesbury Books, 1944.

Widowed Persons Service
AARP, 1909 K Street, N.W.
Washington, D.C. 20049

National Hospice Office
Suite 307
1901 North Fort Meyer Drive
Arlington VA 22209

The Living Bank
P.O. Box 6725
Houston TX 77265

"As Long as There Is Life" (film)
The Hospice Institute
765 Prospect Street
New Haven CT 06511

Society for the Right to Die
250 West 57th Street
New York NY 10107

A Gift for the Dying

by
Jean Loving
Hospice Volunteer

I help dying people. And I help those they love and who love them. I am a hospice volunteer.

Becoming involved with a hospice organization had been my hope for many years. Because of frequent relocation, sometimes to cities with no active hospice, it was an impossibility until my move to Austin, Texas in 1981. The dream was born many years ago, when, as a practicing professional nurse, I recognized that in our ongoing pursuit of the cure of disease, the needs of the dying person were sadly neglected. I was frustrated by our dehumanization of death as we denied knowledge of its nearness, or of its very possibility. After Elisabeth Kübler-Ross publicized her studies and philosophy about the needs of dying people, I began incorporating her ideas as I taught the practice of nursing. I have been committed to the concept of hospice care since that time.

In September 1982, I participated in the educational program for volunteers offered by the Austin Comprehensive Hospice Program. Experiencing the hospice philosophy has become a way of life for me, a gift beyond measure from the dying, to the dying, and for the dying.

To be a hospice volunteer, one must be able to face his or her own mortality, to view death as another stage of life, and to appreciate the value of the gift of living. There must be a willingness to be vulnerable so that those whose time to live is limited may feel comfortable, confident, and free to be unguarded as well. Hospice volunteering is an "activity of the heart," a desire to be a companion and a helper to those in the last days of their journey through life, and to those loved ones who grieve their loss. It is an exceptional way in which an individual can express a deep personal belief in the value of human existence.

An understanding of the activities of a hospice volunteer must be based on an acceptance of how each person faces his or her own impending death. Life *and* death have infinite variety; there are few generalities and no "norms." There is no right or wrong way to think, feel, and act, and there are no rules or checklists. There are far more differences than similarities. In my experience, perhaps the only guide is that people usually face death and die the way they have lived. Their reactions, behavior and outlook are the same as in the earlier stages of their lives when facing a desperate situation. Only rarely do dramatic deathbed changes occur.

Specific fears and levels of grief, anger, and acceptance are as unique as each individual. Fears are varied but sometimes are centered, not on death itself or on the unknown, but on the process of dying: Will they be alone? Will there be pain or air hunger? Will they be conscious? Many grieve for what and who they shall leave behind and for the loss of the years ahead. Some regret words left unsaid and deeds undone, and others have lived only in the past or the future, "putting in time" waiting for a better tomorrow that now will never come. I often hear, "But I still have so much to do." One lovely lady who had often put her own goals and desires behind those of her husband and children asked, "But when will I ever get my turn now?"

Some people are enraged at the injustice of dying and at life's unfairness. They wonder why it has to be happening to them and one patient was even bold enough to name who it should have been happening to instead. Their indignant rage and their struggle toward understanding often interfere with the quality of their remaining days.

Many never lose their sense of humor and often find joy in the smiles they provoke or the laughs they share with others. One stately gentleman had this retort when I introduced myself as a hospice volunteer: "Oh, you're the one who is supposed to make me happy about dying!" Another lady said, "The doctor gave me six months to live and I've made my plans so it better not be a minute more!"

Certain individuals show a calm acceptance, maintaining a dignity of the human spirit even as they experience physical losses and psychological torment, and face their final goodbyes. There are those who are spiritually peaceful and who express their belief, in actions and words, that in joy and sorrow alike, life is God given and precious no matter how limited. Some reach out to others with increasing sensitivity, adding dimensions of love and meaning to their remaining time.

The reaction of others when they discover my involvement with dying people is at times comical. In our supposedly sophisticated society, nothing can stop a conversation or cause a shift of discomfort as quickly as the mention of death. Having passed the boundary of surprise and shock, many ask the question, "But what exactly do you do?" Because we are so task oriented (we want to *do*, not just be), the answer is difficult to express. It cannot be summed up in one sentence, explained in an hour, or found in a reference book.

As a volunteer, I care. I can't take away the anguish nor understand the depth of the despair of dying persons or the grief of their loved ones, but I *care* that they hurt. I offer my help instead of an attempt to save. I'm there, not to lead, but to share, always with an awareness that it is a privilege to be allowed within the intimacy of the precious last months, weeks, days or moments of life.

I'm a friend. And yet volunteers are more than friends because they do not judge. Unlike friends, they expect and demand nothing from the relationship, they need not be protected from the ugliness of physical suffering, from expressions of emotional despair, or from the torment of lost faith. Volunteers don't try to take away the hurt or try to answer, "Why me?" They give no unsolicited advice, use no meaningless slogans, and they never discount what a person is feeling or experiencing.

Hospice volunteers never function without the support and encouragement of others. As a member of the hospice team, they share knowledge and ideas with the physician, the hospice nurse, the social worker and the pastoral counselor. Team members are committed to providing support to the patient and family at home, in one of the participating hospitals in Austin, or in local nursing homes. In addition, volunteers receive reassurance and guidance from a support system which includes other volunteers and the volunteer coordinator.

I often feel my most important function as a volunteer is listening, an *activity* that hears not only words but unexpressed feelings and meanings. I have learned to be comfortable with silence. Words cannot always be formed by someone trying to cope and make sense of it all. But shared silence can be consoling. I recall a past patient, a very proud and private person, with whom I enjoyed a close relationship. On the day she heard from her physician that her disease had advanced beyond further treatment or medicine and that her life expectancy was short, we sat together, holding hands, silent and alone. When I left, she thanked me tearfully and said, "I'm better now." Her words about death and her grief and my expressions of comfort were unspoken, yet there was intimate communication between us.

The spoken words I hear are statements of bitterness, of denial, and of anger against God, physicians, family, and sometimes themselves. On rare occasions, patients become angry at the volunteer, as when one patient asked my age and calculated just how many years I had left to live. I hear the guilts of the past, the anguish of the present, and the regret of leaving things unfinished. I also hear expressions of peace, acceptance, profound and unrelenting faith, and poignant and moving episodes from lifetimes filled with love and sharing. Sometimes the words I hear are spoken just to comfort and encourage me.

By nature I am a "toucher," and many patients welcome this form of communication, though I am careful to respect the feelings of those who might consider it an invasion of their space of privacy. People who are ill feel unlovable and unattractive at times, and a hug can be almost therapeutic as well as a demonstration of my concern. A very special patient, a lovely and gracious lady, always greeted me with outstretched arms asking for her hug of the day, a hug I often needed as well. Another patient whose sight was affected by her disease and by medication would ask as she felt me take her hand, "It's you, Jean, isn't it?" My touch, heart to heart and hand to hand, was a familiar and welcome part of her darkening days.

Touch is especially important in the last hours and moments of life since it is one of the last senses to be lost. It has been my privilege to remain with a number of patients at these times, holding hands, rubbing arms, and stroking foreheads. One patient, whose neurological disease caused numbness in her feet, welcomed a gentle massage of her feet and legs as her illness progressed. During her last moments, she had only the strength to nod yes and smile weakly as I was there to rub her feet for the last time.

As life ebbs from their bodies, speaking to patients is important even if their state of consciousness is questionable. I tell them they are not alone and indicate which of their friends and family members are present. I frequently assure them that they are loved and how much they will be missed. I vividly recall a sweet lady, apparently comatose for hours, who reacted with movements of limbs and eyes when I told her that her only daughter and grandchildren had arrived from their distant home. A sound of pleasure escaped her lips, and she died peacefully a short time later in the loving arms of her husband and daughter.

As a volunteer, I am committed to preserving and enhancing the quality of life of hospice patients, whatever time span that encompasses. I become involved in many activities: arranging and observing heartwarming reunions, smuggling a pet dog into a hospital room, participating in a bedside communion service for a family of sixteen, or helping with a manicure and makeup session for a patient.

Sometimes, and often, it is just having fun together. It's not whispering or tiptoeing around, but telling outrageous jokes and having a good belly laugh. It's arranging (with the physician's approval) for a bottle of favorite wine *and* a crystal glass to be available in a hospital room. It's going for a drive, shopping for a gown or wig, going to a movie. It's shampooing hair or shaving a neglected beard, baking favorite cookies, or hunting down the special mints which are the only things that taste really good. It's going out for a roast beef sandwich or for tacos for the patient who hasn't eaten in days, or arranging for the hospital cook to make old-fashioned chicken and dumplings.

Sometimes it means assisting with funeral plans or arranging for a last family picture to be made. Often it involves making a list of personal treasures and to whom they will be left. It may be providing a journal and encouraging the written expression of feelings too difficult to voice, or helping with letters and tape recordings which will become legacies for those left behind. It's making arrangements for a party or for little gifts to be handmade, perhaps painted bookmarks for each grandchild, or a knitted cap to be completed and remembered with. It's making birthdays and anniversaries special, and having a joyful Christmas celebration even in a hospital room. Little acts of kindness and pleasures of the moment cannot be substitutes for good health and long life, but when moments arc few, they really matter.

Families of dying people often feel isolated and afraid, and helping them cope can mean that the patient is surrounded with gentle, loving, and unafraid loved ones. One family was tired and grieving, yet diligent in keeping a loved one at the bedside at all times. At one point, the sole attendant was a loving 21-year-old granddaughter. When I entered the room, she was obviously distressed and afraid, expressing her fear of being along with her grandmother and of how death would occur. Gently I told her that I thought it would be a quiet and peaceful end, just "like a clock running down." Later we cried together and she thanked me for easing her fear and said, "It was just like you said it would be."

In other ways families can be assisted by arranging the delivery of equipment needed at home, helping with endless forms and papers, providing a break for the primary caregiver or transportation to physician's offices or treatment centers, and being a liaison between the family and the hospice team. Sometimes it is simply providing the encouragement and the opportunity to have a good cry.

Why am I a hospice volunteer? What's in it for me? Without question it keeps my priorities in order, reminding me of what is important in life and what isn't and of how precious a gift each day is. I have discovered inner resources of mind and spirit and a reserve of empathy which had been unknown and previously unused.

Many times my memories are my rewards, because as I give part of myself to others, parts of them remain within me, continuing to teach me about the wonders of the human spirit. And there can be little more satisfying than to hear, "I couldn't make it without you," or "You are the *only* one I can tell how I really feel." It is payment beyond measure to see the drawn face of a grieving spouse light up as I rush back to the bedside of his dying wife, and to hear a patient when readmitted to the hospital ask, not for his physician or for a special nurse, but for me.

Hospice Austin has brought many blessings to my life besides the warm experiences with patients. I have the association of people who are stimulating, supportive, and committed, and I have made special friendships that are and will be a meaningful part of my life. I have a deeper understanding of myself, I treasure my relationships with others more, and I more fully appreciate the value of time. Perhaps the real reward is that I feel that what I am doing really makes a difference.

There are times when I become depressed. I am sad when I fail to establish a relationship with someone in need, and I grieve when death separates me from a special patient. Sometimes I am angry because I've been left behind and will miss the precious opportunities to learn and grow that patients give me. As a dear friend and fellow volunteer expressed it, "If you weren't doing a good job, it wouldn't hurt."

I get my strength and my comfort from my faith in God, my belief in what I am trying to do, and through the support of the hospice team, my family, and friends. I still must strive to keep a balance in my life, often reminding myself that I'm not the *only* one who can help. Periodic breaks allow me to "refill my cup" and replenish my emotional reserves.

As a hospice volunteer, I see grief, pain, injustice, and sad goodbyes. I also see love, caring, goodness, and the miracles of human understanding. And most often, after the special gift of helping someone I care about die with dignity, with the peace of acceptance and surrounded by loved ones, having had the opportunity to say his or her goodbyes, I am eager and impatient to be allowed the privilege to do it again.

IN HER PRIME

IN
HER
PRIME

The Murder of a Political Star

GLENN PUIT

BERKLEY BOOKS, NEW YORK

THE BERKLEY PUBLISHING GROUP
Published by the Penguin Group
Penguin Group (USA) Inc.
375 Hudson Street, New York, New York 10014, USA
Penguin Group (Canada), 90 Eglinton Avenue East, Suite 700, Toronto, Ontario M4P 2Y3, Canada
(a division of Pearson Penguin Canada Inc.)
Penguin Books Ltd., 80 Strand, London WC2R 0RL, England
Penguin Group Ireland, 25 St. Stephen's Green, Dublin 2, Ireland (a division of Penguin Books Ltd.)
Penguin Group (Australia), 250 Camberwell Road, Camberwell, Victoria 3124, Australia
(a division of Pearson Australia Group Pty. Ltd.)
Penguin Books India Pvt. Ltd., 11 Community Centre, Panchsheel Park, New Delhi—110 017, India
Penguin Group (NZ), 67 Apollo Drive, Rosedale, North Shore 0632, New Zealand
(a division of Pearson New Zealand Ltd.)
Penguin Books (South Africa) (Pty.) Ltd., 24 Sturdee Avenue, Rosebank, Johannesburg 2196,
South Africa

Penguin Books Ltd., Registered Offices: 80 Strand, London WC2R 0RL, England

The publisher does not have any control over and does not assume any responsibility for author or third-party websites or their content.

IN HER PRIME

A Berkley Book / published by arrangement with the author

PRINTING HISTORY
Berkley mass-market edition / November 2009

Copyright © 2009 by Glenn Puit.
Cover photographs: *Kathy Augustine and Chaz Higgs* courtesy of the Alfanso family; *Bottle of Succinylcholine* courtesy of Washoe County evidence vault.
Cover design by MC Studios.
Interior text design by Laura K. Corless.

ISBN: 978-0-425-23066-4

BERKLEY®
Berkley Books are published by The Berkley Publishing Group,
a division of Penguin Group (USA) Inc.,
375 Hudson Street, New York, New York 10014.
BERKLEY® is a registered trademark of Penguin Group (USA) Inc.
The "B" design is a trademark of Penguin Group (USA) Inc.

PRINTED IN THE UNITED STATES OF AMERICA

10 9 8 7 6 5 4 3 2 1

Most Berkley Books are available at special quantity discounts for bulk purchases for sales, promotions, premiums, fund-raising, or educational use. Special books, or book excerpts, can also be created to fit specific needs.

For details, write: Special Markets, The Berkley Publishing Group, 375 Hudson Street, New York, New York 10014.

This book is dedicated to
the memory of Kathy Augustine

AUTHOR'S NOTE

If you've read my books before, you know I make my living as an investigative reporter, and much of my time in the mainstream media was spent at the *Las Vegas Review-Journal*, Nevada's largest newspaper, where I covered the Las Vegas Metropolitan Police Department and Las Vegas's most high-profile capital murder cases. I've pretty much been writing—articles and books—about crime for my entire professional life. I've continued to write true crime books because I love doing it, and I believe true crime is the most compelling literary genre out there. There is something about criminal behavior and the human psyche that fascinates me, and it will always fascinate me.

I know it fascinates you, too.

My first book, *Witch: The True Story of Las Vegas's Most Notorious Female Killer*, was a terrifying look into a suspected female serial killer's twisted psyche. My second book, *Fire in the Desert*, is considered the evidentiary handbook for the disturbing murder case against national bodybuilder Craig Titus and his fitness champion wife, Kelly Ryan. My third book, *Father of the Year*, probed the crimes of convicted Las Vegas killer Bill Rundle.

This book, however, is far different from any other I've tackled, because this is not only a true crime book, but also a political documentary and a biography of a remarkable American woman all wrapped into one. The book is about the life of Nevadan Kathy Augustine, a mom, a wife, a politician, and, at one point in her career, arguably the most powerful woman in Nevada state politics. This book, I'm convinced, will be the definitive account of Kathy's life, which included the kind of amazing twists and turns that make for the type of story most nonfiction writers can only dream of chronicling.

In researching this book, I spent several hours with Kathy's family (though her daughter, Dallas, and her younger brother, Tony, declined to be interviewed). After meeting Kathy's parents and her oldest brother, Phil Jr., I understood why Kathy became so successful: her family members are some of the nicest people I've ever met. What has happened to Kathy's loved ones, and the pain they are suffering as a result of Kathy's death, is a terrible injustice. I've spent most of my career in journalism being reminded of the fact that, on a daily basis, terrible things happen to good people, and what happened to Kathy and her family has only reaffirmed that reality of life once again. I hope that in some small way, this book helps to alleviate the pain Kathy's family has endured, because they never deserved it. This book aims to tell the American public who Kathy really was—not just a politician, but a role model, a loving woman, a good mother, and a murder victim.

I wanted to close this note by tossing out a couple of quick thank-yous. Thanks to my employers at the Michigan Land Use Institute, the greatest nonprofit in America, for allowing me to perform meaningful, investigative journalism. The institute has also allowed me to have a work schedule that gives me a chance to pursue my dream of dominating the American true crime market. Thanks to my mom, Dee, who has offered me her support through some very rough times in my life in recent months. Thanks to my English teacher in high school, Letha Henry, who changed my life forever by being tough on me. Thanks to the Washoe County District Courts and the staff in the clerk's office and evidence vault. They are good people who went out of their way to allow me access to thousands of pages of public records.

Most of all, though, I want to thank my children, Garrison, Glenn Jr., and Gracie Lee, who continue to remind me that human beings are inherently good.

Glenn Puit

IN HER PRIME

1 . . . A REMARKABLE MOMENT

The truth always leaves some sort of footprint.
—Kathy Augustine, 2004

In February 2004, Kathy Augustine was enjoying what was perhaps the greatest success of her life. The forty-eight-year-old was one step away from becoming treasurer of the United States.

It was a remarkable moment for a remarkable American woman.

Twenty years earlier, Kathy had been a divorced single mom in Southern California, working as a flight scheduler for an airline company and earning a modest salary to support herself and her daughter, Dallas. After marrying for the third time, the tall, blond woman with hazel eyes and an outgoing personality went to school at night to get a master's degree in public administration. In 1991, a friend urged her to run for a seat in Nevada's state assembly. Kathy decided to go for it, despite having no political experience—and that chance foray into politics would become her calling in life. It was the genesis of a remarkable ascent through Nevada's vicious political arena.

Kathy was elected to the Nevada state assembly as a Republican in a strong Democratic district in Las Vegas. In 1994, through sheer will and, some say, dirty tricks, she repeated the feat when she was elected to the Nevada state senate as an underdog. Then Kathy's career took a huge leap forward when she ran for and was elected to the position of Nevada state controller—a constitutional officer responsible for making sure the state of Nevada spends its money wisely. Kathy succeeded at the job almost immediately, and she was recognized nationally for a program she created to help collect outstanding debts owed to the state. It was clear to anyone who knew Kathy Augustine that she was going places. She was an impressive Republican woman who was on the verge of national politics more than a decade before Sarah Palin became the vice-presidential nominee for the Republican Party and before Democrat Hillary Clinton was on the verge of the presidency.

Kathy's political career was skyrocketing. She'd become one of the highest-ranking female politicians on the state level in just over thirteen years. She was on the fringes of true power, and in 2004, there seemed to be no limits to what Kathy might accomplish.

Kathy learned of her nomination for U.S. treasurer that same year. Her name was forwarded to President Bush by two Nevada men she respected: Republican Senator John Ensign and Republican Congressman Jim Gibbons. The two told the Bush administration that Kathy Augustine was someone special, and they knew she would make a great treasurer for America.

"Please consider Kathy Augustine for the position of treasurer of the United States," Ensign wrote to the chief of staff of President George W. Bush. "The first woman elected Nevada state controller, Ms. Augustine has an exemplary record of public service. She has served as chairman of the Legislative Affairs and Operations Committee and vice chairman of the Human Resources and Facilities Committee in our state. With her numerous experiences, Ms. Augustine has refined the skills of ingenuity that will enable her to excel as treasurer. . . . [H]er time spent in public service and the business community makes Ms. Augustine more than qualified to serve in the . . . administration."

Jim Gibbons, a long term federal congressman who eventually became the governor of Nevada, offered similar sentiments in his pitch to the Bush administration on behalf of Kathy.

"I would like to offer my highest personal recommendation of Nevada State Controller Kathy Augustine to the position of United States treasurer," Gibbons wrote. "Controller Augustine is a nationally respected state official who would serve the Treasurer's Office with distinction. Kathy is the first woman to be elected Nevada Controller. Under Ms. Augustine's guidance, the controller's office has received ten certificates for achievement for excellence in financial reporting under a program established by the Government Finance Officers Association of the United States and Canada.

"As a former state legislator, I served with Kathy when she was a member of the Nevada State Senate," Gibbons wrote. "In the Senate, she was chairman of the Legislative Affairs and Operations Committee and vice chairman of the Human Resources and Facilities Committee. She also served two years as an Assemblywoman. I've known Kathy for several years, and believe her to be a highly qualified individual who has the capability to serve our nation's interests as the U.S. Treasurer."

Kathy was ecstatic about the nomination, and in June 2004, she flew from Nevada's quaint, quiet small-town state capital, Carson City, to Washington, D.C., for an interview with President Bush's chief of staff, Andrew Card, and Treasury Secretary John Snow.

Kathy knew afterward that the interviews with Card and Snow had gone well. She knew she was close to getting the job. Kathy was an impeccable woman in almost every respect. She was organized, she was professional, she was always well dressed, she was personable, and she was tough. Those who worked with her during her rise through Nevada politics said the woman could work a room. That same personable, confident personality came in handy during her interview with Bush's chief of staff.

Introducing the Treasurer of the United States, Kathy Augustine.

She liked the sound of it. She could just tell it was on the verge of becoming a reality. It would change her life forever if she got the job, but for now, Kathy wanted to enjoy the moment as she flew home from Washington, D.C., with her husband, Chaz Higgs. The couple had married in a whirlwind romance a year earlier, after the death of her third husband, Charles Augustine, and now Kathy discussed with her new husband the possibilities of what her life would be like if she got the job. She would be overseer of the U.S. Treasury, and that was no small assignment. She'd supervise the mint and the production of all coins and dollars. The treasury also makes all of the government's payments to its citizens, and it borrows the trillions of dollars necessary to keep the government running. Kathy knew she was more than capable of handling the job.

She returned to northern Nevada from Washington, D.C., and made a round of calls to the people dearest to her. The first two people she called were her parents, Kay and Phil Alfano Sr. Kathy reached them at their La Palma,

California, home to give them the news that the interview with Card and Snow had gone well.

"She was almost positive she had the job," her mother said. "She was in seventh heaven. She thought it was the most marvelous thing in the world. We were so proud of her, because we really didn't even encourage her to go into politics. She did all of this on her own."

Kathy called her brothers, Phil Jr. and Tony Alfano, at their homes in California, and she told them their big sister might end up with her name on the dollar bill.

"A front-runner," Kathy's brother Phil Jr. recalls with great pride of the conversation with his sister. "She was very excited. It was a dream come true for her."

Kathy dreamed of what was possible if she got the job. Someday, she might be governor of Nevada. A federal legislator? Congresswoman or senator? It certainly wasn't out of the question.

Congresswoman Kathy Augustine. Governor Kathy Augustine.

Kathy was a dreamer.

She believed in herself.

She knew all of it was possible.

But it all fell apart in the next four months. Her grasp on the treasurer's job evaporated in the face of a statewide political scandal. Bush named another woman, Anna Escobedo Cabral, as treasurer.

And then, in July 2006, Kathy Augustine was found unconscious in her northern Nevada home.

She died three days later.

This is her story.

2 ... TRUE LOVE AND MOON MEN

Phil Alfano Sr. and his wife, Kay, are wonderful people.

Next to the doorbell of their home in La Palma, California, is a small sign that reads "Grandma's little angels are all welcome here."

That signifies the type of people the Alfanos are. They are kind and caring, and they are all about family. Photos of their three grown children adorn the walls of their home, and they're close to their six grandchildren, too.

Most of Kay and Phil Sr.'s lives have been lived in the Greater Los Angeles area of Southern California—a remarkable collection of big city and old-fashioned American suburbia intertwined with the urban blight, concrete, and freeways that make up the region. The Alfanos' home is an older, well-kept home that was built when tract-home housing in an urban area still allowed for at least a modest backyard. On the back of the home is a screened-in porch that gives Kay and Phil Sr. a place to relax when the day is nearing an end and the sun is setting over the Southern California landscape. The streets there are clean, the lawns are all well manicured, the cars in the driveway are all sparkling, and even in overpopulated, urban Southern California, the people are friendly.

Kay Alfano has auburn hair and a modest, fit frame. She has always been and always will be a beautiful woman. Originally born in Detroit to an English father and an Irish mother, Kay said her parents instilled in her early on the belief that staying busy was an important part of living a fruitful, worthwhile life.

"Idle hands are the devil's plaything," Kay recalls. "My mother said it all the time."

That work ethic persists to this day. It's not unusual for Kay Alfano to get up early, before dawn, to make dinner and have it ready hours before the meal is served. She's always getting a head start through organization and hard work. Her house is meticulous, and Kay is prepared, organized, tough, and graceful through it all. Those closest to her say she is a caring woman who is as sweet as the day is long. She conveys a sense of genuine goodness, and she cherishes her family.

Phil Alfano Sr. is seventy-six years old. He is a former U.S. Marine and a tall, reserved, dignified man. After seven plus decades of life, his hair is thinning, and his frame is starting to thin as well. When he opens up during a conversation, he is kind and soft, but he usually only speaks when he has something to say.

Phil Sr. was born and raised in Chicago to a father who immigrated from Italy and a mother who was born here in America. For the first few years of his life, it seemed that his childhood would be idyllic, but life got hard very quickly for Phil Sr. and his five sisters when their mother died unexpectedly.

"I was eleven when it happened," he recalled. "My dad and older sisters ended up raising the family." When his father subsequently injured his leg badly, the accident put the Alfano family in further straits.

"My father really had the use of only one leg, so he became a switchboard operator," he said. Phil Alfano Sr. credits his father with greatly influencing his life by being a strong role model who persevered in the face of extreme hardship and who supported his family.

"My dad taught us that honesty, hard work, and love of the family were the most important things in life," Phil said of his father.

"We've been married fifty-six years!" Kay Alfano says with pride in her voice.

"Only fifty-six," Phil Alfano Sr. chimes in.

"There's a give and take," Kay said. "You've got to respect one another. With respect, things will iron out."

This couple met in 1950. Kay was working at Bullock's Department Store in Los Angeles at Christmastime when one day she was approached by a handsome, tall man with brown hair. The stranger identified himself as Phil Alfano, and he asked if she would like to have lunch with him.

"I said, 'I'm going to have lunch with my mother,'" Kay recalled.

She was honored that such a handsome man had approached and asked her to have lunch in such a courteous fashion, but she and her mother had brought brown-bag lunches. Phil Sr. then surprised her by pulling out his own brown-bag lunch, too.

"He said, 'Well, I brought mine too, and can I join you?'" Kay recalled. "My mother loved him immediately, and so did my father when he met him."

The couple started to date, and Kay realized very soon that she loved Phil Alfano Sr. She suspected she would marry him one day.

Phil Sr. was a freshman at Occidental College at the time, and he, too, fell in love with the gorgeous woman with auburn hair and a compelling figure. But still, something was nagging inside him: the country was at war with Communists in Korea at the time, and Phil Sr. felt an obligation to serve, so he joined the U.S. Marines in 1951. He was a forward observer for a mortar company in the marines, and his job was to go out into the combat zone with just one other person—a radioman—and call in for enemy fire if he saw North Korean troop movement.

"Scary," Phil Alfano Sr. says of his time in Korea.

He says nothing more.

While Phil was in Korea, though, he missed Kay dearly. To alleviate the fear and the longing, they wrote love letters to one another. The letters were vital to Phil Alfano Sr. They reminded him of the love to be found in a world of combat and killing. In one letter from 1951, Phil Alfano Sr. penned for the future Mrs. Kay Alfano a beautiful love poem on Red Cross stationery. It reads:

My dearest one is all I can say to express myself.
You came to me by fate itself.
I may never see my darling again.
But I love you for things you've done—the things I
*   can't repay.*
I've seen you many times here in this desolate place.
Of course, in my dreams, awake or asleep.
I think of you with all of my heart.
I love you more than life itself.
You won't believe me.
I know you can't but I think of you in my hour of need.

Do you think I can cry?
Well I can, and I try to see the sense in this thing
  called war.
It takes the breath out of old young men. . . .
Forgive me my darling.
Think of me now.
It is you I worship.
You, I adore.

Phil Sr.
Korea

Phil Sr. returned from Korea knowing he was going to marry Kay. The couple married at the San Gabriel Mission on August 10, 1952. They lived in leftover World War II barracks for veterans on the Occidental campus. Phil Sr. got a job in pharmaceutical sales, while Kay worked for Pacific Telephone and Telegraph Company in revenue accounting.

Kay and Phil Alfano Sr. suffered quite a scare in the fall of 1955. Kay was twenty-two at the time, and she became very, very sick. It wasn't clear what was wrong with her, and she was immediately hospitalized.

"I got deathly ill," Kay said. "I mean very sick, and I was put in the hospital. I lost twenty, twenty-five pounds in like two days."

Within a day, however, the doctors had a diagnosis, and it was certainly a surprise for the couple. Kay was pregnant. After two more trips to the hospital for pregnancy-related illnesses, Kathy Marie Alfano, later to be known as Kathy Augustine, was born on May 29, 1956, at Queen of Angels Hospital in Los Angeles. She weighed nine pounds, nine ounces, and was a beautiful baby.

"As long as the baby was healthy, that's all I cared

about," Kay said. "She was just marvelous! I was just ecstatic. I thought she was just the most beautiful thing."

Phil Sr. was enamored with his little girl, too. The baby was born on the day of one of his college finals at Occidental, but he didn't care that he missed the test, because it was a day that brought him one of the most beautiful gifts of his life.

"When I went back to school, the professor said, 'Anyone who had a child in the last twenty-four hours is excused,'" Phil recalled.

The two vowed to do everything they could to give Kathy the best childhood possible. There is nothing like the love that parents have for their first child, and it didn't take long for the Alfanos to realize that Kathy was special. She was sweet and innocent with a loving disposition. Kay also noted that Kathy seemed to be obsessed with helping her mother with household chores even when she was only a toddler.

"She was a happy child," Kay said. "She was always wanting to please, and she was always helping in the kitchen at a very early age. She was a very inquisitive child."

"Always wanting to know everything about everything," Phil Sr. said. "A beautiful child."

Kay noticed something else about her daughter as she grew from a toddler into a little girl: Kathy was consumed with organization. She was meticulous about folding and putting away her clothes in her room. The toys in her room were always stored in an organized fashion. As a young child, Kathy made her bed scrupulously, and she knew from memory where every belonging was in her room. It seemed to her parents that Kathy was a child who had to have structure and organization in almost everything she did, and if things were out of place or in disarray, it bothered her.

"The most organized kid, even when she was little,"

Kay said. "I mean organized. Most kids don't keep clean rooms, but you didn't have to tell Kathy."

"Very driven and very organized," Kathy's brother Phil Alfano Jr. agreed. "Very much a perfectionist. My parents never had to get on her about cleaning her room. My mom used to joke that she could ask Kathy 'Where's your blue sweater?' and Kathy could say 'It's in the third drawer, second one down.' She was that organized."

Kathy excelled in elementary school, and when the family moved from their first home, in Baldwin Park, to the Southern California community of South San Gabriel, Kathy excelled in school there, too.

"She was in Brownies and then Girl Scouts, and she did great in both," Kay said.

Kay and Phil Alfano Sr. both dreamed of having a large family, yet the couple struggled to have another child. They decided to pursue adoption after a doctor told Kay that because of medical reasons she would never give birth to another baby. The couple contacted a local Catholic charity called the Holy Family Adoption Agency and was put on a waiting list.

Kathy was seven at the time.

"When we found out we were going to be able to adopt a child, we didn't know if we were going to get a boy or girl," Kay said. "They called us on a Friday and said, 'We have a baby boy for you. Come in on Monday. The whole family. Everyone has got to come.'"

Phil Sr. drove Kay and Kathy to the adoption agency. They were put in a room with a baby in a bassinet. Kay took one look at the black-haired little baby and instantly fell in love.

"They said, 'If you don't want him, it's OK, and you'll still be on the list,'" Kay said. "Well, we took one look at him . . . and we loved him."

Phil and Kay Alfano named the child—who was born on December 21, 1964—Phil Alfano Jr. They returned home with the new baby shortly after Christmas. The following Monday, Kay got sick. She was rushed to the hospital, where again, she was told she was pregnant. The Alfanos' second son, Tony, was born nine months to the day after Phil Jr. was born.

"It was an incredible blessing," Kay said. "God blessed us. We couldn't believe it.

"When Phil Jr. came home, Kathy couldn't wait to get home from school to play with him every day," Kay said. "She would ask me, 'Can I change his diapers? Can I feed him?' It was pretty incredible. She was always trying to help me with Phil Jr., and it was the same when Tony came home. Kathy was like a little mother."

Phil Alfano Jr. is a kind and gentle man with dark black hair, dark eyes, and an outlook on life that is weighted in kindness. After spending more than two decades as an educator—a teacher for nine years and a principal for both a junior high and high school—Phil Jr. became an assistant school district superintendent in the Fresno area.

It's been a wonderful career for Phil Jr., who got into teaching at the urging of a friend's mother, and the profession suits him.

Phil Jr. remembers multiple moments in his childhood where his parents showed him unconditional love, and with the passage of time, he can now connect those moments in his early life to the kind, decent, and strong man he has become.

One memory stands out in particular for Phil Jr. as evidence of his parents' influence. He'd gotten a pair of expensive walkie-talkies for Christmas as a boy, but they didn't work, and when his mother went to exchange them, the store didn't have any more. Faced with the dilemma, Kay Alfano instead picked an expensive history book set, which would turn out to be a glorious gift for the boy. Phil Jr. read the books constantly, and that fascination with history ended up playing a significant role in his decision to become a teacher.

"I have always been interested in history, and I also had a great uncle who had an antiques store," Phil Jr. said. "He kind of got me interested in antiques. My parents would joke with me that I was born one hundred years too late because I liked stuff from the Victorian period."

Anyone who knows Phil Alfano Jr. unfailingly describes him as a person who cares about others. It is a characteristic clearly learned from the mother and father who loved him from the moment they saw him at the Catholic adoption agency. Phil Jr., in turn, loves his parents dearly. He calls them almost daily, and when he talks about them, the admiration, respect, and thankfulness for his parents is clear. Phil Jr. is also very close to his brother, Tony, but the person he was closest to in his family was his older sister, Kathy.

Both brothers were babied by Kathy, and to this day, Phil Jr. remembers Kathy as an older sister who was constantly looking out for him.

"She was assigned babysitting duties quite a bit when we were growing up," he recalled. "It was kind of an interesting relationship between us and Kathy, because sometimes when older siblings get into high school, they don't want anything to do with their little brothers and sisters, but that wasn't the case with Kathy. She kept us involved in everything. She took us to quite a few places. I know the only time I ever went to the circus was with Kathy and a couple of her friends when she was a teen. I also remember going to a Dodgers game as a little boy with Kathy. She'd just gotten her driver's license, and I'll never forget it because it was an extra-inning game and they were playing the Mets and Willie Mays was with the Mets at that time. My sister took me to that game, so, obviously, she was a really great sister growing up.

"I think we were very fortunate growing up," Phil Jr. said. "We had two solid parents. My parents have been married for fifty-six years, and it is a very traditional marriage. My dad was the quote unquote breadwinner, but my mom did work . . . and we respected them. We didn't want to make my father angry. We knew how to tread lightly. He'd let you know if he wasn't happy about something . . . and my mom would run interference, telling us now [was] not the time to bring something up."

Sundays were magical days for the Alfano family, when they would often go on family drives to places like the Arboretum of Los Angeles County in nearby Arcadia, or the Huntington Library—the former mansion of railroad tycoon Collis P. Huntington, with its formal English gardens and collection of paintings by masters such as Gainsborough and Peale. The Arboretum is a 127-acre botanical garden and historical site that feels much like a beautiful maze through wide green walkways, bushes, flowers, and trails that once served as a set for the old Tarzan movies of the 1930s, starring Johnny Weissmuller.

"Trees, plants, all kind of stuff, and then you can walk through the whole thing," Phil Alfano Sr. said. "It was fun running around through there with the children."

"The kids loved it," Kay Alfano said. "That's where *Fantasy Island* used to be filmed. The home, and the barn, and the lagoon. . . . You could run around. You watched the kids, but you could let them out of your sight and not worry about them."

The Alfano family took summer vacations each August to places like San Diego and Lake Tahoe. From Tahoe, they made day trips to Virginia City and Carson City, exploring the old capitol building that would one day serve as Kathy's office when she became controller.

Kathy, Phil Jr., and Tony were all very close siblings even though Kathy was eight years older than Phil Jr. and nine years older than Tony.

"I know Kathy was very happy to have two younger brothers in the home," Phil Jr. said.

One of his sister's more apparent attributes, Phil Jr. recalled, was her obsession with organization. Everything in life had to have structure for Kathy, but she also had a remarkable sense of humor as a young girl. She was known for "hysterical laughing fits," her brother said, and when the Alfano boys were little, Phil Sr. kept the boys' hair cropped close like marines, prompting Kathy to nickname Phil Jr. and Tony her little "moon men."

"Our hair was cut right down to the nub, and this was right after America put a man on the moon," Phil Jr. said. "And so she said we looked like moon men. She'd come by and rub her hand on my head and call me Moon Man. She came up with other nicknames for us, too, and for our whole lives, we were stuck with them. My other name was 'Willie,' and she called my brother Tony 'Bonzo.' I don't know why we got those nicknames to this day."

When Kathy was twelve, the Alfanos started to notice that the South San Gabriel neighborhood they were living in was deteriorating. A boy who lived across the street from the family was murdered, and the Alfanos felt they needed to move to ensure long-term stability for the family. The Alfanos moved to a brand-new tract-home development in La Palma in October 1969.

"I know they wanted to move before Kathy got into high school," Phil Jr. said.

"Kathy was going into the eighth grade," Kay Alfano said. "She was in choir. She had one of the leads in the musical *Bye Bye Birdie*, and she was also a student body officer."

Kathy enrolled in John F. Kennedy High School in La Palma at fourteen. By then, she was blossoming into a beautiful, well-developed, elegant young lady. She was tall, at nearly five feet nine inches, and she had flowing brown hair that she would later color blond.

"My sister was a very beautiful young lady—a beautiful girl," Phil Jr. said. "Her hair was blond when she was little, then it turned dark, and it wasn't until adulthood when she went back to the blond hair."

It was a stroke of good fortune for Kathy that she ended up going to JFK High School, because the school placed a significant emphasis on its students getting involved in government in the aftermath of JFK's death.

"Student government was a huge part of the culture of that school," Phil Jr. said. "When you walked in, it had JFK's famous quote, 'Ask not what your country can do for you . . .' so they really kind of promoted that, and she got involved in student government right away. I think that is where the bug kind of bit her. She wanted to go into public service."

Kathy knew in high school she was going to be a Republican, like her parents. "We're conservative," Phil Sr. says. "Always have been, and I think that rubbed off on her."

Kathy was popular in high school, and it was clear she was a special person. She got perfect grades. She had her act together, and everyone knew it.

"She was on a weekend swim team, and then another

swim team during the summer," Kay said. "She was always volunteering for everything. Volunteering at church. Volunteering as a candy striper at the hospital. We were so very proud of her. So very, very proud."

"My sister had a type A personality," Phil Jr. said. "Very driven and very organized. Very much a perfectionist. Very driven in school, and interestingly, we didn't grow up in a family where that type of pressure was put on you."

Kathy enrolled in college for a semester at the University of California–Irvine but struggled to get into the classes she wanted. She then transferred to Occidental College in Los Angeles, where she majored in political science. It was the same college her father had graduated from, and Phil Jr. suspects that his sister's decision to go to Occidental was made in part to please her father. According to Phil Jr., Kathy ran with the "in crowd" in college, yet she was constantly befriending nerds and outcasts at school. Phil Jr. sees this as evidence of another characteristic of her sister: that she was a trusting person who always wanted to believe in the best in people.

"She was hanging out with some nerds, and normally people in Kathy's social circle wouldn't do that, but Kathy was very friendly, very outgoing, and she believed in people," Phil Jr. said. "One time, she showed up at our home with a group of guys from the Ivory Coast Olympic Track Team. She was involved in some sort of service group on campus, and she said, 'Hey, I'm going to bring these guys home for dinner.' She was always very, very trusting."

Kathy's ambition shined through during her summers in college. She flew to Alaska and worked as a paralegal on an oil-pipeline project. She lived in Alaska the whole summer. She also received a Toll Fellowship and worked another summer on that project. Her third year in college, she obtained an internship in Washington, D.C., with a Democratic congressman named Gary Patterson.

"I think she was the only Republican working in there," Phil Jr. said. "Every summer she was doing something. She had an aura of something special, and everyone knew it. You knew early on she was going to be someone very successful later on in life. It was obvious to everyone."

3 . . . MEN

This is probably the greatest contradiction. She was so organized. She was so intelligent. She was so smart in her professional life. But when it came to guys, there were times in her life when she had very horrible judgment.

—Phil Alfano Jr.

Phil Alfano Jr. was just ten years old in 1974 when an incident unfolded that troubled him greatly. He admired his sister. He loved her dearly, and she was his closest ally in life. Phil Jr. spent a lot of time with his sister even though Kathy was now in college, and he regularly visited her in a home she rented with two other female students. Few eighteen-year-olds in their freshman year in college would seem likely to spend a lot of time with a little brother eight years younger than them, but Kathy made it a priority to spend time with both of her brothers as much as she could.

"She took me to an apartment in Anaheim, and at the time, she was dating a guy [who lived there]," Phil Jr. said. "We went to the apartment complex pool, and he had a little brother my age, so we were goofing around, swimming, and playing outside. I got kind of bored, so I went back to the apartment to see what was going on. I walked into the apartment, and I heard this guy using some pretty abusive language toward my sister."

Phil Jr. was bothered to hear someone talking to his sister like that. What happened next shocked him, though.

"I saw this guy slap my sister. I couldn't believe it," Phil Jr. said. "So, we left. I remember on the drive home, Kathy was saying, 'Please don't say anything to Mom and Dad.' She was begging me. So I didn't say anything to my parents, and she broke it off with [him] right after that."

In retrospect, this slap was not the first indication that Kathy had bad taste in men. Her parents and brother each said that Kathy had a habit of occasionally dating the "bad boys" in high school.

"She . . . had some very poor judgment when it came to personal relationships," said Phil Jr. "We grew up in a pretty good environment, and the only argument I ever really remember in our home was about some of the guys she was dating. My parents were not pleased with the guys she dated."

Kay and Phil Alfano Sr. said the same.

"In high school, some of the people she went out with . . . bothered us," Kay said. "I'd ask her, 'What are you doing [with him]?' and she'd say, 'But he's a really a good person!' She always tried to find the good in you. So we made a rule that anybody she went out with had to come to the house to pick her up.

"I just didn't like their appearance and the attitudes of some of them," Kay said. "And when we confronted her about it, she'd just say, 'Oh, Mom . . .'"

Kathy graduated from Occidental with a degree in political science, and she quickly fell in love with a young man she'd met in college. The couple planned to marry, but just two weeks before the wedding, they called it off.

"The wedding was cancelled, and then on the day the

wedding had been scheduled for, I was home and the doorbell rang," Phil Jr. said. "I answered the door of our home, and there was a couple at the door. They were all dressed up, and they were there for the wedding. My dad looked at my mom and said, 'I thought you called everyone!' "

After the collapse of her engagement, Kathy couldn't decide what she wanted to do with her life. She moved to Pacific Beach and contemplated becoming a lawyer. She applied to law school in San Diego and was accepted, but before she began, a friend of the family who worked for Western Airlines called Kay and Phil Alfano Sr.

"He called and said, 'Can I get in touch with Kathy?' " Kay recalled. " 'I want to hire her.' "

Kathy was having doubts about law school, and the idea of going straight into the workforce and securing a steady paycheck from Western Airlines appealed to her. She accepted a job scheduling pilot routes and work hours for Western, which at the time was a dominant force in the American airline industry.

"As a pilot, you can only spend so many hours in the air, and you have to have so much rest between flights," Kay said. "Kathy's job was to make sure the pilots didn't get too many hours so that all the rules of [the Federal Aviation Administration] were met. She had to keep track of this."

Kathy was very talented at her job. Her organization skills served her well at Los Angeles International Airport, and she enjoyed it. The job paid well and offered her free travel.

Kathy ended up meeting her first husband while working in the early 1980s. She fell in love with a flight controller named Gary Voss, who'd been married previously. Kathy was twenty-two at the time, and Gary was a few years older. After a few months of dating, they quickly got married, without seeking the Alfanos' blessing. Kay and

Phil Alfano Sr. were not happy about their daughter's decision to marry, because they didn't feel the couple was a good fit.

"They didn't have a church wedding," Phil Jr. said. "My parents were not happy—not pleased at all. They just went to Reno and got married. They came back, and we had a reception. Very impulsive."

"She never even asked us what we thought," Kathy's father said.

The couple lived in Long Beach, then Anaheim, and the marriage produced one of Kathy's greatest joys in life: her daughter, Dallas. Kay and Phil Sr. fell in love with Dallas, their first grandchild, and they showered the little girl with love. Kathy and Gary divorced about two years into the marriage after what Kathy's loved ones described as a difficult relationship.

Kathy and Dallas moved into a condominium in Westminster, California, and Kathy found it difficult supporting the two on her salary. She also wanted to further her education, with the hope that it would allow her to get a better-paying job. Kathy enrolled in a public administration master's degree program at Long Beach State, working full-time during the day and going to class at night.

She relied on the help of her parents to get her through the difficult time.

"I think Kathy was very fortunate," Phil Jr. said. "She had a good support system with my parents. My grandmother was still alive as well, and it was very easy for Kathy to bring Dallas over and drop her off so she could work on her degree. She brought Dallas over to my parents' house whenever she had a class at night."

Kay and Phil Sr. worried about Kathy. It saddened them that their daughter, whose future had been so promising, had put herself in such a tough position. They knew, however, that Kathy was the type of person who would survive the challenge of being a single mom. They also recognized that Kathy was a great mom to Dallas. She fretted over everything about the child.

"Kathy was a strict mother to Dallas," Kay said. "Dallas's room always had to be clean, and Kathy was the type of mother who, when Dallas got up in the morning . . . [made sure Dallas knew she] was expected to get dressed and comb her hair. That was the case even on Saturday mornings. Most kids on Saturday don't want to get dressed. They want to lay around, and Kathy wouldn't put up with that.

"We were always strict with Kathy as parents, and that's the way Kathy was, too," Kay Alfano said.

In 1987, both of Kathy's brothers got married to two wonderful women. Tony married a young woman named Colleen, and Phil Jr. married his wife, Mary. Kathy then dropped a huge announcement on her family within just a few months of her brothers' marriages: she told everyone she was getting married, too. She'd been dating a U.S. Marine named Kevin Hohn for just a couple of months, and she was in love.

Her family was wary again.

"Phil gets married, Tony gets married, and then Kathy springs it on us that she's marrying a marine who was younger than her," Kathy's mother said. "I think she just wanted to get married because her brothers were married."

The couple divorced within a couple of months. It was another reminder to Kathy's family that the seemingly perfect daughter, sister, and mother was someone who jumped into relationships that didn't last.

"She had this idealized view of romance," Phil Jr. said. "She believed in love at first sight. She believed in finding an immediate soul mate, and because of that mind-set, she overlooked a lot of things in the men in her life that were noticed by others."

Kathy was now starting to wonder whether she would ever meet a man who was compatible with her. But despite Kathy's failures with men, she was about to have a significant change of luck. She was about to meet a man who truly loved her and who was willing to spend the rest of his life with her. Within a couple of months of her divorce from Hohn, she met an older man at work named Charles Augustine. She was impressed by him, the man everyone called "Chuck."

Kathy had just gotten her master's degree from Long Beach State, and she was continuing to work at Western, which was later bought out by Delta. Chuck was a pilot for Delta Airlines, and he was much older than Kathy. She was thirty-two and he was forty-seven when they met. Chuck, like Kathy, was also divorced, and he had three children, two sons and a daughter, from a prior marriage. Chuck was also well-off financially, making six figures as a pilot—a lot of money, especially in the 1980s. He owned a modest home off Tropicana Boulevard.

Chuck was a big, strapping man with grayish black hair. He had been raised in the San Francisco area by traditional, Catholic parents, and he, too, was a practicing Catholic as an adult. Chuck had lived an exciting life prior to his meeting Kathy. He'd served in Vietnam as a fighter pilot and attended college at Notre Dame, where he played football when Daryle Lamonica, the famous quarterback for the Oakland Raiders, was at the helm of the Fighting Irish football squad. Chuck eventually blew out his knee on the football field, ending his career, but he remained an avid Notre Dame football fan for life.

"Kathy started dating Chuck right after her divorce," Phil Alfano Jr. said. "But when I met him, I could tell it was going to be the best relationship my sister ever had. Chuck was a real nice guy, and I liked him right away. He was not super outgoing, but he was friendly. He was the type of guy who you could go over to his house, sit down on the couch, watch football, have a beer, and it would be a very enjoyable afternoon. An easygoing guy."

Kathy's parents said they knew their daughter was dating Chuck, but they didn't have a chance to meet him right away. Kathy did, however, call her mother and father to let them know about her new, older man.

"He was older than her, and I knew about him, but I didn't know him," said Kay Alfano, who added that at first, she was slightly concerned about the difference in age between her daughter and her new man. "Kathy told me, 'Mom, you are really going to like him.'"

Kathy and Chuck dated for about a year before they married in 1988 in a ceremony at a private home in Las Vegas. After the marriage, Kathy brought Chuck to La Palma to meet her parents, who liked him right away. They finally felt that their daughter had found a man who would be a good fit for her, and they were proud to welcome Chuck Augustine into the Alfano family.

"Chuck was very intelligent, and he was like us," Kay said. "His home and family meant everything. I liked him from day one."

Phil Sr. was impressed with his daughter's new husband as well. Chuck was a lot like Kathy's father in that he was all business in his professional life. He was an exceptional pilot, and he was committed to a profession he loved. But Chuck was just a normal guy when work was done, and he was also a loving role model in Dallas's life.

"If Chuck wanted things to get done, then they got done," Phil Sr. said. "Then, when he was home from flying all week, he'd kick back and watch the football games. Despite the fact that he was making a lot of money, he cut his own grass. He was just a regular guy, and I really liked him."

About two years after the couple married, they purchased a huge, elegant house in Las Vegas. The home, at 1400 Maria Elena Drive, was large—5,600 square feet of space, in an old, beautiful neighborhood of Las Vegas, down the street from where Howard Hughes had once built a house for a mistress. Kathy moved into the elegant home on Maria Elena and quit her job in the airlines. It was the first time Kathy had lived in Vegas, and she loved the city right away. She spent much of her time caring for Dallas, and she also taught math and science at a local Catholic school. Chuck adopted Dallas as his own daughter shortly after the marriage. He loved Dallas, and he was committed with Kathy to doing everything he could to give her the best childhood he could.

"Chuck was good to Dallas," Kay said.

Kathy's family was happy for her. It appeared that this relationship was different from her prior unions; it seemed like there was a very good chance that this marriage was going to last. Chuck and Kathy had their arguments, like any couple, but they were able to disagree without it affecting their love for one another. Phil Jr. said it seemed that Chuck was able to handle Kathy's perfectionist personality. Chuck just laughed it off when she started to harp on him.

"Chuck used to call my sister 'She Who Must Be Obeyed,'" Phil Jr. said. "My sister certainly could be demanding, and I think that's what was perfect about Chuck. When my sister was demanding, he was just like, whatever. We were over at their house one Thanksgiving, and we were watching Kathy harp on Chuck because he was wearing mismatched colored sweats. We were sitting there going, 'Kathy, give the guy a break,' and Chuck just laughed it off."

The other difference between Chuck and Kathy's prior husbands was the fact that Kathy respected Chuck's opinion, and when he gave her advice, she almost always took it. She felt Chuck's advice was sound.

"If Chuck said something to Kathy, she really took it to heart," Phil Jr. said. "Kathy would often quote Chuck and his advice. She had a lot of respect for him, and I know she loved him very, very much."

4 . . . NANCY VINIK

Nancy Vinik came to Las Vegas from Chicago in 1978 for a change of weather and a change of scene, and she certainly got it. Vegas is certainly a far different place than Chicago. There are no cool, moist, or chilly breezes like the ones that run off Lake Michigan and through Chicago's massive cityscape. In Las Vegas, the summer can be brutal, but Nancy, who was born in Hammond, Indiana, didn't really mind the heat. She loved Vegas when she came to the city *because* it was different from the Midwest. The beautiful young woman with a striking figure, blond hair, and a gorgeous face found the city of neon lights to be intriguing and exciting, always with an edge.

By 1988, Nancy was married, a mom, and working as a nurse, and she began looking for something new to do with her free time. She felt the time she was spending away from the hospital was not as meaningful as it could be. Nancy had been involved in volunteer work throughout her life, and a friend told her about a philanthropic organization for women

called the Junior League of Las Vegas. One of the mottoes of
the organization is "Women building better communities,"
and the organization certainly does that: it enlists an army
of Las Vegas women to do everything from raising money
and collecting goods for victims of domestic violence to promoting public participation in democracy and preserving Las
Vegas's historic sites. Nancy found the work and camaraderie
among the women in the group very exciting; in addition to
offering a chance to give back, Nancy felt like the volunteering for the Junior League also taught her leadership.

"I personally was doing it to meet new people and do
something for the community," Nancy said. "I wanted to
do something different. At the time, I had a daughter who
was two years old, I worked, and pretty much that was it.
Working, taking care of my daughter, and coming home. It
was a cyclical thing, and I needed to get out of the cycle. I
needed to get out and meet new people. I'd always liked to
do volunteer work, and the Junior League was a nice outlet.
I could do things after work, and once you got involved
with Junior League, you could schedule it so it would fit
your own personal schedule."

Nancy Vinik met Kathy Augustine during a 1988 initiation ceremony for new Junior League members, and the
two women hit it off immediately.

"Kathy and I found out that we lived very close to each
other," Nancy said. "I lived in a cul-de-sac, and I could
have climbed my wall, walked through someone's backyard, and her street was literally behind the house where
mine was. We were virtually neighbors.

"She said she was getting involved in Junior League at
the time because she needed to find a purpose for her life,"
Nancy recalled. "She was bored. She hadn't really lived
in Las Vegas all that long, and I sensed she had an itch

to develop a new professional career, but she really wasn't quite sure what she wanted to do."

Nancy saw that Kathy was incredibly organized, elegant, funny, vibrant, and kind. It seemed to Nancy, however, that her new friend was longing for more in life.

"[Kathy was] a beautiful woman," Nancy Vinik said. "She liked to be well-dressed at all times. She was always clean and neat, and she dressed like a million dollars. A very elegant person who always wore her makeup impeccably, but I always said it was more than just skin deep with Kathy. She had a heart that was very big. She was very giving. A wonderful person and a wonderful mom."

What followed for Nancy was the friendship of a lifetime. Kathy was Nancy's best friend, and they confided in one another. They talked on the phone about three times a week, and Nancy's husband, Charles, became good friends with Kathy's husband, Chuck, as well.

"Her husband and my husband were friends," Nancy said. "We socialized together, and we went to dinner [events] together. Our husbands would have lunch together at times. We would go to their home for after-dinner drinks, or in the summertime we had little backyard parties. Things like that.

"Kathy had the best laugh," Nancy Vinik said. "It was infectious. You heard her laughing, and you knew she was coming. You could hear her laughing from three rooms away.

"Kathy was very, very close to her family," Nancy said. "She loved her parents. She was also a person who would never let anyone have a holiday by himself or herself. She would bring people to her home for the holidays who didn't have any other place to go. You could be at her house for Thanksgiving or Christmas, and there would be people there that no one knew. They were invited because they had nowhere else to go."

Kathy and Chuck attended Mass regularly at Saint Viator Catholic Church in Las Vegas, and, like her parents, Kathy was a strong, faithful Catholic. The priest at the church was a good friend of Kathy's and was a regular visitor at the Augustines' home on Maria Elena. Kathy was very involved in her church, and she was very close friends with Father Mike Keliher, who respected her greatly. Kathy, he said, regularly volunteered for the church's philanthropic causes; she was in church most Sundays; and he found her to be an honest, God-fearing Catholic.

Dallas Augustine babysat the Viniks' daughter. Nancy said Dallas was a quiet, studious girl who got good grades in school. She became an excellent golfer as she got older, and she excelled on the golf team at Bishop Gorman—an extremely well-regarded private Catholic school in Las Vegas. Dallas was, by all accounts, a good student and a model daughter. She was very close to her stepfather, Chuck (she uses his last name to this day), and her mother held Dallas to very high standards. She was expected to be organized and follow a rigid structure in life.

"People who knew Kathy well knew that she had to be organized in everything she did," Nancy said. "Everything in their house was organized. For a place, there was everything, and for everything, there was a place. I'd never seen anyone in my life who had everything so organized. All of her shoes were organized by color. She had scarves, and they were folded a certain way. All of her jewelry was stored in a certain way. She would spend a lot of time putting things back to where they needed to be to satisfy her obsessive-compulsiveness, because that's what it was. That's what gave her strength. That's what made her straight in her life. That's how she could function. She couldn't function in chaos, and that's just the way she was. There could be no other way with Kathy."

Nancy Vinik liked Chuck Augustine, and it seemed to her that he was a good life partner for Kathy.

"I think Chuck recognized that Kathy was a person of perfection, and he wasn't going to deny her that," Nancy said.

In 1992, the Viniks and the Augustines were having an after-dinner drink when the topic of politics came up. The Viniks were Republicans, and so were the Augustines. As the couples talked, the Viniks learned that Kathy had been a political science major in college and that she'd gotten a master's degree in public administration. Charles Vinik was somewhat active in politics, in that he occasionally held fund-raisers for politicians he admired, and in passing he suggested to Kathy that she should run for the state assembly in her district—District 12 of Las Vegas. He admired Kathy greatly, and as soon as Charles Vinik mentioned the idea, Kathy appeared intrigued. She started asking Charles some questions about his proposal, and the Viniks quickly recognized that there seemed to be a spark in Kathy's demeanor when she talked about the idea. She perked up almost immediately as the housewife contemplated the idea of running for state office and becoming a politician.

"After my husband found out that she thought government was interesting, he said, 'Hey, why aren't you doing something with politics?'" Nancy recalled. "My husband said, 'We don't have anyone here in the district who is a Republican to even run for the Nevada Assembly.' Year after year in District 12, it was the same shoo-in person who got elected. And when the idea first came up, we were surprised that it didn't take a lot of nudging for Kathy. She said to my husband, 'Would you help me with my campaign?'"

Charles Vinik said of course he would, and he even

agreed to have a fund-raising party to get Kathy started. Kathy was excited by the idea. She had been very active in student government in high school, and she'd loved those experiences. The next day, she filed to run for Assembly District 12.

It was as if a powder keg had gone off inside of Kathy. She'd been through two difficult marriages and was a single mom who'd finally found love in Chuck, but now she wanted to do something more with her life. She became consumed by the idea of running for office. She told everyone around her that she wasn't going to rest until she won. But to do that, she would have to overcome some huge obstacles: District 12 is a narrow but sizeable district of historic neighborhoods in east Las Vegas that runs between Charleston Boulevard and Vegas Valley Drive from north to south and from Maryland Parkway to Nellis Boulevard from west to east in the direction of the Las Vegas Valley's Sunrise Mountain. The district has close to 50,000 people in it, and stretches for more than 6 miles from east to west.

"Everyone knew she was a big underdog," Nancy Vinik said. "The district hugely favors Democrats." Kathy's opponent was longtime Democrat Dora Harris, who was respected in the district and the clear favorite.

But Kathy Augustine was organized, and she was driven. She simply decided to outhustle the entire Democratic operation in District 12, and she told her husband she was going to knock on every door in the district. She developed what would become her signature red and white campaign signs, and within days, she was consumed by politics.

"Right after she filed, there she was, organizing her campaign and doing all of the things she needed to do," Nancy said. "She started getting anyone and everyone she knew to walk the neighborhoods with her, and she started telling everyone what she stood for: Republican values. She started saying, 'This is what I'm going to do.' So I was out there with her, in the middle of the summer, and it's 110 degrees, and we were knocking on doors all day long. She had it all organized by neighborhood and by day as to which neighborhood she was going to canvass. She had it all charted out, and it was a very big district."

Kathy told voters that she would be an accountable representative for the district. If they would give her their votes, she in turn promised to fight on their behalf. Kathy had a knack, Nancy said, for convincing people that she was for real and sincere. She didn't seem like just another politician, and the passion she felt radiated from her. Although Chuck wasn't too excited about his wife running for office, he still supported Kathy's ambitions. He loved his wife, and he could tell that this was very important to her.

"Politics [were] not Chuck's favorite thing," said Kathy's mother, Kay Alfano. "Before this happened, Kathy had really wanted another child, and Chuck's kids from his prior marriage were basically grown. Chuck didn't want any more children. Given that void I think Kathy felt, Chuck realized that this was important to her."

Looking back, Kathy's parents acknowledge that they underestimated how significant an event the assembly run was in their daughter's life. They supported Kathy, and they even volunteered for her campaign, helping to canvass neighborhoods and talk to voters, but they wouldn't realize the true significance of this time in Kathy's life until years later.

"I didn't think much of it," Kay Alfano said. "Dallas was in school all day, and we would walk the precincts with [Kathy]. I enjoyed being with her, and I should have known she was going to win, because Kathy was not one to sit around."

Kathy's brother Phil Alfano Jr. and his wife, Mary, also helped Kathy walk the precincts. They were proud of Kathy's determination, and they, too, sensed that this was very important to her.

"A lot of people have said after the fact that Kathy was always destined for politics," Phil Jr. said. "I don't believe that was the case. She did a political internship in Washington, D.C., when she was young, and she was interested in politics, but from the time she was married to Gary to the time she was married to Chuck, she was not out going to political rallies or walking precincts. She wasn't involved in any of that, and I think she would have been very, very content to simply be a housewife and mom in Las Vegas."

Like his mother, Phil Jr. suspects that his sister threw herself into the assembly race in large part because of the recognition that she was not going to have any more children.

"I know she'd talked about adopting, and Chuck didn't want to adopt," Phil Jr. said. "By this time, Chuck was in his fifties, and I think my sister recognized that if she wasn't going to have more children and be a mom, then she wanted something more to do. If motherhood wasn't in the cards, she wasn't the type of person who was going to sit still."

Kathy's drive and talents always amazed her brothers, but watching Kathy running for the state assembly was nonetheless remarkable to her oldest brother. Phil Jr. knew how Kathy had struggled in life, and he was excited to see his sister realize her success. The woman was relentless.

"She busted her ass," Phil Jr. said. "She was out walking precincts all day. It [was] summertime, and she was walking the neighborhoods from 6 a.m. to 6 p.m. I walked with her when we were over there, and she really, really worked hard. It was a lot of fun to watch."

The race was a tight one, for sure. Kathy pulled out all the stops near the end of the race and put out a mailer that would later earn her a reputation as a vicious campaigner. She put together a flyer that placed her photo next to Dora Harris's, and the flyer was titled "There is a difference." Kathy, who was white, was pictured next to Harris, who was black, and the flyer prompted cries of racism. Kathy listed the policy differences between herself and Harris on the flyer, and she denied any intent to compare the women's racial differences, but the incident helped cement Kathy's reputation in Nevada as a scorched-earth politician who would do whatever was necessary to get elected.

Jon Ralston is a Nevada columnist who founded a statewide newsletter and later became a daily television show host offering political commentary. He's regularly interviewed by CNN and other major networks because of his expertise on Nevada politics. "I just love the personalities, the twists and turns, the machinations," Ralston said. "The only game for adults, a friend of mine says. It's ever-fascinating."

Ralston said Kathy's flyer against Harris got a lot of attention because many really did believe it was racist.

"I had a negative impression from a distance because I thought she had exploited racism in her campaign by running a picture of her black opponent in her brochure," Ralston said. "It was controversial."

One of the most respected writers in Nevada, *Las Vegas Review-Journal* columnist Jane Ann Morrison, would later refer to Kathy's flyer as "skulduggery."

"I looked at the flyer, and I thought it was pretty innocuous," Phil Jr. said. "Dora Harris had used that photo in her own mailers. A lot of people said the flyer was designed to appeals to racists, putting the white woman next to this black woman. I thought that was a bunch of bullshit."

In November 1992, when the voters of District 12 went to the polls to cast their ballot, Kathy pulled off the upset. She received 5,454 votes, or 53 percent of the vote. She won by 707 votes.

Kathy Augustine, state legislator, was now on her way to Carson City.

5 ... CARSON CITY

Abraham Lincoln welcomed Nevada into the union in 1864 in part because the state had a wealth of gold and silver in its terrain, and the value of those raw materials would serve as a boon to the North's fight in the American Civil War. Carson City was chosen as the state's capital, forever giving northern Nevada an anchor to support itself against the unprecedented growth and attention eventually directed to its sinful sister city to the south.

And so it is little Carson City, population 53,000, and not Las Vegas, with its millions of residents and tax revenues and national aura, that serves as the capital of Nevada. Carson City may seem small and out of the way, but it is a city of elegance, cleanliness, and Nevada history—the state's capitol building and governor's mansion seem at their rightful home in the shadows of the high desert pines and mountains of northern Nevada.

Carson City is where the state's most critical decisions are made. Nevada has a state assembly that consists of forty-two members and a senate with twenty-one members. The legislature meets once every two years, and when Kathy traveled to Carson City as a first-term assemblywoman in 1993, she was a complete political rookie. She spent much of her first two years in the assembly building alliances with the state's other Republicans, including longtime northern Nevada Republican Bill Raggio, perhaps the most powerful man in the state. He has served in the legislature since 1973.

Kathy's first term in the assembly was largely uneventful. She did not introduce any major pieces of legislation, and she was not a focus of any major media attention.

"She was never considered a first-rate legislator," Jon Ralston said. "Very ambitious, but no real accomplishments that I recall. The GOP was in the minority in the assembly, so she couldn't do much."

Kathy's family says she was still learning the ropes of political life as she traveled back and forth from Las Vegas to Carson City for the legislative sessions. Since the legislature only met once every two years, Kathy Augustine lived a relatively normal life as a state legislator. She continued to raise her daughter, Dallas, and her relationship with her husband, Chuck, remained strong. In 1994, with her term in the assembly winding down, Kathy set her sights on the next logical step up the Nevada political hierarchy: a run for the state senate. Senators hold more power in Nevada largely because there are fewer of them, which gives their votes more influence. Kathy, however, again faced the same challenge that she had in running for the assembly: Senate District 7, the district that included her neighborhood and eastward to include parts of the city of Henderson, was predominantly Democratic. The district is very large, with nearly 100,000 residents, and its neighborhoods stretch for a length of nearly 9 miles. Many thought

Kathy—a Republican woman with conservative beliefs—
didn't stand a chance of becoming senator in the district.

Kathy filed for the senate race in 1994, and her Democratic opponent was incumbent senator Lori Lipman
Brown. Lipman Brown, a widely respected lawyer, teacher,
and lobbyist, held political beliefs that couldn't have been
more opposite of Kathy's conservative, Christian-based
viewpoints. Lipman Brown is a humanistic Jew and a lobbyist and is the founding director emeritus of the Secular Coalition for America, which describes itself as an
organization that lobbies in Washington, D.C., on behalf
of "atheists, humanists, agnostics, freethinkers and other
nontheistic Americans."

"My first foray into politics was during Gary Hart's
presidential campaign," Lipman Brown recalled. "When I
called Democratic headquarters and told them I had never
volunteered for a campaign before, but I wanted to come
stuff envelopes, they said, 'We need you to go to Reno and
be a delegate to the state convention!' Nevada was such a
small town [then], at least politically. In many ways, even
with millions of people now—it still is easy to get very
involved [in politics].

"When I served Senate District 7 in the 1993 session,
most of its constituents were either middle class or lower
middle class," Lipman Brown said. "Much of the district
included blue-collar workers; many teachers lived in the
district. The district had more veterans than any other senate district in Nevada. I believe the district also had more
manufactured housing than any other part of the state.
Although my neighborhood was pretty diverse, the district
as a whole was predominantly white in the early 1990s."

Lipman Brown had quite a list of accomplishments during her term in the legislature, and she was a formidable
opponent for Kathy. During her term in the legislature,

Senator Lori Lipman Brown was recognized as an outstanding legislator by the American Civil Liberties Union of Nevada.

She said she first met Kathy in 1993.

"[Kathy] Augustine and I served in the Nevada Legislature during the same session," Lipman Brown said. "Although the senate and assembly sides rarely had occasion to interact, I saw her at various events and occasionally at legislative activities. . . . We were polite to each other, but everyone in the legislature knew she had her eye on my senate seat well before the 1993 session came to a close."

In tactics reminiscent of her previous campaign, Kathy Augustine sensed a political opportunity in targeting Senator Lori Lipman Brown as their race neared an end in what was a very tight contest. Kathy proceeded to take a very bold, and some say irresponsible, action to try and secure victory: in the closing weeks of the election, she furthered her barbarous political reputation by sending out ads and placing television commercials that targeted the heavy population of Mormon voters in the district. In the mailers and television ads, Kathy accused her opponent of refusing to "participate in the Pledge of Allegiance during legislative sessions," and she also claimed that Lipman Brown "actively opposed prayer."

They were damning statements, and neither was true.

Senator Lori Lipman Brown was outraged. In an interview with *The Eloquent Atheist* website, Lipman Brown later said that Kathy Augustine's incendiary allegations could be traced back to Nevada's 1993 legislative session, when Lipman Brown was concerned with the "explicitly Christian" prayers being recited before legislators started their daily proceedings in the state's capitol building.

"I was the only Jew in the state senate at the time, and it was clear why these prayers were being said," Lipman

Brown said. "I decided to stop participating in the opening prayer, and 'meditated' on what I was doing outside the chamber while the non-Jews prayed inside during those last few weeks."

In another interview, Lipman Brown also refuted Kathy Augustine's incendiary claim that the incumbent senator refused to pledge allegiance to the flag. "This was false. Not only did I never refuse to pledge allegiance to the flag, but when I wasn't in the legislature, I was saying it [the pledge] as a schoolteacher at the start of each school day."

Lipman Brown asserted that the allegations were bald-faced lies.

"A week before the election, apparently because Augustine was not able to gain a lead on me based on my privacy rights votes, or other attempts to characterize my record negatively, [she] ran an ad in the *Beehive* newspaper claiming that I refused to pledge allegiance to the flag," Lipman Brown said in an interview. "I had heard rumors that she was saying this at campaign appearances, and [I] had sent a letter threatening legal action if this misinformation was published. She also ran TV ads making the same claims. She claimed I was trying to remove prayer from the legislature, and she hired a model [in silhouette] to pace around the foyer of the legislature while a voice-over claimed that my lack of praying and pledging happened each day of the legislature.

"My campaign folks determined, by polling a small sampling of Democrats in my district, that 50 percent of the Democrats in District 7 would vote against Lori Lipman Brown if someone told them she refused to pledge allegiance to the flag," Lipman Brown said. "With this in mind, we held a press conference, flanked by rabbis, Jewish war veterans, and others, to tell the public the claim was untrue. When the press didn't cover it, we paid a substantial sum of money to turn the conference into an ad, which we aired. The day before the election, a letter signed by three Nevada state senators—Bill Raggio, Sue Lowden, and Ray Rawson—arrived via first-class mail to every voting household in District 7. It was in a 'foldover' and the outside said, 'The truth hurts, but the truth is still the truth.'"

When the letter, sent by Kathy, was opened, the header stated, "Here's what three respected state senators have to say about Lori Lipman Brown's attempts to mislead you."

"The content of [Kathy's campaign letter] was that three Nevada state senators claimed that they saw me turn my back on the flag, and that they understood my refusal to participate in the 'traditional' daily prayer, but they were appalled at my lack of patriotism," Lipman Brown told *The Eloquent Atheist.*

"In 1994, there was no early voting, so everyone voted the day after receiving the mailing," Lipman Brown said. "We attempted to get the press to cover it, but when they wouldn't, we had no way to get our message out again before folks went to the polls, and even if we had tried, it would have been my word against three state senators.'"

Lori Lipman Brown sued Kathy Augustine for defamation on the day of the election, but the damage was done, regardless of the settlement. After yet another campaign in which Kathy was accused of vicious, cutthroat behavior, she nevertheless emerged victorious, winning by 2,000 votes.

"We filed the defamation suit and served Augustine and her campaign manager . . . on election day before any results were in, because we were going to clear my name no matter who won the election," Lipman Brown said. "We amended to add defendants Lowden, Rawson, and Raggio shortly thereafter."

The lawsuit prompted a two-and-a-half-year battle that cost Chuck Augustine a lot of money—tens of thousands of dollars in legal fees. In the end, Kathy agreed to basically recant the allegations. Kathy was required to write a letter as part of the settlement. The letter from Kathy read:

> *As you indicated in your speech on the senate floor, your decision to pray separately was actually the result of your discomfort praying to Christ each day, as you are not Christian; rather than an opposition to prayer generally. It is my understanding that, when prayers included you (and were non-denominational), you prayed with the other senators. My statement regarding the pledge was my way of characterizing information received from other state senators who recounted a few occasions in which you were delayed entering the chambers. The term 'refuses to participate in the pledge of allegiance' was an unfortunate choice of words developed during the heat of an election campaign.*

Lori Lipman Brown was satisfied with the settlement. "In the end, we got exactly what we had asked for—letters from each of them [one from Augustine, and one signed by the other three senators]. I was thrilled; we were able to clear my name. Augustine's campaign manager settled for an amount [that] was nearly identical to the total costs of the lawsuit, and since my father, a good friend of mine, and I did all our all legal work, we didn't have to pay any legal fees—so clearing my name was cost-free. Individuals had donated to a legal fund; many with heartfelt letters about injustice and anti-Semitism and patriotism—but since we didn't have to go to trial, I was able to write checks to give back each donation and encouraged them to donate it to another worthy cause."

Lori Lipman Brown came to conclude, however, that Kathy was willing to lie to get elected, and political commentator Jon Ralston called Kathy's techniques brutal.

"The Dora Harris episode . . . left a bad [taste] in a lot of people's mouths," the political expert said. "Same with the Lori Lipman Brown episode, and you know how that turned out—Lori Lipman Brown sued, and they had to settle. I wrote a column about how they lied and got caught. Kathy was ruthless, nasty, and underhanded—but relentless."

Kathy could live with being known as a ruthless, nasty politician as long as she kept winning, and now, people in Nevada were starting to take notice of Kathy Augustine.

Kay and Phil Alfano Sr. always knew their daughter was special, but with her election to the Nevada State Senate, they were starting to realize that their daughter also had the potential for big things in politics. For Kay, the realization came when she visited her daughter in Vegas and witnessed the connection Kathy was developing with voters in Senate District 7.

"Hard work, determination, and personality were the keys to her winning," Kay Alfano said. "She made herself available to the voters at all hours. She made her home number available to everyone, and if you called her, she'd say, 'I'll look into it. I'll get on it, and I'll call you right back.' When Kathy said that, she meant it. She would follow through, and she'd get back to those constituents right away. I know this because I watched her do it."

Phil Sr., too, was incredibly impressed with his daughter. He'd taught her to always believe in herself, and now that lesson was shining through in her relentless political ambition.

"She was going to succeed, and she was going to do it as fast as she could," Phil Sr. said. "I was very proud of her."

The woman who had showed so much promise as a child and who had excelled in college and at Western Airlines was finally realizing the success everyone had predicted for her.

"We worried about her, but at some point, you can't tell your children what to do," Kay Alfano said. "You can only advise them, but we were proud of her, and I think she was thinking about running for governor. I know she thought about running for treasurer."

Kathy's tenure in the state senate ran from 1995 to 1999. She was appointed to several powerful state committees by the Republican power structure in Nevada. Her most notable appointments were as chair of the Legislative Affairs and Operations Committee and vice chair of the Human Resources and Facilities Committee. She was also appointed to the Senate Committee on Taxation, where Kathy took a repeated public stance on lowering taxes on Nevada residents.

The term on the Senate Committee on Taxation gave her an in-depth knowledge of the state's financial system, and in 1998, she decided to run for the position of state controller. The position is a huge leap up from being a legislator. The controller is a constitutional office, and the controller is responsible for collecting the state's outstanding debts. The state controller is responsible for serving as a check on the state treasury and how the state treasurer spends Nevada's money.

Kathy would have to defeat Democrat Mary Sanada to take the job of state controller, and again, Kathy vowed to do whatever was necessary to win. Mary Sanada was a certified public accountant who had actually worked in the controller's office for many years, while Kathy Augustine had no comparable background. She'd had an unremarkable career as a state legislator, but that did not equate to significant experience in financial bookkeeping and performing audits. Kathy was criticized by her opponent for her lack of experience, but Kathy was, as usual, undeterred. She started circulating through Republican circles and campaign events throughout the state to build support for her candidacy. She attended fund-raisers from Las Vegas to rural towns in northern Nevada, and she raised hundreds of thousands of dollars. Anyone who met her on the campaign trail was impressed with her drive and personality.

"[Kathy] just kept going on and winning her elections," said Jerry Bing, a state treasurer for the Nevada Federation of Republican Women and a former Douglas County, Nevada, county commissioner. "She was always at the [Republican women's] events, and contributing. She was good for women. [The way I saw Kathy was] she was always kind of fighting uphill battles in politics. As a woman, she was quite successful, and I admired her."

Bing remembers Kathy as "very feisty, and nobody was going to tell her what to do," though she concedes that Kathy "was a very demanding person. Hard to work for. But she made some great strides . . . [and] did some great things for the state of Nevada."

Kathy Augustine's bid for controller caused Las Vegas media to take even more notice of her, and in the fall of 1998, Kathy Augustine beat out Mary Sanada, officially taking over the controller's office in 1999 and basically becoming the leader of Nevada's fiscal policy. Almost immediately, according to the *Las Vegas Sun* newspaper, Kathy was subjected to false attacks from Nevada Democrats alleging that she'd diverted money from the state's emergency fund to pay for public school instruction. The paper reported that Augustine fought back against the allegations publicly, and "she and her staff proved those charges were wrong."

Kathy also was earning an ally in the form of newly elected Nevada governor Kenny Guinn. Guinn, a Republican, is an affable, kind, and personable man who was previously the top executive of Southwest Gas Corporation. He was also the leader of Las Vegas's massive school district. He is a tall man with a shock of silvery-white hair who rose to the state's most powerful elected office in 1999, and he was known as a moderate Republican during his time as governor. Guinn liked Kathy. He realized she was a tough, ambitious woman, and he repeatedly supported her publicly.

Kathy was now earning $80,000 per year as controller, and she decided she was going to make the controller's office as relevant as possible. She knew that the state had millions of dollars in uncollected debts on items such as unpaid traffic tickets and tax revenues, so she went to the state legislature and got permission to create a program that required motorists and delinquent taxpayers to pay off their debts before they could renew their driver's license. Almost immediately, the program was a huge success, and veteran reporter Ed Vogel, of the *Las Vegas Review-Journal*, who'd covered the Nevada Legislature since the late 1970s, took notice. Vogel interviewed Kathy and penned a story about the program's success, and the story was circulated throughout the state.

"It was actually a pretty good deal, quite successful, collecting debts from people who hadn't paid their taxes to the state," Vogel said. "They collected the money, and it was a worthwhile plan."

Kathy maximized the press she could get for the program by putting out the following press release to all media outlets:

State Controller Kathy Augustine announced today her office has achieved a major milestone by collecting more than $5 million in past due receivables owed the State of Nevada through her aggressive debt collection program. The State Controller's Office is authorized to act as the centralized point of collection for the state, however it can only collect debt voluntarily referred by a state agency. Currently, twenty-eight state agencies, boards, and commissions have contracted with the state Controller's Office for debt collection services. There is no fee or cost to the agencies for the Controller's Office services.

"My office is committed to maximizing revenues, minimizing costs, and serving state agencies through the use of innovative debt collection tools," Augustine said in the press release. "We utilize several methods of collecting including our vendor hold/debt-offset program, in-house collection, and outsourcing of debt."

Vogel said he, too, recognized Kathy was full of ambition when he interviewed her. He'd first met her when she was an assemblywoman, and he also wrote about her a lot during the fight with Lipman Brown.

"The thing with Lori Lipman Brown was nasty," Vogel said. "Very nasty. Kathy was very political . . . and I thought that fight with Lipman Brown was uncalled-for."

The reporter observed that Kathy was relentless in her pursuit of positive press. She was regularly on the phone calling Ed Vogel and his capital bureau colleague, Sean Whaley, in search of ink in Nevada's largest and best newspaper.

"Kathy was constantly calling the news media, including me and Sean, trying to get stuff in the newspaper about her office," Vogel said. "She had delusions of grandeur. She wanted to be bigger than she really was. She had a lot of ambition. You could just tell that when you met her. She wanted to be something more than controller. She wanted to be congresswoman. Governor. Secretary of state. She was going to go as far as she could go."

Ed Vogel saw that behind the cutthroat politician, however, there was a kind, friendly, real person. He was also impressed with Kathy's ability to take criticism. Plenty of politicians and government officials are hypersensitive to press accounts that are critical, but not Kathy. Vogel once wrote a story about how Kathy spent thousands of her campaign money on clothes, and she called him to laugh about it.

"Kathy got a big kick out of it," Vogel recalled. "She was friendly, and she would talk about her life with you. When she became controller, I had more talks with her, and I went to her office every now and then. A very nice person."

Shortly after Kathy took office, however, there was a movement by some in state government, including former Nevada treasurer Bob Seale and current treasurer Brian Krolicki, to consolidate the controller's office into the treasurer's office. The movement echoed a similar, failed movement years earlier in which state leaders argued that having both a controller and treasurer was a waste of taxpayer money. Kathy immediately fought back and spoke before the state legislature as it considered the proposal. She told legislators that the controller served as an important check on the treasurer's office and that the state constitution, which had established the position of controller, was well thought-out. Kathy also wrote a much-publicized letter to the *Reno News & Review* making a case for the importance of having a controller in Nevada. The letter was extensively researched, and Kathy argued that the elimination of the controller's position would prompt an unnecessary voter referendum on the proposal in the middle of June, thus "circumvent[ing] the normal election process, and would result in an unfunded mandate of nearly $800,000 on local governments and townships [to pay for the referendum].

"The only data alleging cost savings has come from a former state treasurer," Kathy said, referring to Seale. "Therefore, it would be prudent to scrutinize [this] more closely.

"I am truly disappointed at the lack of scholarly research and debate [on this proposal] . . . to eliminate a constitutional officer elected by and accountable to the people of Nevada," Kathy wrote. "Changing a document that has withstood more than one hundred years is a serious endeavor. The people of our great state deserve more."

Kathy and Treasurer Brian Krolicki debated the matter further in the *Reno Gazette-Journal*'s July 4, 2000, edition. Krolicki said consolidation of the treasurer's and controller's offices offered efficiencies without compromising the integrity of the state's finances, but Kathy fought back.

"If you combine the two offices, then you have the same person taking the cash, writing the checks, and investing state money," Kathy told the newspaper. "We agree that the likelihood of fraud is small, but considering the dollar volume, it puts Nevada's citizens at risk."

The measure to combine the treasurer's and controller's offices ultimately failed, and Kathy was emboldened by the fight. Kathy was thriving in Carson City, and almost uniformly, people around her recognized that she was hungry for more.

But those who knew Kathy best also knew that her political career was coming with a price. She was now a full-time, daily employee of the state, and this meant she had to be in Carson City five days a week. Her daughter, Dallas, was now in school at San Diego State on a golf scholarship, but her husband, Chuck Augustine, was still back in Las Vegas. He didn't want to move to Carson City, and he had no desire to be a regular in the political social circles. Kathy decided to by a small home in Reno, and she commenced a rigorous commute to and from Las Vegas on weekends to be with Chuck. The schedule proved difficult, and it was a significant strain on the marriage.

6 ... CHUCK

Kathy and Chuck Augustine had been happily married since 1988, but within a few years of Kathy taking the job of controller, the marriage started to show its first signs of fissure. Family and friends said the strains of Kathy's job, her commute to and from Carson City, the distance between the couple, and Chuck's failing health all placed significant stresses on the marriage.

"Chuck was not a big fan of politicians," said Kathy's father, Phil Alfano Sr. "When Kathy initially ran for office, he was very, very supportive, but he never liked going to the fund-raisers or doing all the backslapping that was required. He did, however, go to many of those events."

Kathy's brother Phil Alfano Jr. said he first became aware of problems with the marriage shortly after the millennium. Chuck, he said, had just retired from Delta Airlines and had undergone a double knee replacement. The surgery, by all accounts, did not go well.

"I think Chuck's health was a lot worse than he let on,"

Phil Jr. said. "Chuck's a lot like my dad—he could be at death's door, and he wouldn't tell you. I think Chuck had a lot of physical problems."

Chuck had always been a large man, but after the surgery, his weight escalated to more than three hundred pounds.

"Chuck was always heavy—a big man, six feet four, and he loved to eat," Kay Alfano said. "Whatever you made for him for dinner was fine, and he was an easy man to please. But after the surgery, his weight took off. He blew up like a balloon."

The weight was only a minor issue for Kathy, however. What really concerned her was the fact that Chuck was becoming less and less social. Kathy's family said she repeatedly complained about Chuck's unwillingness to get up and going on a daily basis. Kathy told them that Chuck wouldn't get dressed or showered; he'd just put on a bathrobe, lock himself in a room, and spend the majority of his day reading and watching television. This was intolerable for Kathy, who was a very social and outgoing person.

"Kathy thought that when he retired, he would come up there to Carson City and spend more time with her," Phil Jr. said. "She would be flying home on the weekends, and she did maintain an office in Las Vegas, but they were seeing each other less frequently. Also, the home Kathy bought in Carson City was a modest, quaint home, and the home they had in Las Vegas was magnificent. I know Chuck liked living there."

Kathy confided in her mother that she was miserable in the marriage.

"Because [Chuck] didn't feel good, when he retired, he retired from life," Kay said. "He didn't want to do anything. He didn't want to go anyplace. . . . He was a real history buff and watched sports and the History Channel. He

quit working in the yard, and he quit taking care of the
pool. That's when the marriage started going downhill."

Kathy's best friend, Nancy Vinik, said Kathy repeatedly complained to her about Chuck's reclusiveness.

"I thought he was a nice guy," Nancy said. "I liked him,
and when I first met him, he was working, and he was vivacious and outgoing. He loved to watch Notre Dame football games and have gatherings centered around the game.
Then, once he retired from Delta, it's almost as if he gave
up on himself. . . . It was almost like he just gave up on life.
He put himself upstairs in his office, he closed the door,
and he didn't come out. It was almost like he went into a
bad depression."

Nancy said she and her husband tried to get Chuck
Augustine out of the house. "My husband would call him
constantly," she said. " 'Chuck, Let's go out to lunch. Let's
go swimming.' We lived so close to them, we had a big
backyard, and they had a big backyard. We both had big
pools, and it was like pulling teeth to even get him out of
the house."

Nancy said Kathy often called her crying about Chuck's
downturn in life and his unwillingness to leave the home.
Kathy was frustrated, Nancy said, because she was constantly going to political functions and fund-raisers alone—
and people noticed. This was particularly evident after
Kathy ran for reelection to the controller's office and won a
second term in 1998.

"I think she felt that she was kind of out there on her
own," Nancy said. "She was really into politics, and she
went to just about every event imaginable. Frequently, she
would call and ask if I wanted to go to some of these bigger
events with her because she didn't want to go alone."

Politics were Kathy's life, Nancy said. "She loved it. She
was bubbly and vivacious at these political events. It was

her moment. She networked with people, talked to people, and she loved it. If you told her it was boring, she might smack you. To her, it wasn't boring. It was business, and she liked being the star. She liked everything about it. It was what she was supposed to be doing."

But Kathy, who was still a young woman, in her early forties, was becoming more and more frustrated with her husband. Nancy recalls Kathy complaining that Chuck "is at home, by himself, in his broken-down chair watching television, and he is eating and getting bigger and bigger and bigger."

"'The whole house could fall down around him,'" Nancy quoted Kathy as saying, "'and he'll just sit in there. If I don't come home [on the weekends], I just wonder what would happen to him.'"

An episode at the home in Las Vegas seemed as if it was the breaking point for Kathy. An upstairs water heater gave out, and water cascaded down a stairwell and throughout the residence. Kathy was amazed when she came home from Carson City and learned that although Chuck had known there was a problem, he'd failed to call a repairman.

"She came home," Nancy said, "and the whole bottom floor was completely wrecked. I don't even know if he was aware it even happened. The whole house had to be rebuilt. All of the flooring had to be taken out."

Kathy's mother received a similar account about the water-heater incident and the resulting chaos in the Augustine home. Kathy, always the perfectionist, was incensed at the indifference Chuck was showing to their home.

"The house had the most beautiful floors you'd ever seen," Kay Alfano said. "Real wood, all imported, and Kathy came home, and the floor is sopping all wet, water running down the stairs. I'm sure they had words, and she said, 'Chuck, I can't take this anymore.'"

Still, Kathy's brother never thought that the marriage would end in divorce. He knew Kathy loved Chuck dearly, and he figured his sister would stick with Chuck through these difficult times. That opinion faltered when he got a phone call from Kathy at work in late 2002.

"I remember it well, because she called me at work," Phil Alfano Jr. recalled. "I said, 'How are things going?' And she blurts out, 'I think I'm going to divorce Chuck.' I got pretty upset with her, and I told her, 'That's ridiculous! Chuck's a great guy.'

"She said, 'I need companionship,'" he recalled. "'[Chuck] never wants to come up [to Carson City],' and I got ticked off.

"I started getting on her hard about what she was saying, and what happened next was really telling," Phil Jr. said. "When I was getting on her about it, she started crying. She said, 'No, you don't understand! He doesn't want to do anything! He's like a hermit in that house!' And I had heard a little bit of this from my mom, too. [Kathy] said, 'I can deal with him not going to campaign events, but he's like a recluse.' I know she was very upset. I don't know if it was depression . . . but I think Chuck was in worse health than he was willing to admit."

Kathy and Chuck Augustine legally separated in 2002, after fourteen years of marriage, but Chuck wouldn't live long enough to see the divorce finalized.

7 ... STROKE

Kathy and Charles Augustine's marriage was on the rocks in early 2003. The two said they were getting a divorce, but they had not yet pursued the paperwork to finalize the divorce even though they'd separated. The fate of the marriage remained unresolved for nearly a year, and it seemed to the Alfanos that Chuck and Kathy might somehow work things out.

"I was hoping they would reconcile, which I think might of happened if Chuck could have made it to Carson City more, or if Kathy's job hadn't taken her out of Las Vegas," Kathy's brother Phil Alfano Jr. said.

"They had discussed everything, and there was no hurry for a divorce," Kathy's mother, Kay Alfano, said. "I know if Chuck had just said, 'OK [Kathy], I'll come up there to Carson City and stay a week every now and then,' it would have worked out."

In July 2003, while Kathy was in Carson City, Chuck Augustine walked from the house on Maria Elena to the home of neighbor John Tsitouras. Chuck complained to his neighbor of dizziness, and John could tell something wasn't quite right with his friend. Chuck looked very ill, and Tsitouras called an ambulance.

"[Chuck] was having trouble seeing," Phil Jr. recounted. "His vision was real blurry. Then I guess the neighbor asked him some questions, and he was out of it."

Chuck was rushed to Sunrise Hospital in Las Vegas by ambulance. The sixty-three-year-old's condition seemed to deteriorate rapidly, and by the end of the day, Charles Augustine was diagnosed as having suffered a massive stroke. He was completely incapacitated. Kathy flew immediately from Carson City to Las Vegas. She was shocked and traumatized by what she saw in the hospital: Chuck was unconscious, on a ventilator, and could not recognize visitors, including his wife. Kathy was devastated to see her husband in this condition. Despite their separation, she respected him and loved him dearly. To see him in the shape he was in at Sunrise hurt Kathy.

"She loved him in spite of his shortcomings," said Kathy's father, Phil Alfano Sr. "She loved him very much."

Kathy called her brothers in California to tell them how bad Chuck's condition was.

"Kathy said it was very sad to see him in this condition," Phil Jr. said. "I remember her crying repeatedly about it over the phone. She told me, 'I know he knows I'm there, but he can't acknowledge it.'"

Kathy's best friend, Nancy Vinik, who had worked as a nurse, visited the Augustines in the hospital and was alarmed at Chuck's condition.

"I was shocked," Nancy said. "He was on a ventilator, he wasn't moving, and he had restraints on one side. He couldn't move, and he was trying to move and tug on things. The kind of stroke he had was the worst."

Chuck's family, including his sons and sisters, came to visit him in the hospital. Nancy described Kathy as "devastated" over Chuck's fate. She stayed in Las Vegas for weeks, visiting Chuck, and it became obvious to everyone in the Alfano and Augustine families that Chuck was in terrible shape. Life for him would never be the same again. He was going to need constant care for the rest of his life. Chuck's son Greg Augustine later told the CBS *48 Hours* news show that he discussed the situation with Kathy, including who was going to care for his father after he got out of the hospital. Greg said the culmination of the discussion was that he planned to organize his father's posthospital treatment and that Kathy had expressed concerns about how much his poststroke rehabilitation was going to cost. By late summer, however, the families got some encouraging news. It seemed as if Chuck was starting to show some slight signs of improvement after nearly three weeks in the hospital. Greg Augustine told the television show that his father was improving.

The fact that Chuck was starting to show improvement should not have been a surprise. Sunrise Hospital is perhaps the best hospital in Las Vegas, and it is known for the high quality of its physical-rehabilitation services. It also employs some of the best doctors and nurses available, and the staff was tending to Chuck's needs twenty-four hours a day.

One of those nurses was a man named Chaz Higgs.

By mid-August, it seemed as if Chuck Augustine was going to make at least a slight recovery. He was talking a bit, and he recognized a few visitors. He certainly had a long road of rehabilitation ahead of him, and everyone knew he would never be the same again, but his family was optimistic at the signs of improvement.

Kathy's family agreed with this assessment.

"Kathy told me he'd started to recover," Phil Jr. said. "Kathy was talking about how they'd started therapy, and she said he'd started to blow her kisses when she came into his room. He started to recognize her."

Nancy Vinik, too, said she saw some very modest improvements in Chuck's condition.

"He was starting to respond, and the breathing tube had been taken out," Nancy said. "My husband would go in there and say, 'Squeeze my hand if you know who I am,' and he would. He started to get a little bit better."

And then, without warning, Chuck died.

The death was a shock to everyone, considering his signs of improvement in the week prior.

"He was getting better, and then suddenly all his organs failed," Greg Augustine told the *Las Vegas Review-Journal*.

Kathy, in particular, seemed devastated. She called her loved ones to break the news, and it seemed to them that Kathy was in a particularly bad state emotionally. She'd lost the only man who'd ever truly loved her.

"I threw some clothes in a suitcase, and we were on the road in about twenty minutes for Las Vegas," Kathy's mother said. "We were very, very upset."

Nancy spent the most time with Kathy on the day Chuck died. She said Kathy was an emotional wreck, and she was very concerned about her friend in the aftermath of Chuck's death.

"I happened to be on the other side of town that morning," Nancy said, when Kathy called her with the news. "I couldn't even understand what she was saying. I said, 'Where are you?' She said, 'I'm at Sunrise,' and she was completely hysterical. So I jumped in my car, I got over there, and there she was, all by herself. She said, 'Chuck died,' and I could barely understand what she was saying because she was so upset."

Nancy was startled by the news. She'd recently visited Chuck and had seen slight signs of improvement in his health. She asked some hospital staffers about what happened.

"I said, 'What happened here?'" Nancy recalled. "'He was getting better. All of a sudden, he dies?' They said he got septic. He just got a massive infection throughout his whole body."

Kathy seemed unable to cope with the shock and grief from what had just happened.

"I literally didn't know what to do with her. That's how upset she was," Nancy said. "I got her to sit down, and she wouldn't leave the room. She wouldn't let them take his body out of the room. It was bad—really bad.

"So, then I got her to just sit down and be calm for a while, and we just sat in that room for two and a half hours and cried," Nancy said. "And she was not just crying. She was hysterical. Then a couple of doctors came in, and the chaplain came in."

The official cause of death for Charles Augustine as determined by doctors on staff at Sunrise Hospital was complications due to a stroke. There was no other explanation forthcoming, and because it appeared to be a natural death in a medical setting, which does not require an autopsy under Nevada law, none was ordered.

Charles Augustine was memorialized and then buried in his pilot's uniform at Paradise Memorial Gardens in southeast Las Vegas. It was a fitting final resting place for the former pilot, as the cemetery is literally on the edge of McCarran International Airport, the seventh largest airport in the United States and the lifeblood of the Las Vegas tourism industry. It is impossible to be in the cemetery for more than a few minutes without hearing the deafening roars of huge jumbo jets flying overhead on their approach for landing to the airport.

"We went to Chuck's funeral in Las Vegas, and it was very sad," Phil Alfano Jr. said, but "very dignified."

"I cried. Chuck was a good man, and he was very good to my sister. I was one of the pallbearers along with his sons and some of his friends. It was very hot, and right as they were getting ready to lower him into the ground, a Delta plane flew overhead and landed at the airport. We all thought Chuck would have liked that."

Chuck's death had made Kathy Augustine a very wealthy woman. He left her the house on Maria Elena, which was completely paid off. He also left her a $500,000 annuity. Kathy would likely never have to worry about money again.

"When I first got there, there was clearly some tension between Kathy and Chuck's son Greg. As far as I know, they got along fine, but when it came to the funeral, he had already been there for a day or two, and there was some friction," Phil Jr. recalled. "I think that was understandable, given the fact that everyone knew Kathy and Chuck had separated and seemed to be divorcing."

A reception followed at the Bootlegger's restaurant in Las Vegas, and virtually everyone was still reeling from shock that Chuck had died. His death had been a complete surprise.

But what happened three weeks later in Hawaii was even more surprising.

Kathy Augustine got married.

8 . . . FOURTH HUSBAND

He wasn't very smart as far as leaving evidence around.
He's not very smart when it comes to covering his tracks.
He's actually very stupid.

—Kirstin Lattin, Chaz Higgs's second wife

Chaz Higgs was the man who would become Kathy
Augustine's fourth husband.

William Charles Higgs and his twin brother, Michael,
were born on June 2, 1964, in Washington, D.C., to two
loving parents, William and Shirley Higgs. The Higgs
brothers grew up in Virginia and North Carolina. Their
father was a former U.S. Marine and had been the chief of
police in Jacksonville, North Carolina.

Chaz has said that the reason he didn't go by his first
name was that in his family, "there were four people named
William Higgs, and the only differentiation was the middle
name. . . . That created a lot of problems, as you can imagine, [with] all of us getting our documents mixed up." So,
he decided, "I dropped my first name, since everyone went
by first and last name, and I shortened my middle name."

His mother said that both Chaz and Michael were good
kids growing up in the seaboard states of the Southeast.
"[Chaz] and his brother were like most kids growing up.

They participated in Cub Scouts, and Little League, and when they got into junior high and senior high, it was football, track, golf, and swimming. He and his brother were just always very close-knit. They always did things together. They were very good kids."

Chaz's father recalled that his son was an outstanding golfer growing up. "He loved it," the elder Higgs said. "He was almost going to be a pro, but he decided to go into the military."

Chaz Higgs joined the military in 1983 to pursue a career in medicine and spent sixteen years in the U.S. Navy. Chaz spent most of his time as a hospital corpsman, basically the equivalent of a military nurse. The experience in the navy served him well, giving him the knowledge that later helped him become a critical-care nurse in the private sector.

"[I] started out in basic hospital corps school," Chaz said. "Then I went to battlefield medical school to learn how to work with the Marine Corps. Then I went to what is called independent duty hospital corps school, which was a little over a year long. What we do there is we learn how to function independently with units like SEAL teams or the Marine Corps, or the army, or navy, or anything. It's comparable to a nurse practitioner. I love helping people, and [the military] was an avenue for me to be able to do that."

Chaz said he actually trained to be a Navy SEAL in the late 1980s but dropped out of the rigorous military training school in Coronado, California, because of an injury.

"I broke my arm, and I was unable to finish training," Chaz said. He still stayed associated with SEALs, though, by becoming a medic for the navy's special forces.

Curiously, after all those years of service, Chaz left the

military just four years short of being eligible for significant retirement benefits. He said he left because he wanted to go into the private nursing field.

"I had become interested in nursing along the way," Chaz said. "I liked critical-care nursing . . . and I had worked in intensive care, emergency rooms, and was an emergency medical technician for a few years. I really wanted to be a critical-care nurse."

Chaz was muscular, tanned, and known to wear muscle shirts. His appearance was polished and groomed, and he was repeatedly described by women as being very "into himself" and his looks. Chaz usually wore his brown hair neatly cut, with puffed-up bangs in front, and he often had bleached-blond highlights as well.

The meticulous attention to his appearance led many people to speculate at first glance that Chaz Higgs might be gay. He was not.

He was a ladies' man.

The public knew very little about Chaz Higgs until well after the time he and Kathy ran off to Hawaii. That changed with an in-depth *Las Vegas Sun* piece published on July 10, 2006, written and researched by Ed Koch and Mary Manning. Both reporters had decades of experience in the Las Vegas newspaper business, and both were tenacious journalists.

"Mary and I were assigned this piece because we were both veteran reporters who had worked well together in the past, and we are both known for our good research skills and patience, which were essential for a complicated, in-depth story like this," Koch said.

"We spent at least three weeks gathering information," Manning said, "and once we learned that he had been married four times and gone through two bankruptcies, we knew we had quite a story." The paper also tracked Chaz's frequent moves, listing his prior places of residency over the previous twenty years as "Virginia, North Carolina, Florida, Tennessee, Reno, Las Vegas, San Diego, and Eureka, California."

"We had to extensively surf the Internet and review a number of public records, lengthy financial documents, and bankruptcy court filings, among other data, to piece together Chaz's life," Koch said. "It was at times complicated because he left paper trails with seemingly conflicting information as he crisscrossed the country and went overseas while in the service.

"There naturally were some rather large gaps in his drifter-type life that were difficult to piece together, but we were aggressive in our research and interviews and were pretty much able to fill in the blanks for most of his adult life," Koch said.

"As a reporter trying to be down-the-middle fair with a particular subject, you bend over backward trying not to be judgmental or draw hard and fast conclusions from what you find," said Koch. "You just print the facts and let the readers decide for themselves what to make of them.

"But, personally, what kept coming back to me was that this guy truly lived the stereotypical life of a scumbag— at least three prior broken marriages, an unstable family life, bouncing from one home or one state to another under suspicious circumstances, large and unwise purchases with credit cards and loans that resulted in more than one bankruptcy—that kind of stuff," Koch said.

"Also, from interviews with those who knew him both intimately or casually, a clear image of a narcissistic—for lack of a better word—asshole quickly emerged," Koch said. "This was a vain individual who cared only about himself."

Digging up all of those facts and the portrait of Chaz Higgs earned Manning, Koch, and the *Las Vegas Sun* an honorable mention in investigative reporting from the Nevada Press Association in 2006.

"It was like earning a Ph.D. in Chaz Higgs," Manning said. "We spent at least a week going over every single fact in [that] story."

Among the facts that they uncovered was that Chaz Higgs had been married three times—just like his future fourth wife—when he and Kathy Augustine met in 2003.

Chaz's first wife, Dawn Renee Brown, told the *Las Vegas Sun* that she'd met Chaz at Camp Lejeune, North Carolina. They were wed on September 15, 1984, in Brown's hometown of Dillon, South Carolina. She described her former husband as "always into himself" and alleged she caught Chaz in bed with a nursing student shortly after they married. Brown told the paper Chaz "was a little womanizer."

In 1990, he was briefly married to his second wife, Kirstin Lattin. From July 1993 to 1997, he was stationed in Manama, Bahrain, and sometime during or after that period, the *Las Vegas Sun* reported, Chaz married his third wife, Lorelei Sagmit Gueco. Chaz is listed in public records as stepfather to Gueco's daughter. Family and friends said Chaz remained very close with the young girl, who lived in Vegas. He visited her regularly even after divorcing Gueco, and he maintained a fatherly relationship with his stepdaughter for years to come.

Chaz secured an associate's degree in nursing from Craven Community College in New Bern, North Carolina, and passed the National Council Licensure Examination test in Nevada in 2002. According to the paper, Chaz then received a state nursing license, and by November of that year, he was working as a nurse in Las Vegas and living in a trailer park.

Las Vegas Sun reporter Ed Koch came to conclude that Chaz had basically lived a drifter-type lifestyle and that at least some of the women in his life had accused him of cheating on them.

This was Chaz Higgs's situation—living in an older-model, beat-up RV—when he met Kathy Augustine, at the time one of the most powerful women in Nevada state politics.

Kirstin Lattin, who had the less-than-envious distinction of being Chaz Higgs's second wife, is a witty, intelligent, and very attractive woman who lives in a nice master-planned community in Las Vegas and is now married to a law enforcement officer. She has long, straight brown hair and a stunning figure. Lattin is just a few days older than Chaz, and she originally hails from Boise, Idaho. She, too, went into the military because she wanted to be a nurse.

In an interview conducted with the *Las Vegas Review-Journal*, Lattin said she met Chaz Higgs, whom she originally knew as "Chuck," while she was stationed at the Jacksonville Naval Air Station in Florida. She was a petty officer in charge of administration at the medical clinic, while Chaz was in charge of medical supplies. They worked together regularly, and the two were just friends for years.

"I was a Navy Corpsman," Lattin said. "The same as Chaz . . . basically the equivalent of a licensed nurse or a medic. I met Chaz in my mid-twenties. I worked with him for quite some time. We worked in the same facility together—the Branch Medical Clinic, which was a Naval clinic. It was for dependents of active duty, and they also ran all of the ambulance services for the base out of the clinic."

At the time, Lattin was the mother of a newborn boy and was having "very serious problems" in her first marriage.

"We were heading for divorce," Lattin said, "and I think [Chaz] just saw an opportunity." She and her husband ended up divorcing in 1989, and she said Chaz basically swept her off her feet in the weeks and months after her divorce. The romance with Chaz, she said, happened "very fast."

"I thought he was very suave," said Lattin. "He was a [ladies'] man. A very sharp dresser. He cared a great deal about his parents, and he was charismatic. He was one of those people who likes to be around other people. He liked to go out, and that generally involved [going out with] his brother and his friends. He liked to go out and dance. He liked to tan. He liked to bodybuild.

"He's very much about himself," Lattin said. "His appearance was everything. He kind of exuded this [ladies'] man thing, very much a smooth talker."

Chaz did have some drawbacks as a boyfriend. He was a drinker who was known to get seriously intoxicated every once in a while. And, Lattin said, Chaz was obsessed with his appearance. His hair and clothes had to be perfect before he went out in public.

"I think the [bodybuilding] was something that turned me on about him because I had never been around that before," Lattin said. "That was fascinating to me. He was very much into bodybuilding, and he tanned a lot. . . . He was terribly consumed [with appearance]. It took him longer to get ready than it did me. This was back when it didn't take me that long to get ready to go out . . . but it definitely would take him much longer than it would me. Every curl in his hair had to be perfect . . . [and every piece of clothing] had to be perfect when it touched his body.

"The lotions and potions on the hair and the curls . . . had to be just . . . right," Lattin said. "Lotion all over his body. He would shave his body, and that was time-consuming as well. I would say Chaz was metrosexual before *metrosexual* was a term."

Despite his obsession with his appearance, Chaz Higgs was not, however, a very neat person when it came to his apartment. Kirstin Lattin noticed this when she first visited Chaz's apartment.

"It was very odd when I first met him, because his bedroom specifically had a very strange smell of tuna fish," Lattin said. "I couldn't tell where it was [coming from but] it was offending. His bedroom was just a horrid mess." She eventually discovered the source of the rank smell. "There were cans of tuna fish in the shower," she said. "I can't remember if it was for a cat, or for him . . . [but the] smell was just terrible. He was a very unkempt person in his physical surroundings."

Chaz convinced Kirstin Lattin that he was madly in love with her after her divorce was finalized. It was a very tough time in her life. She was leaving the military to go into the private sector as a nurse, and she was going to be a single mom. Lattin was vulnerable and on her own, and Chaz spent hours and hours counseling her and telling her how he believed in her. He repeatedly promised her that he would be there for her for the rest of her life.

"Coming off of this divorce, Chuck, being my friend, honed right in," Lattin recalled, "and he and I started having long conversations about my marriage, about me, [and] about my life.

"We would have [these] conversations that would [literally] last from the time I got off work at my private job until I would have to get ready for work the next morning," Lattin said. "Several times I did not go to sleep. I lost a tremendous amount of weight while we were dating. The conversations that we would have were so intense. He would tell me things, and [I believed] he [wanted to] take me away from everything in my life. . . . Why did I have to stand for what my ex-husband was doing to me? Chaz was better than that. I needed to better myself."

Kirstin Lattin said she found herself changing while dating Chaz Higgs. She started listening to different music. She wore different clothes. "He got me into tanning," she said. "[I] even redecorated my house based on him.

"If I had to put my finger on one thing, I'd say brainwashing," Lattin said. "This person knows how to get into somebody's head and rearrange the thought process to get you thinking exactly what he wants you to think. [He was] somebody who was better than a girlfriend, and someone who was better than a boyfriend, and he was someone who was going to be there to make things OK. And why did I have to put up with the things I was putting up with? 'I'm going to make things OK. I'm going to make things OK for you.'

"I thought [at the time] he was above me," Lattin said. "He was such a catch, when I knew him as a friend [and] not as a husband. . . . Everybody wanted to date him. He was charismatic. He was good-looking. He's slick. He's just kind of like the way Brad Pitt is to so many women. There is something . . . that women just see . . . in celebrity men, and many don't understand what it is. That's what it was with him. Nobody could see what it was, but women wanted to be with him.

"There were so many jealous women when I started to date him," Lattin said. "There were a couple [of women] that got very, very upset. One in particular who I know . . . was very upset [about our relationship] and she came to his house."

Lattin, in retrospect, wonders why Chaz was so interested

in her. She was a divorcée with a very young child, and
Chaz was a single, good-looking man who was being
chased by multiple women.

"I came with baggage. I had issues with a divorce. I did
have a child. Why would someone want to pick up those
pieces . . . when he could get numerous single women
who had no attachment? The only thing I can think of was I
had property, and I had items in my house. I had stability, and
those were things he craved. He had no personal property.
He had no real estate, and he had no stability whatsoever."

The dating period for Kirstin Lattin and Chaz Higgs
wasn't long. The couple started talking about getting married within months of Lattin's divorce, and rumors swirled
among friends and family that they were considering marriage. Lattin's parents had already met Chaz, and they
warned her not to marry him.

"My dad told me specifically, 'That would be a bad mistake,'" Lattin said. "He could tell. My parents repeatedly
told me, 'Don't do this.' My parents thought my relationship
with him was bad from day one. They thought he was slick,
and my dad picked up on it right away. My mom, to this day,
is pretty forthright about the fact that she told me right from
the get-go to not have anything to do with him. She tells me
to this day, 'See what you get? I tried to tell you.'"

Nevertheless, despite her parents' warnings, Lattin
accepted Chaz's marriage proposal in 1989. She had no
idea at the time that Chaz had been married previously.

"I honestly thought I was the first wife," she said.

The couple planned to marry at the stroke of midnight
on January 1, 1990, at a New Year's Eve party in an apartment the couple was sharing with two friends.

"The marriage was a complete surprise to everyone,"

Lattin said. "I mean, we told no one, including our families. We dressed in these now very hideous costume-like outfits from the 1980s. They looked like a cross between hip-hop dancers and prom outfits. We had it arranged so that at midnight, we would have a minister come into our apartment and administer the ceremony [in the middle of the New Year's Eve party]."

The first sign that the marriage was a mistake came in the hours before the actual wedding took place. Lattin said Chaz got incredibly drunk the night of the marriage, and he passed out in the front yard of the apartment before the vows were exchanged.

"He was completely smashed drunk during the ceremony," Lattin said. "They basically had to wake him up to get married. I know it was raining outside, and he'd been outside in the rain, lying down because he'd passed out."

Lattin decided to overlook the grievous slight, and married him anyway.

She got pregnant but lost the baby to a miscarriage. She then proceeded with what she characterizes as the biggest mistake of her life: she let Chaz become the legal father of her then two-year-old son. Soon after, she said, she started to suspect Chaz was cheating on her.

"There was a card that I found," Lattin said. "It was a card that was written by a girl, and she had given it to him. He wasn't very smart as far as leaving evidence around. He's not very smart when it comes to covering his tracks. He's actually very stupid."

There was another aspect of Chaz Higgs that bothered Kirstin Lattin: his bad temper. Chaz, she said, would fly off the handle for no reason, and at first she was at a loss to explain why.

"It was different than somebody just getting mad," Lattin said. "It was different than getting mad in traffic or just getting mad at your spouse. This was a totally different kind of mad. This was a mad that virtually nothing sets you off, and you go off into a rage. You want to hurt something. You want to get away from that person when they are like that. That's the way he was, and it would happen just like that. It was all of a sudden, and it was verbal.

"Also he started breaking out in [acne] a lot," Lattin said. "The acne got really bad."

Lattin said she eventually found a needle and bottles of steroids in the bathroom the couple shared.

"He admitted [using steroids]," Lattin stated. "He had no problem admitting it. He injected them. He admitted he did them in cycles to help him with his bodybuilding. He didn't have any problem admitting that to me whatsoever. What surprised me . . . was he wasn't concerned about it.

"When he was on the steroids, he was in the gym all the time, and he would never come home," she recalled. "Was he seeing someone? Or, was he in the gym? I mean, he was in the gym all the time. Sometimes he wouldn't come home at all. To my knowledge, I didn't know you could work out all night long."

Lattin said in addition to the steroids, she also found a huge stash of medicines in their closet. It appeared to her that the medicines had been taken from the naval medical branch where Chaz worked.

"He had scissors, stethoscopes, hurricane kits. Large bottles of medication. I mean, pharmacy bottles of medication. He had a jar of ephedra that was huge. What was he going to do with this stuff?"

Eventually, Lattin kicked Chaz out of the apartment they shared, and she decided she was going to pursue a divorce.

"I had had enough," she said. "I couldn't take it any-more. The marriage was a huge, huge mistake. I had just gotten through this with my ex-husband, and why was I doing this again?"

There was a brief period of reconciliation in which Chaz moved back in with her. Chaz then announced he was moving from Florida to the San Diego, California, area to begin training for the Navy SEALs. Lattin thought she, too, needed a change, and she wanted to move to the West Coast. She, Chaz, and a close female friend of Lattin's rented a large RV and drove across the country. Lattin still believed that she and Chaz might be able to work through the problems in their marriage, but during the drive, Lattin started to suspect that Chaz and her friend were having an affair.

"I was thinking, maybe he's changed, and then I started to have very strong suspicions he was having an affair with my friend," Lattin said. "He was still the same old slick Chaz. The next thing I know, he's taking off to go to the grocery store with this girl, and they are coming back a half day later. It didn't take a rocket scientist to figure out there was an attraction between these two. It was extremely hurtful."

Lattin said the trip in the RV was a miserable one. The toilet on the recreational vehicle backed up, and all three of the travelers got sick. When the trio arrived in Las Vegas, Chaz announced he had some medical supplies with him, and he wanted to hook Lattin up to an IV because she was feeling so ill.

"He had all these medical supplies, and he wanted to give me some fluids because I'd been throwing up so bad," Lattin said. "I got very, very sick, so instead of taking me to the [military] base to get some treatment, he decided to plug me up to an IV in the living room."

Lattin eventually recovered from her illness, and she filed for divorce. More than a year after the two saw each other for the last time, Lattin received a letter in the mail from Chaz that was dated April 22, 1991. The letter was actually addressed to her son, then three years old, which Lattin found odd. Although Chaz was the boy's legal father, the child was very young, and she said Chaz had hardly spent any time with her son when the couple was together.

She would come to conclude the letter was nothing more than another attempt at manipulation by Chaz.

The letter from Chaz began with a declaration of how much he missed and loved the boy and included promises to see more of him in the future. It then went on to praise Lattin, calling her "a terrific woman" with "a lot going for her."

"You mean the world to your mom, so be good to her," Chaz wrote. "I really loved your mom when we were together, and I still love her dearly now. We just had a very difficult time with our marriage. I feel as though I really wanted a marriage, but [I] wasn't ready."

After more declarations of love for the child, Chaz wrote to the boy that "I will be there for you as much as I can." He talked of the supposedly close bond he'd developed with the boy and begged the child to "please try to understand what is going on. I am sorry that all of us can't be together as a family, but we will both do as much as we can for you. . . . When you can, please respond."

Chaz asked Lattin to keep the letter for her son until he was old enough to read it.

Lattin found the letter revolting.

"He'd had no contact with my son whatsoever," she said. "He had nothing to do with [him] ever. He adopted this child, and then he had nothing to do with my son."

It was obvious to her that the contents of the letter were

written for her and not for her three-year-old. "What was he thinking writing this to me? Is he apologizing to me or my son? That's what I think he is doing, apologizing to me. Again, it's just his slick way of doing things."

The letter made her sick. Higgs's attorney, Alan Baum, would later describe Lattin's account of Higgs as completely inaccurate, saying Lattin was bitter over the couple's failed marriage. Lattin, however, stood by her account of Higgs and, in retrospect, said there was one thing about Chaz Higgs that bothered her even more when she looks back now and contemplates their brief marriage.

According to Kirstin Lattin, around the time Chaz was on steroids, he also insisted on injecting her with what he termed vitamin B shots. The shots, he said, had to be injected into the skin of her buttock, and he promised they would make her feel better when she was tired or listless.

"The IV was not the first time he'd stuck a needle in me," Lattin said.

9 ... ITALIAN AMERICAN OF THE YEAR

Kathy Augustine received a prestigious honor in October 2003: the Augustus Society in Las Vegas had decided to name Kathy its annual Italian American of the Year. It was an easy choice for the organization, given Kathy's meteoric rise in Nevada politics and the expectations that she was eyeing a much larger political position. Kathy was honored to receive the award, and she invited her entire family to attend the ceremony at the Venetian resort. The Augustus Society presented a large audio and video presentation in honor of Kathy, and it was obvious that the award was cherished by the single mom turned power broker in the Silver State.

The entire Alfano family traveled to Las Vegas to attend the function. The event was just two months after Charles Augustine's death, and they wanted to be there as a show of support for Kathy. Phil Alfano Jr. was extremely proud of his sister, but shortly after arriving, he noticed that his sister seemed to have a date with her. He was a tan, muscular man who was obviously younger than Kathy.

"He had highlights in his hair," Phil Jr. said. "His hair-style reminded me of the Pet Shop Boys. I thought he was her date."

The thought crossed his mind that it was a little early for his sister to be dating, but, then again, she had been separated from Charles for nearly a year when he died. Phil Jr. didn't give this individual much more thought until the next morning, when the bombshell dropped at a family brunch. Kathy arrived with the same man, whom she introduced as Chaz Higgs. At the conclusion of the brunch, Kathy stood up and again introduced Chaz, then announced to everyone that he was her husband, and they'd gotten married in Hawaii a month earlier.

Everyone in the room was astonished. Kathy's husband had only been dead for three weeks, and she'd run off and married a bodybuilder named Chaz in Hawaii?

Kathy's brother was certainly startled. He was also on the edge of being angry.

"I was completely shocked," Phil Jr. said. "She said, 'He was a nurse when Chuck was sick, he'd taken care of Chuck, and he'd been an angel to me. He swept me off my feet.' I was shocked. I thought it was very inappropriate to get married that quickly after your husband has died, regardless of whether you are separated or not.

"I wish I had a videotape of her introducing him to us," Phil Jr. said. "It was like listening to a seventeen- or eighteen-year-old kid giddy with excitement. She was talking about how wonderful this guy . . . [is] and what an angel he is. From a male's standpoint, I was sitting there gagging, but she believed it could be true love just like that."

Phil Jr. decided not to confront his sister. She was an adult woman, forty-five years old, and she could take care of herself. He also knew from past experience that his sister was a woman subject to rash impulses when it came to men.

"She's a grown woman, and it would have been very awkward to confront her," Phil Jr. said. "Plus, I risked alienating her over that. Keep in mind that I had similar misgivings when she married Chuck. She'd just gotten divorced. She [was] marrying a guy fifteen years older than her, yet that worked out very well. The best relationship she ever had."

Then the moment came where Phil Jr. introduced himself to Chaz Higgs. Phil Jr. is by his very nature a kind person, and he decided to give the guy the benefit of the doubt and went over to shake his new brother-in-law's hand. But Phil Jr. couldn't help noticing that Chaz didn't have much of a handshake.

"My dad had always taught me that you don't want to break somebody's hand, but you want a firm shake," Phil Jr. said. "His was limp. It was like a dead fish. That kind of stood out. It was very strange. The other thing I noticed was [when we were] conversing in a group; say there are three or four people there, we are all sitting around talking, and Chaz wouldn't say anything. He was just drifting off in his own world. Very quiet. It was almost like he was detached.

"You kind of kick yourself initially," he said. "Maybe I'm just judging this guy. Maybe I'm being unfair.

"But I didn't say to my sister, 'What the hell are you doing?' which, in retrospect, I wish I had," Phil Jr. said. "I was like, maybe it will work out for her, but I found it very distasteful. Even if she had been on the outs with Chuck, and there had been an attraction with this guy and they'd dated for a while and then got married, OK. But to run off and get married right away? I thought it was very distasteful."

In retrospect, the quickie marriage to Chaz Higgs was yet another example of Kathy Augustine's poor judgment—and inability to control herself—when it came to men.

"The more I look at it, this [was] not out of character for her," Phil Jr. said. "She married Chuck six months after she'd divorced her previous husband. I'd seen her rush into relationships before and regret it. It's just a real contradiction in her character, because she could be so organized and so thoughtful about things professionally, and then in her personal relationships, she was reckless."

There was at least one person who was not completely surprised by the marriage. Kathy's mother, Kay Alfano, had heard a rumor circulating through some of Kathy's old friends in California that Kathy had gone on a long-planned trip to Hawaii and that a "nurse from the hospital had followed her over there." Kay was mortified at the very suggestion.

"I said, 'Whaaaat?'" Kathy's mother recalled. "I immediately said, 'I hope she doesn't marry him.'"

Kay Alfano decided to confront her daughter about the rumor at the first possible chance. Kay, perhaps the sweetest woman one could ever meet, was pissed off. The whole situation seemed very inappropriate.

"From what I had understood, she had gone to Hawaii, and he followed her," Kay said. "When she got back, she called me, and the first thing out of my mouth to Kathy was, 'Did you get married?'

"Mom, how did you know?" Kathy responded.

"Mother's instinct," said an angry Kay Alfano.

"She begged me, 'Please don't tell Dad,'" Kay said. "She said, 'I'm going to introduce him at the Italian American banquet.'"

Kay then proceeded to ask her daughter, the controller for the state of Nevada, if she had any common sense at all.

"Have you lost your mind?" she asked.

" 'But mom, he's so nice,' " Kay quoted her daughter as saying. " 'He's been so good to me.' "

Kay loved her daughter, but she was furious with her. It seemed too soon after Chuck's death to get married.

"I was thinking he must have gotten her at a vulnerable moment," Kay said. "And, being he was Chuck's nurse, he must have heard conversations, so he knew what's going on [in Kathy's life]. Chaz is an opportunist, and I know she did not know he had been married at all [before]. I'm positive. Then, all of the sudden, she found out he was married previously to a gal who has a little girl. Then the other marriages he had would come out. I told her she was crazy."

Still, Kay Alfano decided to keep the secret until it was unveiled at the Italian American of the Year dinner. She couldn't tell her husband herself "because I was afraid it would kill him." Kathy, after all, was the one who went off and got married, and Kay decided that Kathy was going to be the one who would have to look her father in the face and tell him that she'd run off with a bodybuilding nurse and gotten married three weeks after her husband's death. Kay knew it was going to be a difficult moment for her daughter because Kathy valued her father's opinion dearly. She'd always wanted to please her father since she was a little girl.

Phil Alfano Sr. said he, too, was shocked when he learned of the marriage, and he didn't like Chaz Higgs from the moment he met him. It was hard to fathom that his daughter had run off and married this man.

"I really didn't think that much of him," Phil Sr. said. "He wasn't real friendly. He wouldn't look you in the eye. There was just something about him that I really didn't care for. I couldn't put my finger on it."

Kay Alfano's meeting with Chaz did not go better. And, when she saw him in person, she realized she had met him before. Chaz, Kay recalled, had been at Kathy's house two days prior to Chuck's funeral.

"That night he came over . . . with pizza," Kay said. "He supposedly came over to offer his condolences."

Nancy Vinik hadn't seen Kathy for a few weeks after Chuck's death, in August 2003, and she and her husband agreed it would be a good idea to check on how Kathy was holding up. They looked forward to seeing her, and they also wanted to make sure that she wasn't depressed in the aftermath of the loss of her husband. The couple decided to invite Kathy to their home for dinner when she came to Las Vegas from Carson City for the weekend, and Nancy prepared a nice meal of lamb chops and asparagus for her best friend.

Kathy arrived at the Vinik home in northwest Las Vegas in good spirits. The couple and Kathy had a wonderful evening together. Nancy said she had to walk her dog as the evening was winding down, and she asked Kathy if she would like to come along. The two were walking on a circular route through Nancy's neighborhood when Kathy told her good friend that she had a bit of a surprise for her.

"She said, 'I've got something to tell you,' and she proceeded to tell me that she was married," Nancy recalled. "I said, '*Whaaaat*?'"

Nancy had to do a double take on that one. She asked Kathy if she was kidding.

She wasn't.

When she realized that Kathy was serious, she became angry. Kathy was one of her best friends, and Nancy was insulted that Kathy hadn't told her anything about it. The thought was also whirling through her head that the idea of marriage was a little preposterous, given that Chuck had died just a few weeks ago.

"I said, 'Kathy, how could you not tell me?'" Vinik said. "'Who did you get married to? Someone I know?'"

"'Well, I don't think so,'" Nancy quoted Kathy as saying. "Then, she said, 'Are you going to be happy for me?'"

"I said, 'How can I be happy for you when you just run off and get married and don't tell me? Who is this person?'" a dismayed Nancy asked.

"Then, she proceeded to tell me who he was," Nancy said. "She told me it was the nurse that took care of Chuck."

Nancy was flabbergasted, and she found it hard to believe what she was hearing from the controller of the state of Nevada.

"I stopped in the middle of the street, and my eyes were bugging out of my head, and I said, 'Huh?'" Nancy recalled. "And then she said, 'I got married a while back.'"

"'A while back!'" Nancy said. "'How could you get married a while back? Chuck just passed away.' I said, 'Kathy you have always been a person who always thinks things through, and the only thing I'm going to say to you is I hope you didn't make a bad mistake or a wrong decision because this is not you.'

"And, she said, 'There is such a thing of not wanting to be by yourself, and I've been by myself for a very long time because when I was married to Chuck, I was still by myself,'" Nancy recalled.

"She said, 'He's flying down tomorrow and his name is Chaz Higgs.'"

But Kathy could sense the conversation was not going well.

"I don't think I said much more to her than that, and then she said, 'Well, I've got to go because I've got a long ride home,'" Nancy said. After Kathy left, Nancy told her husband about the marriage, and he, too, was stunned.

"You should have heard my husband," Nancy said. "He couldn't believe it either."

Nancy Vinik saw Chaz Higgs a few days later, at the Italian American of the Year festivities. She didn't like him from the moment she met him.

"The first thing I said was, 'They don't go together,'" Nancy said. "I actually thought he was gay at first. There was something about him that looked feminine. [He wore] a diamond earring, and he had his hair bleached. When he was introduced to everybody, he didn't talk to anyone. He just seemed very uncomfortable."

10 . . . STORM CLOUDS

Gerald Gardner is a veteran prosecutor who spent nearly nine years as a deputy district attorney with the Clark County District Attorney's Office in Las Vegas. His successes prosecuting criminals at the district attorney's office in Las Vegas drew the attention of state officials, and in 2002, he was asked to join the Nevada Attorney General's Office in Las Vegas. A successful prosecution by Gardner of a North Las Vegas city councilman on insurance fraud received a great deal of media attention, and in 2003, Gardner was named the leader of the attorney general's office in Las Vegas.

It was an appointment that put him on a direct collision course with Kathy Augustine.

In 2003, after Kathy was reelected to a second term as controller, some of her employees at the controller's office were privately complaining that Kathy was making them work on her political campaign while they were supposed to be working for the state. State politicians in Nevada are specifically prevented by law from doing political work on the state's time, and that same year, two of Kathy's top employees at the controller's office—Jeannine Coward and Jennifer Normington—spoke with the attorney general's office. Coward and Normington said they were supposed to be working on behalf of the state at the controller's office, but in reality, it seemed to the two women that they were more like staffers for Kathy's political campaign.

"Gradually, I came to realize that I was spending most of my official hours working on the controller's reelection campaign and unable to make up for it by skipping lunch and staying late," said Jennifer Normington, who was Kathy's executive assistant from October 4, 2001, through January 31, 2003. "I became concerned that I was in gross violation of the law."

Jeannine Coward was Kathy's assistant controller from February 8, 1999, to January 31, 2003, and she made similar allegations. Coward, a former Nevada assemblywoman, also provided Nevada Attorney General Brian Sandoval's office with a computer disc that she said contained records indicating campaign work was being done on state time in Kathy's office.

"I was the one who delivered the disc to Attorney General Brian Sandoval's office with the comment, 'I think the State Controller may have broken the law, but I think it should be your decision to decide,'" Coward said.

The complaint was a little stale—nearly a year old—but it was eventually determined that the matter warranted further investigation, and the case was given to Gardner.

"I had maybe been at the attorney general's office for eight or nine months at the time," Gardner said. "Brian had been sworn in, and . . . it was decided at that time it should be looked at by an investigator, and that's when I was notified."

Gardner, forty-three, is a medium-sized man, with dark hair and hazel eyes. He was born in Maine, the son of a career executive at IBM. He said his father's career ended up taking the family all over the world.

"It was disruptive to have to pull up roots every three years and move, but I can't complain," Gardner said. "The overseas experience in particular was very valuable, because it gave me a view of the world I would have never had otherwise."

Gardner is what you would expect from a prosecutor: clean-cut, meticulous, thorough, and honest. He gives off an aura of being organized, and he is a very talented lawyer. Gardner found the allegations against Kathy credible as he and the attorney general's office investigators interviewed the witnesses and reviewed computer evidence, which included campaign speeches and donation lists that were taken from computers at the controller's office.

"[Kathy] was running for reelection in 2002, and the witnesses were very high-level employees, including her deputy controller, Jeannine Coward, and her personal executive assistant, Jennifer Normington," Gardner said. "In the last year or so of Kathy Augustine's first term, while she was running for reelection, she basically enlisted them as her campaign staff. They were working a substantial number of hours to help her with her campaign reelection. Jennifer Normington said that during the last few months of the campaign, that's pretty much all she was doing. . . . [She] organized campaign party events, stuffed envelopes, and replied to contributions and wrote thank-you letters. All of this was being maintained on her state computer, on state time.

"Ultimately, we had seven or eight witnesses, including her [chief] deputy controller, Jim Wells, whom she told to do her campaign finance expenditure reports," Gardner said. "She told him, 'I want you to complete these campaign finance forms,' and anyone who is familiar with politics in Nevada knows that those forms are a huge part of your responsibility as a politician. To ask a state employee to do that on the state clock is a pretty shocking thing.

"It took a good year to figure it all out," Gardner said of the investigation. "There was a significant review of computer evidence, and the attorney general's office had a computer forensics expert . . . [who produced] three thousand pages of documents in the case. We had contributor's lists, campaign speeches, political scripts, and it was all right there on [Kathy's] office computers. We interviewed probably a couple of dozen people."

One of the witnesses interviewed was Kathy Augustine herself. Kathy, flanked by a civil attorney from the attorney general's office, denied any wrongdoing, and she told investigators she'd always acted appropriately in her office. She would later portray Normington as a disgruntled employee who was angry because Kathy had once issued her a written reprimand. She also said she'd told employees who worked on her political campaign that the work was strictly voluntary and that those activities needed to be performed after hours. Kathy could not, however, deny the computer evidence that convinced authorities she was basically running her political campaign out of her controller's office in Carson City.

Gardner said he was also bothered by witness testimony that indicated Kathy had been abusive to her employees. She screamed and yelled at them, and when Normington complained that she couldn't work on campaign tasks all night because she had to go home to feed her cat, Kathy supposedly told her, "You need to kill [that cat]."

"What I felt had happened was that Kathy Augustine [had] consciously decided that she could use her state employees as her own personal staff," Gardner said. "She had developed a sense of power to the point where she felt that they were her own personal servants . . . and I really believe she didn't think there was anything wrong with what she was doing.

"One of the ironies of this was that she was treating these people very poorly," Gardner said. "If you are going to misuse your staff, at least treat them nicely. She didn't. She was tough on them. She belittled them, insulted them, and threw things at them."

Gardner closely scrutinized the allegations to try and determine if it was possible that the allegations were made for political reasons. He concluded that, to the contrary, the witnesses were very credible, and it seemed to him they had no ulterior motives.

"Were these people doing this for politics or personal animosity?" Gardner said. "There were so many witnesses who had seen this, and with some of the primary witnesses, there was some personal anguish . . . about coming forward to testify. We had witnesses in tears because they were so conflicted about coming forward and telling us, but they felt they had to."

The evidence and witness testimony convinced Gardner that Kathy had clearly violated state law, which prevents state employees from performing political activities while being paid by the state. The next decision was whether to criminally prosecute her.

"We weren't quite sure what to do with it," Gardner said. "We reviewed it for the possibility of criminal charges, and the charge that we felt fit was misconduct of a public officer, which is a felony. Even now, as I think about it, the technical aspects of that charge were probably met, and we talked about actually filing a criminal complaint. However, because she [was] a public employee, sending it to the Ethics Commission was another option, and that is the way we opted to go."

The complaint was forwarded to the Ethics Commission in the summer of 2004.

By July 2004, Chaz Higgs and Kathy Augustine had been married for less than a year, but the marriage was already showing strain. Chaz said he offered as much support to his wife as possible while she was facing the ethics proceedings, yet at the same time, he was beginning a flirtatious relationship with one of his coworkers.

Chaz was working at the Washoe Medical Center at South Meadows in Reno as a critical-care nurse when he met Linda Ramirez, a very attractive young woman with dark hair who was an admissions clerk at the hospital. He did not mention to her initially that he was married. Ramirez struck up a friendship with Chaz, and the two started exchanging e-mails. Ramirez described the relationship as "flirtatious" and said that when Chaz learned that her birthday was that month, he brought her a rose with a note that said "Linda, Happy Birthday."

"It was sweet," she said.

She said she later learned Chaz was married but that he was miserable in his relationship. She said Chaz repeatedly vented to her about his wife being a "bitch," and she was willing to listen because she thought he was a nice, decent person.

"'I hate my wife,'" Ramirez quoted Chaz saying about Kathy. "'She's a controlling, manipulative bitch. Vindictive.'"

The Nevada Commission on Ethics was established in part to make sure government officials in the state don't use their public office for personal gain. The commission consists of eight members appointed by the Nevada governor and legislature, and the commission does have some real power in the form of the ability to impose significant fines. The commission is a hugely important aspect of keeping government officials in Nevada honest, and it is a function that many Nevadans take for granted. There is no such thing as an ethics commission in some other states. The case file from the attorney general's office for Kathy Augustine was sent to the commission's executive director, Stacy Jennings. Jennings, too, interviewed the witnesses against Kathy, and she also concluded that Kathy had clearly violated state ethics law. She penned a ten-page report to the Nevada Commission on Ethics panel in August 2004.

"[State law] prohibits a public officer from attempting to benefit [his or her] personal interest through the influence of a subordinate," Jennings wrote.

All of the employees knew it was against the rules to do campaign work on state time, but it was made clear to them that their job depended on it, and the employees felt compelled to do what Kathy said.

"Several of the controller's office employees indicated she frequently requested state work be put aside or demanded campaign tasks be performed immediately during state work hours," Jennings said. "The controller, Augustine, expected campaign work to be the top priority, [and this] was understood by staff in the mercurial work environment. After former [Chief] Deputy Controller Jim Wells refused to work on Augustine's re-election campaign, the working relationship between the two significantly changed such that he subsequently left. In light of this, other employees seemed convinced that Controller Augustine was not to be confronted regarding campaign work on state time. The egregious nature of this conduct should be viewed through the perception of at least one employee who felt the necessity to choose between making her monthly mortgage payment or performing blatantly unethical tasks at the direction of an elected constitutional officer of this state who could hire or fire her at whim."

Jennings wrote that the witnesses clearly felt as if they were under duress when asked to do the political work. Each witness contacted by the Commission on Ethics said he or she was directed by Kathy to perform campaign work.

"The conduct of Controller Augustine appears to have instilled in several employees a legitimate belief that performing campaign work was a condition of employment," Jennings said. "Conversely, the employees appear to have had a legitimate fear that failure to perform campaign work as directed by Controller Augustine, whether on or off [the] state clock, would result in termination."

The Nevada Commission on Ethics decided to schedule a full hearing for Kathy Augustine in September 2004 to determine if she'd broken state ethics law.

Any chance of Kathy Augustine being named treasurer of the United States officially slipped away when news of the ethics complaint against her became public. The press in southern Nevada treated the allegations against Kathy as if it was the story of the century, and Kathy's problems with the Commission on Ethics were daily fodder for the papers. The *Las Vegas Review-Journal* reported that "if found guilty of a willful violation, Augustine could be liable for a civil fine amounting to $5,000 for a first offense, $10,000 for a second and $25,000 for a third."

Southern Nevada's political columnists were especially harsh on Kathy. Steve Sebelius, a longtime Las Vegas political columnist who had worked at the *Las Vegas Sun* and the *Review-Journal* newspapers, at one point penned a column that mockingly labeled Kathy "evil."

"As we discover the dimensions of the depths of state Controller Kathy Augustine's true evil—she allegedly told an employee to kill a sick cat that was interfering with overtime work!—one thing is clear: It's going to take explosives to dislodge her from office."

Review-Journal columnist Jane Ann Morrison predicted as early as July 2004 that Kathy's political career was over because of the ethics allegations. In a column headlined "Augustine's impending political end rooted in past skulduggery," Morrison recounted all of the rough-and-tumble political races that Kathy had run as well as her nefarious political tactics against opponents Dora Harris and Lori Lipman Brown.

Morrison interviewed Lipman Brown for the column, which basically made the case that what goes around comes around in Nevada politics.

"Comeuppance is such a delightful Victorian word," Morrison wrote. "It doesn't get enough use because it doesn't happen often enough. State Controller Kathy Augustine is finally going to get hers. But for two Las Vegas women, Dora Harris and Lori Lipman Brown, it is more than a decade overdue. Augustine engaged in foul deeds against them both."

Kathy knew she was in trouble upon reading those accounts in Nevada's largest newspaper. She realized it was going to be a tough fight to clear her name, but she thought the allegations against her weren't very serious and that voters would eventually forgive her. She told her family that almost every politician she knew in Carson City performed political functions while at work.

Her buff, weightlifting, young new husband would later

say that the allegations took a toll on Kathy behind the scenes. He claimed that he'd offered his support for her as the allegations flew but said he had also started to believe that Kathy needed to get out of politics. She was too consumed by being at the top of the political game. She was obsessed with the power, the attention, and the thrill of the political race, and it was hurting their relationship.

Chaz said he urged his wife to consider buying an RV so the couple could travel the country—an idea Kathy's family would later say would have been laughable to Kathy. Chaz, however, said he and his wife planned to go on the road in an RV. He would become a traveling nurse, and the strain of political life would be gone.

Kathy's brother Phil Alfano Jr. said Kathy kept him up to speed on the ethics case against her as it was unfolding.

"She would always call me and let me know how it was turning out," Phil Jr. said. "It was hurtful for her. She would call and just let us know what was happening, and we talked a lot about it. I spoke to her by telephone in early June or July, and she said, 'I don't think anything's going to come of it. It's from a disgruntled employee. The charges were filed more than a year ago.'

"Personally, I thought the whole thing was peanuts," Phil Jr. said. "A lot of what this employee and another employee said had some basis . . . [of] truth in it, and Kathy acknowledged that there was some basis of truth in it. She said, 'I did use the office equipment. I should have monitored it more. It's my fault.' Given that, I figured it wasn't that big of a deal."

Kathy, nonetheless, took the necessary precautions, considering that if rumors were flying, it was at least possible that the attorney general's office could criminally charge her. She was also interested in trying to protect her political future as much as possible and limit the damage in front of the Commission on Ethics. To defend her, she hired two of the most respected attorneys in Nevada: John Arrascada, an accomplished, well-connected Reno attorney, and Dominic Gentile, a long-haired fireball of an attorney who is widely recognized as perhaps the best litigator—and the biggest-profile attorney—in the entire state of Nevada.

The attorneys began their defense of Kathy by again telling the Commission on Ethics that Kathy had repeatedly told her employees that any of the political tasks she'd assigned were voluntary and were to be performed after-hours. Kathy also produced the letter of reprimand she'd written Jennifer Normington on January 9, 2003, which indicated she'd reprimanded Normington for poor job performance. The reprimand, the attorneys said, was proof that the employee was out to get Kathy.

"It is with great regret that I find it necessary to write you this letter of reprimand," the letter began, "due to your negligence in handling State Controller's Office personnel files and Diner's Club summaries. . . . I questioned you on several occasions regarding the status of these files, and you assured me they were up to date and being maintained. When you were absent on sick leave last month, three personnel files were found *under* your desk, as were a folder of unfiled personnel documents dating back to April of 2002. Diner's Club summaries were also found unopened back to December of 2001. This is totally unacceptable." The letter closed with a reminder that the files in question needed to be reviewed weekly, "or future disciplinary action will be taken."

Normington resigned from the controller's office less than two weeks later via a letter to Kathy on January 22, 2003. "It is with mixed feelings that I submit my letter of resignation as your executive assistant," the resignation letter began, going on to say that she had accepted another position elsewhere. "It is a difficult move for me to make, but one that I feel is necessary," Normington wrote, adding, "I will always appreciate you bringing me into the state and mentoring me both in government and in the realm of politics."

Kathy Augustine's attorneys were trying to make a case that Jennifer Normington was a disgruntled employee who had it out for her boss. They arranged for Kathy to take a polygraph test administered by Dennis Arnoldy, a former agent with the Federal Bureau of Investigation. Arnoldy summed up the results of Kathy's polygraph—which questioned whether Kathy felt she had ever pressured any state employee to work on her 2002 campaign and if she believed Normington to have worked less than ten hours a month in the office on her campaign—as "not indicative of deception."

Kathy, however, was mistaken when she'd told her family that Normington and Coward's allegations and the ethics case against her would eventually blow over. They wouldn't. Kathy was soon standing in a river of negative publicity in the Las Vegas and Reno papers that mostly portrayed her as just another politician who preferred political ambition over following the rules. There were repeated calls for her resignation.

In the fall of 2004, the damaging media reports continued to take huge chunks out of Kathy's political flesh by the day. Kathy's attorneys decided it was time to try and limit the damage. They cut a risky deal with Jennings and the Commission on Ethics in which Kathy agreed, upon the advice of her attorneys, to enter into a stipulation with the commission that she'd committed three ethics violations. In return, Kathy would pay a $15,000 fine.

Kathy's lawyers, Arrascada and Gentile, recognized that the deal carried with it a dangerous unknown: under

Nevada law, any constitutional officer who admitted to an ethics violation was automatically subject to impeachment proceedings in the Nevada Legislature. An impeachment is essentially viewed as a decision on whether to remove a political official from office because of a violation of the public trust. Kathy's attorneys were aware of the possibility of an impeachment trial of Kathy in front of the state assembly and senate, but at the time the deal with the Commission on Ethics was struck, they were more concerned by the possibility of the attorney general's office filing criminal charges against Kathy. It also seemed at least possible that an actual impeachment over what, to the attorneys, seemed to be some relatively minor offenses was unlikely to run its full course in both the state assembly and senate. They suspected that the politicians in the legislature might merely issue a strongly worded reprimand.

Arrascada, Gardner, and Jennings negotiated for weeks over the potential solution with the Commission on Ethics, and on September 21, the agreement between Kathy and the commission was released.

The following are relevant, edited excerpts from the lengthy legal document:

On July 8, 2004, a request for opinion [ethics complaint] was filed with the Nevada Commission on Ethics [hereinafter the "Commission"], alleging that Kathy Augustine, Controller of the state of Nevada, violated certain provisions of Nevada's Ethics in Government law. Kathy Augustine acknowledges that the Commission provided her with notice of the allegations against her and an opportunity to file written responses. She is fully advised of the allegations.

The Commission's executive director investigated

*the complaint and rendered a written recommen-
dation that just and sufficient cause exists for the
[C]ommission to conduct a public hearing and render
an opinion, [and] Kathy Augustine hereby freely and
voluntarily waives her right to a hearing. Kathy Augustine stipulates to the following findings of fact:*

*Jennifer Normington was employed by the state
of Nevada as executive assistant to Kathy Augustine
from October 4, 2001, through January 31, 2003. During this period of time, Kathy Augustine caused Jennifer Normington, on state time, to perform, from time
to time, functions related to Kathy Augustine's 2002
re-election campaign, including, but not limited to,
maintaining campaign records for official filing, coor-
dinating certain campaign fundraisers, designing certain campaign invitations, and maintaining databases
for campaign contributions.*

*Throughout the 2002 election campaign, computer
equipment owned by the state of Nevada and located in
the office of the controller was used, from time to time,
for creating, maintaining, storing, and printing documents relating to Kathy Augustine's 2002 re-election
campaign.*

*Throughout the 2002 election campaign, equipment
and facilities provided by the state of Nevada for use by
the office of the controller were used, from time to time,
for business and purposes related to Kathy Augustine's
2002 re-election campaign.*

*Kathy Augustine, as the elected controller of the state
of Nevada, at no time sought guidance from the Nevada
Commission on Ethics on questions of the propriety of
her past, present, or future conduct as a public officer
using state resources for her campaign activities.*

Opinion

The Nevada State Legislature has declared that a public office is a public trust and shall be held for the sole benefit of the people of the State of Nevada, and that public officers must commit themselves to avoid conflicts between their private interests and those of the general public whom they serve.

By a preponderance of the evidence, Kathy Augustine willfully violated [state law by] causing state employee Jennifer Normington, on state time, to perform functions related to Kathy Augustine's 2002 re-election campaign.

By a preponderance of the evidence, as a second act, Kathy Augustine willfully violated [state law by] causing computer equipment owned by the state of Nevada and located in the office of the controller to be used for creating, maintaining, storing, and printing documents relating to her 2002 re-election campaign.

By a preponderance of the evidence, as a third act, Kathy Augustine willfully violated [state law by] causing equipment and facilities provided by the state of Nevada to be used for business and purposes related to Kathy Augustine's 2002 re-election campaign.

As a result of Kathy Augustine's three separate willful violations, the Nevada Commission on Ethics imposes a civil penalty of fifteen thousand dollars.

Kathy was humiliated and, for the moment at least, ruined politically. She was ordered by the commission to start making "thirty consecutive monthly installments of five hundred dollar [payments] payable on the first day of each month commencing October 1, 2004."

Kathy issued a public apology the day the resolution was reached. She addressed the possibility of impeachment proceedings in a brief interview with the *Las Vegas Sun* newspaper, saying, "As an elected official beholden to the people of Nevada, I will allow the process to run its course."

According to the paper, Kathy said she took "full responsibility for the actions that occurred" and apologized for her conduct.

She refused, however, to resign. "I will continue to perform my duties as state controller."

Kathy later explained her reasons for reaching a deal with the Commission on Ethics in letters to the editor that were sent to various papers throughout Nevada. Those writings and related commentary appeared on the Nevada political website newsdeskbynancydallas.com.

"If I had not signed the ethics stipulation, the Attorney General had threatened to convene a grand jury to try and criminally indict me," Kathy wrote. "If that had occurred, I would have had to immediately resign my position as State Controller."

Kathy provided documentation to the website to back up her claim. In a letter from Chief Deputy Attorney General Gerald Gardner to her attorney Arrascada, dated September 16, 2004, Gardner stated:

I previously advised you, in my letter dated May 19, 2004, that if your client failed to admit fully to the allegations, or failed to acknowledge that the violations were willful, the State would retain the right to file criminal charges and/or to proceed in any manner within its statutory authority. We also state that if, for any reason, the Commission fails to accept the stipulation, the State would retain the right to proceed criminally.

"This is why there was no need to even have an ethics hearing," Kathy wrote. "Had we fought the charges in front of the Ethics Commission and won, the AG would still have filed charges against me."

Kathy attempted to defend herself further in a letter written to the *Las Vegas Review-Journal* and other newspapers across the state a little more than two weeks after the deal with the Commission on Ethics was struck. The tone of the letter was defiant, given her admission to the ethics charges just a couple of weeks earlier, and she called out what she portrayed as the media's incomplete coverage of the ethics proceedings. Once again, Kathy acknowledged her mistakes, but anyone who read the letter to the editor came to realize that her resignation was out of the question. It wasn't going to happen.

"Sometimes, small bits of fragmented information can be more misleading than no information at all," Kathy wrote in her letter. "I have learned this to be the case with media coverage of my recent appearance before the Ethics Commission. Reporters have taken the published findings of the commission and have had no choice but to arrive at conclusions on an incomplete record because I have not yet spoken publicly."

Kathy then went on to say that "I want everyone to know that even my accusers admit that I told them over and over again, 'Don't do this on state time.' The record is clear on that point." She later returned to the topic, insisting that "many of my staff volunteered to assist [in my re-election campaign]" and lamenting that "I should have known that some of them were expending state time on the campaign. However, I had no intention or actual knowledge that any ethics rule or law was being breached.

"Any incumbent running for re-election knows the line between official business and campaign business can be blurred," she later admitted in the letter before blaming her actions on not having known any better. "My past campaigns were as a legislator, a position specifically excluded from the dictates of the ethics statute involved in this matter.

"In hindsight, I should have known my employees' time spent on my campaign crossed the line. That, I admit. I was not fully aware of the allegations against me until attorney general investigators questioned me over a year after my accusers lodged their complaint with that office."

As for those accusers, Kathy pointed the finger firmly at her former executive assistant, detailing the incident that had led to the reprimand in Normington's file and baldly stating that the woman lied. "I was then faced with what managers and supervisors have to deal with at one time or another: a disgruntled employee with an ax to grind."

Later in the letter, she again returned to the theory of the vengeful employee. "If you are truly interested in finding the truth in this case, ask yourself this: Would someone who thought . . . [she] had done something wrong reprimand anyone who could become a witness against . . . [her]? Persons involved in a nefarious plot do not make their scheme public or intentionally create witnesses against themselves.

"I have spent the past 12 years of my life in public service for only one reason," Kathy wrote. "I feel I have the talent, integrity and judgment to do a good job in public service for the people of Nevada. It isn't glamorous work, but it is a chance to improve the way our state operates." She backslid from her previous admissions of unethical conduct, stating that she'd cooperated with the investigation and agreed to the $15,000 fine because she "value[d] ethics in government, and when these things occurred on my watch, I took responsibility. I did not submit any excuses," she claimed, though her letter repeatedly did just that.

Kathy finished with a typically aggressive stance, asserting that "I will not stand silently and have my integrity dragged through the mud. I'm ready to fight."

Back in California, the furor over Kathy's troubles was astonishing to her family. Kathy's brother concluded that the firestorm over his sister's ethical misdeeds was being fueled by politics.

"I will always question whether there were some other folks in Nevada [whose names never surfaced publicly] who wanted to see this go through," Phil Alfano Jr. said. "You had a Democrat-controlled assembly who's thinking, 'Ah hah, we can get back at this person who has won four consecutive elections against Democratic opponents who she wasn't supposed to beat, on shoestring budgets.' They wanted to embarrass the Republicans, and it was 2004— an election year."

Phil Jr. said the ethics proceedings against Kathy gained steam just as she was starting to ask questions about the management of an education investment fund in Carson City that was heavily promoted on television by Nevada treasurer Brian Krolicki. Kathy and Krolicki had previously clashed when the treasurer had advocated for the elimination of the controller's office. Krolicki was himself a rising star in the Nevada Republican Party at the time, and Kathy, Phil Jr. said, was starting to ask questions. That questioning clearly fell under her job responsibility of making sure the state's money was being spent wisely.

"She knew some things that were going on in the treasurer's office that turned out to be absolutely true," Phil Jr.

said. "I think [the Republican Party hierarchy in Nevada] saw this as an opportunity to get rid of her."

Kathy had hoped that the deal she reached with the Commission on Ethics and her letter to the editor would resolve her problems, blunt any impeachment effort, and give her an opportunity to salvage her political skin.

They wouldn't.

In fact, Kathy's political problems weren't even close to over.

11 . . . IMPEACHMENT

Let us pray. We ask in this very difficult time that you provide this Body, [the Nevada Assembly], not only with the wisdom to reach the correct decision in the matters before us, but also with the ability to do it with understanding and compassion. And, we pray that the newest members of this august Body, as well as the seasoned members, and all else who work here or participate in these functions, find fulfillment in the public service that they are about to render. We ask this in whose name we pray. Amen.

—Prayer by Nevada Assembly Chaplain Terry Sullivan at the commencement of a special session to impeach Nevada Controller Kathy Augustine, November 10, 2004

Kathy Augustine was clinging to the hope that her plea deal to ethics charges with the Nevada Commission on Ethics would allow her a second chance in politics. But in politics, no one wants to be associated with a loser, and in the aftermath of Kathy's impeachment, her Republican colleagues abandoned her like she had the plague.

One of the first high-profile Republicans to abandon Kathy was Senator John Ensign. Ensign, who'd once written to the chief of staff of President Bush a recommendation for Kathy for the job of U.S. treasurer, said in a press release issued September 23, 2004, that he could no longer support her.

"An impeachment proceeding would be embarrassing and distracting for the state, the legislature, and our constitutional officers," Ensign said. "For the good of everyone involved in this case and in order to put it behind us as quickly as possible, I have urged Kathy Augustine to resign as state controller immediately."

The press release went on to say that Ensign had called on Augustine to resign "during a telephone conversation with the controller from Washington this afternoon."

In addition, Kathy's former adversary, Treasurer Brian Krolicki, called for her resignation, as did Nevada Secretary of State Dean Heller. Perhaps the most important Republican colleague and supporter to turn on Kathy, though, was her former ally Governor Kenny Guinn, who also called for her to resign. Guinn had waited a couple of weeks to make the request, saying he believed Kathy was under stress and that he didn't want to make the request for her resignation immediately out of concern for her well-being. In the first week of October, however, Guinn stepped forward and called for Kathy to step down. The governor was in a tough spot politically, and he was unable to justify supporting her, given Kathy's admissions to ethical lapses.

"If she's still there and hasn't resigned as a controller in the second week, I will call a special session," Guinn told Las Vegas television station KLAS–Channel 8.

Las Vegas Sun columnist Jeff German picked up on the theme of Republicans abandoning Kathy, and he pointed out in a column that Nevada Attorney General Brian Sandoval, who was Gardner's boss and who would eventually be named a federal judge, certainly didn't do Kathy any favors, either.

"Members of her own party don't even like her," German wrote in his column. "Fellow Republican Gov. Kenny

Guinn pushed for the costly special session. And, another Republican, Attorney General Brian Sandoval, kept Augustine on the hot seat for more than a year until she agreed to admit to ethics violations."

The media attention was relentless. The press was smothering Kathy, given the persistent calls for her resignation and her apparent unwillingness to do so. The story's value was magnified further by the fact that Kathy's impeachment was a historic event in Nevada: for the first time, the Wild West state was considering impeaching a constitutional officer. Kathy's case was also widely viewed as one that would test whether Nevada was going to stand up and enforce the ethics laws it has on the books, thus guaranteeing the integrity of state government.

Ed Vogel, a reporter at the *Las Vegas Review-Journal*'s capital bureau, said the impeachment was certainly a historic event, and it was intriguing to watch the governor and other top Republicans clash with what now seemed like a rogue Kathy Augustine.

"It wasn't worth an impeachment," the veteran reporter said. "It seemed more political than not. But because it was a willful violation of ethics laws, it was automatically referred to the legislature. I thought a lot of people had done [what Kathy had done], but apparently they hadn't used their office [like she had]. I felt the people [who worked on Kathy's campaign] did [so] voluntarily and that they weren't really forced. It was incredible, though, because this was the first time in state history that someone had been impeached."

Kathy was in the midst of a political crisis. She certainly didn't want to resign. She called her brother Phil Alfano Jr. and talked about what to do. She was considering stepping down. Phil Jr., though, told his big sister to fight.

"It seemed like a pretty trivial thing for an impeachment," Phil Jr. said. "I think a lot of people see that."

At the same time as the impeachment process, Kathy was also struggling in her relationship with her daughter. Dallas, after graduating high school, had gone off to college in San Diego, and there were times when she clashed with her mother over her grades and her future. Though Dallas has spoken very little publicly about this time in her life, in one television interview, she admitted that her relationship with her mother was at times stormy. Kay and Phil Alfano Sr. also said Kathy harped on Dallas a lot about her grades and her future and was simply worried about her daughter because she wanted her to have the best future in life possible. Dallas, however, was a grown woman, and, the Alfanos said, she was rebelling.

Chaz, meanwhile, was likely wondering what he'd gotten himself into. He'd married a politician who was on the verge of impeachment. During the times he spent with Kathy in Reno and Las Vegas, he saw the life being drained out of her. She was stressed out to the max and facing ruin in a field that had come to be an important part of her identity. The impeachment changed his wife and their relationship.

"She became very defensive," Chaz would later recall. "I said, 'Well, you know I'm here for you,' but she was just so cold, so hard, so scared, so defensive. I didn't know how to deal with it."

Kathy's brother Phil Jr. said he had always been impressed with his sister's ability to shrug off the criticisms and nastiness that come with being in public office, but Phil Jr. could tell that Kathy was hurting from the strain of the pressure of imminent impeachment. Her very integrity and worthiness as a public servant were being questioned, and despite Kathy's tough public image, it gravely wounded her on a personal level, her brother said.

"It was very, very rough on Kathy," said Phil Jr.

"I think that toughness was a part of the personality she'd cultivated in public office," he said. "She was a type A. I know she was a good manager and had high standards. She used to refer to Nevada politics as a good-old-boys network. If somebody called her a bitch, she laughed about it. It was fine if people perceived her that way because it didn't really matter to her. I think she was tough to a certain extent, but that was more of an image she created."

Phil Jr. told his sister to be strong. Don't resign, he said. He sincerely felt the impeachment was unwarranted, and he urged his sister to scrap it out all the way to the end of a full impeachment hearing if that's what would be necessary to clear her name.

"After the governor asked her to resign, and [she asked me], 'What do you think I should do?'" Phil Jr. recalled the heart-to-heart he had with Kathy over her political future. "I said, 'If you've got the wherewithal to fight it, I would fight it. What have you got to lose?' Her attorney told me the amount of stuff they did on the computers couldn't have amounted to more than a hundred bucks. Who else may be doing what? The line between campaigning and working for an elected official gets blurred all the time."

Kathy agreed with her brother.

It wasn't in her to quit now in disgrace.

She was going to fight.

Governor Guinn found himself in a difficult spot with Kathy's refusal to step down. He couldn't back down after calling for her to resign. The governor, according to media accounts, debated for weeks with attorneys and legislators about whether to proceed with an impeachment proceeding and, if so, how to do it. It seemed the governor really had no choice. State law dictated that if a constitutional officer was found guilty of an ethics violation, then an impeachment was mandatory.

Guinn decided to call a special session of the legislature for the purposes of the impeachment, and he suspended Kathy with pay. Kathy's fate in the legislature would be decided in a two-phase process. The first step would be a hearing in the Democratic-controlled assembly to determine if there was enough evidence to forward the charges, known as the Articles of Impeachment, to the state senate. If the assembly forwarded the allegations to the senate, then the senate would hold what amounted to a full trial to determine if Kathy should be impeached. Twenty-one state senators would sit in judgment on whether Kathy should be kicked out of the controller's office in complete disgrace.

The actual procedure for pursuing impeachment against Kathy was groundbreaking.

"This was the first time the impeachment of a constitutional officer had ever taken place," prosecutor Gerald Gardner said. "The process was as much of a job as the time it took to organize the charges and the facts. We sorted through the various constitutional provisions of the statutes and the statutory principles that say the attorney general shall assist in the impeachment hearings, but it doesn't say who does what, so we thought of the assembly as a lower court and the senate as a trial court."

Everything seemed to be crumbling around Nevada state controller Kathy Augustine. If the defections of her supporters weren't bad enough, she was also tallying up staggering legal bills to pay for a legal team that now included six attorneys. The governor had also made clear to Kathy that she could be found liable for as much as $200,000 in costs for the special session, which would be a huge chunk of money even for Kathy. She faced the possibility of losing as much as half of her wealth, if not more, when tallying up the combination of attorneys' fees and a possible levy of the special session's cost.

Gerald Gardner disagreed with those who felt that the impeachment proceedings against Kathy were unwarranted. The law is clear: a constitutional officer found in violation of an ethics provision is required to face impeachment proceedings. It is not OK, he said, for someone to view state office as his or her political campaign headquarters, nor is it OK for politicians to spend the state's money on their own political ambitions. He said the estimate of the costs of Kathy's actions was at least ten thousand dollars, and the bill for that political activity was not what the taxpayers of Nevada signed up for in their agreement to pay for the position of Nevada controller.

"The violation of the public trust is paramount," Gardner said. "The people elected her to serve the public, and she used her office to give herself an unfair advantage."

The veteran prosecutor also refuted allegations that the impeachment was political or that it was an attempt to slow down Kathy's career. Simply not true, he said. The complaint lodged against Kathy with the Commission on Ethics was supported by facts, and he never took a single step against Kathy to further anyone's political agenda. He did what he did, he said, because it was the right thing to do.

Gardner also pointed out that although Kathy was clearly fighting her impeachment "tooth and nail," she also seemed to willfully forget that she had already admitted to the violations. "There were a number of members of the legislature who pointed out that she basically stipulated to these violations [in front of the Commission on Ethics], so I don't know how we could not find her to have violated the principles that would lead to an impeachment. It was something she never seemed to acknowledge, that she had previously stipulated to these violations."

Gardner knew Kathy's prosecution was making history, but he wasn't enjoying it. He viewed it as an unfortunate event for Kathy, and he was taken aback at the amount of press coverage Kathy's impeachment received.

"It was very controversial," Gardner said. "Heavily reported. People were very interested. Kathy Augustine had her share of supporters and her share of critics. By the time we got to the assembly hearing, it was huge news. Banner headlines. I was amazed by the coverage, and it was certainly a growing experience for me. I'd never been involved in something so high profile. It teaches you on many levels, not so much on how to conduct yourself in public, but it was a good experience to learn how careful you have to be at the initial stages of the investigation."

Gardner knew there was a slight flaw in the case against Kathy as he prepared the evidence for the state assembly to consider. When Kathy was interviewed as part of the investigation and denied any wrongdoing, she'd called a deputy from the attorney general's office civil division to accompany her to the interview. All constitutional officers, such as governor and controller, are assigned a deputy from the attorney general's office to represent them on matters in their office that require legal review. In this case, Kathy called upon the deputy attorney general, Shane Chesney, for advice in the face of the investigation. This would complicate matters immensely, because in essence it meant she'd been represented during the interview by the same agency that had been investigating her.

"There were mistakes made that in a normal case wouldn't have been anything, but they were made into a big issue," Gardner said. "If there was one thing I wished we could do over, it was the interview of Kathy. [The attorney general's office investigators] called up her office to schedule the interview, and unbeknownst to the investigators, she'd called her deputy attorney general counsel to be at that meeting. When Kathy called her deputy attorney general to the interview, the investigators saw this deputy sitting there, and they didn't know what to do. Nothing she said during the interview was of any materiality, but Dominic [one of Kathy's attorneys] was able to rave about it to make it sound like some convoluted conspiracy."

In fact, Kathy's attorney Dominic Gentile was making the case that the entire impeachment would be invalid because of that apparent conflict.

"Chesney advised Augustine against waiving her right to be silent and asked her questions and had her expand upon her answers to the attorney general," Gentile told the Eureka, Nevada, *Sentinel* newspaper, in explaining what he viewed as the significance of the conflict.

Gardner said, however, he had no reservations about pursuing the impeachment further in the assembly. The law required it.

"I had an important responsibility to do this right," Gardner said. "It was not a good thing for anybody. It was an unfortunate thing for everyone. For her, for our office, and for the people."

The Assembly Speaker, Richard Perkins, a Democrat, headed the Nevada Assembly's impeachment proceedings in 2004 alongside Democratic Majority Leader Barbara Buckley. Perkins is a tall, dignified man with blondish hair who is also a longtime police officer in Henderson, Nevada. He rose all the way to the top of the Henderson

Police Department, and then he rose to the head of the state assembly. At the time of Kathy's impeachment, he was considered one of the most powerful men in Nevada and a possible candidate for governor one day.

The assembly proceedings would not allow Kathy's attorneys to cross-examine her accusers, and witnesses read prepared statements. A committee would hear the allegations and determine whether the allegations should be organized in an article of impeachment document to be voted on by the entire assembly. Perkins defended the process, saying the committee members would ask questions of witnesses after the statements were read and that if the full assembly approved the Articles of Impeachment for Kathy, she would still get her day in court, so to speak, in a full trial in front of the Republican-controlled senate.

Without the ability to cross-examine witnesses and challenge their credibility, Kathy's attorneys said the process was being rigged. The defense attorneys refused to call any witnesses, and Gentile called the process "polluted" by politics.

The impeachment proceedings opened on November 10, 2004, in the historic halls of the state assembly building. The assembly was packed with an astonishing number of journalists: one hundred and thirty-one reporters and related media staffers. The *Las Vegas Sun* newspaper alone brought seventeen reporters, producers, and staffers to the spectacle.

"As we move into this proceeding, let me just indicate to everybody that this is a legislative committee and not a court of law," Perkins said. "The rules of evidence are, as many of you well know, much different in the legislative setting. The committee will receive testimony from witnesses. . . . Any testimony given will need to be relevant to this proceeding and the actions of Controller Augustine.

There will be no cross-examination, as you would find in a court of law. Again, this is a committee hearing."

Prosecutor Gerald Gardner presented Perkins with a list of eight witnesses, and a binder with forty-two exhibits, including the computer records from Kathy's office, was entered as evidence. Gardner then gave a statement.

"We are here today to uphold the Nevada Constitution," Gardner said. "Article 7 of the Nevada Constitution provides that state officers shall be liable to impeachment for misdemeanors and malfeasance in office.

"Kathy Augustine had no authorization whatsoever to make state employees work on her private campaign on state time," the prosecutor said. "She had no authorization to use state facilities and equipment and computers to run her campaign out of her state office. Kathy Augustine's acts fall squarely into the category of malfeasance—the commission of acts that are unlawful in themselves, [and] which are completely unauthorized, illegal, and wrongful. Kathy Augustine, from approximately October 2001 to November 2002, literally ran her campaign headquarters out of the Nevada State Capitol."

Gardner told the legislators that "former and current employees of the Controller's office . . . will lay this case out for you. They will testify how state employees were directed to keep track of campaign donations, write campaign speeches, create invitations to fund-raisers, keep lists of lobbyists, attend campaign events, deliver campaign stump speeches, and hand out campaign literature, all on state time, all while their salaries were being paid out of the state treasury.

"You will hear how Kathy Augustine's demeanor and treatment of her employees caused them to believe that they had no choice but to obey her commands to do her campaign work; how employees who refused to comply with her demands to do her campaign tasks were berated, belittled, and, ultimately, shunned from Kathy Augustine's inner circle."

Gardner reiterated to the forty-two assembly members present and Perkins that the proceeding was "not a criminal trial" and did not require proof beyond a reasonable doubt. All that was required was that a majority of the assembly vote that there was sufficient evidence to issue the Articles of Impeachment, or charges, which in turn would prompt a trial before the senate.

"Kathy Augustine's stipulations [to the Commission on Ethics] are, in themselves, sufficient to support impeachment on three Articles of Impeachment," Gardner said.

Gardner's testimony ended, and the assembly called Jeanette Supera, a chief deputy investigator with the Nevada Attorney General's Office, to testify. Supera has been an investigator since 1983, specially trained in examining computer systems for evidence. On February 18, 2003, Supera said she was asked by another investigator at the attorney general's office to examine twelve computer floppy discs that had been provided to the attorney general's office by former employees of the state controller's office. She was also asked to examine a Zip drive that had been obtained from the state computer system that contained backup data from the controller's office.

"Before examining these discs, I knew absolutely nothing about this case," Supera said. "It took me approximately two weeks to conduct the full forensics examination. In examining all of these discs, I found dozens and dozens of documents that appeared to be related to a campaign and reelection for state Controller Kathy Augustine."

The next witness was one of Kathy's chief accusers, her former executive assistant, Jennifer Normington. She politely read for the assembly her written statement.

"I must preface my remarks with the statement that I am not here today as a 'disgruntled employee,' as I have been characterized by Ms. Augustine in statements to the press," Normington said. "In fact, contrary to what she told reporters when first questioned about the charges several months ago, I did not file a complaint with the attorney general's office. Rather, I turned over documents, on the aforementioned twelve floppy discs, to be reviewed at the attorney general's discretion. I did seek counsel from the State Department of Personnel in late summer of 2002 because I believed I was being forced to violate state ethics guidelines, but [I] was informed by them that the only way they could provide assistance was to help me find another position, which ultimately led to my departure from the controller's office in February 2003.

"In any case, my appearance is not as someone seeking retribution . . . [for] a former supervisor, but as a former state employee who was forced to break the law under the implicit threat of loss of job," Normington said.

Normington said she'd first met Kathy Augustine in December 2001, when Normington was giving a luncheon address on presentation skills and image management to the Carson City Republican Women's Club. They were seated next to each other at the head table. Kathy was impressed with Normington and invited her to the controller's office to discuss the possibility of Normington becoming her executive assistant. Kathy was especially interested in capitalizing on Normington's public-speaking and speech-writing skills to assist in promoting the public image of the controller's office. Normington was offered a job within a day.

"When I first started work, Ms. Augustine was traveling in Europe," Normington told the assembly. "I was trained by her former assistant, Susan Kennedy. . . . When Kathy returned to the office two weeks later, I was immediately asked to perform various campaign support duties, which I initially agreed to without question. . . . I do not recall whether or not the controller initially asked me to perform the work on my own time or not, but, as a matter of practice, I tried to do so because my workday hours were busy with regular, non-campaign-oriented duties."

Normington said that at first, she obliged her boss's request to perform campaign work, but as time passed, Kathy's requests grew more extensive.

"I also began compiling . . . the donor tracking reports that needed to be submitted to [the Secretary of State's Office]," Normington said. "On occasion, the controller did mention that campaign work should be performed on my own time, which is to say before 8:00 a.m. when I started work and after 5:00 p.m. But the increasing workload and increasingly short due dates imposed on me by the controller meant I could no longer perform all of these duties in my so-called off time."

Making Kathy's demands even more trying was the fact that Normington had a diabetic cat that needed insulin twice a day. The state employee had hoped for understanding from Kathy about the pet, but instead the situation "became problematic vis-à-vis the controller's priorities," Normington said. "Often, I was forced to work on the campaign during my scheduled work hours, after which the controller would tell me I could not go home until my regular state work was completed. . . . [T]he controller became incensed if I told her that I had to be home by 7 p.m. [and] told me, 'That cat is interfering in your life. You need to kill it.'"

Normington said she gradually came to realize she was spending most of her official hours working on the controller's election campaign, and she was unable to get caught up on her regular workload by skipping lunches and staying late.

"I became concerned that I was in gross violation of the law," Normington said. "I still tried to do what I could during off-hours, but often the controller would fax me handwritten notes from her Las Vegas office midmorning and want them fleshed out into full campaign speeches and faxed back by early afternoon. Or she would review a report that was due to the secretary of state's office and want it updated within a few hours or a few minutes. Given the frequency with which the controller gave me campaign work in the middle of my workday with a same-day deadline, it is clear that she was fully cognizant that I was working on her election campaign during state time and on state-owned office equipment. Campaign-related work I performed at Ms. Augustine's request on state time included, but are not limited to, writing campaign speeches; delivering campaign speeches; attending community and Republican events; organizing fund-raisers; maintaining a database of potential contributors; creating invitation lists for fund-raisers based on geographical location; formatting request-for-contribution letters and mailing them all over the United States; designing fund-raising invitations; and stuffing envelopes and mailing them to contributors."

Normington portrayed the controller's office as a political machine and Kathy as a woman who expected her staffers to support her ambitions. Normington recalled that in one instance, it was briefly discussed that Kathy would hire someone to handle all the political work for her reelection campaign that Kathy's state employees were doing. When weeks passed and no one was hired, Normington asked Kathy why not.

"She told me, 'I do not have enough money to hire any staff. We are going to run everything out of this office,' "

Normington quoted Kathy as saying. "Another time, the controller asked me to begin e-mailing reminders of upcoming fund-raising events to a database of prospective contributors. I suggested to her that it might not be appropriate to send such a message from the controller's e-mail address. She responded, 'Are you refusing to do something I have told you to do?' I told her no, that I was just offering a concern about appearances. Ultimately, she agreed with me and told me to e-mail the database and event schedule to her daughter to send out."

Normington said Kathy always instructed her to carry contribution envelopes to Kathy's public speeches as controller, and Normington was ordered to "remind the audience to vote for [Kathy] in November" after Kathy's speech was over.

"The one instance when I was not able to remind them to vote, I was chastised for it enormously," Normington said. "As I grew more and more concerned about my involvement in what I believed to be unethical campaign practices, I began to consider what to do about it. About that time—I think it was somewhere in the June 2002 time frame—Judy Hetherington, from the controller's Las Vegas office, told [Kathy] she wanted to stop attending campaign events because she was uncomfortable doing so on state time. The controller told us in the capitol office that, while that might be OK for the Las Vegas office, that was not the way it was going to work up here . . . [in Carson City]. She told us that, since we were unclassified employees, our job security for the next four years depended on us helping her get reelected."

Normington said the issue of state employees doing Kathy's political work came to a head when Kathy's chief deputy controller, Jim Wells, refused to comply with a request to compile Kathy's political donations and file the list with the Nevada Secretary of State's office.

"[Kathy] became enraged by his refusal," Normington said. "She started yelling and throwing things around the office and said to me, 'Jim is no longer in the circle. You, Jeannine, Sherry, Judy—you guys are in the circle. I just wish I could fire him now, but I will have to wait until after the election or it will look like retaliation.' Fortunately for Jim, he located alternate employment and resigned on his own initiative. But, based on this event, I knew that, as a mere secretary, I would be fired in a heartbeat if I did not comply with the controller's demands."

Normington was concerned she was breaking the law by doing Kathy's political bidding. She went to the Nevada Personnel Department to see if she could get a transfer. Because she was an unclassified employee with limited time with the state, she was told she had limited rights and that the personnel department had no authority over the actions of constitutional officers such as the controller.

"They offered to help me find another position, but I was unable to secure a new job until the following January," Normington said.

Normington portrayed Kathy as someone riveted by the challenge of collecting political donations that dwarfed her opponents. She said Kathy would sit "at her desk midday calling donors to pressure them for more money. She routinely reviewed donation . . . tracking reports filed by her main opponent in the election as well as the state treasurer to see if they received larger donations than she did. If the donor made a larger contribution to either of these two people, she would call them asking for more money. She would then tell the contributor that if he or she expected access to the controller's office after the election, they needed to give her a larger donation. I know this to be fact, because the controller conducted these conversations in her office, over her speakerphone, with her door wide open.

"She even filmed a campaign commercial in her office during state working hours, using two state employees—myself and Jeannine Coward—to fill the seats in a mock conference," Normington said. "When Ms. Coward suggested that would be a violation of campaign ethics laws, we were told to keep our backs to the camera so no one could identify us."

Normington started to suffer health problems because of the stress that came with working for Kathy.

"I loved working for the state of Nevada and serving the public in my own small way," Normington said. "However, what I had thought was a career breakthrough turned out to be just the opposite. My health suffered greatly as a result of the stress I faced between Ms. Augustine's oppressive management style and the ethical conflict I faced on a daily basis. But the issue before this Body is not me. It is whether or not elected officials should be allowed to misuse public resources, as Ms. Augustine has, and still remain in office. Over the course of the 2002 year, I was forced to devote at least 75 percent of my state time to working on the state controller's reelection campaign. If that is not an impeachable offense, I do not know what is."

That last statement seemed to indicate that Jennifer Normington was not only offering testimony, but also actively advocating for Kathy's impeachment. Speaker Perkins immediately addressed the comment.

"Thank you, Ms. Normington, for your testimony," Perkins said. "I suppose, fortunately or unfortunately for us, it is our judgment that will determine whether or not we will issue these articles [of impeachment]."

Perkins proceeded to ask Normington questions about the work atmosphere in the controller's office.

"The threats were on a daily basis," Normington said. "If there was a mistake made in the office with a typographical error on a report, she would come out, throw it across my desk so it would slide across [and] hit me in the chest, and say, 'You had better get this right.' If she did not like the way my files were organized, she would say, 'Do you not have any secretarial office skills at all?' to which I responded to her on one specific occasion, 'I have office experience, but not as a secretary, just as a manager. You read my résumé.'"

Perkins questioned Normington as to whether she felt threatened with dismissal if she did not do Kathy's political work.

"She sent me an e-mail once asking that I provide her with the salaries for the chief deputy controller, the assistant controller, as well as my position," Normington recalled. "During that time, that was after Jim Wells had resigned and she was interviewing other candidates. I took that e-mail to mean that she was also looking to replace myself as her assistant and Jeannine Coward as assistant controller. Repeatedly, throughout the entire time I worked with her, she reiterated to me that I had better do everything I can to get her re-elected because, otherwise, I would not have a job."

Another assemblyman questioned Normington about how the computer discs documenting the campaign finance reports ended up in the hands of the attorney general.

"I copied the discs off of what was on the hard drive on my computer at the . . . controller's office," Normington said. "And, I turned those discs over to Jeannine Coward, who had an appointment with Attorney General Sandoval so he could review them and decide if any action should be taken on them."

The next witness called by Perkins was Kathy's former assistant controller, Jeannine Coward. The woman is professional by all accounts, and she has worked with several Republican political campaigns in Nevada. She worked as a state employee for Kathy from February 8, 1999, to January 31, 2003. She started off her testimony by addressing how the computer discs ended up at the attorney general's office. She said she made the decision to get the discs to the attorney general's office in consultation with Normington.

"When I knew I was going to resign from the controller's office, and I knew Jennifer was going to move over to another office in the state government, we had some serious discussions about what had taken place during the prior year and a half and all of the campaign work that was done on state time," Coward said. "And, we seriously discussed, do we owe our loyalty to our boss, who hired us, or do we owe our loyalty to the citizens of this state? Ultimately, we decided we owed our loyalty to the citizens of this state, and it was our responsibility to report the misdeeds of the controller.

"I directed Jennifer to copy all of the campaign files that were on her computer, on the C drive," Coward said. "I copied all of the campaign material that was on my computer, on the C drive. Those were the twelve discs that we delivered. I also found out, at that time, that every Friday night they would back up the F drive, which was the controller network where we could access anyone's files that were in the controller's office. It was normal procedure, . . . after about three weeks, to just copy over those files. The day I left, I instructed the person in the basement who made the file copy not to destroy that file, not to copy it over. That, at some point, it might be very important because it would be the key evidence that would show that the computer files that we were going to give to the attorney general's office were not copied off of home files and transferred to our computers at . . . [work]. That they were, in fact, files created at the computer's office that would show the time dates, the stamps, times that they were edited, and whose computer they were initiated on, and then whose they were transferred to. So, I was the one who delivered the disc[s] to Brian Sandoval's office with the comment, 'I think the state controller may have broken the law, but I think it should be your decision to decide.' And, that was the last that I heard of it until I was called in for my first interview with them."

Jeannine Coward's testimony was convincing, and damning for Kathy.

"I believe [state controller Kathy Augustine] deliberately—and with little regard for the ethical standards of an official elected by the citizens of this state—required and expected certain employees of the state controller's office to work on her 2002 re-election campaign during normal working hours and, on their own personal time, after work," Coward said.

Coward portrayed Kathy as a tyrant prone to throwing tantrums over minor issues.

"Controller Augustine had a history and a reputation for losing her temper, throwing things, losing control by screaming and yelling when she was angry about something," Coward said. "[This] included anything from not being at your desk when she happened to phone you, to not liking the size of a label on an envelope [or] not liking the size of the font on a letter.

"Since the controller's personnel had seen and been a victim of these tantrums, everyone tried to do exactly as . . . [he or she was] told," Coward said. "Yelling in her office was also heard by the Treasury's Assistant and the Capitol Police on a regular basis."

It was an ominous sign for controller's office staffers, Coward said, when Deputy Controller Jim Wells refused to work on Augustine's reelection campaign. Wells later left the office in a move that Coward said "reaffirmed to other employees that controller Augustine was not to be confronted regarding campaign work on state time."

Coward testified that since Normington was the one who worked the most on Kathy's campaign, Coward encouraged her to address the issue of performing campaign work on state time with Kathy. Coward said Normington felt certain that if she complained about the campaign work, she would lose her job and be ostracized. Coward said the topic of whether it was appropriate for her to do campaign work on state time came up only twice in Coward's own conversations with Kathy. The first was in August 2001 when Kathy directed her to call a secretary of a lobbyist who was going to host a fund-raiser for Kathy in Las Vegas.

"I was supposed to get the details of the event," Coward said. "I had been waiting for the issue to come up, so I was ready with an answer, which was, 'I do not really think this is appropriate for me to do on state time, do you, Kathy?' Her response was [that] I should do it at 5 p.m. then.

"From that time on, I never questioned her again," Coward said. "Many times I took my office work home since I was expected to do campaign work during the day. The second time the issue came up was when she told me to have two women, who worked for me, stay late and stuff envelopes. Both of these women were classified employees, and I was not going to ask them to stay after work. I did ask them to help us during the lunch hour, stuff some envelopes, and that is what they did."

Coward said Kathy was inconsistent as a manager, and she employed double standards concerning work versus her campaign.

"She had no problem letting [my assistant] Sherry [Valdez] leave work early . . . to stuff envelopes, nor did she have a problem when she asked Jennifer and Sherry to stop by a jewelry store, after an event in Reno honoring administrative assistants, in order to check on a fund-raiser the owner of the jewelry store was having," Coward said. "But a year later, after the same event, when Sherry [and another controller's office staffer] returned late to the office, she screamed and yelled and told them that they had to take annual leave for going to the luncheon that she'd directed me to take them to.

"I personally drafted invitations, helped Jennifer with the campaign contribution reports, wrote answers for campaign questionnaires, made personal phone calls related to potential fund-raisers, and attended events during and after state hours," Coward said. "She also required me to fill out forms nominating her for awards. Also, the controller wanted to have a presence at every event for which she received an invitation, including ribbon cuttings, award dinners, dedications, political functions, et cetera. The purpose of these events, I believe, was more related to her political ambitions and increasing her personal visibility than it was in representing the state controller's office."

The next witness was Susan Kennedy. Kennedy had worked at the controller's office as an executive assistant to Kathy from February of 2000 to September of 2001.

"I did fear for my job during that period of time," Kennedy said. "In June of 2001, my position moved from a classified status to an unclassified status, and, again, I felt my job was in jeopardy every day. During my time with the state controller's office, I was directed by Controller Augustine, on at least three occasions, to perform functions related to her campaign for reelection. I estimate this time frame occurred from October of 2000 throughout the remainder of my employment, and resulted in about sixteen hours of work."

Sherry Valdez, an accounting assistant with the state controller's office, was hired by Jeannine Coward in 2001, and her primary responsibility was debt collection. She, too, was involved in doing campaign work for Kathy.

"In 2002, I helped do a few campaign tasks for the controller during work hours and also off-work hours," Valdez said. "I also witnessed Jennifer Normington and Jeannine Coward doing campaign work during work hours. I saw Jennifer Normington working on campaign tasks almost daily. On one occasion, Jennifer, Jeannine, and myself stuffed envelopes for the campaign in the controller's office during work hours.

"On another occasion, I was also asked to attend a function with Jeannine, Jennifer, and the controller one evening in Incline Village," Valdez said. "We were going to attend the event and stay at Jeannine's home in Incline and return to work the next day. I did not find out until later, after I agreed to attend, that we were going to be staying up late after the event to stuff campaign letters for the controller."

Valdez said she personally witnessed the office's chief deputy controller, Jim Wells, get into a dispute with Kathy over Valdez being assigned to political functions.

"The controller assigned me a task working on some envelopes," Valdez said. "At the time she assigned me the task, I did not know it was campaign-related [work]. She brought the envelopes to my desk and gave me the instructions to black out with a marker some information on an envelope. I never questioned her."

Valdez said a few moments later, Wells saw Valdez working on the envelopes.

"He approached me," Valdez said. "He seemed very upset and said, 'You should not be doing that on state time.'

I explained that the controller just told me to do this task. He then said he would discuss this with the controller. A short time later, Jim returned looking very frustrated and went back to his office. I was never told by the controller to stop. I completed the job as requested and returned the envelopes to the controller."

The next witness to be called by Perkins was Michelle Miles. Miles is a Carson City resident who retired from the controller's office on December 13, 2004, after serving for twenty-seven and a half years. At the time of the retirement, she was chief accountant of operations, and her primary duties were to supervise the operation of the controller's office's accounting system.

"In the year 2002, during Kathy Augustine's run for re-election, it was a matter of common knowledge that state employees were working on the campaign during work hours," Miles said. "I personally saw state employees working on campaign envelopes for Kathy Augustine's re-election. I also learned from employees that they were being asked or told to work on Kathy Augustine's campaign.

"One of these employees was Jennifer Normington," Miles said. "Jennifer was Kathy Augustine's executive assistant during this time, [and] one of Jennifer's normal duties was to receive and route the mail and log in the incoming checks. It was important that Jennifer do this job to maintain the proper separation of duties regarding the handling of the checks. The people I supervised were not allowed to log in the checks. They would deposit the checks in the bank and then do the accounting for the checks.

"When I am talking about checks, I am talking about quarterly and monthly returns from all of the counties of the different revenues that they collect and send to the state," Miles said. "Jennifer was a competent and hardworking employee. However, it became clear that Jennifer was having trouble keeping up with her duties. Jennifer became so bogged down with Kathy Augustine's campaign assignments that she was unable to keep up with processing the incoming checks. Checks that should have been processed and deposited on the same day were not being deposited on time."

Miles said the controller's office became three to four days behind on depositing the checks.

"Jennifer came to me and complained that she could not keep up with the check responsibilities because she had too much campaign work to do for Kathy Augustine," Miles said. "Eventually, Kathy Augustine came to me and told me that Jennifer would no longer be processing the incoming checks because she was too busy with other work."

Jim Wells, the former chief deputy controller, would close the deal against Kathy in the Nevada Assembly. Wells is an accountant who was working for the Nevada Public Employees Benefits Program when he took the witness stand against Kathy. He had joined the state controller's office in 1998 and served as the chief deputy controller to Kathy from November 2001 to November 2002. His primary duties were to oversee the daily business of the operations, financial reporting, information technology, and financial systems of the controller's office. During Kathy's campaign for reelection in the summer of 2002, he said he frequently witnessed her executive assistant, Jennifer Normington, working on campaign-related matters during state hours.

"It was not uncommon to see Ms. Normington working on a stack of campaign fund-raiser event invitations or other campaign-related materials in her office," Wells said. "To the common person, it was obvious that Ms. Normington was working on campaign-related matters.

Ms. Normington was a dedicated and hardworking employee, and it was not uncommon for her to put in fifty- to sixty-hour work weeks. During peak periods of Ms. Augustine's reelection bid, I estimate that half of her time or more was spent on campaign-related activities."

Wells said he also witnessed Sherry Valdez, the debt-collection accounting assistant, working on campaign envelopes emblazoned with the logo "Augustine for Controller." Valdez, Wells said, was working with several stacks of these materials at her desk in the center of the Capitol Annex, and because of the openness of this area and the undeniable appearance that Valdez was working on campaign-related activities during work hours, Wells decided to confront Ms. Augustine.

"Upon entering Ms. Augustine's office, I reminded her it was inappropriate for these activities to be conducted during normal business hours," Wells said. "Upon hearing this, she replied, 'I did not tell her she had to do it on state time.' "

The implication of the testimony was clear. Kathy knew that it was inappropriate to have a state staffer doing campaign work, and she didn't seem to care that it was happening.

"To my knowledge, Ms. Valdez continued to work on that activity over the next several hours until it was completed," Wells said.

Wells said that in late 2002, Kathy came into his office and asked him to complete her campaign expense reports for filing with the secretary of state's office.

"The request was worded as, 'I need you to do something for me in your free time,' " Wells recalled. "And, the tone of her request was that associated with delegating a work assignment, as opposed to requesting a favor. I was concerned at that time it was improper for me to complete the report, but I did take the work home with me and consider her request overnight. After reviewing [state law], and considering the tone and manner of Ms. Augustine's request, I came to the conclusion it was inappropriate for me to complete the report on Ms. Augustine's behalf."

Wells drafted an e-mail the next day outlining his concerns about the assignment. The e-mail also included a message meant to be a subtle reminder to Kathy about the prohibitions regarding campaign-related activities being conducted on work time that were included in both the Nevada Administrative Code and the Controller's Office Policy and Procedures.

"The e-mail was an attempt to inform Ms. Augustine that not all the staff considered their campaign assignments as voluntary," Wells said. "Ms. Augustine responded to the e-mail by portraying me as a disgruntled employee and criticizing my lack of commitment to her re-election campaign, stating that others had had to pick up the slack on my behalf. To my knowledge, Ms. Augustine requested and Ms. Normington completed the expenditure report for submission to the secretary of state's office. Ms. Augustine was clear in stating that the report should be completed on my free time, and I do estimate that it would have taken ten to fifteen hours to complete that task."

Wells said he knew his relationship with Kathy was "finished" after he refused to fill out the campaign finance reports.

"She barely spoke to me unless it was necessary for state business, and her [previously] frequent visits to my office all but ceased," Wells said. "She also reportedly stated to Ms. Normington that she would have fired me if she thought she could have gotten away with it. Our relationship was strained to the point where I felt no other option but to resign. I had worked for the state of Nevada for ten years at the time these events took place. I worked my way up through the ranks and considered this to be an important position and a dream job for myself.

"I resigned after the 2004 elections and took a cut in both pay and prestige in accepting a job with the City of Roanoke, Virginia," Wells said.

The culmination of the testimony was a death knell for Kathy. The assembly voted unanimously to impeach Kathy.

Kathy's attorneys reiterated their belief that their inability to cross-examine witnesses made the hearing unfair.

"Basically what they did was create pure hyperbole in their canned presentations to the Assembly," Arrascada said of the witnesses in an interview with the *Review-Journal*. "The Senate is a more deliberative body where we will be able to conduct proper and effective cross-examination and address their credibility and their biases."

12 ... SENATE

We thank You, Lord, that there is no weather in heaven.
Let not the cold of this day get into our hearts or minds.
May we be warm and cheerful, secure in the knowledge
that You are still here, that no clouds can blot You out,
no rain, sleet, or snow drive You away. As winter blows
her icy breath along the city's streets, our love goes out
to all who need encouragement, to all who lack food and
clothing, to all who are cold and cheerless, to all who long
for home and friendship. Help us, in our blessedness, to
be more willing to share the good things of life. Give us
generosity and concern for others that shall mark us as
Your disciples.
Amen.

—Prayer by Senate Pastor Albert Tilstra at Kathy Augustine's
   senate impeachment trial, December 2004

Kathy Augustine's impeachment trial in the senate commenced just as a bitterly cold and snowy weather system
bore down on Carson City on December 1, 2004. The senate
appointed a special prosecutor, Dan Greco, a twenty-year
prosecutor with the Washoe County Chief Deputy District
Attorney's Office, to oversee Kathy's prosecution, given
state senators' plans to call prosecutor Gerald Gardner as a
witness as well as clear indications that Kathy's attorneys,
Dominic Gentile and John Arrascada, were trying to make

an issue of the attorney general's office's independence in the proceedings. The defense attorneys, in addition, complained about their inability to cross-examine witnesses in the assembly. Gentile promised the *Las Vegas Sun* newspaper that things were going to be different for Kathy during her trial in the senate.

"Anytime I have a right to confront and cross-examine and discredit a witness, I've got what I need," Gentile told the paper. "I sure as hell didn't have that [in the assembly]."

Greco's task in the senate was to present evidence that would secure a conviction of Kathy on the three charges of "malfeasance" outlined in the Articles of Impeachment forwarded to the senate by the assembly. Greco needed only two-thirds of the twenty one legislators in the senate to obtain a conviction.

The proceedings actually started with what amounted to a pretrial hearing on November 29 in front of a senate committee. Arrascada argued what he portrayed as technical flaws in the charges. He questioned the validity of the witness accounts against Kathy, and he told senators the prosecution was overkill, given that she'd already been beaten up by the Commission on Ethics and admitted to the violations in that venue.

"Removal from office is simply not necessary or just based upon the law and evidence in this case," Arrascada said. "No matter how dissatisfied her accusers are with the way they have been treated, Kathy Augustine has done nothing to harm the citizens who elected her."

Gentile reminded the legislators and attorneys that they were making history and that the legislators would be sitting in judgment of another legislator. Gentile described it as a true jury of one's peers.

"No impeachment has ever taken place based on the

facts such as those alleged in the Articles of Impeachment before you," Gentile said, adding that "the Commission on Ethics did not find this case to be of the magnitude to impose the maximum fine; therefore, how can you even contemplate impeachment and removal from office?"

Questions quickly surfaced from the senators about the validity of the assembly proceedings. Kathy found an ally in the form of a Democrat, longtime state senator Bob Coffin, who clearly seemed baffled by the methods used for the assembly hearing. He questioned why the witnesses in the assembly hearing were not separated from one another during the hearing. It seemed to the senator, in watching the proceedings in the assembly, that the charges were already drawn up against Kathy before the hearing in the assembly had even started.

"Looking at the assembly process, I was amazed at the methods used and the construction of the Articles of Impeachment," Coffin said. "The witnesses were sitting in a group and allowed to converse among themselves. I surmised they were discussing the case. In addition, the witnesses were allowed to observe the testimony of each other. It was my assumption the assembly operated under the pretense they did not need the testimony of the witnesses, and the Articles of Impeachment had been prepared in advance of the testimony. If that is the case, why should we go through the guilt phase, then the trial phase, and last the penalty phase? Why all these different phases if guilt has . . . already been predetermined by the assembly?"

"Senator Coffin, the Controller's guilt has not been determined," Greco responded.

A motion to dismiss the charges was eventually tossed by a vote of twenty to one in the senate. Kathy entered a plea of not guilty through her attorneys, and opening statements in the trial kicked off December 1. Gentile, Arrascada, and

Kathy all believed they had a shot at winning and clearing Kathy's name, but that shot depended largely on the cross-examination of Kathy's accusers.

"It is an honor and a privilege to address you in this unique and historic constitutional exercise," Greco told the senators in his opening remarks of Kathy's impeachment trial. "The evidence presented in the state's case will show that four employees were directed to do campaign work during normal office hours on the taxpayers' dime. They did as they were told because they were afraid of losing their jobs, afraid of retaliation, afraid of the controller of the state of Nevada, [and] Kathy Augustine's famous temper, which, as you will see, could explode instantly for no good reason.

"In its simplest terms, the state's evidence will show you that the controller's office was, in fact, campaign central for Controller Augustine for 2002."

Arrascada, in his opening statement, said the movement to kick Kathy out of office should have stopped with the Commission on Ethics' plea deal.

"Why are we here?" Arrascada said. "That question has been asked throughout this legislative building from the beginning. Why are we here? None of you wants to be here; Controller Augustine never envisioned she would be here, nor does she want to be here. . . . The Ethics Commission decided the evidence by preponderance. What is important is that you have a higher burden. The burden to do justice."

The defense agenda became perfectly clear in Arrascada's opening remarks. Gentile and Arrascada were going to portray Kathy's accusers as people who hated her because of her bullying management style. As a result, those accusers were now dead set on destroying her. Arrascada told the senators that Jeannine Coward was angry with Kathy because she'd been removed from the position of supervisor of the controller's office debt-collection program.

The attorney produced a letter for senators that Coward wrote to Kathy describing her removal from the debt-collection program position.

"[Coward] stated on the last page [of her letter], 'The decision made regarding debt collection was seen by staff as a demotion for me, and the fact that you told some that you offered me the accounting position under [another staffer] was even more humiliating,'" Arrascada said. "We are here because an employee became humiliated and felt she was demoted.

"[The accusers] find fault in every action [Kathy] does, which you will see throughout Jeannine Coward's statements," the attorney said. "Jeannine Coward said something [else that was] significant in her statement to the attorney general. She stated . . . in her statement, 'Kathy Augustine wants higher office. She does not deserve it. She should be stopped.'

"But why is Controller Augustine here?" Arrascada continued. "Controller Augustine is here because she had courage to not favor employees who did assist on her campaign. . . . We know Controller Augustine may be many things, but one thing we do know for sure is she is not dumb. As you hear the testimony, and the fact [that] there was a reprimand, ask yourself, if this was a terrible plot, a nefarious plot, that Controller Augustine planned to carry out . . . would she punish her co-conspirator? The answer is no."

Arrascada acknowledged Kathy had a "unpopular personality," one that had "a polarizing effect," but he said "a bad personality and being mean in office do not rise up to the level [of] impeach[ment] and remov[al] from office."

Stacy Jennings, the director of the Commission on Ethics, was the first witness of the trial. She testified about Kathy's stipulations to the ethics violations. The next witness was controller's office management analyst Susan Kennedy, who reiterated the same allegations she lodged at Kathy in the assembly, though she added a few more details and twists. She said that Kathy had changed her position and that of four others from "classified" to "unclassified," meaning the employees had less job security. Kennedy implied that this was a move to allow Kathy more control over her employees. She said Kathy also directed her to solicit donations from area construction companies to pay for the controller's trip to Harvard for an educational class and that Kathy was even willing to hawk Asian pearls from her office for the purpose of bringing in campaign cash. Ten percent of the take from the pearls sale by a pearl dealer invited to the controller's office went directly into Kathy's campaign coffers, Kennedy said.

"I resigned because it was very hard to work for Controller Augustine," Kennedy said.

Kennedy said she just didn't feel it was right to perform Kathy's political tasks, such as keeping track of her campaign contributions, while being paid by taxpayers, and she documented why she thought Kathy was a bully.

"In the very beginning of the employment, I was ostracized at least six times a day," Kennedy said. "You know, I did not file this record right, I did not type this record right, I was not going fast enough. There was one day where I was in her office and she said, 'You know, if you were working for any other elected official, you'd be fired.'

"The last thing I remember, she screamed at me one day over the telephone in her car because I had told the assistant controller about an appointment first instead of telling Controller Augustine about the appointment first," Kennedy said. "Controller Augustine also talked to me about campaigning in the months coming up. She really wanted me to campaign with her out in Elko. She could hardly wait to show me the scenery and have me meet people out there. I knew I did not want to go there."

Gentile cross-examined Kennedy and pointed out that Kathy had signed off on a positive job performance review for the woman. He also produced a greeting card from Kennedy to Kathy that said, "For a fabulous boss, Kathy. . . . Hope your day is a great one. You're the best." In addition, Kennedy acknowledged that Kathy, when asking her to perform campaign work, said, "Try to do it after work; try to get it done after 5 p.m."

Another management analyst at the controller's office, Judith Hetherington, testified that she considered Kathy Augustine her friend. However, Hetherington testified that Kathy had asked her on one occasion, via e-mail, to put labels on campaign envelopes. Hetherington bluntly responded to the e-mail by saying she was prohibited from doing so.

"I would not be able to assist her with that because it was on state time. It was against our policy, and I would not be able to do it," Hetherington recalled.

The e-mail exchange was entered as evidence by Greco, and it offered insight into the way the campaign requests were being made by Kathy of her employees. The requests were usually bundled in the middle of other routine, non-political tasks. The first e-mail was sent from Kathy to Hetherington on March 5, 2002, at 4:59 p.m.:

I hope your schedule is light enough on Friday morning to assist me in labeling and stamping two hundred and fifty envelopes. I have both the return and addressee labels ready to go. I will pick up the invitations and the RSVP cards around noon at Century Graphics and then my friend Jenny and I will get them stuffed Friday afternoon. I will put them in the mail before I leave on Sunday. I also have the calling list. Hopefully you can drop it off at State headquarters on West Sahara and Durango sometime next week. Did Jennifer tell you I was scheduled to speak at the county convention on Friday night at 6:15 p.m. at Castaways? Also I will be coming down again on the 18th for the DRI [Desert Research Institute] dinner at Caesar's Palace since I will miss their dinner here in Reno on the 20th. Will you please RSVP to the NDA [Nevada Development Authority] breakfast for me on the 19th at the Stardust, and for both of us for the Women's History tea at the Las Vegas Academy . . . ? Thanks. Did you want to join us for dinner on the 20th with Tom Creal and Mark Doyle from Prime Recovery?

Hetherington responded to the e-mail on the following day at 11:17 a.m.:

Good [m]orning. I have made your reservations for the NDA breakfast on March 19th and the Women's History tea. . . . I will not be able to attend the tea with you as I am taking a class that day and it is not over until 3:30 p.m. Will attend the dinner on the 20th. Where, when, etc.? Has Jennifer RSVP'd for the DRI dinner on the 18th at Caesar's Palace? Or do you want me to do that? Regarding the envelopes since our employee manual states 'No employee shall engage in political activity in or about the office of the state controller during the hours of state employment,' I feel that I should not work on your campaign at the office. I believe this is also in the Nevada Revised Statutes.

Government employees' working on campaigns during
working hours has been an issue in some past races
and I would not want it to have a negative impact on
your reelection. But I will be happy to drop off the call-
ing list to the state headquarters on my way home from
work. Hope you are having a great day. Jh.

Hetherington was willing to stand up to Kathy. Kathy
called her on the phone the next day and said she didn't
mean to imply that the work was to be done on state time.

"She said she did not mean for me to put aside my regular work. She thought I could do it on my break," Hetherington said, adding that break time was still state time, and
she thought Kathy was trying to backtrack on her original
e-mail request. Arrascada questioned Hetherington about
whether Kathy ever ostracized her or yelled at her for not
performing the campaign tasks. She never did. Instead,
Hetherington was promoted and got a raise.

The next witness, Sherry Valdez, recounted how she
was asked to attend a speaking engagement in Incline Village and then was expected by Kathy to stuff eight hundred envelopes while staying the night at Coward's house.
She estimated the total amount of state time she'd spent on
Kathy's campaign as a "few hours," but, Valdez said, she
saw Jennifer Normington doing campaign work for Kathy
almost daily.

Michelle Miles, the twenty-seven-year veteran of the
controller's office, also said she'd seen Valdez stuff "a lot"
of Kathy's campaign envelopes. That was the entirety of
her direct examination testimony against Kathy. Under
cross-examination, Miles said that she never went to the
attorney general's office to complain about Kathy. Instead,
they came to her.

The following morning, on December 2, Jim Wells

was called to testify. Wells reiterated what he'd said in the assembly: that he'd witnessed Normington and Valdez performing Kathy's campaign tasks and that he'd been asked to prepare Kathy's campaign contribution reports. He found the request to be inappropriate.

"Our office manual prohibited those activities," Wells said.

Wells read for the senators his e-mail to Kathy declining to compile the report, and it seemed to be a polite, reasoned notification to Kathy that she could not mandate her employees to do her political bidding. The e-mail was sent to Kathy on August 1, 2002:

Kathy, while I don't mind preparing your campaign expense report, I do not appreciate feeling like it is a condition of employment because it isn't. If it was a job requirement, it would violate Nevada Administrative [S]tatute 284.770 as well as our office policies, whether you require it to be done during or after office hours. Since I am a salaried employee, I don't have fixed hours. I get a job done. Requiring me to complete the report qualifies as work, and as such violates the prohibition of engaging in political activity during the hours of an employees' employment. However, if you ask me to prepare the report on my own time, and I agree, there is not a problem. It is all in how you ask. Free time is a valuable and limited commodity. Many of us have outside interests and hobbies, which quickly fill up what free time we have. When I or any other member of your staff volunteer our time to assist you either with your campaign or by attending an event on your behalf, we do it because we want to [and] not because we have to. We all have to be able to choose what we do during our free time without fear of repercussion. If

a member of your staff does not want to do something,
they should be able to tell you, and you need to respect
their decision. I cannot speak for others, but the more
you expect, the less I feel like volunteering. This is just
some information I needed to share with you.

"I thought very hard about it before I sent it," Wells said
of the e-mail.

"Was it difficult for you at the time to actually press
your send button and send it to Controller Augustine?"
Greco asked.

"Yes," Wells replied.

After the e-mail was sent, there was an obvious change
in Kathy's demeanor and the way she treated him.

"Conversations, except for those required for day-to-day
activities, were all but cut off," Wells said, adding he'd
heard secondhand from Jennifer Normington that Kathy
wanted to fire him.

"[Normington] informed me Controller Augustine said
she would fire me if she could, but that she would have to
wait until after the election," Wells said. "I considered it
hellish during August, and I believe I actually resigned in
late September."

Under cross-examination, Gentile pointed out that
Wells had once left the office for another job, then returned
at Kathy's request. Wells also acknowledged that he was
the one who requested Jeannine Coward be replaced as the
supervisor over debt collection in favor of an accountant,
not Kathy. The defense attorney was trying to show that
Coward's alleged hostility toward Kathy, and her subsequent turning over of evidence against her to prosecutors,
was misguided and should have been directed at Wells.

Wells said he and others occasionally went to Kathy's
"public relations appearances, which in my personal opin-

ion were not necessarily tied to the job," but Wells said they weren't forced appearances by Kathy.

"They were just kind of something that was, you know, again, something that if we did it, that was great; if we did not do it, then, you know, there should not be any repercussions for it . . . because we want to do these things," Wells said.

"When you refused to work on this campaign, you were not fired; were you?" Gentile asked.

"No, I was not," Wells said.

"You do not know of one person, in all the years Controller Augustine has been state controller, who has ever been terminated by her; do you?" Gentile asked.

"No, I do not," Wells said.

"I do not have any further cross-examination," Gentile said.

Greco asked just a couple of questions on redirect of the witness.

"No one was fired by Controller Augustine; correct?" Greco asked.

"Not to my recollection, no," Wells said.

"But, many people left of their own volition; correct?" Greco asked.

"Yes."

"That is all I have," Greco said.

Jeanine Coward, the former assistant controller, was next. She was a critical witness because she had provided the computer evidence to the authorities and had posed the initial question to prosecutors of whether Kathy had broken state statute. Coward said Kathy was the person who hired her at the controller's office in February 1999. She described how she later helped craft the legislation that

Kathy Augustine was a rising political star in Nevada until some of her former employees alleged she was making them perform political tasks on state time. (Courtesy of the Alfano family)

Kathy was described by her brothers and parents as a sweet, caring child who was curious about everything. (Courtesy of the Alfano family)

Phil and Kay Alfano raised three children in Southern California and watched with great pride as their daughter Kathy became a high-ranking politician in Nevada. (Courtesy of the Alfano family)

Kathy Augustine and her third husband, Charles, are pictured in this family snapshot. Kathy's fourth husband, Chaz Higgs, was accused of poisoning her. Suspicions surfaced as to whether he could have poisoned Charles, too. (Courtesy of the Alfano family)

Kathy Augustine and her fourth husband, Chaz Higgs, a critical care nurse, are pictured together on a cruise to Alaska a year before Kathy's death. (Courtesy of the Alfano family)

Chaz Higgs at a press conference shortly after his wife became gravely ill. (Courtesy of *Las Vegas Review-Journal*)

Kathy Augustine posed for this newspaper snapshot that accompanied a story about her attempt at a political comeback in her bid to become treasurer of Nevada. She was murdered shortly after this photo was taken. (Courtesy of *Las Vegas Review-Journal*)

Kathy Augustine's bedroom in her Reno home is pictured in this police photograph. Augustine was found unconscious in the bed and rushed to the hospital because of what was originally believed to be a heart attack. (Courtesy of Washoe County evidence vault)

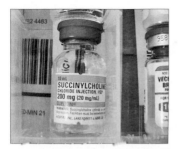

A bottle of succinylcholine is pictured in a police snapshot taken at a Reno hospital. Authorities accused Kathy Augustine's husband, Chaz Higgs, of using the powerful analytic agent to kill his wife. They suspect he accessed the drug while working as a critical care nurse.
(Courtesy of Washoe County evidence vault)

An autopsy photo depicts a slightly bruised area. Prosecutors and defense attorneys for Chaz Higgs later argued over whether the bruised area was an injection site. (Courtesy of Washoe County evidence vault)

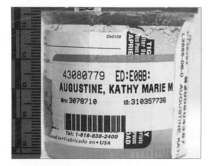

Kathy Augustine's urine sample was taken shortly after she was rushed to the hospital and fell into a coma in 2006. The Nevada politician died two days later, and authorities determined she was poisoned.
(Courtesy of Washoe County evidence vault)

Chaz Higgs addresses reporters during a press conference after his wife was found unconscious in the couple's home. Second from the left is *Las Vegas Review-Journal* reporter Ed Vogel. To the rear of Higgs is Kathy's brother, Phil Alfano Jr., and Kathy's daughter, Dallas Augustine. (Courtesy of *Las Vegas Review-Journal*)

Kathy Augustine's daughter, Dallas, speaks to reporters after her mother's death in a Reno hospital. (Courtesy of *Las Vegas Review-Journal*)

Dallas Augustine walks to a press conference after Kathy's death.
(Courtesy of *Las Vegas Review-Journal*)

Kathy Augustine's brother, Phil Alfano Jr., mourns the death of his sister
at her funeral in 2006. (Courtesy of *Las Vegas Review-Journal*)

Clark County Coroner Michael Murphy removes a dead rose from the casket of Kathy Augustine's third husband, Charles Augustine. Charles's body was exhumed in an effort to determine if he had been poisoned by Kathy's fourth husband, critical care nurse Chaz Higgs.
(Courtesy of *Las Vegas Review-Journal*)

Chaz Higgs is pictured in this police mug shot shortly after his arrest on charges he murdered his wife, Nevada politician Kathy Augustine.
(Courtesy of Washoe County evidence vault)

allowed for the creation of the successful debt-collection program that Kathy was always taking credit for during her public appearances on the campaign trail.

"During the 2002 campaign, did Controller Augustine tout the success of that debt-collection unit that you headed in her campaign?" Greco asked.

"That was probably her number-one accomplishment she talked about in her reelection campaign," Coward said.

"Did you ever consider yourself a campaign volunteer for Controller Augustine?" Greco asked.

"I did not," Coward said.

"Nonetheless, in the period of late 2001 and 2002, did Controller Augustine ever direct you to do campaign-related tasks?" Greco asked.

"Yes," Coward said. "The general tasks would be to help draft invitations. Sometimes to contact people who might give a [fund-raiser] and make the connections with them or to answer any questions about details for an event; filling out campaign questionnaires that candidates normally get. I think at the beginning of the campaign season, I just handed over some [discs] to Ms. Normington that were mailing lists that had been used in two previous campaigns I had worked on. They were somewhat outdated, but they established a base of people. The list could be edited and updated. There were Republican [w]omen's clubs, central committees, women that lived in [n]orthern Nevada—that kind of list."

Greco asked Coward to be more specific about Kathy's temper tantrums, and he inquired whether Coward feared a tantrum if she didn't perform the political work.

"[Kathy] could get very angry when she did not like something. She had thrown things at me before, when she did not like the way I wrote some notes for her for a speech," Coward said. "She slung them on my desk and told me that was not what she wanted. I suppose that was very cowardly, and I just took the easy way out and tried to go along."

Kathy, Coward said, was a supervisor who created "an atmosphere . . . where feedback or discussion was not welcomed or tolerated. If you did disagree, you might as well be talking to a blank wall. . . . It was obvious if you got on her bad side, she ignored you," Coward said. "It was one way of creating an atmosphere where people she did not like would leave on their own."

Arrascada handled the cross-examination, and it was clear from his first questions that he intended to scorch Coward with his portrayal of her as an angry, disgruntled woman out to get Kathy. He immediately asked about Coward being removed from the debt-collection program.

"[Kathy removed you from the position] because you were getting too much notoriety and popularity for the debt-collection program. Is that right?" Arrascada asked.

"No, I do not think that at all," Coward said.

"Would it surprise you to know it was actually recommended six months before to remove you from debt collection by Jim Wells and [another employee]?" Arrascada said.

"I had no knowledge of that," Coward said.

"Would it surprise you though, if you learned it just now?" Arrascada asked.

"I do not think I had thoughts of it either way," Coward said.

Arrascada questioned Coward about her history serving in the state assembly and as chief of staff for Nevada lieutenant governor Lonnie Hammergren. She'd also coordinated special events and meetings for Governor Guinn

while working on the governor's campaign, and she'd
worked on Congressman John Ensign's campaign as well.
The attorney was making a point that the witness herself
had done a lot of political work and had been actively
involved in politics, but she'd never filed any complaints
against those individuals.

"You also told [the attorney general's office] Controller
Augustine was not a very nice person?" Arrascada asked.

"Her screaming and yelling in the office to me indicated
that she could not be a very nice person. She could also be
a nice person," Coward said.

"After you left Controller Augustine's office, you were
very unhappy; is that correct?" Arrascada asked.

"For about a month, I was not pleased Controller Augustine had taken the job away from me without any discussion and made the decision without letting me have any
input into it at all," Coward said, adding, "I thought after
four years, I was deserving of a little more input in her
decision."

"You do not like her; do you?" Arrascada said.

"There is an old saying 'Love the sinner, but hate the
sin,'" Coward said. "I did not like the way she treated our
staff or me. It had nothing to do with my personal feelings
about her. As I have said, she can be very charming in a
social occasion. She was witty and a lot of fun to be with.
Someone you would want to be your best friend."

"When you interviewed with [the attorney general's
office investigator], you told him, 'She is not a very nice
person,'" Arrascada said.

"That is true," Coward said.

"When you met with the [attorney general's office
investigator], what really concerned you was that Controller Augustine could be elected to a higher office. In your

opinion, she did not deserve to?" Arrascada asked, adding Coward told the investigator, "She could be in Congress before we know it."

"I thought her behavior in our office indicated a complete lack of respect for the law," Coward said.

The next witness was Kathy's other major accuser, Jennifer Normington, who recounted all the allegations that she'd lodged against Kathy, including the details of the political work she was required to do for Kathy and the temper tantrums. There was no mention of the diabetic cat that Kathy had wished dead.

"I felt I had no option because of the way Controller Augustine treated me," Normington said. "The controller expects absolute perfection in all aspects in the controller's office, in her campaign work, in her assistants. We are expected to look appropriate, hair and makeup done. Everything has to be done perfectly. Otherwise, you are screamed at, you are yelled at, papers are thrown across the desks so they hit you. She on more than one occasion yelled at me and said, 'Can you not get anything right?' . . . She said, 'I do not care how long you have to stay here, tonight, to get everything done; I do not care if you have to sleep here; you are going to stay at your desk until everything is completed.' Because of that, I had no choice. If she told me to do something, I did it. If she told me to attend something, whether it was before work, during lunch, after work, on the weekend, I did it out of fear of what she would do and say to me when I returned to work if it was not done."

On the final day of Kathy's impeachment trial, the senators considered another motion to dismiss the charges by Gen-

tile, and this time, Kathy got a break. After her longtime
ally, Senator Bill Raggio, outlined for the senate the actual
standard of proof, the senators voted to dismiss one of the
three charges. Kathy, in the audience and wearing a sharp
blue business suit, seemed overjoyed. But when the senators continued their debate, they refused to dismiss the second and third charge in the Articles of Impeachment. The
attorneys were then asked to present closing arguments.

"You should not ignore the obvious, which is . . . the
Nevada Commission on Ethics stipulation," Greco said.
"In that stipulation, you can see she admitted to these
same two violations. In an Ethics Commission hearing, the
burden of proof is the preponderance of evidence. That is
not the burden in this case, but she has admitted to these
things. That is the strongest evidence before you.

Gentile told the senators that "the burden is to justice
according to the law and evidence.

"I have to ask you to ask yourself what public trust or
public interest is at stake here that needs to be protected—
some space on a computer?" Gentile said. "I suggest to you
that if you return the verdict of guilty on the articles of
impeachment that are based upon having personal information on your computer in a state office; then, you are
going to have a new administrative agency that is going to
be called the computer police. There is going to be monitoring, or there should be if you are going to apply this
fairly and equally to everybody in office. I ask you to think
about that."

Gentile suggested that Kathy be censured with a strong
letter of reprimand instead of impeached. That request
seemed to gain momentum when the senators debated
what to do with the charges against Kathy. Senator Bob
Coffin, a Democrat, went to bat for Kathy.

"The public does not know the difference between

impeachment and conviction," Coffin said. "We have put the stain of impeachment on Controller Augustine for the rest of her life. That is no small punishment. Forever, she will always be the 'former State Controller' impeached in 2004 by the Nevada State Assembly. This will always be with her name. She is a young person who will spend the rest of her life with this impeachment hanging over her head. In the public's mind, it is the same as conviction. I believe the impeachment process was not correct. The flaws are evident to all of us here that nearly every witness from the opposition was discredited in some fashion."

Coffin remarked that he did not like some of the political campaign tactics Kathy had used in the past, but he said that had no relevance to the proceedings of the day.

"None of us has been perfect angels in our campaigns, as none of us is a perfect angel in our lives," Coffin said. "That is why we are human beings and proud to serve. That is why we have been picked to be here. We did not hold ourselves up to such a high standard that we would then become like archangels. It cannot be bestowed on us."

Coffin said when he read the initial media accounts of the allegations against Kathy, he presumed she must be guilty. But after hearing the evidence, he criticized what he described as the media's mob mentality and the calls for her resignation.

"I became a bit worried about my own sentiments when, starting late in the summer, people were calling for her resignation," Coffin said. "They said she should go. She did something wrong. She admitted it. . . . [But] when you take someone who is a little unpopular and you single them out in a crowd, as her own party appears to be deserting her, it is easy to take these positions.

"I believe in acquittal," the Democrat said. "I believe

in a clean judgment. If you cannot convict, I believe in acquittal. Some have discussed censure. I have suggested an apology. She owes an apology to employees who she throws a piece of paper at. But did she hurt anyone? Did she hit anyone? Did she threaten anyone physically? No. Did she say, 'I will fire you?' No. Did she say, 'If you do not do this, I will fire you?' No. Has she fired anyone in the six years she has been there? By testimony, the answer is no. The street language is that maybe her bark is worse than her bite. The work of the office is being done. Every two years, an undercurrent comes forth to get rid of the office and to merge it into the Treasurer's Office. It could be that some of the resentment for this controller comes from the fact that she opposes that. She believes her office is a check. It is part of the checks and balances set up by the founders of this state."

It was a powerful, eloquent speech by all accounts, and it clearly helped Kathy. When the votes were tallied on one of the remaining two charges, eleven voted in favor of conviction and ten voted against. That tally fell short of the two-thirds vote required for a conviction, and another charge against Kathy was tossed. But on the final charge, Kathy was not so lucky.

On a vote of fourteen to seven, Kathy was found guilty of having "willfully diverted equipment and facilities for use in her campaign for reelection rather than for the interests of the general public whom she has been elected to serve."

Kathy was crushed. She openly sobbed in the senate chambers as the television cameras rolled.

The media, however, didn't view it as a defeat. Kathy had beaten two of the three charges, and the senate issued her a strongly written censure. Kathy was not kicked out of office. She would be allowed to finish her term as controller. Most of Nevada's newspapers portrayed the events as a win for Kathy and a defeat for the state's ethics laws.

Kathy told columnist Steve Sebelius afterward that she "absolutely" felt vindicated. Despite this, however, everyone predicted that Kathy's political career was now over. Everyone believed Kathy's political career was dead.

Everyone, that is, except Kathy Augustine.

Phil Alfano Jr. and his wife, Mary, had watched with dismay as Kathy was put through the political meat grinder via an impeachment. They were terribly saddened by what happened to Kathy, and they offered their support for her through the difficult time. They also decided that they weren't going to judge Kathy based on her decision the year prior to run off and marry right after Chuck Augustine's death. Phil Jr. found the move tasteless, but the couple also decided to give Chaz the benefit of the doubt because they loved and respected Kathy, and they wanted the best for her.

Phil Jr. and his wife invited the couple to their home in central California on more than one occasion, but there were some incidents with Chaz that, in retrospect, were concerning. The first was in late 2004, when Kathy and Chaz visited the Alfanos' home as the impeachment was proceeding against Kathy.

"There was an incident where Chaz and I went to the Department of Motor Vehicles together, and he was talking about how demanding Kathy [was]," Mary Alfano recalled. "I said, 'Yeah, well, that's Kathy. You married her.'"

When they returned home, Chaz and Kathy were bickering. Mary later talked to her sister-in-law briefly about the status of her marriage, and she said Kathy admitted she was unhappy. She said Chaz was threatening to divorce her.

"Kathy was like, 'You have no idea what is going on. You don't understand,'" said Mary Alfano, who questioned Kathy about why she didn't just divorce Chaz.

"'I don't want to be alone,'" Kathy told her.

"There was a lot of tension in that visit," Mary said. "I kept saying, 'Why are you with him?' She said she still wanted to have a companion, and she didn't want to go through another divorce."

Kathy told Phil Jr. something else that, in hindsight, was troublesome to Kathy's brother. Kathy mentioned her will and trust to her brother.

"She said, 'Did you get a copy of the trust in the mail? It should have been sent to you,'" Phil Jr. said. "I said, 'No, I haven't,' and my sister said, 'That's odd; the attorney said it was sent to you. Anyway, I just want you to know, Chaz is not to get a dime.'"

Phil Jr. asked his sister if Chaz knew he wasn't going to inherit anything if she died.

"She said, 'No, he doesn't,'" Phil Jr. recalled. "She said, 'Dallas will get a substantial amount of money, and I don't want to see her piss it away.'"

Phil Jr. said he didn't think much about the conversation at the time.

"My sister was in her late forties, and I wasn't thinking about her will," Phil Jr. said.

In January 2005, Chaz Higgs and his coworker Linda Ramirez continued to e-mail one another back and forth repeatedly for a brief period, but the hospital's Human Resources Department quickly stepped in to inform them that they were misusing hospital computers, and the content of the e-mails between the two was determined to be an inappropriate use of the hospital's resources. Chaz was suspended, and Ramirez was let go from her job. Ramirez said that the e-mails, along with the fact that she'd taken a day off from work without being sick, were the reasons the hospital fired her. But how did hospital HR even know that the two were e-mailing each other? According to Ramirez, it was because Kathy found out about her husband's friendship with the admissions clerk and reported her to hospital authorities.

"I believe his wife got ahold of the e-mails I had sent him and turned them in to human resources," Ramirez said.

Ramirez didn't hear from Chaz again until November 2005. By then, he was using a new e-mail address with the handle "Kumustakana," which means "How are you?" in Tagalog, the language of the Philippines, which Higgs may have learned while in the navy. In an e-mail sent to Ramirez on November 4, 2005, Chaz wrote that he had missed her every day and that "the other person" (i.e., his wife, Kathy) was driving him crazy. "It has been a nightmare. I am planning on leaving every day. I am looking for a place to live. There's so much I want to tell you. I did what I did with us to protect you from her. I did not want to. I had to. . . . It is a secret e-mail. Miss you."

Another e-mail Chaz sent to Ramirez in December read, "There are prying eyes here as always, so I will write more soon. *Miss na miss kita.*"

Ramirez said *Miss na miss kita* was Tagalog for "I miss you a lot."

Chaz wrote Ramirez again on December 8, 2005, telling her, "I have missed you every day and thought of you every day since we last spoke or saw each other. You touched my heart, and I want to be with you. I've never let go of the hope of being with you again. . . . I feel so much for you. I want to give you the world. You have made me feel things that I have never before. So I made a pact with myself that I would see you again and tell you how I felt. True feelings, true caring, true love only comes around once in a lifetime. I know the situation is not ideal, but you cannot hide true feelings regardless of the situation."

Again, he vented about Kathy:

"Let me say the other party in this is very vindictive and has a lot of power. She is incredibly controlling and wants to control everything in her life. She lost control of me when you came along and has not regained it since. She made my life a living hell in the past by manipulation and threats. . . . She is crazy. . . . She has the power to make peoples' lives hell if she wants." Chaz goes on to explain that he's decided to "live every day making her life a living hell. I live every day manipulating her and driving her crazy. It is working, and she wants to kick me out at the beginning of the year. I hate this woman, and I will make her break. . . . It is my quest in life to drive this bitch crazy. And it is working. She is losing her mind.

"I do not care anymore what she tries to do to me. I was scared before, but not anymore. I could not leave. She manipulated all of my friends. She manipulated the people I worked for. So I was stuck. But I have things in motion. . . . I will be free, and I will be with you. That is what I want. You have my heart. Chaz."

In late 2005, Kathy, Phil Jr., and Mary planned a couple's trip to Italy with Kathy and her husband. They knew Kathy needed a break in the aftermath of the impeachment proceedings, which crushed Kathy and left her exhausted. The trip plans included a rendezvous between the Alfanos and Kathy and Chaz at the San Francisco airport. The Alfanos were planning to drive their children to Oakland to put them on a plane to Long Beach so they could stay with Kathy and Phil Jr.'s parents, Kay and Phil Alfano Sr.

"We were packing, just about ready to go out the door, and the phone rang," Phil Jr. said.

Mary answered the phone. Kathy was on the other end of the line, and she was hysterical.

"She said, 'Where's Phil! I need to talk to Phil, and I need to talk to him right now,'" Mary recalled.

Phil Jr. got on the phone and was alarmed at what his sister told him.

"Apparently they were in the Sierra [Nevada mountain range], and I said, 'What's wrong? What is up?'" Phil Jr. recalled. "She was in tears, crying, and she was saying, 'I don't think we are going to go now.'

"I said, 'What's the matter?'" Phil Jr. said. "She said, 'It's Chaz! He's trying to kill us! He's trying to kill both of us!' She was very upset. I could hear her saying, 'Pull over; pull over!'

"I said, 'Kathy, what's going on, and what do you want me to do? Do you want me to meet you?'" Phil Jr. recalled. "She said, 'He's driving like a maniac, and he is trying to kill both of us!' She kept saying, 'He's trying to kill both of us!' I could hear him mumbling something in the background, like 'Ohh, we are going to be all right.'"

Phil Jr. asked Kathy what she wanted him to do. She kind of calmed down and ended the conversation without saying much more.

"I had never heard her like this," Phil Jr. said. "If you asked me if this sounded like someone who was in fear of her life, I'd say absolutely. That's why it was so disturbing."

"I had seen her mad, and this wasn't mad," Mary said. "She was hysterical."

Phil Jr. and his wife debated what to do next. Their trip to Italy seemed like it might not happen now, but they decided to start driving to Oakland anyway in the hope they would eventually hear from Kathy.

"So we are looking at each other, saying what are we going to do, and I said, 'Lets just get in the car,'" Phil Jr. said. "'We are going to be no worse off taking the kids to the airport and getting them on the plane. We are not going to be any further away in Oakland,' so we started on the trip, and we are trying to call Kathy a couple of times, and there is still no answer. That was even more disturbing."

Kathy eventually called Mary back and said she and Chaz would meet the Alfanos in San Francisco as planned. She said little more. The couples eventually met in San Francisco that night as planned, and the topic of the frightening phone call immediately came up.

"It was very awkward when we got to the motel," Mary said. "Chaz kind of pulled me aside and said, 'I'm sorry. I apologize. It was really no big deal. I was driving fast and she got upset.'

"I said, 'OK,' and Kathy was behind him," Mary said. "I said [to Kathy], 'Is everything OK?' She was looking at the ground and saying, 'Everything is OK,' but the tone of her voice was such where you wouldn't think things are fine."

Phil Jr. and his wife remained concerned, but Kathy and Chaz seemed to be getting along fine the next day when the couples flew to Italy.

"What was so strange was that then, for the rest of the trip, they did seem fine," Phil Jr. said. "They gave all appearances of a being a happy, loving couple. Holding hands and normal affection. There wasn't any arguing in front of us."

Mary said she thought Chaz was a little "odd" during the trip. She observed Kathy and Chaz having a minor debate about whether Chaz needed to head back to Las Vegas and the States early because of his work schedule at a hospital in Carson City.

"She made a few comments throughout the trip about how . . . [Chaz] wouldn't be there if it wasn't for her and how it was her money paying for it," Mary said.

There was one other episode on the trip, however, that Phil Jr. and his wife remember vividly. The moment unfolded during dinner at a restaurant stopover on a bus trip to Pompeii. Mary and Chaz were drinking some wine when Kathy basically ordered her husband to stop drinking.

"I didn't want any wine, and Kathy didn't want any wine, but Mary and Chaz were going to have some," Phil Jr. recalled. "So they bring out a small bottle of this wine, Tears of an Angel, and I pour some for Chaz, and I poured some for Mary. We're eating, having a fine time, and when I went to pour some more for Chaz, Kathy said he didn't need any more.

"I didn't say anything, and I just left it at that," Phil Jr. said. "So we are finishing our meal, and there is still some wine left, and I said, 'Come on, let's finish this up,' and I went to pour some for Chaz, and Kathy literally grabbed my hand, and I put the bottle down. I spilled some of it. She said, 'He doesn't need any more! He gets mean when he drinks, and he's on medication. He's not supposed to be drinking.'

"It was very awkward and I didn't know what to say," Phil Jr. said.

Chaz didn't say a word.

After the couples returned to the States, another incident happened, but the Alfanos did not know about it until after Kathy's death. It happened at a Christmas party held by one of Kathy's friends. During the party, Chaz offered the hostess's teenage daughter some marijuana. The teen's father found out about it and threatened to kill Chaz, but no one told Kathy about the incident.

"I think Kathy would have been very upset," Phil Jr. said. "Kathy was not a partier. She rarely drank."

On February 15, 2006, Chaz wrote Linda Ramirez via e-mail:

"Just wanted to say *mahal na mahal kita* ['I love you very much' in Tagalog]."

On February 18, Ramirez wrote back to Chaz:

"*Kalbigan ko kinakano ko.* How are things with the wife?"

Ramirez said the Tagalog reference in her e-mail means "I am your friend, and I want to sleep with you."

Despite the impeachment, Kathy Augustine wasn't going to go away quietly. She'd been trashed in the assembly hearing and emerged from the senate trial badly scarred, and she was hurt by it. She was impeached on only one of three charges and censured—not kicked out of office— but the entire affair was widely considered a lethal blow to her political career. Everyone knew that Kathy's role as the most powerful woman in Nevada was over. But Kathy was a fighter, and she was convinced that she could make a come-back. She wanted to restore her name and reputation. With her term as Nevada controller winding down, she made the surprise announcement that she was going to run for trea-surer of Nevada in 2006. It was hailed as a long-shot bid in the Nevada press, but Kathy was OK with that. Kathy was

back where she'd started in politics. She was on the outside and an underdog again. This was when she was at her
very best. She appeared on the Nevada political television
show *Nevada Newsmakers with Sam Chad* shortly after
announcing her bid for the state treasury job. She wore a
bright red suit and a stunning diamond necklace, and her
makeup was perfect. Kathy looked simply elegant, and her
strengths as a politician were once again abundantly clear:
she was tough, composed, convincing, and even charming as she deflected Chad's grilling questions about how
she could run for treasurer after the impeachment. Kathy
stood her ground throughout the interview. She said she'd
taken responsibility for the "mistakes" in the past but that
the scandal had been way overblown and that it was "time
to move on."

"It [has] been two years, and I apologized to the people
of the state," Kathy said. "I don't think that . . . [the media]
knew and the general public knew what actually had
occurred," Kathy told the reporter. "The way the investigation first came out in the press, it was much more egregious
than it [really] was.

"The whole process was very polluted," Kathy said of
the impeachment.

She also seemed to imply that the entire investigation
had been merely a political attack when she pointed out
that the attorney general's investigation into the ethics allegations didn't start until after she'd interviewed for the job
of U.S. treasurer.

"I was being interviewed for U.S. treasurer, and it [was]
just a couple of weeks later that the AG's investigators came
into my office and began their investigation," Kathy said.

Kathy had made a similar comment to the *Las Vegas
Review-Journal* during a press conference in December
2005.

"I had been interviewed in Washington, D.C.," Kathy was quoted as saying. "Secretary of the Treasury John Snow said: 'How soon can we get her confirmed?' Two weeks later, the nightmare began."

Another nasty Nevada political fight was still in store for Kathy, however. When it was announced that she was running for state treasurer, the Republican Party of Nevada, under the leadership of Chairman Paul Adams, made it clear that they wanted nothing to do with Kathy. Under no circumstances, Adams said, should the Republicans support someone with a stained record of impeachment. The move was controversial within the party, because a lot of Republicans throughout the state in 2006 truly liked Kathy and were sympathetic to her in the aftermath of the impeachment.

Nonetheless, during a conference call with conservatives throughout the state in February 2006, Adams assailed Kathy about how she could be running for office, given her stipulation to the ethics violations and her subsequent impeachment. Kathy was mortified. Adams was harping on her while campaign supporters listened in from all across Nevada. She repeatedly tried to deflect Adams's questions, saying the conference call was not the appropriate time to discuss the issue.

According to a report by *Review Journal* reporter Molly Ball, the issue got downright ugly when Adams later gave a speech tearing Kathy apart even as she sat in the room.

"We have to say, 'This is someone who, because of what they've done, should not be running as a Republican,'" Adams was quoted as saying.

Ball, an intrepid and fearless reporter, interviewed Kathy about the Adams ambush. Kathy's response was quite tough, saying, "This is a free country, and everyone's entitled to run for whatever they want to, whenever they want to," she told the paper.

Ball asked Kathy if she would ever abandon the Republican Party, considering that the Republican Party was abandoning her.

"I've been a lifelong Republican," Augustine said. "I'm not considering leaving."

But despite the stewing controversy, and even a banning from Republican events, Kathy seemed more motivated than she'd ever been in her political career. She went to war with Adams, blistering him in a subsequent speech at the statewide Republican convention, and she combined with another Republican in the race, Henderson resident Joseph Pitts, to attack the party-supported candidate, Mark DeStefano. Kathy portrayed Adams's actions as an insider's power play, and she continued campaigning relentlessly. Some people were starting to give Kathy a chance at a remarkable rise from the political dead.

"One, it's a down-ballot race and she ha[d] good name recognition," University of Nevada, Reno, political scientist Eric Herzik said. "Two, there was a backlash against the opposition she was encountering from the party and people who didn't want her to run."

Herzik told the *Review-Journal* that because of that backlash, Kathy was actually becoming "somewhat sympathetic." He also said Kathy was never someone who could be counted out, describing her as "incredibly tough."

Nancy Dallas, at the online website newsdeskbynancy dallas.com, questioned Adams's persistent scorn.

"Is Ms. Augustine's candidacy that much of a threat to the party; or, is it that her candidacy is a threat to certain political interests within the party?" Dallas wrote. "Are the forces pushing Mr. Adams in his efforts to discredit Ms. Augustine the same as those that pushed Republican legislators in their bumbling efforts to disgrace and embarrass her?"

Even so, Jon Ralston of the *Las Vegas Sun* said in an

interview that Kathy's chances in the treasurer's race were not stellar. He personally doubted she could win, but he had learned to never count Kathy out.

"She was not going to get any money, but she was working the circuit," Ralston said. "I never thought she actually would have won a big race. But she was so indomitable."

Ralston actually penned a column about the treasurer's race and Kathy's bid for a comeback. In his column he compared Kathy to the black knight in the movie *Monty Python and the Holy Grail*. In the film, the black knight is a character who refuses to give up on his efforts to defend a bridge even as the overconfident knight, in a fight with swordsmen, has his limbs severed one by one by his attackers.

The knight continues to fight even when all that is left of him is a bloody torso, and Ralston thought the black knight comparison was a fitting one for Kathy.

The woman just refused to give up.

"[She was] like that knight in Monty Python," Ralston said of Kathy. "I wrote about how I compared her to that knight, and she called me about it."

Ralston said Kathy started doing impressions of the black knight during the phone call.

"'It's only a flesh wound!'" Kathy quoted from the movie.

Ralston said he and Kathy also discussed the topic of whether it was possible that Kathy could actually win the race for state treasurer.

"Anything . . . [is] possible," Kathy told the veteran newsman.

Two women who witnessed Kathy Augustine's political toughness in person in the aftermath of the impeachment and during Kathy's race for treasurer were Jerry Bing and

Heidi Smith. Both women, active in Republican political circles in northern Nevada, said Kathy went through an impeachment that badly damaged her career, yet afterward, Kathy was out fighting to make a comeback. Kathy, at least, believed she could come back from the political dead. What impressed them most about Kathy on the political trail was her constant politicking. Even in off years, when she was not up for reelection, Kathy was always present at small Republican gatherings in rural Nevada, and she was continuing that trend in her race for treasurer even though the Republican Party leadership had abandoned her in light of the impeachment. She was relentless on the campaign trail, they said.

No other Republican candidate, they said, consistently showed up at the events like Kathy did. No one had the energy and tenaciousness that Kathy did.

"Very feisty," Bing recalled. "Nobody was going to tell her what to do. It was a good feisty."

Despite their favorable opinions of Kathy, however, Bing and Smith did notice something strange about Kathy as she was in the twilight of her political career: her husband, Chaz Higgs. The man seemed completely out of place at Republican dinners and political functions. The two just didn't seem to go together. Bing and Smith observed that Chaz was much younger than Kathy, he wore his hair with blond highlights, and he was muscular. Kathy was nearly fifty years old by then and consumed by politics, while Chaz seemed like he could not care less about his wife's political career.

"We were at some function, and he was with her, and she introduced him to me as her husband," said Bing, a state treasurer for the Nevada Federation of Republican Women. "It was a strange relationship. [They] did not seem to go together. He didn't seem to be the type of person that the Kathy Augustine I knew would have chosen as a husband. I was very surprised.

"[It was] very strange," Bing said. "The first time I met him, I walked away shaking my head. He was just kind of there. He couldn't carry on a conversation all by himself, either. He was shy and uninterested. I just thought, 'Well, I guess she's got some young stud.'"

Smith had similar impressions of Chaz, remarking on his "funky hair."

"He never spoke," Smith said. "Maybe a couple of words here and there. We were really surprised when we met him. He was the exact opposite of Kathy. Kathy was vivacious, and this man never talked. You never could get anything out of him. Once . . . [in] a while, you might get a smile. We just figured he was a [ladies'] man, and that's all we thought he was good for.

"He was just weird," she said.

Although Kathy's best friend, Nancy Vinik, may have been one of the last people to know about Kathy's whirlwind marriage to Chaz Higgs in 2003, she was one of the first to know when the marriage started to falter.

Kathy had been married to Chaz for only a few months when she told Nancy that she suspected Chaz was cheating on her.

"I talked to Kathy I can't tell you how many times when she was crying, upset about things that he had done to her and his running around with other women," Nancy said. "Talking, chatting online with other women, and going behind her back [and] opening up post office boxes. Changing deposits on his checks at work so he wouldn't have to contribute to the household finances."

Kathy told her she and Chaz got into explosive fights and that Chaz had gotten violent with her. Kathy never reported any incidents of domestic violence to authorities.

"He was physical with her," Nancy said. "He gave her a black eye at one point. She called me to ask, 'What kind of makeup can I use to cover a black eye?' He threw cell phones at her. She would find things out about him . . . about his indiscretions and about other women, and he didn't even care if she found out."

Nancy advised her friend to get out of the marriage.

"I said, 'Kathy, leave him. Tell him to get out. It's your house,'" Nancy Vinik recalled. "I told Kathy, 'You are going to collect all his things throughout that house, put it in a big pile in front of the door, and when he comes back, he can pick up all his garbage and be out of there.' And I said, 'You are going to be done with this. You are done with him. Call the locksmith in the morning and change the locks on the house.'

"I talked to her until one or two a.m.," she said. "So Kathy went through the whole house, she piled all his stuff up by the door, and she told me when she was done, 'I feel so much better. He'll be gone.'"

But when Nancy called her friend the next morning to find out how Kathy was doing, Kathy surprised her.

"She said, 'He's so sorry; he just doesn't know why he does these things,'" Nancy quoted Kathy. "She said, 'He's got a thyroid problem, and that's hormonal.'"

Nancy was upset and challenged Kathy on her weakness when it came to Chaz.

"'Why won't you just walk away?'" Nancy asked her friend. "She said, 'I truly am in love with him,' and I was like, 'In love with what? He's a piece of trash. No human being deserves to be treated that way.'

"She said, 'But I'm getting older. I'm getting to be fifty,' " Nancy recalled. "I said, 'I don't care if you're seventy and you don't want to be alone. It's better to be alone than be treated like that.' "

The conversations led Nancy to conclude that Kathy—her incredibly tough and impressive friend who had risen to the top of Nevada's political world—could not make good decisions when it came to men.

"I just think that when it came to men, she had no smarts upstairs," Nancy said. "I don't know why. Her father is a good person. She had good role models in her life."

Nancy said the marriage between Kathy and Chaz Higgs unraveled further, and Chaz repeatedly told Kathy he was going to leave her. Kathy told Nancy she missed the stability that Chuck Augustine gave her in her third marriage, and she missed Chuck's love. It was clear to Nancy that Kathy regretted marrying Chaz.

"I was her sounding board. I was her friend through good and bad," Nancy said. "She said, 'I never really knew how much [Chuck] loved me . . . He left me so well off.' "

Nancy said she wasn't the only one to tell Kathy to divorce Chaz.

"No one was afraid to tell her," Nancy said. "A lot of people said, 'Kathy, what's wrong with you?' "

Still, despite the stormy marriage, Kathy continued to buy Chaz expensive gifts, such as a new BMW and a cruise to Alaska.

"The Alaskan cruise . . . was a gift she was giving to him as an anniversary gift," Nancy said. "Right before they were supposed to go, he told her he was divorcing her, and she had asked me if I wanted to go. Then, the next thing I knew, everything was hunky-dory, and they went on the cruise together."

It was clear to Nancy that the marriage was destined to fail. She advised her friend to get her will and finances arranged so that Chaz would not stand to inherit her wealth if they divorced or if anything happened to Kathy.

"She was very, very comfortable [financially]," Nancy said. "After Chuck died, there was a lot that was left to her.

"I told Kathy early on in the marriage, 'You better go get your life straightened out,'" Nancy said. "'Think about it: He's going to be sitting there . . . sitting at that Maria Elena house, and he's going to be having such a good time with all of your things. All of your nice, pretty things. Chaz would have all your things. Doesn't that kind of make you sick?'

"There were some other people who told her, 'Put it all in a trust. At least do something,'" Nancy said.

Kathy took her friend's advice early in the marriage. In 2004, just a year into the marriage, Kathy consulted with an attorney and changed her will and trust to leave Chaz the BMW and all of the sports equipment the couple owned, but she arranged to leave the vast majority of her belongings, including the $500,000 annuity and the massive home in Vegas, to her daughter, Dallas, in a living will.

Phil Jr. offered the following summary of his sister's financial condition at the time of the change in the will:

"I . . . came up with a ballpark figure of about $1,200,000, but this included the equity on both homes. The bulk of the liquid assets were in a TSA and mutual funds worth about $400,000. Kathy also had $50,000 in a trust checking account. Kathy and Chaz also had a joint checking account with Wells Fargo, but I don't know how much was in it.

"I also discovered that Chaz and Kathy had a joint account with the Naval Federal Credit Union in Virginia. I never learned how much was in this account.

"Keep in mind that I was never able to inventory the Vegas home. I know that Kathy did have some expensive jewelry that probably had an insurance value of about $100,000. . . . Chaz was left all the vehicles and sports equipment."

13 ... GOOSE BUMPS

Kim Ramey is about as good a nurse as there is. She is a caring woman, a hardworking employee, and also a woman who has endured the pain of a truly nasty divorce with her former husband in Virginia.

Ramey, who has been a nurse since 1998, chose to take a slightly different approach to her career in patient care—instead of working for years at the same hospital, Ramey works as a traveling nurse, which means she contracts with a hospital to work a certain amount of time. When that time is up, she and her boyfriend pack their stuff up and move on to the next community with a hospital in need of a nurse who specializes in caring for patients recovering from open-heart surgery.

It is a lucrative career although it requires a willingness to be on the move constantly.

"I travel," Ramey said. "I specialize in open-heart recovery. If you come in and you need a heart bypass, and you come out of heart bypass, most places after surgery would go to what we call recovery. Open-heart nurses actually [help patients] recover [from open heart surgery].

"I choose to not work on staff for a hospital," Ramey said. "I choose to be a traveler. And, because of the nursing shortage in the United States, and because of my specialty, I'm very blessed that I can basically work anywhere. I don't work for any particular company at one time. I just work through different multiple companies, and I choose where I want to go. Sometimes a contract is as short as two weeks. Sometimes a contract is a month. And sometimes it's renewed and renewed if I choose to do so or the hospital asks me to stay."

In January 2006, Ramey and her boyfriend took a travel assignment in Carson City at the main campus of Carson Tahoe, which was opening a brand-new open-heart center. Ramey and her boyfriend—also a nurse—agreed to work at the hospital to help open the new heart center and train their nurses. On July 7, 2006, Ramey was working the day shift—a twelve-and-a-half-hour shift—and she arrived to work at fifteen minutes before seven in the morning. She learned that she would be floating over to the Intensive Care Unit that day.

"As the patient load census goes up or down, they have to shift so they have the correct staff on one unit or another. As a critical-care open-heart nurse . . . [we] can float over to the ICU, but ICU nurses can't float to the open-heart [center] because they don't have that specialty. So, of course, it was my turn to float over there, and I did."

Ramey walked across a hallway to the Intensive Care Unit and met a new nurse at the hospital, Chaz Higgs, who had recently hired on after working for two years at the Washoe Medical Center at South Meadows campus. Chaz was assigned to help Ramey with medical equipment and gloves as she tended to patients.

"I just started talking to him, and then he started talking to me," Ramey said. "He asked me, you know, if I worked there, and I told him I was a traveler, and we had four days left on our contract."

Ramey said she was working with Chaz on a crazy day in the Intensive Care Unit. They were very busy.

"I needed assistance in getting equipment," Ramey said. "I can remember vividly the two patients I had. . . . One of them, we were ruling out whether she had spinal meningitis, the bacterial type, which is worse than the viral type. . . . The other patient was a long-term patient with all kinds of [problems]," Ramey said. "She had a ventilator. She had frequent suctioning. She had severe emotional problems because she had been in the hospital over a month. And, you know, every time I went in there, she wanted me to stay in there. And I'm trying to go back and forth and take care of her and then [I'm dealing with] the other family, who thinks their mother has bacterial meningitis. I'm calling the health department. So I'm in and out of there; I'm asking [Chaz] to get me stuff. And that's how we got engaged in conversation."

Ramey prides herself in a special ability to assess people on a moment's notice. It is a skill that comes in handy as a nurse, and when she met Chaz, she concluded pretty quickly that he was a "player." She made a point of mentioning that she was involved in a relationship and that she and her boyfriend would be moving back to Virginia in a few days. Chaz, in turn, mentioned that he was married but that he hated his wife.

"Throughout the day, it was this vicious, mean, hateful, every word in the book [to] describe her," Ramey said. "She was a 'stalker.' She was an 'f-ing bitch.'"

Ramey mentioned she had endured a nasty divorce, and Chaz responded, "Oh, I'm getting a divorce, too."

Chaz mentioned to Ramey that his wife "was high profile: Kathy Augustine." Ramey said she didn't know anything about Kathy, and he said, "She's the state controller . . . [and] she's running for treasurer." In retrospect, Ramey said she never saw Chaz express a single term of endearment about his wife. He was continually bad-mouthing her throughout the day.

" 'She's a fucking stalker,' " Ramey said, quoting Chaz. " 'I'm looking for an apartment because she's a fucking stalker. She's a bitch. She's a psycho.' That's the only emotion I saw. Anger [and] rage."

Ramey also witnessed Chaz yelling at Kathy on the phone.

" 'I will fucking talk to you when I get home,' " Ramey quoted Chaz as saying. " 'I will fucking talk to you when I get home. I said, I will fucking talk to you when I get home.' And [he's saying] this . . . in the middle of [the Intensive Care Unit], which to me, it was inappropriate. Especially with an employee that had just started. He wasn't even off orientation.

"I said, 'What was that all about?' " Ramey said after the phone call was over.

Chaz responded, saying, "I can't fucking believe it. She found out that I opened an account with Wells Fargo. And I was told that it was only my name and she wouldn't find out about it."

"I felt bad for him because that's the sort of thing, the same thing that happened to me [in my divorce]," Ramey recalled. "I said, 'Yeah, it sucks. You're supposed to have all this protection through the banks and stuff now.' And I said, 'The same thing happened to me. My ex went in and canceled an account of mine [and] took the money out. It sucks.' "

But near the end of the day, Chaz's ranting about his

wife took a bizarre twist when he and Ramey were talking about the shocking murder case of Reno businessman Darren Mack. Mack had recently shot his wife to death, then went to the Washoe County Courthouse and shot a judge who presided over Mack's divorce trial. The judge was critically wounded. Instead of expressing the shock that most felt over the details of the crime, Ramey said that Chaz called Mack an idiot and suggested that the ideal way to kill someone was to inject him or her with the drug succinylcholine. "Succs," as the drug was called, is used in emergency rooms to briefly paralyze a patient to insert a breathing tube.

The drug, he implied, was the perfect murder weapon.

"He said, 'That guy did it wrong,'" Ramey recalled. "He said, 'If you want to get rid of somebody, you just hit them with a little succs.'"

Chaz made a gesture with his hands to make it look as if he was injecting someone.

"Because they can't trace it postmortem," Chaz said.

Ramey was shocked. A chill went through her body.

"My bodily response was my hair rose up sort of, like, woo," Ramey recalled. "I said, 'Chaz, wow, that's too much anger to carry around.' . . . I mean, you could touch it [the anger]. I don't know if you've ever gotten a physical response to something horrible. That's what I got. A physical response. Like goose bumps."

14 ... A PULSE

About twelve hours after Kim Ramey's troubling conversation with Chaz Higgs, Nancy Vinik had a terrifying experience. She was at home sleeping at about 3 a.m. on Saturday, July 8, when she awoke to a chill.

"I woke up and I swear . . . there was somebody standing in my bedroom," Nancy said.

Nancy's husband had fallen asleep on the couch. She sat up in her bed, petrified, for about ten minutes before she crept out of her bedroom and went to find her husband.

"I was in shock," Nancy said. "I saw someone in my room. My clock said 3 a.m., and I told my husband, 'There is somebody in the house!'"

Nancy's husband told her she was probably dreaming or having a bad dream.

"I said, 'No I'm not!' I was scared out of my frigging mind," Nancy said. "I was drenched. I was shaking, and my husband said, 'The alarm's on. No one's in here. You are having a bad dream.'"

Nancy still isn't sure who was in her bedroom that morning, but thinking back now, she believes it was her friend, Kathy Augustine.

"To this day I tell myself it was Kathy . . . [and that] she was here," Nancy said.

Benjamin Pratt is a firefighter and paramedic with the Tahoe-Douglas Fire Protection District in Washoe County. He also works part-time with the Regional Emergency Medical Services Authority, which is a paramedic ambulance service operating in northern Nevada. Pratt has seen a lot of remarkable things as a paramedic and firefighter, but few compare to what he saw on the morning of July 8, 2006, when he witnessed Kathy Augustine come back from the dead.

At 6:45 a.m.—one day after Ramey's conversation with Higgs—a caller phoned 911 and told dispatchers that his wife was unconscious and that he'd tried to administer CPR to no avail. The caller was Chaz Higgs, and the person who was unconscious was his wife, Kathy Augustine. Dispatcher George Meade was the one to take the call, and he noted that there didn't seem to be any urgency in Chaz's voice, given the perilous situation.

"He was just very calm in that situation, where most would not be," Meade said. "The conversation was just very lengthy. Usually when somebody is doing CPR, it's very brief, because they're getting back to it."

Pratt and his partner, Manny Fuentes, were dispatched to the home. They flipped on the lights and sirens on their ambulance and raced through the northern Nevada dawn to Kathy's house.

"We had a gentleman out front waving us in on the curb sidewalk area," Pratt said. "We also had the Reno

Fire Department following right behind us. We all kind of arrived together, [and] it was the four firefighters, me and Manny, and Mr. Higgs."

Pratt was in a hurry to get to the patient. He noticed that Chaz seemed unusually calm as he told paramedics that his wife was unconscious in a rear bedroom.

" 'She's in the back room. She's right by the kitchen in the back room,' " Pratt quoted Chaz as saying. "Kind of nonchalant, but not like an emergen[cy] . . . you know, yanking on your sleeve. . . . [No] screaming [or] yelling. More of a calm demeanor."

Pratt, Fuentes, and the firefighters scurried through the house and found Kathy on the bed in the master bedroom of the home. She appeared to be dead.

"Unresponsive," Fuentes said of Kathy's condition. "Supine on the bed."

"We went and felt for a pulse, and we didn't feel a pulse, nor was she breathing," Pratt said.

The paramedics knew they couldn't give Kathy CPR on the bed because the surface was too soft, so they dragged her off the bed, put her on the floor, and started pressing on her chest in the hope of bringing her back to life. The paramedics put a device into her mouth and down her throat to try to help her breath. They continued the CPR as they set her up with an IV and hooked her up to a monitor to see if they could detect any vital signs.

"Then we give medications," Pratt said. "We do CPR for two minutes in between each medication and check for a pulse or any changes on the monitor. If there are no changes, you continue CPR with the [breathing] bag assisting, and you push more medications."

Despite these efforts, Kathy still showed no signs of life.

"She was flatlined," Pratt said. "A straight line across

the monitor. And with that [situation], you would give one milligram of epinephrine and one milligram of atropine."

Fuentes administered the drugs into Kathy's IV as Pratt performed more CPR, and what happened next startled the paramedics.

Kathy's heart started beating.

She was fighting for her life.

"Most commonly you'd go up to three rounds [of the medication], which is three milligrams of each. And then at that point, we usually call the code," Pratt said. "But with this patient, we only gave two milligrams because we got a pulse back. We did get a heartbeat back."

Pratt was startled and excited to see the blip on the monitor that told him Kathy's heart was beating again. These were the types of calls that Pratt had trained hundreds of hours for, and he wanted to do everything he could to help Kathy. She was still unconscious and in a terribly grave condition, but at least her heart was beating.

"These don't happen very often, where you get pulses back," Pratt said. "It's just an upbeat call. You know, you actually bring someone from the dead back, and you know, your adrenaline is pumping, and everything is going."

Pratt said Chaz entered the room and "asked if we were going to be transporting" Kathy to the hospital.

"Same calm demeanor," the paramedic said.

The men put Kathy on a gurney and wheeled her to the ambulance. Chaz got into the ambulance with them and said very little as they raced Kathy to the Washoe Medical Center at South Meadows. It was the hospital where Chaz had worked as a critical-care nurse until just a few weeks prior. Kathy, upon admittance to the hospital, was treated for a little more than an hour before she was transported to Washoe Medical Center's main hospital campus because that facility was better prepared to handle Kathy's gravely critical state. Chaz again rode with the paramedics in the ambulance, and Fuentes noticed that Chaz picked up a newspaper in the cab of the ambulance and started reading it. Considering his wife was near death, Fuentes thought that was a little unusual.

"He was sitting in the passenger seat next to me. Pretty quiet. Didn't really say one word. Just kept to himself. We had a newspaper sitting on the dashboard, and during the ride . . . he grabbed one of the sections of the newspaper and started flipping through it."

Marlene Swanbeck has been a registered nurse for eighteen years. She works in Reno, at Washoe Medical Center at South Meadows, the same hospital where Chaz Higgs had worked for the last two years until he quit and took a job at Carson Tahoe hospital, where he'd worked for only a few weeks when Kathy fell ill. Swanbeck said that, for some reason, her colleague had always made her uncomfortable.

"I always felt a little suspicious. Something was never right," Swanbeck said. "I was not ever comfortable [with] the way he talked about his wife. He would call her a bitch. If she would call on the phone, he would be irritated. You know, he was going to just let her sit on hold for a little bit."

On July 8, 2006, Swanbeck said she was working in the emergency room of Washoe Medical Center at South Meadows when the hospital staff was informed that an unconscious fifty-year-old woman was being brought in. The patient was in cardiac arrest, but the paramedics had been able to bring the woman back from flatlining and had detected an apparent heartbeat.

"When they arrived in the emergency room, we had a

young-looking fifty-year-old with no health history," Swan-beck said, adding that she was surprised because "you don't expect a fifty-year-old person with no health history to arrive down [on their back] and intubated."

Swanbeck was on a team of medical professionals that included fellow-nurse Chris McCabe and Dr. Guy Gansert. Kathy was wheeled into a treatment room, and the team started tending to her.

"We cleansed the patient with Betadine, a cleansing solution, to clean her off, and then we just put the catheter into her urethra, into her bladder," Swanbeck said. "We drew a whole panel of blood, and we drew some urine. We left the catheter in place, but we sent a urine specimen [to the lab].

"We hooked her up to a heart monitor," the nurse said. "We were giving her oxygen by way of a round device that inflates her lungs. It's handheld. I don't remember exactly at what point blood was drawn, but that would be some-thing that we would do when a patient comes in."

The medical professionals were interested in what the eventual results of the tests would be, given Kathy's condi-tion. It was a mystery to the doctors as to what was wrong with her.

Kathy's medical records would show a urine sample was taken at approximately 7:35 a.m.

"I . . . [took] the urine from the tubing," Swanbeck said. "I took a label off the patient's armband and wrote the date, time, and my initials and then put it on the container. [I] put it in a biohazard bag, in a sealed bag that closes, and sent it off to the lab.

"Because we had a healthy patient, we were trying to figure out what was going on with her, so we sent that urine for a toxicology screen," Swanbeck said. "We didn't have any answers. We were running the gamut."

The team was mulling over what could be wrong with Kathy when something unusual happened: Chaz Higgs, who had worked at the hospital until just a few weeks prior, pulled back the curtains.

"I looked up and said to him, 'What are you doing here?'" a startled Swanbeck said. "He said, 'That's my wife, Kathy.'"

Swanbeck almost immediately picked up on the way Chaz carried himself, "the way he was standing," Swanbeck said. Like it was "just another day." He wasn't sobbing or excited or even asking any questions about Kathy's well-being.

Dr. Gansert asked Chaz what had happened.

"He [said that he] had been out in the garage earlier in the morning [working on his car]," Swanbeck recalled of Chaz's answers to the questions. "Kathy had been under a lot of stress, so he was letting her sleep in. And he went into the bedroom after having made coffee. [He] was bringing her coffee, and the room was dark, and he tried to arouse her, and she didn't arouse. So he opened up the curtains, checked her . . . and found that she had no pulse."

Swanbeck said Chaz's nonchalant demeanor and his account of what happened both struck her as odd.

"She had been healthy, and now suddenly she's down, [and] he was removed from what was happening, it seemed."

Swanbeck talked about the incident with her colleagues afterward, and they, too, found their former coworker's behavior to be curious.

"I think that we were all sufficiently suspicious, and we had been talking among ourselves," Swanbeck said. "It didn't feel right to us."

15 . . . LOSING KATHY

Phil Alfano Jr. and his eldest daughter had traveled to Orange County to attend her freshman orientation for college in the summer of 2006. They planned to spend the weekend at his parents' home in La Palma. Phil Jr. learned that Kathy and Chaz would be there as well, attending a political fund-raiser for Kathy in Marina Del Rey that same weekend. Kathy's youngest brother, Tony, and his wife, Colleen, lived just two miles from Kathy's parents. That weekend Chaz struck up a conversation with Colleen Alfano while visiting her home. Although Colleen did not always get along with Kathy, she reported to her loved ones that weekend that she'd had a conversation with Chaz Higgs that really bothered her.

"My brother's wife, Colleen, had . . . a very bizarre conversation with Chaz when we were down for that fund-raising event in June," Phil Jr. said. "He had said some pretty nasty things about Kathy to Colleen, and she was really put off by it."

At Kathy's fund-raising event, which Phil Jr. and his daughter attended that weekend, Phil Jr. recalled that some of Kathy's friends reminisced with her about her late third husband, Charles Augustine.

"There were some of Kathy's old friends there from the airlines, and they all started talking about Chuck, and I could see Chaz getting very uncomfortable," Phil Jr. said. "And Chaz was drinking like I'd never seen him drink before."

Everyone was having a good time that night, and Kathy, in particular, was in a good mood. She was vibrant and excited as she talked to her oldest brother about her bid to become treasurer of the state of Nevada.

"She was talking about the campaign," Phil Jr. said. "She was in great spirits. I was telling her she didn't have a chance, and she said, 'Actually, the polls are kind of tight,' so I was kind of shocked at that. It was good news."

As the night came to a close, Phil Jr. and his daughter, as well as Kathy and Chaz, returned to the home of Kathy's parents in La Palma. Chaz passed out drunk on the floor of his in-laws' residence.

"He came back, and he was plastered," Kay Alfano said. "Drunk wasn't the word for it. He laid on the floor in front of the television set in the family room. Finally, Kathy went upstairs, and the next morning, [Chaz] didn't remember coming home. He got drunk on wine because it was a wine-and-cheese fund-raiser. I guess everyone who met him that night was telling Kathy, 'What in the heck did you do?' Friends and relatives were saying it."

That evening was the last night Kathy's family would ever have with her outside the cold walls of a hospital room.

Two weeks later, on the morning of Saturday, July 8, Kay Alfano said she was cleaning the kitchen cupboards and her husband was outside, presumably working on the lawn, when the phone rang. It was Chaz.

"He said, 'Kay, Kathy just had a heart attack,' " Kay recalled. The news sent a current of grief through Kay's body.

"What happened?" Kay asked.

"He said, 'I got up, and I went out in my car, I came back in [and I] went to get her a cup of coffee, and then I got into bed and I started snuggling next to her, and I realized she was not breathing,' " Kay recalled of the conversation.

"We'll be right up," Kay told him. "Chaz said, 'No, you don't have to come up,' " Kay recalled. "Yes we do!" she replied.

A flood of emotion, alarm, and horror washed over Kay like a huge, vicious, indiscriminate wave. Her beloved daughter—the person she was closest to in life—was in danger.

Kay called her sons and told them the horrible news.

"I went and got my husband right away," Kay said. "I couldn't believe it. I called Philip. I called Tony. And then I called [Kathy's daughter] Dallas."

Phil Jr. got the call from his mom at his home at about 8:30 a.m. He said that when he heard the tone of his mother's voice over the phone, he knew something was terribly wrong.

"I could tell right away," Phil Jr. said. "I'm thinking a relative has passed away or my dad is sick. She said, 'Chaz called, and your sister had a massive heart attack.' "

Phil Jr. almost dropped the phone from shock. He had just seen Kathy at the fund-raiser in Marina Del Rey two weeks earlier, and she had looked as healthy as ever. He'd also gone to Italy with her a few months ago and watched in amazement as she scaled the famous Spanish Steps in Rome in high heels, without missing a beat or even breathing very hard. Kathy certainly didn't seem to be the type of person that was a likely candidate for a heart attack.

She didn't smoke and rarely drank, and she was only slightly overweight.

"I said, 'What happened?'" Phil Jr. recalled saying to Kay. "My mom said she didn't know—that Chaz found her unconscious, and right away, I knew it was bad."

That Kathy had been unconscious indicated to Phil Jr. that his sister was in bad shape. A colleague of his had had a heart attack and been found unconscious; the man lived but was left a vegetable by the medical episode. Phil Jr. was overcome with alarm and grief, but he did not let on to his mother right away that he knew that Kathy was in huge trouble.

"I knew it wasn't going to be good," Phil Jr. said, holding back a wall of emotion and tears as he talked. "I didn't let on to my parents."

He had been planning to drive to his parents' home that morning and then catch a flight to Phoenix for a conference, but he put the trip off. "I said, 'Let me cancel my flight,' but what really stands out is that Chaz had told my mother that we didn't need to come up. Why would he tell her parents that they didn't need to be there?

"I found that suspicious from the get-go, but then again, you keep blocking that stuff out," Phil Jr. said.

No way. It couldn't be. People with no history of heart problems do have heart attacks, he thought, brushing aside his suspicions.

Phil Jr.'s wife, Mary, booked a flight for her in-laws to Sacramento. Phil Jr. met them at the airport, and the three drove to Reno. Kathy's youngest brother, Tony, was en route as well. Throughout the drive to Reno, the Alfanos tried to contact Chaz, but for some reason, he was using Kathy's cell phone and not his own. Dallas Augustine had already gone to the hospital, and she talked to Tony Alfano over the phone and told him Kathy was in very bad shape.

Tony communicated that message to Phil Jr.

"When my parents got off the plane, I just said to them, 'I want to prepare you for what you might see,'" Phil Jr. said. "So we drove over there, and we [finally] got ahold of Chaz. We weren't even sure what hospital Kathy was in. The information hadn't been really forthcoming."

What followed was a frantic, tortuous drive for the Alfanos back and forth through Reno. They couldn't seem to find the Washoe Medical Center. When they finally did, they rushed in to see Kathy. What they found in her hospital room was a horrifying sight. Kathy was unconscious, and her eyes were open, but they were rolled back into her head so that the whites of her eyes were exposed.

"It was just a horrible sight, to see in her in that condition," Phil Jr. said. "Unconscious, on a respirator, and what was most disturbing was the fact that her eyes were wide open, and she couldn't blink. At that point, I wasn't sure if it was something she could recover from. I knew she'd have permanent brain damage."

Dallas was present, and she was crying. Kay was crying. Phil Jr. was crying. So was Phil Sr. The only one person in the room who wasn't crying was Chaz. He showed no emotion.

"He was beyond clinical," Phil Jr. said. "He was like an unassociated observer."

In contrast, Kay was frantic and beside herself over her daughter's condition. She was heartbroken like never before in her life. She'd had three beautiful, wonderful children in life, and to see her only daughter, Kathy, in this condition was completely devastating. It was an overwhelming grief: the kind of grief that, when it struck, you knew your life would never, ever be the same again. Kay said to herself that she wasn't going to leave her daughter's side; she knew, in the back of her mind, that there was probably not much time left to spend with her first child. The tears streamed down her face. Her body was racked with sorrow as she clasped her unconscious daughter's hand.

"The only thing she had was involuntary twitching in her leg," Kay said through tears as she, too, recalled the day she learned that she might lose Kathy forever. "No movement at all. She was paralyzed.

"We were tired," Kay said. "Phil [Sr.] was tired, and the stress [was overwhelming]. Mary had gotten a hotel room for everyone, and I said, 'No, I'm not leaving the hospital. I'm staying.'"

Kay's family tried to convince her to go back to the hotel, but she wouldn't budge. "That was my daughter. I couldn't leave her."

Kay's family relented and let her stay because they knew there was no changing her mind, and a chair-bed was moved into the room for her. Phil Sr. and Phil Jr. returned to their hotel rooms, and Kay stayed behind with her daughter. The nurses caring for Kathy repeatedly advised Kay to take it easy.

Then a doctor entered the room and said, "Is this the overdose victim?"

Kay was startled by the comment. She then learned something else that further surprised her: a preliminary review of Kathy's blood test indicated the presence of barbiturates in her system. It would later turn out that the results from this blood test were in error, and authorities later concluded after further forensic testing that Kathy did not have barbiturates in her system. Nonetheless, this was the first time Kathy's family had ever heard the premise that, perhaps, Kathy was the victim of a drug overdose. However, Kay also learned from the doctor that Chaz had been told of the preliminary positive test for barbiturates hours earlier, on Saturday morning, yet he hadn't even mentioned the important development to Kathy's family.

"[The nurses] kept asking me questions," Kay recalled. "I was out of it. I'd been up for over twenty-four hours, and the emotional strain was terrible. They said, 'What kind of medications does she take?'

"Nothing," Kay responded.

"'What does she take for pain?'" the nurses asked, and it was clear to Kay that they were trying to figure out if it was possible that Kathy had attempted to kill herself via a drug overdose.

The very idea seemed shocking to Kay, and out of character for Kathy. She was also shocked because Chaz had indicated Kathy suffered a heart attack, yet now medical professionals were telling her that Kathy was showing signs of a drug overdose, and they were contemplating the possibility of an attempted suicide.

"I said, 'Suicide? No way!'" Kay said. "I was told by someone that, 'You know she had barbiturates in her system,' and I said, 'No, she doesn't take anything like that!' My mind was in overdrive at this point, and we are talking three, four o'clock in the morning. I was delirious. They said, 'You've got to have something to eat.' The cafeteria was closed, and all they had in the fridge was sherbet and crackers. I told them I didn't want it, and they said, 'No, you are going to eat it,' and they brought me more coffee."

Kay was completely exhausted. Her mind was racing. She wasn't thinking straight. Yet despite everything that was going on, she was able to come to the mind-numbing conclusion that night in the hospital that Kathy was going to die. There was just no way she was going to recover from the devastating condition she was in, and Kay knew it.

"I knew she wasn't going to live. She had the ventilator on," Kay said.

Kay asked the nurses if a priest could come to the hospital room the following morning. The priest came, and he and Kay prayed together for Kathy.

"I said [to the nurses], 'She's had the last rites, hasn't she?'" Kay recalled. "I figured they would have done that right away. The nurses told me, 'Her husband said she doesn't have a religion,' and I said, 'I want a priest down here.'

"Within a half hour, the priest was there," Kay said. "He stayed with me and Kathy . . . and the next morning, we all went to Mass."

Kathy's condition did not improve on Sunday. The Alfanos also noticed that day that Chaz Higgs and Dallas Augustine had been spending some time together, and it seemed to them that the two were friends. Dallas had even mentioned at the hospital that Sunday that she and Chaz had been drinking together the night prior.

According to the Alfanos, Dallas and her mother had been somewhat estranged at this point. Dallas was an adult, and, they said, she was now in a relationship with another woman.

Phil Jr. said Chaz "kept talking again very clinically" at the hospital that Sunday. Phil Jr. eventually sat down with both Chaz and Dallas at the hospital to ask if they knew what Kathy's desires were for life support under such a circumstance. Chaz indicated that he and Kathy had both drawn up a power-of-attorney document, and the document dictated Chaz would be the one to decide whether Kathy should be removed from life support. Phil Jr. told Chaz he would like to get a copy of the power-of-attorney document for the doctors, and Chaz told him, "OK, I got it back at the house, and I'll get that for you."

Phil Jr. said he then sat down with Dallas alone and informed her that Kathy had asked him to be the executor of her estate if she passed away. Phil Jr. told Kathy's only child that he knew the basic contents of Kathy's will, and he informed her of the fact that Dallas would be a wealthy woman if and when Kathy passed away or was removed from life support.

"I sat Dallas down and told her, 'Your mother had set it up so you'll inherit a lot of money if she passes away,'" Phil Jr. said.

The doctors were indicating to the family that Kathy was basically brain-dead, but they still wanted to see if it was possible that she might show some signs of improvement. "At that point, we were waiting for the doctors to do one more EEG to see if there had been any further improvement," Phil Jr. said.

By this time the doctors were concluding that Kathy had not had a heart attack.

Dr. Stanley Thompson, a physician and cardiologist who works with Reno Heart Physicians in the Reno area, was asked to perform an angiogram on Kathy. The test involves the insertion of little tubes into the heart and an injection of contrast material (a dye visible under X-rays) to determine whether the heart has a blockage that might have caused a heart attack. The procedure usually involves inserting the tubes through the big arteries in the groin to get to the heart, and this is what Thompson did with Kathy.

"We inject the dye into the arteries to see if there's a blockage there, because heart attacks are produced by a blockage in the arteries," Thompson said. "[We concluded] that she did not have any coronary artery disease and no blockage. The arteries are perfectly normal. This is not what you would expect from someone having a heart attack."

The doctors still did not know what had caused Kathy to go into a coma, but they suspected it was possible she was the victim of an overdose.

At some time on Sunday, the Alfanos, in discussion with Chaz and Dallas, decided it was time to make Kathy's condition public. They knew the information about Kathy's grave condition would be in the media soon anyway, and it was agreed that Phil Jr. and Chaz would deal with the public attention. Kathy's hospitalization would be in all of Nevada's newspapers and on television the following morning. They agreed to hold a press conference the next day to tell the public about Kathy's condition. Chaz and Phil Jr. agreed to meet the next morning at the hotel and then go to the controller's office to hold the press conference on the steps of the Nevada State Capitol.

But before they even left the hotel, Chaz made a comment that immediately caught Phil Jr.'s attention.

"[Chaz] showed up about a half an hour late," Phil Jr. said. "So, we got in the car, and Chaz said, 'Hey Phil, I've got something to tell you. One of the nurses called me last night and said they found trace amounts of barbiturates in Kathy's system.'"

Phil Jr. officially became suspicious of Chaz the moment that he uttered those words: Kay had already told Phil Jr. about the false-positive test for barbiturates, and she'd also told her son that Chaz was informed of this on Saturday morning—not Sunday night.

"That was the tipping point for me," Phil Jr. said. "I knew he was lying. Why would you lie about that?"

Phil Jr. kept his suspicions to himself. He and Chaz drove to Kathy's office, and the phones were ringing off the hook. Reporters were calling constantly after learning that

Kathy was in the hospital. The press conference was called
on the steps of the state capitol building that afternoon.
All of Nevada's major news organizations were present. A
press release was read that documented Kathy's condition,
and Chaz told the reporters present what happened when
he discovered Kathy unconscious.

"I basically found her unresponsive," Chaz told reporters. "She wasn't breathing. She had no pulse. I started CPR
and called 911 . . . Obviously she had been complaining
about being stressed out about the campaign and the whole
sort of thing.

"She came to work everyday," Chaz told the Associated
Press. "She did her job; then after work she would go to
one or two [political] events in the evening, and then in the
weekend she had two or three [political events] a day."

Chaz continued to imply that Kathy had a heart attack.
He talked about all of the stress she had been under, and
he also said that she had been complaining of a stomach
ache and heartburn, which can sometimes appear as symptoms in individuals who end up having heart attacks. Phil
Jr. stood quietly in the background as the cameras recorded
Chaz's words. With each of those words, Phil Jr.'s suspicions about Chaz got stronger. The two had just had a suspicious conversation about barbiturates in Kathy's system
that Phil Jr. concluded Chaz was lying about, and now here
he was talking about a heart attack and stress being the
cause of Kathy's sudden illness.

"I've described him as kind of being like a bad actor,"
Phil Jr. said. "When he would attempt to show he was being
sincere, it was very, very contrived."

There were other people at the press conference who
were suspicious, too. Ed Vogel, the dogged veteran reporter
for the *Las Vegas Review-Journal* who knew Kathy, said
the idea of her having a heart attack didn't sit right with

him. He knew Kathy to be a vivacious, healthy woman. Something about Chaz's comments were strange to him as he wrote them down on his notepad.

"He told about what happened to her, how he tried to revive her, and that he'd called the paramedics," Vogel recalled. "It seemed fishy from day one—from that first press conference. Really odd."

Vogel couldn't quite put his finger on why he was suspicious, but the first thing that stood out to him in retrospect was Chaz's appearance. It was the first time Vogel had seen Chaz, and Vogel was struck by how the younger man was groomed to the max, tanned, and a bodybuilder. Vogel knew Kathy, and he quickly thought that Chaz didn't seem to be the type of man Kathy would hang out with, let alone marry.

"It just . . . seemed odd that Kathy would be with that guy," Vogel said of Chaz. "I was talking to everybody [else], and everybody thought it was weird."

Another aspect of the press conference that Vogel keyed in on was that Phil Jr. and Chaz were standing next to one another, but it did not appear "that the two were together."

Phil Jr. and Chaz returned to the hospital after the press conference. The doctors informed the family that Kathy's condition had worsened, and Phil Jr. sensed that Chaz was trying to avoid him. That night, Phil Jr. could contain his suspicions no longer. He pulled his mother aside and let it all out. He had to tell someone that he suspected Chaz might have harmed Kathy in some unknown way even though he had no proof.

"Based on these conversations that my mom had with the doctors, based on the behavior I observed in him, and the lies, it was Monday night that I could bring myself to share my suspicions with somebody else," Phil Jr. said. "I sat down with my mom and said, 'I think Chaz had something to do with this.'

"Without blinking, my mom said, 'I've been thinking the same thing,'" Phil Jr. recalled.

By the next morning, Tuesday, July 11, there were still no signs that Kathy stood any chance of recovering. Instead, she was getting worse. There were no signs of brain activity in the tests the doctors performed, and Phil Jr. was getting frustrated because he still didn't have the power-of-attorney document that Chaz had promised to provide.

When he finally got the document, from Dallas, it showed that Chaz was not the person responsible for deciding if Kathy should stay on life support or not. Kathy's father, Phil Sr., was the one Kathy wanted to make the difficult decision about life support.

"Sure enough, [Chaz] lied about that, too," Phil Jr. said.

The suspicions were mounting on the same day that the realities of Kathy's condition were being determined. The doctors had no optimism about Kathy's potential for recovery, and the Alfanos concluded that her life was over. She was not coming back. There was just no chance.

As a family, they talked to Phil Sr. about the decision to remove Kathy from life support. The Alfanos are strong Catholics, and they dreaded the idea of Phil Sr. struggling with such a difficult decision.

"By Tuesday morning, we were all looking at this situation, and we knew she wasn't going to recover," Phil Jr. said through tears. "She wasn't going to be mentally there. She would be dependent on others for the rest of the time she had. [For] my dad . . . it was real hard . . . and we said, 'Dad, we all know what needs to be done, so don't feel like it's all on your shoulders.' He had some real struggles with that. It was really, really hard."

Phil Alfano Sr. said the decision was a terrible one, but

he knew removing his daughter from life support was the right decision because it would end Kathy's suffering.

"She was breathing only with the respirator," Kathy's father said. "She was not absorbing any food. She was gone."

Chaz, meanwhile, continued to act strangely at the hospital by explaining to everyone in clinical detail about how Kathy would die when the life support was turned off.

"He went through the whole process," Phil Jr. recalled. " 'They'll hook you up to a morphine drip,' and he went into detail about how it will reach such and such a level. 'The respirator is removed and she won't feel a thing.' He was talking to us like a nurse, and he was saying stuff a nurse would say to comfort a family. He was not talking like a husband."

The Alfanos agreed to spend time with Kathy, one by one, in her final hours. It was a devastating, tearful afternoon for everyone—except Chaz, who, the Alfanos said, remained completely stoic.

"We took turns holding her," Phil Jr. said through tears. "We knew it was just a matter of hours, if not minutes. I was thinking of all the memories, but I also couldn't believe this was actually happening."

As Kathy lay dying, her youngest brother, Tony, witnessed Chaz removing Kathy's wedding ring from her finger.

"My son Tony saw him take her wedding ring off after they stopped the life support," Kay said. "Chaz . . . kept leaning down . . . and saying something to her, and he took off her wedding ring."

Kathy Marie Augustine's heart stopped beating shortly after 4 p.m. on Tuesday, July 11, 2006. As the grief-stricken Alfanos emerged from the hospital room, Phil Jr. observed two detectives with the Reno Police Department in the wing of the hospital where Kathy had just died. The detectives were asking doctors and nurses questions about Kathy. The sight was an encouraging one to Phil during a very difficult time.

"We'd thought about going to the authorities, but the problem was we didn't have anything to go on," Phil Jr. said. "We were very comforted by the fact that literally, as soon as she expired and they wheeled her out, I saw two detectives standing there in the nurse's station. We knew someone had called."

The next morning, Phil Jr., Phil Sr., Kay, and Dallas were scheduled to meet with Kathy's attorney to discuss Kathy's will and trust. Everyone in the group was grieving and seriously depressed over Kathy's death. After they arrived at the attorney's office, Phil Jr. was surprised when Chaz showed up at the meeting with Dallas. Everyone sat down at a table in the attorney's office, and the attorney went through the details of the inheritance and the fact that Dallas was due to inherit pretty much everything. Phil Jr. said he watched Chaz as the attorney spoke, and it seemed to him that it came as a surprise to Chaz that he wasn't due to inherit anything from Kathy's death.

Chaz would later dispute this claim vehemently.

"I could see the look in Chaz's eyes," Phil Jr. said. "He was glaring at me across the table. I can't be convinced 100 percent that he didn't know what was in that trust, but my sister told me he didn't know what was in it as of December 2004. Unless he found out between then and 2006, he wouldn't know. The expression on his face that morning was such that I don't think he knew. The body language and the expression on his face indicated to me that that was the first time he knew he wasn't getting a payout."

At the attorney's office afterward, Phil Jr. said he found a moment where he and Dallas were alone, and the two started to talk. Dallas revealed to him that she, too, suspected Chaz might have had something to do with her mother's death.

"I said, 'Dallas, you don't know how glad I am to hear you say that,'" Phil Jr. recalled. "'Your grandmother and I have been thinking the same thing.' Apparently, [Dallas had] already had some contact with the police."

The Alfanos went to Kathy's office that day to collect her belongings. Phil Jr. said they were packing Kathy's stuff when Dallas stopped in and let them know she'd found two guns in the home. She had the weapons in her vehicle trunk, and she was going to take the guns with her because she didn't want Chaz to have them. She said she'd also talked to the detectives, and she'd given them the keys to the house because they were going to search it.

Phil Jr. took his parents to the airport, and Dallas was going to organize and plan her mother's funeral in Las Vegas.

"The next morning, we all headed to Vegas, and that's when things really started to heat up," Phil Jr. said.

Mary and Phil Alfano Jr., along with their three children, arrived in Las Vegas on Thursday, July 13, 2006. They intended to stop at Kathy's house on Maria Elena, and Kathy's parents—en route to Las Vegas—would arrive at the house a short time later. Dallas was staying at the massive house, which she was due to inherit. Kathy's visitation and funeral would follow in Las Vegas on Friday and Saturday, respectively. The plan that day was for the entire family to gather at Kathy's house to talk and share memories, although when the Alfanos arrived at the house, Dallas wasn't there. Kathy's longtime friend, Nancy Vinik, came to the house a short time later, and a cousin of Kathy's who lived in nearby Henderson, Nevada, came by, too. No one in the Alfano clan had communicated with Chaz Higgs the details of the rendezvous, because no one in the family wanted to be around him.

Then, suddenly, the door to the home flew open, and Dallas walked in with her girlfriend—and Chaz.

"They were laughing and giggling, and we heard the wine bottles and glasses clinking," Phil Jr. said. "It was Dallas, her girlfriend, and Chaz."

Phil Jr. was uncomfortable that Chaz, whom they were all suspicious of, was there in the presence of Phil Sr. and Kay. His parents had been through enough, and he didn't want them exposed to Chaz for another moment. The elder Alfanos were incredibly brokenhearted, and having Chaz around certainly wasn't going to help matters any. Phil Jr. pulled Chaz aside and asked him to leave.

What followed was a bizarre series of events that left the entire Alfano family shocked and mortified.

"We were sitting in a little area off one of the main hallways," Phil Jr. said. "I was very low-key, and I said, 'I know my mom had told you she wanted to be here with just the family' . . . and I could smell the liquor on him. I said, 'Chaz, I don't want to cause a bunch of problems here, but I think it would be best if you leave.'"

Chaz flipped out. He started screaming, yelling, and waving his hands.

"This is bullshit!" Chaz yelled. "This is my house!"

"That's not the point," Phil Jr. told Chaz. "My parents have a lot of memories here, and they wanted to spend some time with Dallas."

Chaz continued to scream and cuss.

"I can't believe this!" Chaz yelled. "This is bullshit!

This is fucking bullshit. This is my house, and I lived here, too! I never cheated on her! Well, OK, I did have one affair, but that was it."

Phil Jr. tried to calm Chaz down, saying, "Chaz, I just want to keep the peace," but Chaz continued to curse and rant.

"This is fucking bullshit!" Chaz yelled. "I loved that fucking woman!"

Dallas walked into the room and asked what was going on. Phil Jr. said he started to explain to Dallas that he'd asked Chaz to leave, and Dallas started yelling, too.

"She starts saying, 'This is my house! I'm so sick of this!'" Phil Jr. paraphrased Dallas as saying.

Dallas, according to the witnesses, stormed out the back door of the home and threw a drinking glass to the ground, shattering it. She started yelling and fell to her knees. Her girlfriend was comforting her. Meanwhile, Chaz was in the kitchen, still yelling.

"Everyone thinks I fucking did something!" Chaz was yelling. "Maybe I should just leave. I loved that woman! I loved that fucking woman!"

Phil Jr. and his cousin were keeping their distance, when suddenly, Chaz bolted for the front door. He ran out of the house and slammed the door behind him, making a very large banging sound that rang throughout the house. Everyone heard it, which prompted Dallas's girlfriend to run back into the home and scream at everyone present.

"Are you guys fucking satisfied? He just shot himself!"

Everyone knew that Chaz hadn't shot himself and that the loud bang was just Chaz slamming the door. But witnessing the theatrics and Chaz's screaming was enough for Nancy, who suspected Chaz might actually have a gun. She retrieved her phone and called the police.

"A big, huge freak show," Nancy said. "Dallas [came

in] with Chaz, [and] they were dripping drunk. Just awful. Chaz went crazy, he started screaming, and he took a door and almost ripped it off the hinges. Everybody got scared to death. Phil and Mary's daughters were there, and they [each] turned white as a ghost. They were scared. They didn't know what to do. Everybody was shaken by it."

What bothered Nancy was hearing Chaz use vile cusswords to bad-mouth Kathy as he talked to Kay. Chaz continued to use foul language to describe Kathy, and Nancy was sickened by what was hearing.

"I won't even repeat what he said to me," Kay would say later of the conversation with Chaz.

The Las Vegas police showed up at the home within a matter of minutes and spoke with Dallas. Dallas told the police she wanted everyone out of the house, and the Alfanos and Nancy were happy to oblige that request, given the afternoon's bizarre events. The Alfanos booked a hotel room, and everyone remained dumbfounded over Chaz's actions. Kathy's funeral was scheduled for Saturday morning, and Chaz was melting down in front of everyone.

16 ... HOMICIDE COP

Dave Jenkins comes from a long line of cops, and he's proud of the honorable profession. He recognizes he lives in a world where a certain percentage of people spend the vast majority of their time trying to figure out how to hurt others and get away with it. He takes the responsibility of catching those people very seriously.

"I was raised to believe that it is just fundamentally wrong to victimize people," Jenkins said.

Jenkins is a medium-sized man with a moustache and clean-cut brown hair, and he was raised in a very religious family. His mom is a devout follower of the Church of Jesus Christ of Latter-day Saints. His dad is a longtime Sparks, Nevada, police officer. Being a cop is what Jenkins always wanted to do, and he joined the Reno Police Department on April 5, 1976. Since then, he's worked pretty much every assignment in the police department, from undercover narcotics to his current position as homicide detective. He and his wife, Theresa, have two children, of whom they are both extremely proud: their son is going to school and working at a local hospital, and their daughter has followed in her father's footsteps. There are now two officers named Jenkins on the Reno police force.

"The only remembrances I have of wanting to do anything is to be a policeman, like my father, like my grandfather, and like my uncles," Jenkins said. "My mom has two brothers, both of whom were policemen, and now my daughter is a police [officer] right here in Reno. We [at the Reno Police Department] work very, very hard, and the people here are as honest as the day is long. I think it's a good, honorable profession, and I've done well."

Jenkins often wears a tie to work with a well-pressed suit, and he carries about him an aura of both organization and determination. His passion is the investigation of violent crime.

"I've been involved in two hundred and fifty to three hundred homicide investigations," Jenkins said. "The one that bothers me the most, and the one that I have the most gratification from solving, is in 2000 I was involved in solving a twenty-three-year-old child abduction-murder. A six-year-old girl [had been] kidnapped from a local city park, sexually assaulted, and murdered in Reno. [She had been] abducted in September 1977, and we started looking at it again in the mid-1990s, when DNA technology was becoming available. The evidence yielded good DNA evidence even after all those years. We started working with the DNA evidence, and we were able to match the DNA to an offender, who is currently spending the rest of his life in prison. [He was] a previously convicted serial child rapist who had been out on parole at the time of the murder."

Another case stands out in Jenkins's career as well. Jenkins played a significant role in nabbing murderer David

Middleton, who abducted two women, sexually assaulted them, and disposed of their bodies in northern Nevada.

"That was particularly frightening because, had he not been caught, I have no doubt he would continue to offend," Jenkins said.

On Sunday, July 9, 2006, nurse Kim Ramey showed up for work to finish one of the three remaining shifts she needed to complete to finish her contract at Carson Tahoe. It was two days after her disturbing conversation with Chaz Higgs. As the traveling nurse was making the rounds and going in and out of patients' rooms, she saw a copy of a newspaper on a desk. The top story in the paper indicated that Kathy Augustine was found unconscious by her husband and was in the hospital. A chill went through her entire body when she read the headline, and it was the same exact feeling she'd had when her coworker—Kathy's husband, Chaz Higgs—talked two days earlier about how the emergency-room drug, succinylcholine, was the perfect murder weapon because it was so hard to detect during autopsies.

"Oh my God, the same bodily feeling," Ramey said. "I couldn't believe it. My gut, my intuition [told me] that he had done something to her. I thought that immediately. I thought he had killed her."

Ramey was tormented about what she should do. She was trying to tell herself that perhaps she was just paranoid and perhaps the discussion she'd had with Chaz and the fact that Kathy was now clinging to life in a hospital room were just coincidental. She finished her shift and went home and did not call the police immediately. She said she was hoping that others would come forward with evidence against Chaz. Also, she was reluctant to get involved because she'd just gone through a horrendous divorce in Virginia in which lawyers had eviscerated both parties in the legal dispute with her husband.

"You have no idea how much I despised lawyers," Ramey said. "I didn't want to deal with any more lawyers. And I was praying I would watch TV, and watch the newspaper, and that they would just arrest him, and I would be off the hook."

That didn't happen. By July 11, 2006, Ramey was back at work, struggling with what to do regarding her conversation with Chaz. She was visibly upset about what she should do, and a doctor she worked with, Richard Seher, noticed. He highly respected Ramey as a nurse, and he could tell Ramey was upset, which he found unusual. He'd never seen her struggle like this at work.

"I think she's great," Seher said of Ramey. "I'd be happy to have her take care of any of my family members. She's really on the ball."

Seher pulled Ramey aside and asked what was bothering her. Ramey told the doctor that she suspected Chaz Higgs had killed his wife by injecting her with succinylcholine.

"She said, 'I know. I know that Chaz Higgs killed her. I know what he did,'" Seher recalled. "She recounted that [when] they had worked together, she'd heard him arguing with his wife on the phone, and he [told Ramey] something to the effect of, 'I'm going to leave my wife and take the money out of the account.' Then he said, 'You know, Darren Mack was stupid. He should never have been caught. He should have used succinylcholine. He wouldn't have been caught.'"

Seher's response to Ramey's account was immediate.

"I said, 'You have to call the police,'" Seher said.

Seher, upon hearing the story, also called a colleague, Dr. Richard Price Ganchan, and told him to go to the hospital's toxicology lab to order a test for the presence of succinylcholine in Kathy Augustine. The hospital had already tested for the presence of standard drugs in Kathy's urine, but testing for succinylcholine at the hospital was simply not possible because testing for the drug is reserved for the most sophisticated forensic labs.

Seher's request, however, proved to be a critically important step in the investigation into Kathy's death because a lab technician ordered that some of Kathy's urine samples be placed in a freezer as a result of the doctor's inquiry.

Detective Dave Jenkins was sitting at his desk when the call from nurse Kim Ramey came in. Jenkins had been following the news that state controller Kathy Augustine was unconscious in the hospital and on the verge of death, but he'd assumed she was felled by a heart attack. That, after all, was what her husband had been saying in public, and that's what all the media accounts he'd read indicated. Jenkins had no involvement in Kathy's case at the time and no reason to believe he would have any involvement.

"I assumed it to be exactly what the media had portrayed it as," Jenkins said.

A nervous Ramey, speaking four days after her conversation with Higgs, recounted all of the details of her conversation. She said that on the day prior to Kathy's hospitalization, Chaz had talked about what an idiot Darren Mack was for stabbing his wife and that he would have been smarter if he "would have just hit her with succs."

Jenkins had no idea what "succs" was, and Ramey explained that the drug is succinylcholine, which is commonly used to momentarily paralyze a patient in an emergency room for the purposes of inserting a breathing tube or device.

"'Succs' is the term that all nurses know who work in emergency and critical care," Ramey said of the abbreviation for the drug succinylcholine.

"We use it as a paralytic," Ramey said. "We use it only when the patient is ready to go into a respiratory arrest or a cardiac arrest. It paralyzes you so we can safely get the breathing tube down someone's throat, so we can ventilate, breath for them. I administer it intravenously. It's . . . immediate."

Jenkins was very curious about the information he was receiving. He made the determination that Ramey sounded believable, and the information she had was very specific. The tip warranted further investigation, which had to be done immediately. Jenkins and a fellow homicide detective, Scott Hopkins, traveled to Washoe Medical Center that Tuesday, July 11, to ask the doctors some questions.

"Kim Ramey sounded credible," Jenkins said. "My initial reaction was I'd never even heard of succinylcholine. I didn't even know if it was a viable method capable of causing [Kathy Augustine's] hospitalization."

Jenkins tracked down the nurse supervisor in the ICU at Washoe Medical and asked if it was possible that an injection of succinylcholine could have caused Kathy's condition.

"I said, 'Let me run something by you: I just got this phone call that raised the possibility that she had been administered succinylcholine,'" Jenkins recalled of his conversation with the nursing supervisor. "'Would that seem possible or viable? Could you eliminate that based on what you know about Kathy's medical condition?'"

The response the nurse gave Jenkins was very telling.

"'OK, that would make sense because her condition at this point makes no sense at all,'" Jenkins recalled the nurse saying. "'Yeah, succs could do that.'"

The nurse also told Jenkins that some other nurses had expressed concerns about Chaz Higgs's behavior in the hospital and that he didn't seem to be appropriately concerned for his wife's condition. And then the nurse added, "Oh, by the way, they've made the decision to end life support. She's expected to expire today."

Jenkins contemplated the information he had in front of him. Kathy was one of the most powerful people in state government, and she was on the verge of death. He had a tip that her husband had poisoned her with succinylcholine, and he knew very little about the drug other than the fact that it seemed plausible that it could have left Kathy unconscious, in a hospital bed, with her eyes rolled back into her skull. Jenkins's heart was pounding because, after three decades of police work and nearly three hundred murder cases, this was the first time he'd ever investigated a possible poisoning homicide.

He was assured that urine and blood samples had been taken and were preserved.

"Most of my cases involve someone obviously dead and obviously dead by criminal means," Jenkins said. "When you have five or six gunshot injuries or a knife sticking out of your back, you can say, 'OK, that's a murder.' This one didn't start like that."

Steve Woods, a deputy coroner investigator for Washoe County, Nevada, arrived at the Washoe Medical Center's Intensive Care Unit on July 11 at the request of police. He saw Kathy Augustine in her hospital bed, he talked with nurses, and then he spoke to her family members. He specifically talked to Kathy's husband, Chaz Higgs, and her daughter, Dallas Augustine, and learned that Kathy was going to be removed from life support that afternoon.

"[I discussed] basically a history of what might have been going on in her prior health . . . and I advised Mr. Higgs and Dallas that I felt that an autopsy should be done, and we would do one tomorrow at the coroner's office," Woods said.

After Kathy was taken off of life support and she passed away, Woods photographed her body and sealed it in a body bag. He accompanied the body to the hospital morgue, and he was met there by people from the funeral home. From there, the body was transferred to the Washoe County Coroner's Office, where it was weighed and measured in preparation for autopsy. Woods then returned to the hospital and went to the facility's lab, where he picked up blood and urine samples taken from the time of Kathy's admission to the time of her death.

"I thought there could be a possibility of an overdose, so I requested them," Woods said. "Several samples were frozen, and the rest were cold."

Traditionally, Woods said, such samples are placed in a refrigerator and chilled but not frozen. He noted that receiving urine samples in a frozen state "[was] very unusual."

The autopsy on Kathy Augustine was performed by Dr. Ellen G. I. Clark, of the Washoe County Coroner's Office. Reno Police Department detectives Dave Jenkins and Scott Hopkins were now the lead investigators on the case, and they were also present for the autopsy. Kathy's medical records were again reviewed by authorities, and by her doctor, Jerry Jones, who had treated her since 1991. He'd last seen her a month prior, in June 2006. He'd reported her to be in "good health. Her blood pressure was normal. I listened to her heart and lungs. They were clear. Her heart rhythm was normal." A doctor at Washoe had previously performed an angiogram that showed Kathy's heart was healthy. The autopsy by Clark then confirmed what the medical records were telling her: that Kathy had no significant heart problems.

"There was not evidence of the typical hardening of the arteries or . . . clogging of the arteries that we often see associated with so-called heart attacks or myocardial infarction," Clark said. "That . . . was relevant in my opinion, because Ms. Augustine had reportedly presented to the hospital having suffered a heart attack. There [was] no evidence of . . . significant obstruction of the coronary arteries, or the arteries which carry blood to the heart muscle."

The autopsy did show Kathy had a modest defect with a heart valve. The valve that had the defect allows blood to pass out of the large muscular chamber on the left side of the heart into the main circulatory system, that is, the aorta and the large vessels in the heart.

"In my determination, the change in the . . . valve was minimal," Clark said.

The interior examination of Kathy showed a significant amount of brain swelling.

"A swollen brain can be associated with decreased blood flow or decreased oxygen to the brain, so that became a significant finding," Clark said.

Finally, during the external examination of the body, Clark noticed a peculiar mark on Kathy's left buttock. It looked to her like a possible injection site. The small spot on Kathy's buttock was blue-green in color with some purple and red tinges. Clark thought the mark was significant, and she noted it in her autopsy findings.

"There were actually two punctuate areas of discoloration that are potentially significant [and] they have an overall configuration in appearance that would be consistent with needle punctures or injection sites," Clark said.

The irregularity on Kathy's skin was photographed, and Clark performed an autopsy procedure called a cut down, which amounts to a straight surgical incision with a scalpel to examine the skin underneath the surface injury.

"That was done for this wound, and [it] demonstrated a very narrow track of bleeding into the tissue that was directly beneath the very small injuries on the surface," Clark said.

This looked to Clark like further evidence of an injection site, although she was unable to measure how far a needle would have protruded into Kathy's body. Jenkins witnessed Clark perform the cut down and secure tissues in the area of the site for further testing. Jenkins said he, too, observed what looked to him to be physical evidence consistent with an injection site on Kathy's left buttock.

"I saw the hemorrhage underneath the skin," the detective said. "I looked at its placement and its location, and it was consistent with a small and subtle puncture. It looks like a lot of injection sites."

The one curiosity surrounding the purported injection site was its location. It was on Kathy's buttock, meaning if succinylcholine was injected there, it would not have been administered through an IV, which is the standard way of administering the drug. If Kathy was injected with succinylcholine into her buttock, this would have constituted what is known as an intramuscular injection as opposed to an injection of the fluids directly into her veins, and an intramuscular injection, the investigators learned, would mean that it would take longer for the bloodstream to absorb the drug through muscles and fatty tissues. Nonetheless, the investigators with the police department and the coroner's office found the injection site to be highly suspicious. They further examined Kathy's medical records and found no evidence that the injection site was the result of medical treatment Kathy received from paramedics, nurses, or doctors. There was no medical explanation for why the injection site would be there. It was a highly suspicious clue, and it seemed to fit with Ramey's account.

Now Chaz Higgs's wife was dead, she had what looked like an injection site on her buttock, and nurses at the hospital had told the detectives that succinylcholine poisoning would fit with Kathy's symptoms. Detectives Jenkins and Hopkins, Dr. Clark, and the coroner's investigator all consulted with William H. Anderson, the chief toxicologist for the forensic science division of the Washoe County Sheriff's Office. They agreed that the obvious next step in the investigation would be to initiate the testing of Kathy Augustine's blood and urine to determine if she had, in fact, been poisoned with succinylcholine. The problem, Anderson told his colleagues, was that succinylcholine was notoriously difficult to detect in human bodies. He decided against the idea of the sheriff's office performing the drug screen for succinylcholine because they had never done it before. He performed an extensive amount of research and determined the Federal Bureau of Investigation's toxicology lab in Quantico, Virginia, would be perhaps the only lab in the country capable of testing Kathy's blood and urine for the presence of succinylcholine.

"This was a case," Jenkins said, "that would be made or fail based on science. We all knew that if the tests for succinylcholine came back negative, it was over."

The detectives agreed as well to search Kathy and Chaz's home to see if more evidence could be obtained. Jenkins returned to his office and drew up a search warrant application for the home in Reno. It read in part:

Detective Dave Jenkins . . . your affiant, has become familiar with facts and circumstances involved in the alleged crime of furnishing a controlled substance, a felony violation of Nevada [law].

On July 8, 2006, at about 6:44 a.m., Reno Emergency Medical Services' paramedics Pratt and Fuentes were dispatched to the report of an unconscious female. . . . The paramedics reportedly administered CPR until Ms. Augustine began breathing and had a pulse. Ms. Augustine was subsequently transported by ambulance to the Washoe Medical Center where she was admitted for treatment. . . . Upon her admission into the hospital, medical personnel obtained and submitted blood samples from Ms. Augustine to the Washoe Medical Center Laboratory in an attempt to diagnose and treat her.

On July 11, 2006, at approximately 3:30 p.m., your affiant was contacted by a citizen complainant who alleged that he/she had information that caused him/her to believe that Ms. Augustine had been intentionally administered a controlled substance in an attempt to kill her. . . . The same citizen complainant alleged that he/she had personally been told by that individual that he/she had considered administering/providing a controlled substance to Ms. Augustine that would result in her dying from cardiac arrest.

After being admitted to the hospital, Ms. Augustine never regained consciousness and was pronounced dead on July 11, 2006, at 4:35 p.m.

The warrant summarized the autopsy by Dr. Ellen G. I. Clark on July 12, 2006. Clark said the death of Ms. Augustine was suspicious and that she did not observe the typical evidence of coronary disease that is present in a heart attack victim. After receiving the search warrant from a justice of the peace, Jenkins, Hopkins, Anderson, and a team of crime-scene investigators descended on the Augustine home. Prescription medicine bottles in the names of Chaz Higgs and Kathy Augustine were collected, as were plastic Visine bottles containing the clear liquid. Bedding and sheets were collected from the bed in the master bedroom, and a date book–journal containing handwritten notes was confiscated.

Jenkins said there was one discovery during the serving of the search warrant that was critical to the investigation: in the bedroom where Kathy was found unconscious, the police found Chaz's backpack. In a pouch in the backpack was a glass vial of a drug known as etomidate. Etomidate, the detectives learned, was a drug commonly used in conjunction with succinylcholine in a hospital setting. It was not the type of drug anyone would or should have sitting around the house, and it seemed to indicate that Chaz had taken it from a medical setting.

"No one could explain to me why he would ever have a vial of etomidate with him," Jenkins said. "Certainly, in my mind, there was every reason at that point to go forward with the investigation."

17 ... MELTDOWN

Las Vegas Review-Journal reporter Ed Vogel had stood about three feet away from Chaz Higgs during the press conference and listened to the man talk about finding his wife, Kathy Augustine, unconscious. Vogel had heard Chaz characterize his wife's illness as a heart attack, and he included those contentions in his stories for the *Review-Journal* reporting on Kathy's death the next day.

Vogel, though, was still mildly suspicious of Chaz. He didn't know quite why, but something wasn't quite right. Others in the media were somewhat suspicious, too, but there was no known information to indicate there was anything other than a heart attack to blame for Kathy's demise. Vogel's suspicions were heightened further, however, on Friday, July 14, 2006, when he received a tip that indicated that the Reno police were investigating Kathy's death. Vogel also learned some very specific information: that police thought it possible Kathy had been poisoned with a hard-to-detect drug and that Chaz was a suspect.

Vogel was startled. If true, it would be a shocking story. The undeniable pulse of a story was brewing, and Vogel knew it.

"Suspicions are swirling," Vogel said.

Vogel called *Review-Journal* managing editor Mary Hynes in Las Vegas, and the two discussed what steps they should take next. The source of the tip seemed credible, and the two discussed the possibility of Vogel calling Chaz and asking him if he'd been notified of any type of investigation.

Vogel agreed to do it.

"I talked to Mary Hynes about whether we could use the information . . . that people were accusing him of murder," Vogel said. "We decided to approach . . . [Chaz] about it."

Vogel called Kathy's cell-phone number because he knew Chaz was using it, but the reporter was surprised when Chaz actually began answering Vogel's very pointed questions.

"I told him that, 'We heard this rumor that you had taken a drug out of the hospital and you'd used it to kill Kathy Augustine,'" Vogel recalled of what he bluntly told Chaz. "'Everyone's saying you killed her.'

"He said he was shocked," Vogel said, paraphrasing Chaz's response. "'How could anyone ever think that of me? No, no, no. . . . My wife was great.' He defended the relationship . . . [and] he was somewhat tearful, almost crying."

Vogel said during the brief conversation Chaz mentioned to the reporter that Kathy had been in a long-running dispute with Treasurer Brian Krolicki and former treasurer Bob Seale.

"I loved this woman who died, and now there is all this [expletive] coming up," Chaz told Vogel. "It is just crazy for people to assume I had something to do with it. I asked for the autopsy. I want to clear it up. My wife was a healthy fifty-year-old woman who dropped dead. I want to find out what happened. People don't know what went on in our home. She was frazzled and stressed out."

Vogel wrote down everything Chaz said, then hung up.

Chaz tried to kill himself a few hours later.

Chaz Higgs had apparently been drinking into the wee hours of the morning of Friday, July 14, 2006. Kathy's funeral was scheduled for the following day in Las Vegas, and her viewing was that afternoon. On that Friday, hours after Vogel called, Dallas Augustine reported to police that Chaz had dressed himself in a suit, locked himself in an upstairs bedroom of the Augustine home, and slit his wrists.

Dallas busted through the doors of the bedroom and found Chaz in a pool of blood.

She immediately called 911.

Chaz was wheeled out on a gurney into an ambulance. The critical-care nurse was hospitalized with non-life-threatening gashes to his wrists. He was released from the hospital that Friday evening.

Authorities collected a suicide note that Chaz wrote. In the note, Chaz alleged that Kathy's political enemies had killed her. There was no mention of a heart attack in the note. He named Kathy's political adversary, Brian Krolicki, and former treasurer Bob Seale, who had butted heads with Kathy in the past, as Kathy's enemies. Krolicki had tried to eliminate Kathy's position at the controller's office years earlier, and Krolicki was Seale's protégé at the treasurer's office. Chaz also mentioned the rumors of a mismanaged education fund at the treasurer's office that Kathy had been asking questions about and implied this was a possible reason for what really happened to Kathy. Chaz added in the suicide note that the Republicans were putting forth a "patsy" candidate, Mark DeStefano, against Kathy in the treasurer's race. Chaz addressed his suicide note to the media. The following excerpts are from the actual suicide note:

Media, this is the story.

Brian Krolicki and Bob Seal [sic] have had investments in an Atlanta company for sixteen years. Brian is about to leave the office: so how can they continue these investments by putting a front, a patsy, whatever you want to call it, into office? Mark DeStafano [sic] just throws money around and people do what he wants. Has anyone investigated his background? It looks very interesting. Kathy and I have been looking at it for months. Isn't it interesting that the complaints that marked the impeachment proceedings sat in the AG's office for over a year before [they were] acted upon? Isn't it interesting that a week after Kathy and I returned from DC from an interview [with] John Snow, for the position of the next US treasurer, that the impeachment investigation started? Isn't it interesting that eight years ago, when Kathy became controller, Bob Seal [sic] told her, "[Y]ou are going to fuck it all up." What was she going to fuck up, perhaps some money deals in Atlanta? The whole impeachment was contrived to get rid of Kathy over money. Just ask Brian, Bob, Mark, and do not forget about Paul Adams. Does the story come together now? I am truly looking forward to seeing these gentlemen in the afterlife so we can have a few words. Thank you for taking my wife away from me.

Of course, they will deny all of this, but just take a

*look. If you need more info. Ask Joe Pitts, who is also
running for treasurer. He and Kathy corresponded on
numerous occasions about this and all that they found
by investigating DeStefano.*

When Ed Vogel came into work the following day and
learned Chaz had tried to kill himself, he was overcome
with guilt at the possibility that he'd played a role in Chaz
losing it.

"I was like, 'Oh my god! Did I push him over [the
edge?]' " recalled Vogel. "That was my concern. I talked to
Mary about it. 'Good God, did I do that to him?' "

Vogel was assigned to a team of reporters working on
a follow-up story about Chaz's attempted suicide, and the
story would drop a bombshell: the *Review-Journal* interviewed Chuck Augustine's son Greg by cell phone. Greg
Augustine told the paper he thought Kathy's death was
suspicious, and he recounted how his father, Chuck, had
been in the care of Chaz Higgs when he died suddenly and
unexpectedly.

"He was getting better, and then suddenly all his organs
failed," said Greg Augustine, whose father was married to
Kathy for fifteen years. "There never was an autopsy. His
body should be exhumed."

The attempted wrist slitting seemed to show a possible
consciousness of guilt by Chaz, and a pent-up flood of suspicions about the nurse came into the open.

Kay, Phil Sr., and Phil Alfano Jr. learned of Chaz's
attempted suicide on Friday as they were driving to the
funeral home to help with arrangements. Kathy's longtime
neighbor, John Tsitouras, called Phil Jr. to let him know
that there was an ambulance in front of Kathy's house, and

Chaz was being hauled out on a gurney. In shock, Phil Jr. called Detective Jenkins. Jenkins called the Las Vegas Metropolitan Police Department and learned Chaz had slit his wrists. It was already a traumatic day for Kathy's family because her viewing was that afternoon, and the funeral was the next day. Now, Chaz had apparently tried to commit suicide.

The Alfanos thought Chaz's suicide was another bizarre act, and they didn't believe for a second that Chaz was trying to kill himself. Instead, they believed he was trying to deflect attention. After all, he was a critical-care nurse. He'd know how to slit his wrists to kill himself if he really wanted to do it.

"I didn't know what to make of all of it," Phil Jr. said. "One more thing going on, and the funeral is the next day. We went to the viewing. The whole thing was very, very hard to get through with all this weird stuff going on."

There was, however, one person who came to Chaz's defense. Kathy's daughter, Dallas, asked the public not to pass judgment on Chaz. Despite public opinion that the suicide attempt made Chaz look very suspicious, Dallas stood up for him. She told veteran Las Vegas television reporter George Knapp that she did not believe Chaz had killed her mother. Instead, she thought the suicide attempt was likely the act of a "grieving husband, and certain things had pushed him over the edge, I guess."

"That act makes a lot of people think he's gotta be guilty, but not you?" Knapp asked Dallas.

"No. It's in a couple of papers that there was a suicide note, but it was not a confession," Dallas said.

When questioned by Knapp about Chaz's legal status with Kathy's estate, Dallas said Chaz was not in a position to benefit financially from Kathy's death.

"We already knew what my mom drew up, her paperwork, two years ago, what was entailed then," Dallas said. "As far as financial gain, there was no reason that I can see."

Kathy Augustine was memorialized at the Guardian Angel Cathedral in Las Vegas on Saturday, July 15, 2006. More than two hundred people attended the event at Desert Inn Road and Las Vegas Boulevard. Kathy's body was then buried at Davis Cemetery. Several prominent Nevadans were on hand, including Governor Kenny Guinn and U.S. Congresswoman Shelley Berkley, a Democrat. Kathy's longtime priest and friend, Father Mike Keliher, of Saint Viator Catholic Church, where Kathy was a member, addressed the mourners.

"I never thought in a hundred years I'd be here standing before you for the funeral of Kathy Augustine," said Father Keliher. "The sudden and unexpected death of Kathy Augustine confronts us all."

Kathy's brothers, Phil Jr. and Tony, were among the pallbearers. Her daughter, Dallas, had spent hours organizing the ceremony. The Alfanos were exhausted and sorrowful, and they were disappointed by Dallas's decision to sit next to Chaz's parents. Phil Jr. said Dallas was "not talking to anyone" in the Alfano family. Phil Jr. said the family was also shocked when Chaz's twin brother, Michael, showed up, but Chaz was a no-show. Everyone present at the funeral was devastated by the loss of Kathy, and Kathy's mother, Kay Alfano, remembers little of the day.

"In the Catholic religion, they present the crucifix," Kay said. "Father Mike gave it to us. I was at the funeral service. I know I was there. People came up to me, talked to me, I was there, but I don't remember it."

Phil Jr. said he, Tony, and his parents decided not to attend the reception afterward. The Alfano brothers were concerned about their dad's ability to endure any more stress on what had already been a stifling hot, grief-stricken day.

"We did not attend the reception at all," Phil Jr. said. "We left directly from the cemetery and drove back to my parents' home in Southern California. We apologized to a few family members before we left and asked them to explain to others why we weren't there.

"I was afraid my dad wasn't going to make it," Phil Jr. said.

18 . . . SUCCINYLCHOLINE

They shoot monkeys out of the trees with darts coated with it. Shoot the monkey and within about five minutes the monkey can't hold on.

—Dr. Brian Andresen, founder, Lawrence Livermore Forensic
 Science Center, on the drug curare, which later was synthesized by scientists into succinylcholine

If you walk into a bar or club in California, there's a chance you might see Brian Andresen jamming on the drums, and you would have no way of knowing that the man pounding the skins in front of you is one of America's most brilliant scientists. In fact, you'd be hard-pressed to find someone with a more impressive résumé than Dr. Brian Andresen. He is a tall, thin, brown-haired, humble, and polite sixty-one-year-old who has spent his life trying to make the world better through science. As a professor at Ohio State University, Andresen's significant contribution to society was the role he played in the discovery of the cause of Reye's syndrome—a devastating affliction that caused the brains of children to swell inexplicably until death. The killer of children was especially prevalent in the Midwest, and it was a mystery as to what was causing it.

"Between Michigan, Ohio, and Wisconsin, they were having tremendous problems," Andresen said.

Andresen was working as a full tenured professor at Ohio State in 1979, and he started studying the blood samples of all the children afflicted by the disease. He used an amazing piece of scientific equipment called a gas chromatography–mass spectrometer, or GC-MS, to analyze the blood. The technology of the GC-MS was actually fathered by Andresen's mentor, Klaus Biemann, at the Massachusetts Institute of Technology. It involves spinning a test sample one wants to analyze at high speeds and putting it under gas pressure. The procedure serves to separate compounds, allowing for extensive analysis of the presence of the materials in the test sample.

Andresen relied on the lessons taught to him by Biemann at MIT to look for a cause of Reye's syndrome.

"These kids were presenting just like they'd been poisoned with some sort of drug or agent," Andresen said. "Their blood was analyzed, as were their body fluids, and they didn't show anything unusual."

Andresen used the gas chromatography–mass spectrometer to test all of the children's blood. A clear pattern was identified in performing the tests: all of the children had aspirin in their systems.

"In every case, there was aspirin," Andresen said. "Pediatric departments canvassed parents . . . and when the kids got sick, they always got aspirin. They never got Tylenol. Aspirin."

It turned out that certain children could not tolerate a cold virus or fever in combination with aspirin.

"It goes to the liver, and intoxicates their liver, the liver makes bad chemicals that go into the brain, and the brain starts swelling," Andresen said. "Some kids have a predisposition when they are sick from a common cold virus combined with aspirin."

The discovery led to an extensive informational campaign to inform parents not to give their kids aspirin under those circumstances, and today, the affliction is a rarity.

"The disease is virtually gone now," Andresen said. "No one knows about it. It's something I've done, but nobody really knows about it."

Andresen's repeated successes in the scientific lab led to his recruitment to start up the Lawrence Livermore Forensic Science Center, a premier, world-class scientific lab in every respect. It serves a critical function to federal agencies such as the Department of Energy, the Federal Bureau of Investigation, and the Central Intelligence Agency in understanding how organic chemical analysis can help the agencies solve all sorts of problems. One part of the lab's many responsibilities includes helping law enforcement solve complex forensic cases.

In 1997, Andresen was overseeing the forensic lab at Livermore when he got a call from police in Glendale, California. The police were investigating a respiratory therapist, Efren Saldivar, who had allegedly confessed to killing up to fifty patients with the muscle relaxant Pavulon and the paralytic agent succinylcholine. The police had a dilemma on their hands because Saldivar recanted after confessing, and police had no other evidence to prove that the drugs had been used on the patients.

"The city of Glendale gave our lab money . . . and we exhumed twenty bodies," Andresen said.

Pavulon is a full skeletal muscle paralyzer often used in conjunction with the placement of a patient on a breathing device in an emergency room. The exhumations proved successful when Andresen developed a specific scientific protocol for testing for, and identifying, the presence of Pavulon in a human corpse. Of the twenty deaths deemed suspicious under Saldivar's watch, Pavulon was found in six of them, and eventually, Saldivar pleaded guilty to murdering six patients and was sentenced to life in prison.

Of particular interest to Andresen, however, was the scientific detection method he developed for the presence of succinylcholine in dead bodies as well. Succinylcholine, he said, is truly unique in the world of drugs. Its origins can be traced to the jungle, where it occurs naturally in trees in the form of curare. The basic structure of the drug was synthesized by scientists into its synthetic form, succinylcholine. The drug, he said, consists of two nitrogens separated by ten carbons. It is a big, bulky molecule that, when injected into the body, completely paralyzes the muscle system by fitting perfectly into muscle receptors and stopping the contraction of muscles.

"The muscles just don't contract," Andresen said.

The medical application for the drug is most often found in emergency rooms when a patient needs an immediate insertion of a breathing device to live. In those cases, succinylcholine may be administered to paralyze the patient temporarily while the breathing device is inserted.

Given a large-enough dose of succinylcholine, without the use of a respiratory device, the drug eventually paralyzes the muscles that allow for breathing. The patient is deprived of oxygen and dies.

Andresen said what makes the drug unique is not only its molecular size, but also its quick metabolism in the human body, which makes succinylcholine one of the hardest drugs in the world to detect in humans. Succinylcholine, he explained, is made up of succinic acid and choline, and both are naturally occurring in the body.

"The body is totally used to seeing [succinic acid and choline] . . . in the body, and it has enzymes to break [succinylcholine] apart," Andresen said. "The body immediately detoxifies it. It disappears real fast."

Complicating the matter further for police investigations is the fact that as succinylcholine degrades, it produces succinylmonocholine, which is naturally found in decomposing bodies. This means that proving a decomposing body had succinylcholine in it is profoundly difficult. Pretty much the only way to do it is to prove that the exhumed corpse in question had elevated levels of succinylmonocholine in the remains. To do that, Andresen said, he has recommended that investigators exhuming a body in a succinylcholine-poisoning investigation should also consider exhuming other bodies in the area to compare their succinylmonocholine levels. Then, a determination can be made as to whether the suspected victim has elevated levels in the remains.

"I tell coroners they have to exhume a control sample, either an animal or patient, to compare," Andresen said.

History told Andresen, as well, that succinylcholine is an extremely dangerous drug when in the wrong person's hands. The drug has been commonly linked to medical professionals accused of murder, because it is so hard to detect. Time and again, medical professionals have been accused of using succinylcholine to kill, and time and again, there were problems prosecuting the accused because of problems in the forensic testing for succinylcholine.

In 1961, Dr. Carl A. Coppolino, an anesthesiologist, was accused of murdering his wife, Dr. Carmela Coppolino, and William Farber, the husband of Coppolino's ex-lover, in a double love triangle. He was accused of poisoning and smothering Farber and poisoning his wife. He was convicted of second-degree murder and served twelve and a half years despite serious questions about the forensic testing that identified the presence of succinylcholine in bodies.

In the 1980s and 1990s, one of the world's most notorious medical serial killers—Dr. Michael Swango—was investigated in connection with thirty to fifty deaths. He went from hospital to hospital, occasionally under an alias, and patients started dying mysteriously. His crime spree is alleged to have stretched from West Virginia to Africa, and one of his many methods of killing was the injection of epinephrine, a heart stimulant, and succinylcholine.

In 1981, authorities said Texas vocational nurse Genene Jones started poisoning children in her care. Children went into cardiac arrest so often under Jones's care that she earned the nickname "Death Nurse" from her colleagues. Evidence showed she'd purchased succinylcholine in one case involving a child's death, and she was convicted of murder. In another case, she was convicted of killing a child with the blood-thinning agent heparin. She was sentenced to sixty years.

In 1992, a nurse named Richard A. Williams fell under suspicion after authorities said forty-one patients at a veteran's hospital in Missouri died while under Williams's care. Nearly a decade later, Williams was arrested and charged in ten deaths after forensic testing on exhumed bodies indicated what authorities said was the presence of succinylmonocholine in the bodies of Williams's patients. The charges were later dropped when questions were raised about the scientific validity of the tests.

In 1998, a nurse named Kimberly Hricko went on a mystery weekend retreat with her husband. The couple watched a play about a fictional poisoning murder and was then asked, as members of the audience, to help solve the crime. Hours later, authorities said Hricko injected her husband with succinylcholine and set the hotel room on fire. She was convicted of murder and sentenced to prison.

In 1991, a medical examiner, Dr. William Sybers, reported that his wife, Kay, had died at their Florida home.

The woman had an injection site on her arm, and a prosecutor pursued charges against Sybers in the face of evidence he was having an affair and stood to benefit from his wife's death by avoiding a costly divorce. A jury determined in 2001 that Sybers was guilty of killing his wife with an injection of succinylcholine, but the verdict was overturned by an appeals court because it was determined that the testing for succinylcholine had not been adequately scrutinized and proven over time. Facing retrial, Sybers pleaded guilty to manslaughter and was sentenced to the time he'd already served—two years. The scientist in the case later acknowledged that he'd been wrong about the significance of his finding of succinylmonocholine in the victim's remains.

Andresen said a very large dose of succinylcholine would be fatal if the patient is left unattended, and the chances of detecting the drug in the body rapidly decrease in just a matter of hours. The best way to detect succinylcholine in blood or urine is to test for it right away, before it degrades and becomes succinylmonocholine. But the difficulty in detecting the drug is not the only disturbing aspect of succinylcholine when used as a potential murder weapon.

Andresen said equally disturbing is the torture that a person goes through if he or she is fatally poisoned with succinylcholine.

The victim, he said, would be totally conscious up until the last moments. The muscles are paralyzed, he said, but the victim would be completely aware of his or her surroundings for several minutes until the oxygen deprivation becomes too much for the brain to endure.

"If you were in the hospital and it was injected into your IV line, you wouldn't be able to move your arms, or feet, and you can't move your diaphragm, so you can't breathe,"

Andresen said. "You are wide awake, you can see, but you can't breathe. The feeling must be terrible. You know you should breathe, but you can't move for the last few minutes. You must be completely crazy before you die."

Andresen believes there should be much stricter controls on succinylcholine. It is a drug that is not handled as stringently in hospitals as other dangerous drugs are, and it is usually within relatively easy access to doctors and nurses.

19 ... FBI

Behind every case is a victim—man, woman or child, and the people who care for them. We dedicate our efforts . . . [at the] FBI Laboratory building to those victims.

—The dedication of the FBI's new lab in Quantico, Virginia

In the Tom Clancy novel *Teeth of the Tiger*, a fictional intelligence agency invents a hypodermic needle disguised as a pen. The intelligence agents then use the pen to poison terrorists with the drug succinylcholine because succinylcholine is difficult to detect and, oftentimes, people think the victim has had a heart attack. One terrorist's terrifying death from succinylcholine poisoning is described in the book in detail. Detective Dave Jenkins of the Reno Police Department coincidentally happened to read the book as he investigated Chaz Higgs, and he found the contents of the Clancy thriller scary and ironic, given the case he was investigating.

"The description in that book of what happened is pretty frightening and pretty accurate," Jenkins said.

The wait for the results on Kathy's blood, urine, and plasma samples, along with the flesh from the suspected injection site on her buttock, that had been sent to the FBI lab in Quantico, Virginia, for succinylcholine testing would take an agonizing two months. Jenkins said that shortly after the samples were sent off, he got a call from a top-notch defense attorney out of California named Alan Baum, who said he was calling on behalf of Chaz Higgs.

"He was fishing, saying, 'What's going on?'" Jenkins recalled. "'And by the way, detective, what type of investigation is this?'"

"'It's a death investigation,'" Jenkins said he told him. "'There were some allegations made. I don't know if they are true or false. We are looking into it.'"

Detective Jenkins reflected after the call on the fact that he'd pretty much been in contact with everyone in Kathy's case with the exception of Chaz Higgs. Kathy's brother Phil Jr. called him regularly. Dallas Augustine seemed genuinely shocked at the thought that there was a police investigation, and she was concerned. Even Chuck Augustine's family had been in touch with him, but the only inquiry he ever got from Chaz was through a defense attorney.

"If my wife were to die, and I thought it was a natural death, and someone were to suggest she was murdered, I'd want to know what was going on immediately," Jenkins said. "But he never came forward to us, and the only contact we had with him was with his attorney."

Jenkins found the timing of Chaz's suicide attempt at Kathy's home to be important as well: it was after the police search of Kathy's home, and after the bottle of etomidate was found, but before Kathy's funeral.

"At that time, he was very aware of the circumstances of the police involvement," Jenkins said.

The detective did not know at the time that *Review-Journal* reporter Ed Vogel had confronted Chaz that very morning about suspicions Chaz had poisoned Kathy.

"As we started interviewing the neighbors in Reno and the neighbors in Las Vegas, we started to realize that the relationship [between Chaz and Kathy] was certainly rocky and tumultuous at best," Jenkins said. "There was a neighbor in Reno Kathy had confided in, saying if anything happens to her, they should look at Chaz. Coworkers had described Chaz's marriage as a troubled relationship. They talked about him being very derogatory about her. None of them could understand why he could stay in the relationship for such a long time if he was so unhappy and displeased.

"We continued to talk to [Chaz's] associates," Jenkins said. "We continued to field calls, follow up on tips, and do background investigation."

Jenkins talked to Kirstin Lattin, Chaz Higgs's second wife, who told him about Chaz's propensity to hook her up to IVs and even give her vitamin B injections in her buttock. Jenkins found the information relevant.

"A critical-care nurse certainly would be capable of administering an intramuscular injection, and Mrs. Lattin's statement showed he had a propensity to do injections outside of the hospital," Jenkins said.

Reno detectives were at the same time "discreetly" tracking Chaz, and they knew their suspect, who had not yet been arrested or charged with anything, had not only missed Kathy's funeral, but had then left Nevada within a few weeks of her burial. Now he was staying in both Virginia and North Carolina with his brother and parents, respectively.

The detectives examined the inheritance left behind to Dallas and learned that Chaz stood to inherit very little: some sports equipment and a BMW. The detectives knew that Dallas stood to inherit most of Kathy's riches. After interviewing Dallas, they determined she had had nothing to do with her mother's death.

All of the evidence pointed to Chaz.

"If succinylcholine was the mechanism, who would have been in the position to administer it?" Jenkins said. "If you are to believe Chaz, in his initial statements to the paramedics and in his 911 call, all of the evidence suggested that he was the only person who could have administered succinylcholine at a time that would have rendered her unconscious."

The detectives were also in touch with Chuck Augustine's sons from his first marriage. Greg Augustine and Jenkins agreed that Chuck Augustine's death, while under Chaz Higgs's care, needed further investigation. That responsibility would fall to Las Vegas police, Jenkins said, because Chuck Augustine died at Sunrise Hospital in Las Vegas—not Reno.

"The Augustine family was very concerned about how their father had died," Jenkins said.

On July 30, 2006, just two and a half weeks after Kathy's death, Linda Ramirez sent an e-mail to an old friend, Chaz Higgs. She mentioned in the e-mail that she'd broken up with her boyfriend. She did not know at the time that Kathy had died. Chaz responded to her via e-mail on August 3, 2006.

"Hey, good to hear from you," Chaz wrote. "I am single also now." He told her that his wife had died from a sudden heart attack and that he was thinking about moving to California. "Sound good? Want to go with me? I have never forgotten about you. . . . Miss you," he wrote.

Ramirez was startled to hear that Kathy was dead. She surfed the Internet and learned about the suspicions swirling around Chaz. She was amazed. She wrote him back asking if it was true that he'd tried to kill himself. Chaz responded on August 26.

"I told you a long time ago that I was in love with you, and it is true," Chaz wrote. "It does not go away. You only have one true love in your life, and you are it. Whatever it takes, that is what I will do," he told her, before going on to say that although he'd love to give her the details about Kathy, his lawyer wouldn't let him talk to anyone yet. He boasted about all of the media that has been chasing him, "like *People* magazine, Fox News, *48 Hours,* Geraldo, the *New York Times.*"

Chaz then reiterated how much he loved and missed Ramirez and said that after two years, he could no longer hold back his emotions for her. He again brought up the idea of them running off together.

"Lets go to Mexico. Or, why don't you go to San Dog with me?" Higgs said, using a slang term for San Diego. "We can run to Mexico all the time. Or we can go to Sedona, or Santa Fe. You tell me. I'll take you anywhere. I can make you the happiest woman on this earth. I know I can. I know me, and I know what I am capable of and what I can do for you in every way.

"Again, I'm not trying to freak you out here. I just love you, and that's a fact. You are all I've ever wanted since I first saw you. . . . I wanted to run away with you and never look back."

Ramirez heard nothing more from Chaz.

Madeline A. Montgomery is a forensic chemist and toxicologist at the Federal Bureau of Investigation's lab in Quantico, Virginia. The lab is a massive complex of 500,000 square feet filled with the most advanced scientific testing equipment in the world. The lab provides scientific analysis for federal law enforcement agencies and other American law enforcement police and sheriffs' departments free of charge. Some of the nation's most intriguing criminal cases have been solved here using the latest technology to analyze everything from DNA to fibers to fingerprints. One scientific technology the FBI has mastered at the building is called liquid chromatography–mass spectrometry, or LC-MS, which is a slight twist on the scientific methodology Dr. Brian Andresen used to help identify the cause of Reye's syndrome. Liquid chromatography–mass spectrometry uses high-tech machinery to identify chemicals, usually contained in a mixture of other chemicals. Dr. Montgomery, a forensics examiner at the lab, would be the person responsible for using the LC-MS to process the forensic samples submitted to the FBI by the Reno Police Department. The samples of Kathy Augustine's urine, blood, and plasma, along with the flesh from the suspected injected site on her buttock, arrived at the lab on dry ice on July 21, 2006. The samples weren't inventoried until July 26, and it would take Montgomery two months to announce the results on the samples.

Montgomery is an expert in chemistry, toxicology, and forensic chemistry. She was pleased to see that the samples were frozen, given the inherent instability of succinylcholine, and the test she would perform for the presence of succinylcholine was certainly not one she performed every day. In fact, the FBI only had a protocol to identify succinylcholine's metabolite, succinylmonocholine. Montgomery, in her testing for the actual presence of succinylcholine, would have to use her own judgment, and some oversight by her supervisor, Marc LeBeau, to tweak the FBI's protocol for identifying the metabolite succinylmonocholine so that it could also be used to identify its parent chemical, succinylcholine.

"Succinylcholine is a unique drug," she said. "It's one that's not tested for in every forensics laboratory, which is why it came to us." Even at the FBI lab, however, "It's not something that we run [tests for] every day or week in the lab."

Traditionally, the search for succinylcholine in criminal cases actually involves a hunt for succinylmonocholine, because succinylcholine degrades and disappears incredibly fast. Usually, scientists like Montgomery are left merely searching for the metabolite.

"Succinylcholine is not a very stable chemical, either in the body or just in a liquid form in the test tube," Montgomery said. "If it's in a test tube, it will break down by a chemical process that's called hydrolysis. And, it will break down to that marker . . . succinylmonocholine. It will also break down to succinylmonocholine in the body.

"We would expect to find breakdown product [succinylmonocholine] wherever succinylcholine itself is present. We look for the breakdown product first, because if that's not there, we wouldn't expect the succinylcholine to be there, either," she explained.

It is important to understand, Montgomery said, that the original form of the drug, succinylcholine, would not be found in a human body unless it were administered as part of medical treatment. It just doesn't occur naturally in the body.

Montgomery followed the FBI's procedure and protocol for identifying the presence of succinylmonocholine in Kathy's urine. The LC-MS helped Montgomery separate the chemicals in Kathy's urine, and it also allowed for a chemical fingerprinting technique to specifically identify those chemicals. She ran the tests for succinylmonocholine three times on Kathy's urine, and it came back positive for this by-product of succinylcholine each time. Next came the tests for succinylcholine, and these tests were trickier because the FBI didn't have a specific protocol for the search of the drug in urine.

"The procedure that I followed to look for the succinyl-monocholine that we have validated and used in our lab for a number of years just looks for the breakdown product," Montgomery said. "Typically, we are looking at autopsy samples, and that's the only chemical we would expect to find present because the succinylcholine itself is so unstable. So, I had to do a little bit of research in the lab in order to figure out what succinylcholine itself would look like if it was run through this method that we use for the succinylmonocholine."

Montgomery sought guidance from her supervisor, and he approved of her modifications to the FBI protocol to search for succinylcholine. Montgomery collected urine samples from herself and from other people in her office.

"I got fifteen different urine samples [from my coworkers]," Montgomery said.

Montgomery used the urine to run three tests. The first test, what she called the blank urine test, which utilized urine from Montgomery and her coworkers, was run through the LC-MS and tested to make sure succinylcholine did not show up in the test results. This demonstrated that there has been no contamination of the LC-MS. The next test performed was on concentrated extracts from the suspected victim's urine sample to look for the presence of succinylcholine. The third test was what is called a "spiked" sample. In the final, "spiked" test, urine from Montgomery and her coworkers was spiked with succinylcholine to demonstrate what a positive test looks like.

Montgomery tested Kathy's urine.

"I ran this . . . [test] two times for the succinylcholine and three times for the succinylmonocholine," Montgomery said.

The tests came back positive for both succinylcholine and succinylmonocholine. The fact that the FBI found succinylcholine—in its original form—in Kathy's urine meant Chaz Higgs was in a huge heap of trouble. Montgomery's tests are believed to be one of the first times, if not the first time, that tests in America identified succinylcholine in a suspected homicide victim's urine. Montgomery also tested the tissue samples from the purported injection site on Kathy's buttock. She tested Kathy's blood and plasma, and she found no succinylcholine or succinylmonocholine in any of the other samples.

She was not surprised.

"Succinylcholine is excreted from the body and broken down very, very rapidly," she said. "So it can be just a matter of hours, and it can be gone."

On September 27, 2006, Detective Dave Jenkins was enjoying a day off. It had been a long time, two months, since Kathy Augustine's urine, blood, and plasma (along with the flesh from the suspected injected site on her buttock) were sent to the FBI. He and Detective Scott Hopkins and a team of Reno police detectives had done a lot of investigating of Chaz Higgs in those two months, and they weren't sure yet if there was going to be proof that Kathy died at the hands of another.

"I was very cognizant of the fact that if the tests did come back negative, and if succinylcholine was not present, then the evidence of murder would be gone," Jenkins said.

Jenkins got a call on his cell phone from William Anderson, the supervisor of the Washoe County Crime Lab. The test results were back, Anderson said, and everyone was going to meet at his office to discuss the results. Anderson, Hopkins, Homicide Division Supervisor Doug Evans, Dr. Clark, Washoe County Coroner Vernon McCarty, and

Washoe County Chief Deputy District Attorney Thomas Barb were all present when Anderson announced that the FBI found succinylcholine and its metabolite, succinylmonocholine, in Kathy's urine.

"I think that those lab results were extremely significant," Jenkins said, "Not only did it identify succinylcholine, but also the expected metabolite. My reading of it was that there is no potential there for a misidentification. Succinylmonocholine might be explained in some circumstances, but having both the metabolite evidence and the whole drug [in the urine] . . . was very compelling."

Everyone agreed it was time to get an arrest warrant for Chaz. They discussed the evidence and concluded it was enough to file a murder charge. His strange behavior, Kim Ramey's witness account, the purported injection site, and the succinylcholine in Kathy's urine were clear evidence of murder to the authorities. Jenkins returned to his office and drew up a warrant that mimicked the application for a search warrant he'd drawn up two months earlier. This time, he also inserted a summary of the forensic testing on Kathy's urine:

The urine sample collected from Ms. Augustine on July 8, 2006 was forwarded to the Federal Bureau of Investigation forensic laboratory in Quantico, Virginia, where it was analyzed by Dr. Madeline A. Montgomery. On September 27, 2006, your affiant received a written report generated by Dr. Montgomery in which she documented that she had identified both succinylcholine and succinylmonocholine (a breakdown product and metabolite of succinylcholine) in the urine sample from Ms. Augustine.

Your affiant ascertained that Mr. Chaz Higgs was a registered nurse in the state of Nevada and had worked at the Carson Tahoe Hospital on July 7, 2006. Your affiant also ascertained that Mr. Higgs had access, during his employment at the hospital, to a variety of drugs to include succinylcholine and syringes and needles to administer . . . them.

Your affiant met with Dr. William Anderson of the Washoe County Crime Lab, Dr. Ellen Clark, and Washoe County Coroner Vernon McCarty on Sept. 27, 2006. They all agreed that, based on the totality of the facts, circumstances and evidence developed to this point caused them to believe that Ms. Augustine's death was a homicide and as a result of her being intentionally administered succinylcholine. Further, they opined that the succinylcholine had been administered to her very soon before her admission to the Washoe Medical Center.

Wherefore, your affiant prays that a complaint and warrant of arrest be issued for Chaz Higgs charging him with first degree murder.

Washoe County Judge Barbara Finley issued the warrant the very same day, and the detectives contacted both the FBI and local law enforcement in Virginia, where Chaz was believed to be residing with his brother. Jenkins and Hopkins flew to Virginia, and the detectives got legal permission to track Chaz's cell phone.

"He had a Nextel GPS-enabled phone, so we were doing real-time monitoring," Jenkins said. "I was literally on the phone with the police giving them the GPS coordinates. We were about twenty-five minutes behind him on the highway. We called ahead of us and [told local law enforcement], 'He's ahead of us, and he's coming your way.' They actually were waiting for him at his brother's house when he pulled in the driveway, and they physically took him into custody. We arrived a few minutes later."

A television camera captured images of Chaz, in a dark shirt and jeans, as he was being escorted to a police cruiser in Hampton, Virginia.

Chaz appeared to be polished and relatively relaxed, given the circumstances.

"When we got him to the local police department, we sat down with him, and we offered him a chance to tell his side of it, and he declined," Jenkins said. "He said he had nothing to say except he was not involved. Legally, that was it."

The detectives booked Chaz into jail and returned to the scene of his arrest. Crime-scene analysts and the detectives scoured his vehicle for clues, and they found two very significant items of evidence. Chaz had a stack of three-by-five-inch cards in his possession that documented different types of drugs and how they are administered.

"Right on top [of the stack of cards] was succinylcholine," Jenkins said.

Chaz also had in his possession a medical book bookmarked to a page describing intramuscular injections.

"The location of the injection site was intramuscular," Jenkins said. "The reference book was to intramuscular— not intravenous. It was extremely significant. It was how he chose to administer the succs."

Jenkins acknowledged that after all his years in law enforcement, the chase and apprehension of Chaz in Virginia and the collection of that evidence from the car was still quite the thrill.

"That's the fun of it even after thirty years," Jenkins said.

The news was a relief for Kathy's family. They believed Chaz to be guilty. Dallas Augustine gave an interview to *Las Vegas Review-Journal* columnist John L. Smith, saying she was avoiding the media on purpose. She also seemed to be distancing herself from Chaz. After hanging out with him in the days after Kathy's death, it was now clear that Dallas had turned on Chaz.

"I'm not out for the publicity of it," she told Smith. "I'm not after my fifteen minutes of fame. I want to seek justice for my mom and move on with my life."

If there was any doubt about Dallas turning on Chaz, those doubts were erased when Dallas granted another interview, this time with KLAS–TV 8 in Las Vegas, on September 30, 2006.

Speaking of the suicide attempt after Kathy's death, she said, "At that point, I thought he was a grieving husband. I got him to the hospital. I stand by what I did. Now, he can rot."

Dallas also addressed the loss of her mother and her grief over the way she was taken from her.

"[I'm] very angry at the fact that she could be standing with me here today," Dallas said. "So, it's brought up the whole grieving process all over again."

Kathy's mother, Kay Alfano, said she felt like a huge weight was lifted off of her when Chaz was arrested. She was overcome with emotion when Phil Jr. called her and told her Chaz was being charged with Kathy's murder.

"It did my heart good," she said.

20 . . . EXHUMATION

On the morning of October 10, 2006, a large excavator cracked grass and dirt in the southwest corner of the sprawling Paradise Memorial Gardens cemetery in Las Vegas. There were no Edgar Allen Poe–like overcast skies or stormy weather for this exhumation in Las Vegas. It was sunny, clear, and hot—T-shirt and shorts weather. The grave was dug as an army of cars whizzed by on nearby Eastern Avenue, on the edge of McCarran International Airport and next to the cemetery where Chuck Augustine's body had been buried underneath the rumbling jumbo jets overhead. Now, some three years later, the sounds of the airplanes again pierced the sky as authorities brought Chuck's casket and body back to the surface in search of evidence of a murder.

Clark County, Nevada, coroner Mike Murphy stood by the grave in a dark suit. Murphy is a stocky man with a shaved head and a sharp sense for media relations. He wanted to make sure this was done right. He was joined at the gravesite by a team of general-assignment and homicide detectives from the Las Vegas Metropolitan Police Department. Also present were Clark County Deputy Medical Examiner Gary Telgenhoff and Senior Crime Scene Analyst Joe Matvay. The best and brightest of Las Vegas Valley law enforcement were on hand for the exhumation of Chuck's body. Murphy ordered the approximately fifteen reporters and cameramen who showed up at the exhumation to be cordoned off at a distance of about forty yards away from the gravesite. Exhumations themselves are rare for law enforcement purposes, and they almost never happen under these high-profile circumstances. One photographer for the Associated Press snapped photos from the roadside on the other side of a brick wall. Murphy made no effort to prevent the media from attending Chuck's exhumation because he knew he'd never be able to keep them away from the sight of Chuck's coffin rising from the grave. He also knew that the task of trying to fend off the media could turn the event into a circus. The news that Chuck Augustine's body was going to be exhumed had leaked days earlier, and it was a huge story in Vegas. It was on the front page of the state's biggest paper, the *Las Vegas Review-Journal*, and it was the lead story on every television news broadcast throughout Nevada. The positive tests for succinylcholine in Kathy Augustine's urine were known. Chaz was under arrest, and there was now rampant speculation in the newspapers and on television about what had really happened to Chuck Augustine three years ago.

Was he, too, dosed with a huge injection of succinylcholine as he was recovering from his stroke?

Chuck's son Greg told reporters that it had seemed his father was getting better when he died. Even more intriguing was a largely unspoken suspicion that perhaps—just perhaps—Kathy could have been in on Chuck's death. Of course, Kathy stood to inherit all of Chuck's money when he died, but what made her fall under suspicion was how she'd run off to Hawaii to marry Chaz Higgs in a stunning, whirlwind romance. Given those details, the idea of Kathy being involved in Chuck's death was certainly not beyond the realm of possibility.

Clark County, Nevada, district attorney David Roger, Las Vegas's top prosecutor, told reporters from the *Las Vegas Sun* that he specifically remembered seeing Chaz and Kathy together at a Republican function nearly nine months before Chuck's death. Roger said he was pretty much certain he'd seen the two together.

If true, that would be a direct contradiction of what Kathy said: that she'd met Chaz at the hospital while Chuck was ill. Chaz had said the same.

Roger is certainly not some anonymous witness with no credibility. He is a Republican district attorney who has one of the most respected records of successful prosecutions of murderers in the state. He and the sheriff of Clark County, Nevada, are the two top law enforcement officers in Las Vegas. Roger is a man of his word—a tough, sharp, honest individual—and his word carries weight. He told the *Las Vegas Sun* he was convinced he saw Chaz and Kathy together at a Republican function in October 2002—nearly nine months prior to when Kathy and Chaz had said they'd met at Sunrise Hospital.

Roger, despite diligent questioning from reporters, was convinced his memory was correct, although he acknowledged it was possible he was mistaken.

"He wasn't very talkative," Roger said of Chaz at the function. "He seemed somewhat standoffish, and it appeared that he didn't want to be at the function."

To this day, Roger is the only person who claims to have seen Chaz and Kathy together prior to Chuck's hospitalization. Kathy's family members and Chaz's attorneys would eventually say that Roger must have been mistaken.

But regardless of the accuracy of Roger's account, Las Vegas authorities knew they needed to investigate Chuck's death further. Greg Augustine was not opposed to an exhumation, and Murphy signed an exhumation order to determine if it was possible that Chuck had been poisoned with succinylcholine or murdered in any other fashion.

"We don't take this lightly, and I mean that with as much sincerity as I can possibly convey," Murphy said in an interview published in the *Review-Journal*. "We are in a unique situation. The family wants answers, the public wants answers, the media wants to cover it, but there are other people who have loved ones in that cemetery, and they may be there, grieving.

"What we are hoping to do is answer questions, and one of the big ones we have to answer is whether what the doctors believed . . . [Charles] died of is what he died of or not," Murphy said.

Greg Augustine says he supported the investigators' actions.

"The reason we are doing the exhumation is to see if there is any foul play," he said. "I'm completely convinced . . . [the Las Vegas authorities] are doing their job in a very, very professional manner."

Chuck Augustine's casket was transported in a hearse to the funeral home. Matvay, along with a team of crime scene investigators, took forensic samples from the grave, the casket, and from Chuck's remains. The body was shipped to the coroner's office for autopsy.

Telgenhoff, the medical examiner, is a man with long gray hair and a matching goatee. He has performed hundreds of autopsies in Las Vegas. Telgenhoff was raised in a conservative, religious family, and he spent the early years of his life traveling in rock cover bands. When not doing autopsies, he has an affinity for playing rock music after hours in the basement of his home. He plays all the instruments himself. Telgenhoff is also a longtime consultant for the CBS television show *CSI*.

Telgenhoff found Chuck's remains to be remarkably well preserved despite the fact that Chuck had been in the ground for three years. He observed evidence during his internal examination that indicated Chuck had, indeed, suffered a massive stroke. Telgenhoff determined that Chuck was also suffering from pneumonia at the time of his death. There were no signs of unusual or misplaced puncture wounds on Chuck's body. The medical examiner ordered samplings of Chuck's tissues to be sent to a forensics laboratory in Pennsylvania for a full toxicology screen for traditional poisons such as arsenic. He also ordered tests for more obscure ones like succinylcholine. The tests looked for the presence of succinylcholine's metabolite and common drugs of abuse that can cause an overdose. The results came back two months later: there was no succinylcholine, succinylmonocholine, or any other drug found in Chuck's body.

The results were not a surprise to investigators because they were all aware of how difficult a task it would be to find forensic evidence of succinylcholine poisoning in a man who had been buried for three years.

"The cause of Augustine's death is a stroke," Murphy told the Associated Press.

Evidence gathered from Las Vegas police also cast further doubt on whether it was possible for Chaz to have killed Chuck. Police secured payroll records and employee time sheets from Sunrise, and they showed Chaz was not working at the hospital the day Chuck died, and authorities said they had no evidence to show foul play.

21 . . . FOLLOW-UP

The prosecution of Chaz Higgs was in the hands of Washoe County, Nevada, district attorney Dick Gammick, and he assigned the high-profile case to two of his best prosecutors, Thomas Barb and Christopher Hicks. The deputy district attorneys are both family men and long-time northern Nevada residents with multiple successful murder-case prosecutions. The negative tests for poisons in Chuck's body meant little to the prosecutors.

"It doesn't impact our case at all," Barb told reporters.

The two prosecutors set about following up on the investigative efforts of the Reno detectives in the Higgs case, and their efforts soon paid off. They secured and sorted through all of Chaz Higgs's computers and e-mail accounts, and they uncovered the name Linda Ramirez—the young woman to whom Chaz was e-mailing love letters while they both worked at Washoe Medical Center at South Meadows campus, where Chaz worked up until the summer of 2006.

The courting had occurred while Chaz was still married.

Ramirez said she just basically wanted to be friends with Chaz, but the prosecutors felt the e-mails were significant evidence that Chaz was a philanderer who hated his wife.

Another task for the prosecutors in preparing for the murder trial of Chaz was to reinterview his coworkers. Doing so revealed even more accounts of Chaz's outward dislike for his wife and his seemingly detached behavior in the aftermath of Kathy's hospitalization.

Marlene Swanbeck, the nurse who treated Kathy when she was rushed into Washoe Medical Center at South Meadows, found Chaz's nonchalant demeanor—as the team of doctors and nurses hovered over his wife—concerning.

Swanbeck recounted for prosecutors how, the very next day, on July 9, she was back at work when she got a phone call from Chaz. He said he was in the parking lot of Washoe Medical's South campus and asked Swanbeck to grab a paycheck that he had not picked up since he left Washoe Medical South to work at Carson Tahoe Hospital, three weeks earlier. Swanbeck agreed to grab Chaz's check, exit the building, and meet him in the parking lot. Swanbeck found the request to be extremely odd, considering Chaz's wife was in another hospital, unconscious, and barely clinging to life.

"I said to [a coworker named Jennifer], 'That was Chaz on the phone,'" Swanbeck recalled. "'He asked me to meet him outside in ten minutes. You know where I am if I don't come back.'"

Swanbeck arrived in the parking lot with Chaz's paycheck in hand, and he presented her with a dozen donuts, which she said added to the strangeness of the encounter.

"'Thank you for taking care of [my] wife,'" Swanbeck said Chaz told her.

Swanbeck thought the gesture was weird.

"To need your paycheck when your wife is ill and to bring us donuts, the timing didn't feel right to me," she said.

Kathryn Almaraz was Chaz's supervisor at Washoe Medical South, and she described Chaz as an excellent critical-care nurse with exceptional skills. She said she was especially impressed with Chaz's interaction with patients. But Almaraz said during the last six months of Chaz's employment, she noticed "his demeanor started becoming more stressed out," and she concluded the stress was related to his relationship with his wife. Chaz, she said, often called his wife a bitch, and she said it seemed he didn't want to go home because of his wife. He also referenced the fact that he had a stepdaughter in Las Vegas (from his third marriage, to Lorelei Gueco) and that his concerns over the future well-being of his stepdaughter— and his ability to provide for the child—were the only things that kept him from killing Kathy.

"He said to me . . . 'If I didn't have a daughter in Las Vegas, I would kill my wife and throw her down a mine shaft,'" Almaraz said.

Almaraz, along with nursing manager Tina Carbone, urged Chaz to get counseling "because he was so unhappy with his marriage."

Winifred Cindy Baker, a registered nurse at Washoe Medical South's emergency department, said Chaz was her mentor. She did not know he was married, however, until Chaz showed up at the emergency room with Kathy one day when he was having an allergic reaction. Baker said Chaz talked negatively about his wife.

"We always asked him if he needed some help [with patient care], and he said, 'Take care of my wife,'" Baker said, adding she, too, had heard Chaz call Kathy a bitch.

Baker said she was working at Washoe Medical South the day Kathy was brought to the hospital by paramedics. Kathy was later transferred to Washoe's main campus, and Baker drove to the hospital. She went because she wanted to make sure she was available for Chaz if he needed emotional support from his coworkers. Kathy was unconscious, in the Intensive Care Unit, and Chaz was talking to a nurse.

Baker walked up to the unconscious Kathy and held her hand.

"I just wanted to make sure she was OK," Baker said. "At the time, her eyes were twitching, and the nurse said she was having seizures. I said [to Kathy], 'I'm so sorry.' I think it was more [an act of] compassion because it was my coworker's wife. And, Chaz has been part of the emergency room department [so he was] part of our family."

Baker said Chaz approached her as she was standing by Kathy's bed. He put both his arms around her and said, "I know; it's OK."

A thought of concern briefly entered Baker's mind.

Is it possible he could have hurt her? Baker wondered.

Jennifer Dado, a registered nurse at South Meadows, heard Chaz call his wife a bitch as well, and she witnessed Chaz talking about getting "rid" of his wife.

"The implication in my mind was that he's not happy, and he doesn't want to be with her and, 'Get rid of her, do something with her,'" Dado said. "A 'Get her away from me' sort of thing."

Dado said on one occasion, she called Chaz's house to see if he could come in to the hospital to cover a shift of a sick coworker.

"Kathy answered the phone, and she didn't seem to be too happy," Dado said. "And [Chaz] came on the phone, and I asked him, 'Chaz, are you interested in working a shift or part of a shift?' He said, 'You know, I can't.' The next day, when he came to work, I kind of apologized and I said [to Chaz], 'Sorry if I had called at a wrong time. Seemed like you guys were both a little upset.'

"He said, 'No, she's just a bitch,' " Dado recalled.

The prosecutors felt the scientific evidence against Chaz was solid as well. They knew about the past difficulties involving succinylcholine poisoning in homicide cases, but their case seemed different because they had a positive urine test for succinylcholine—not just succinylmonocholine—and they had an injection site. The prosecutors did, however, still have one problem: they did not know where Chaz got the drugs that they believed were used to kill Kathy. The source of the succinylcholine was investigated by police. An audit was performed at the hospitals where Chaz worked, and the police knew he had had access to succinylcholine for years. He had worked at Washoe Medical South for two years, and an audit there could not confirm that he'd accessed succinylcholine there. Chaz had left Washoe Medical South and gone to work at Carson Tahoe Hospital just three weeks prior to Kathy's death. Officials at Carson Tahoe said he'd worked only five shifts at the facility. Chaz was essentially on a probationary period at the hospital, and given this, he would have been accompanied by another nurse during his time in the facility, and it would have been very difficult for him to access any medicines without anyone noticing.

Prior to working at Washoe Medical South and Carson Tahoe, Chaz had also had sixteen years of access to medicine in the U.S. Navy, and his prior wife said he had taken medicine home from the navy's supplies. Chaz was also employed at Sunrise Hospital in Las Vegas for a year.

An inquiry by the authorities seemed to indicate Washoe Medical Center and its South Meadows campus had less than adequate oversight of succinylcholine. The drug was stored in a refrigerator that was easily accessible to all nurses and doctors where Chaz worked. All the staffers had to do was enter a password into the refrigerator. The drug could also be found on so-called crash carts in the emergency room for even quicker access. Nurses told authorities how, if some succinylcholine was used, it was simply restocked by an employee responsible for refilling all medicine stocks in the hospital that day. There appeared to be minimal monitoring and no way to track who had used the drug, much less determine if a theft of the drug had taken place in the critical-care area of the hospital where Chaz worked.

The district attorney's office concluded that they would likely never know where the succinylcholine came from.

Washoe Medical officials announced in December, three months after Chaz's arrest, that they'd changed their protocol for handling succinylcholine in their hospitals. They restricted access by requiring nurses and doctors to get succinylcholine from a single source at the hospital's pharmacy.

"We evaluated the protocol, and decided we could add more accountability for this medicine," said hospital spokeswoman Alexia Bratiotis to the *Reno Gazette-Journal* newspaper.

22 ... TRIAL

David Houston is a defense attorney who walks into court during a murder trial fully expecting to kick the prosecution's ass. He's that good, and he takes great joy in winning. Houston operates under the rightly held belief that the prosecution has to prove their case. If they don't do that job and convince a jury of a defendant's guilt beyond a reasonable doubt, then that's their problem. Houston gets paid well to win, and that's exactly what he does. He is a well-prepared, tenacious litigator, and his track record would make any prosecutor nervous. He's won murder trial after murder trial in northern Nevada. Time and again, Washoe County authorities have watched Houston walk defendants accused of committing murder.

Houston is a high-priced, top-level, national defense attorney headquartered in a small office just down the road from the neon lights of the casinos in downtown Reno. He's represented Joe Francis, the infamous *Girls Gone Wild* video series owner, on a myriad of legal issues, including both civil lawsuits and criminal charges lodged against Francis; he also represented Hulk Hogan's son. He is fifty-six years old, six feet tall, and physically fit, with reddish blond hair parted on the side. The man has a relentlessness about him that's quite remarkable, and he talks about Chaz Higgs's case, in particular, with passion. Houston can talk about the technicalities of succinylcholine testing as if he were a scientist himself, and he is completely convinced that Chaz is wrongly accused. When asked why, Houston's answer is straightforward and to the point:

"Junk science," he claims.

Houston is one of two attorneys hired in 2006 by Chaz's family to defend against the charge that Chaz murdered Kathy. They also hired highly regarded attorney Alan Baum, of the United Defense Group law firm out of California. Baum is a sharp-looking, well-dressed, dignified man with silvery hair. He has thirty-eight years of trial experience and has been dubbed "attorney for the stars." Baum is an expert at guiding a client through a criminal proceeding that takes place in the media spotlight. Both men said when they first met Chaz Higgs, he was adamant about his innocence, and Houston said Chaz was very concerned about "certain politicos" in the state having it out for Kathy.

"Quite frankly, Chaz believed there was some sort of conspiracy involved in his wife's death," Houston said. "Very reserved, very depressed, but very cognizant of his position and wanting to get a statement out about what happened. [He was] more concerned about finding out [who] was responsible as opposed to his own welfare. I thought it was consistent with his being innocent."

Chaz waived extradition after his arrest in Virginia and was brought back to Reno by Detectives Dave Jenkins and Scott Hopkins. The defense team found out early on that part of their job in this case was going to encompass dealing with a relentless onslaught of media inquiries. Those calls and inquiries came from reporters not only from Nevada, but also from the *New York Times*, the *Washington Post*, and major crime news programs including CBS's *48 Hours* and *Dateline NBC*, which both aired programs on the case. With Baum at his side, Chaz granted an interview to CBS's *48 Hours* and told the show he didn't kill his wife.

Chaz's defense attorneys, meanwhile, spent a lot of time analyzing the relationship between Chaz and Kathy. Chaz told his lawyers that he and Kathy had first met at the hospital, but it wasn't until after Kathy's third husband Chuck's death that they struck up a conversation. Kathy came to the hospital after Chuck's death, Chaz said, with thank-you cards for all of the nurses who'd cared for her husband. Kathy realized upon arrival she was one thank-you card short. The one person who didn't get a thank-you card was Chaz, and when the two spoke, sparks flew.

Houston said his client told him they agreed to have coffee, and the whirlwind marriage followed. After the marriage, Chaz found himself at Republican events, being "dragged around like a little poodle" by Kathy, according to Houston, who also said that Chaz knew he was perceived as Kathy's "boy toy" at political functions, and he hated it. Chaz was a respected, talented critical-care nurse, but he knew that Kathy's Republican colleagues simply viewed him as some young stud who'd swept Kathy off her feet for her money.

"He hated it," Houston said. "It wasn't his world. He couldn't talk politics. He knew the undercurrent in the room, the murmur was, 'Look at him; that's her boy toy.' It was horribly embarrassing [for him], and it got to the point where he didn't want to go. People wanted to portray him as the blond bimbo for Kathy's ego. He was a highly trained, highly competent medical professional. Whatever you want to say about Chaz Higgs, he was excellent at what he did, and people denied him his due in order to create that image of him."

The marriage between Chaz and Kathy was real, Houston said. It was not some sham relationship, and the defense attorney said it was Chaz who suggested that Kathy alter her will and living trust to leave all her belongings to her daughter, Dallas. Chaz loved Kathy, but he was also devastated by having to watch Kathy endure the impeachment proceedings. The impeachment was a strain on the couple's marriage, and one moment in particular at a Republican dinner made Chaz realize politics had destroyed her.

"It was the only time I'd ever seen . . . [Chaz] get emotional," Houston said. "[He said it was at] a party affiliation dinner [after the impeachment], and he shows up to this dinner with Kathy. They go to the table, Chaz and Kathy sit down, and to a person, everyone gets up and leaves. No one will sit with Kathy Augustine from her own party. It crushed her, and Chaz got teary eyed over it."

Chaz urged his wife to quit politics completely, according to Houston, and she agreed. Chaz told him that the couple planned to buy an RV and travel the country. Chaz would become a traveling nurse, and the strain of political life would be gone. The marriage was already rocky, but Chaz believed this would solve the couple's problems.

"He agreed to stick with her through all of the impeachment, and afterward, he thought it was over—that she was done [with politics]," Houston said.

Chaz said that he pretty much gave up on the marriage when Kathy abruptly announced to him that she was going to run for treasurer. At that point, Chaz claimed, he realized Kathy would never give up on politics, and he wanted out of the relationship.

"It was his opinion that everything happening in her life, her bad moods, her issues, her inability to communicate with him on a level that was conducive to being husband and wife, were all related to Kathy's goal of, 'I've got to get back on top. I've got to get back on top. They aren't going to keep me down,'" Houston said.

Chaz said his frustration with his marriage led to the e-mail exchanges he had with Ramirez.

"He's not the first guy to send flirty e-mails to other girls," Houston said.

The defense team analyzed all the evidence against Chaz as they prepared for a preliminary hearing and trial. It quickly became apparent to the defense that Chaz was a suspect in large part because of his seemingly strange behavior. The attorneys, however, said much of that behavior could be explained, and that strangeness does not make someone a killer. They contend that the accounts of Chaz acting detached at the hospital were overblown and largely irrelevant.

"The [authorities] complain of Chaz Higgs's demeanor at the time his wife was being admitted," Houston said. "They complain that he was too casual and not emotional enough. Of course, they leave out the fact he's a battlefield medic. He's got war training. He's seen people get blown to pieces. One thing he's learned, when emotions take control, you are ineffective. Had Chaz been blubbering like a six-year-old kid at the hospital, the authorities would be yelling, 'Fake! Fake! He's had all this training!'"

Nurse Kim Ramey's account of the conversation was not accurate, claimed Houston. Houston blames Ramey's nasty divorce in Virginia and that she is a woman who "hates men." Chaz gave his lawyers a far different account of the conversation he'd had with Ramey on the day prior to his wife's sudden illness.

"[Chaz and Ramey] talked about divorce settings," Houston said. "[Ramey talked about] how terrible her divorce had been. It raged on for years. She hated lawyers. She hated divorces, and Chaz said he was very thankful his divorce wasn't going to be like that. It was [going to be] very amicable.

"Kim Ramey's story and the truth are a little bit different," Houston said. "Kim Ramey was the one raging on about divorce, how terrible they are, how it's going to be a terrible experience. According to Chaz, the Darren Mack case was reported in the press, and if you ask Chaz, it was Kim Ramey talking about succs—not Chaz. He agreed with her, but he didn't bring the subject up."

The most important aspect of the case, however, was obviously the positive test for succinylcholine in Kathy's urine. The defense attorneys did a comprehensive analysis of the evidence that led to the FBI's positive test results, and Houston and Baum concluded that a grave error had been made. There was just no way that the succinylcholine could be administered in the way the state was saying it happened. The reason? The authorities were alleging that the puncture wound on Kathy's buttock was an injection site for the succinylcholine, but experts hired by the defense team raised doubts. Houston said injecting someone in the buttock with succinylcholine would be the worst way to try and kill someone with the drug; if you want to kill someone with succinylcholine, it really needs to be injected directly into the bloodstream. Houston said consultations with the defense experts led him to believe Chaz would need to have injected Kathy with a massive amount of succinylcholine—at least 40 ccs of the drug. That would be four syringes full, which would have seemingly left a huge lump of fluid in Kathy's skin. No such lump of fluid was found. The state's theory, Houston said, would also mean Chaz would have had to inject Kathy with 10 ccs of succinylcholine and then reload the syringe three more times while she lay there, compliant with his plot to slowly poison her to death with four separate injections.

"It burns, and the person would be very uncomfortable," Houston said. "There was no tearing around this supposed injection site, which means the person wasn't moving. I guess it would be [the state's theory that] she allowed him to inject her while conscious, and she continued to let him inject this burning material into the fat pad on the buttock where, Chaz the nurse would know, it is about the worst place to administer succinylcholine because of the enzyme reaction in the blood."

Houston probed the intricacies of their marriage, and he knew Kathy had a stronger personality than Chaz. He said one nurse told his investigators that Kathy bossed Chaz around like she owned him.

"If you believe [Chaz], Kathy was hell on wheels," Houston said. "When you talk to his coworkers at the hospital, she'd pick him up in a BMW, get out of the car, and start screaming, 'What the fuck are you doing? Get the fuck in the car.' It was absolute control. So, there is no way she would have laid there and let him inject succinylcholine into her ass. Everybody understood she'd have beat the shit out of him if he tried it. She would file complaints against the nurses he was talking to at the hospital. She literally tried to get [at least one of them—Ramirez—] fired. It was that type of woman we are dealing with."

To Houston, the idea of Chaz, a critical-care nurse, choosing to inject his wife with succinylcholine in the buttock seemed ludicrous. But what bothered defense attorneys the most was the way in which Montgomery came to her conclusions that succinylcholine was present in the blood. Houston said the method Montgomery used to identify succinylcholine in the urine had never been done before, and Montgomery's supervisor at the time—who had signed off on the methodology—had testified in the analysis of the succinylcholine tests in the poisoning case against Dr. William Sybers of Florida. In that case, the FBI got it wrong.

"Sybers went to prison because the FBI showed up and said, in no uncertain terms, succinylmonocholine cannot exist in the human body absent the introduction of succinylcholine," Houston said. "It is a breakdown metabolite; therefore, succinylmonocholine cannot exist naturally. It's impossible. The FBI, five years later, published their own bulletin saying, 'Oops, it can; sorry we made a little mistake here.' The FBI has this nasty habit of absolutes until they find out they are wrong."

Houston said the defense expert, Chip Walls, of the University of Miami, was bothered by what he saw when he analyzed the testing. When the FBI charted out the presence of succinylcholine and succinylmonocholine in Kathy's urine, they charted the succinylcholine at a higher level than its metabolite, succinylmonocholine. Walls was baffled by this, given the way the drug rapidly degrades.

"You should have a greater peak for succinylmonocholine," Houston said. "The only way that could be avoided was if the blood concentrate for succs was so high that it was literally feeding into the urine. That would be the only explanation, but the blood had zero succinylcholine. The blood had zero succinylmonocholine. Our expert was like, 'There's something wrong with the test. It makes no scientific sense.'"

The case of *State of Nevada versus Chaz Higgs* went to trial in the courtroom of District Judge Steven Kosach on

June 18, 2007, and started with jury selection. The trial took place in downtown Reno. Reno is a vibrant, mostly thriving city with a good side and a dark side. The good side is that it's an attractive city, and a few blocks from the renaissance area of downtown Reno is a nice stretch of coffee shops and restaurants along city roadways that connect by bridge across the Truckee River, a beautiful flow of water where the city was first founded. The city of Reno has constructed a lovely walkway along the river, and it is the nicest spot in Reno. The river's blue waters cascade down a path right through the center of the city, attracting wildlife and kayakers alike to the heart of the municipality.

Sometimes, though, in the spring after the thaw or after a ton of rain, the Truckee can run wild.

A brisk walk away from the courthouse is the darker side of Reno, the side found in pretty much every major gambling town in America. Red and yellow neon lights illuminate the western sky. It is like a mini Las Vegas strip here, where a lot of shady types and "tweakers" (agitated methamphetamine users) walk the streets from their weekly rent apartments in search of the next high or gambling buzz or dope deal.

Prosecutor Christopher Hicks has prosecuted crime in Reno, but this would be his most high-profile case. His was the first opening statement of the trial. Hicks came out swinging with an elegant, calm presentation in which he relentlessly detailed the scientific evidence and witness testimony. There was no doubt that the state of Nevada and the prosecution were convinced that the FBI's succinylcholine testing was solid, and they were going to use it to their advantage.

"Succinylcholine, or succs as it's commonly called in the medical setting, is a paralytic drug that has devastating effects," Hicks told jurors. "It's commonly used in emergency situations when a person needs to be intubated, they need to have a tube run down their throat so that a machine can breathe for them. It is administered both intravenously and intramuscularly. And, when it is administered, it renders a patient totally paralyzed.

"They cannot move, they cannot breathe, they can't even blink their eyes, and yet they are totally awake," Hicks said. "Without the assistance of another person in helping that person to breathe, they will suffocate, their heart will stop, and their brain will likely suffer irreversible damage due to oxygen deprivation."

Chaz Higgs, who was dressed in a dark suit and blue tie, sat just a few yards from where Hicks spoke to the jury. The prosecutor recounted the witness statement that on July 7, 2006, while referring to a high-profile murder case in which a man allegedly stabbed his wife to death, Chaz had mentioned the drug.

"Mr. Higgs said, 'That guy did it all wrong. If you want to get rid of somebody, you just hit them with a little succs,'" the prosecutor said of Chaz's conversation with Kim Ramey.

"The very next morning, his wife, Kathy Augustine, a woman who he admittedly hated, who he commonly referred to in real nasty terms, and who he desperately wanted to leave, was found in their home with Mr. Higgs, not breathing and without a heartbeat," Hicks said.

The prosecutor recounted Chaz's calm 911 phone call and told the jury how Chaz, a critical-care nurse, had said he'd given Kathy CPR, yet when paramedics arrived at the scene, Kathy was found on the bed. Any medical professional knows it is best to give CPR to someone on a hard surface. Hicks recounted how others had found Chaz strangely unemotional in the face of his wife's sudden and unexpected demise. He was a nurse who had access to succinylcholine and talked about using it to kill a spouse a day before his spouse turned up unconscious. He talked a lot to colleagues about getting rid of his wife. He had a bottle of etomidate—a companion drug to succinylcholine—in his backpack. He had three-by-five-inch cards in his car, and the top card in the stack referenced succinylcholine. He had a medical book bookmarked to a page on intramuscular injections. He'd been e-mailing a young woman love letters, and most importantly, succinylcholine was found in Kathy's urine.

"[The medical examiner will] tell you that she discovered a puncture mark on the left buttock of Kathy, a nontherapeutic puncture mark," Hicks said. "What that means is that the puncture mark cannot be attributed to any of the treatment [Kathy received]. And that [the urine was] tested not once, not twice, but three separate times, and every time the urine came back positive for the presence of succinylcholine."

Defense attorney David Houston was next. He told the jury there was another side of the story that they hadn't heard, and he urged them to meet their obligations as jurors and to follow the law.

"It is the duty of jurors to honor what we call the presumption of innocence and the idea of burden of proof," Houston said. "Truly, you are the finders of fact. All that we ask is that you listen to [witness testimony], you evaluate it, [and] you analyze it. Because, witnesses are like everyone else. They come with human faults. They come with human frailties."

Houston outlined for the jury a narrative of Chaz's love for Kathy, their relationship, and the struggles that came with living with her.

"When they returned from Hawaii, they returned each to their own individual criticisms of, 'You acted too quickly.

What were you thinking?'" the defense attorney said. "But they didn't care because, you see, Chaz and Kathy had created what we would call their own world. And, in that world all that mattered is they cared for one another, they were in love with one another."

Houston told jurors that Chaz had not been aware of Kathy's stature as a Nevada politician when they met. He was not aware that she was considered a very important person in the state.

"He was not aware to some, it consumed her life," Houston said. "It defined who she was. That lesson would come, but it would come slowly, and it would come over a period of years. Their marriage and their union together, despite the criticism from others, was, to at least Chaz, wonderful. The happiest he had ever been in his life.

"And, you will hear from some of the very nurses, hospital employees, the state has referred to, that Mr. Higgs was happy-go-lucky. He was constantly in a good sense of humor. A great frame of mind. But that changed. That changed [in] . . . 2004."

The defense attorney told jurors that in 2004, Chaz and Kathy were notified by the state of Nevada that it was the intention of the attorney general's office to make a case against Kathy Augustine for using state resources for her campaign activities. Houston implied that Kathy had enemies in the state.

"There was some question as to why the impeachment was occurring at that time, since Kathy had just been invited by George Bush to be considered for the U.S. treasurer," Houston said. "Some believed it was because she knew too much. Others believed the impeachment was viable and appropriate."

The impeachment proceedings tore through Kathy and Chaz's marriage, the defense attorney said. Chaz was miserable, and Kathy's attitude started to change from all of the stress and "others' attempt to literally tear apart [her] life and everything [she] had worked for.

"Mr. Higgs began to see that this small world that they had created for themselves was not impenetrable, and certainly was not one that could not be touched by others," Houston said. "And, as the pressure increased, as the momentum of this impeachment campaign against her increased, you will hear that the mind-set of Kathy Augustine as it pertained to virtually everything was no longer as pleasant or certainly as happy-go-lucky as it had been when they first met."

Chaz decided he didn't want to live the life of a political spouse. Kathy, however, wasn't going to give up politics. Chaz finally concluded he was going to divorce Kathy.

"It matters not how much you love somebody, but at some point something that can happen educates you to the knowledge that no matter how much you may love someone doesn't matter," Houston said. "That person isn't going to change. It doesn't mean you hate them. It certainly doesn't mean you want to murder them. But it means that you have to go your separate way, pursue your own dreams and allow them to pursue their own goals. That decision was made by Mr. Higgs."

Houston addressed the conversation Chaz had with nurse Kim Ramey by saying jurors would have to decide what the two really said and that Chaz had planned to tell Kathy that night he was divorcing her.

"Mr. Higgs, after going home, talked with Kathy," Houston said. "He explained what he was doing. Kathy had indicated to him she didn't feel well. Kathy went to bed. Mr. Higgs joined her a short time later.

"Early in the morning on July 8, the evidence will demonstrate that Chaz Higgs woke first, went out into the garage, came back in to the bedroom, and he noticed something," the defense attorney said. "He noticed that the breathing sounds of his wife that he had become so accustomed to over the years that he was married to her weren't the same. And, he got close enough to her, like snuggled to her, to listen. And he was alarmed enough to where he went and he opened the blinds of the room to allow some light to come in. And, he could tell that there was something wrong."

The couple's bedroom was not originally viewed as a suspicious crime scene by paramedics and police, Houston said. "Nothing was askew. Nothing was overturned. No one's clothes were ripped. No blood. None of the typical things that you would think would accompany a passionate battle for life.

"Would it make sense that a healthy woman would allow someone to jab her with a needle and inject a quantity of a drug under your skin that would burn, and simply lay there during the period of time it receives onset, that it gets into your system, without trying to put up a struggle?" Houston said. "With your breath being taken from you? Are you simply going to lay there? It is a drug designed to be administered through an IV. It is administered intramuscular on only very rare circumstances."

Houston briefed the jury on Chaz's attempted suicide and the e-mails he'd sent to Linda Ramirez by saying, "You'll have a chance to evaluate loneliness and grief and perhaps how that may manifest itself."

Houston officially notified the jury that the defense planned to call its own pathologist, Dr. Anton Sohn, and there would be doubts cast about the injection site and the method of murder the state was alleging.

"The state's case will not survive beyond the defense pathologist," Houston said.

The first witness called was Kim Ramey. The blond

nurse started off somewhat shaky and had to pause because she said the room was spinning.

"I just feel dizzy," she told prosecutor Christopher Hicks from the witness stand. "You were spinning. I'm not good with rides."

She steadied herself and talked about how she'd thought Chaz was a player. She recounted the phone conversation where Chaz seemed to be yelling at Kathy. She said Chaz talked as if he was filled with hate toward his wife, and he told Ramey that "succs" was the perfect way to get rid of someone, "because they can't trace it postmortem."

Defense attorney Alan Baum questioned Ramey carefully on cross-examination. He asked about the methods for tracking succinylcholine.

"It can be missed," Ramey said. "They might not see it missing out of the refrigerator maybe from one shift to the next."

The defense attorney got Ramey to acknowledge that she did not give Chaz much credibility because multiple statements from him "didn't add up. He told me he's getting a divorce. Then later on in the day I find out he's not even, you know, filed, or even told her. So . . . his credibility as the day goes by is not very high with me."

Ramey also acknowledged that she waited to call authorities after learning Kathy was gravely ill.

"In hindsight, Mr. Baum, I should have called," Ramey said. "But, you know, hindsight is twenty-twenty. I should have listened to my intuition, and I didn't."

Ramey, however, was steadfast in her account that Chaz had talked about dosing someone "with a little succs," and she said the conversation bothered her.

"I had the goose bumps, because nurses don't kill people," Ramey said. "We save people."

Witnesses in the following days of the trial testified

how Kathy's urine was collected and stored at Washoe Medical. William Anderson, the chief toxicologist for Washoe County, testified about sending the urine, blood, and plasma samples to the FBI. A string of nurses testified about Chaz's bizarre behavior as his wife was being tended to in the emergency room, and they consistently told of how Chaz bad-mouthed his wife.

Nurse Marlene Swanbeck told of bringing Chaz's paycheck to him and getting the dozen donuts in return in the parking lot of Washoe Medical South as his wife lay dying in a hospital room across town.

"He was removed from what was happening, it seemed," Swanbeck said. "I always felt a little suspicious. Something was never right. I was not ever comfortable with the way he talked about his wife."

Linda Ramirez told jurors about the sultry e-mails Chaz had sent, and the rose he gave to her, but said she'd only wanted to be friends with Chaz.

"It was just a flirtatious relationship," she said.

Detective Dave Jenkins told the jury about finding the etomidate in Chaz's backpack, and the medical book with the flagged page in his car, as well as the three-by-five-inch cards referencing succinylcholine. Dr. Ellen Clark told jurors of the suspicious needle mark.

"There were actually two punctate areas of discoloration that are potentially significant because they have an overall configuration in appearance that would be consistent with needle punctures or injection sites," Clark said, adding she performed the cut down of the punctured area and detected "a very narrow track of bleeding into the tissue that was directly beneath some of the punctate or very small injuries on the surface."

She said under a diligent cross-examination that Kathy had only a minor defect in a heart valve and no signs of coronary disease. Clark said she'd determined Kathy's death was caused by "succinylcholine toxicity" due to the FBI tests and the apparent needle injection site.

Madeline A. Montgomery, from the FBI's lab in Quantico, documented for the jury her methodology for testing Kathy's urine, blood, and plasma for the presence of succinylcholine. She recounted the extensive steps she'd taken to ensure that the LC-MS was working properly, and she noted that her supervisor gave her permission to modify the FBI's scientific search for succinylmonocholine so that succinylcholine could be identified. Houston pursued an aggressive line of questioning with Montgomery as he tried to show the scientist's testing was flawed.

"Is Marc LeBeau your supervisor?" Houston asked.

"Yes, he is," Montgomery said.

"Are you aware that LeBeau testified in the Sybers case?" Houston asked.

"Yes," Montgomery said.

"Were you aware that Mr. LeBeau had testified that succinylmonocholine does not exist in the body [naturally?]" Houston asked.

"Actually, our lab was the lab that reported that succinylmonocholine was found in autopsy samples from individuals who had not been exposed to the drug," Montgomery replied.

"Would you agree with me that the science surrounding succinylcholine is an ever evolving science?" Houston asked.

"Absolutely," Montgomery said. "That's why I did my own test in the lab to show that succinylmonocholine is not present in urine samples, because to my knowledge, that had never been tested before."

Under questioning from Chaz's attorney, Montgomery conceded that her methodology for identifying succinylcholine had not been published or subjected to peer review.

"I got permission from my supervisor after he reviewed the data . . . before I ever looked at the urine in this case for the succinylcholine," Montgomery said. "He agreed that the testing I was doing was adequate and acceptable. The adaptations that were made to this method were not very different."

The prosecution also called Paul Mailander, a surgical anesthesiologist for Sierra Anesthesia in Reno. He described for jurors how succinylcholine works and how it would affect someone injected by it.

"Any muscle you can voluntarily control, your breathing, your eyelids, shrugging your shoulders, anything you voluntarily control, will be paralyzed and unable to move," Mailander said. "Your heart will work. Your intestines will work. Other muscles that you don't normally control voluntarily will continue to work. But the skeletal muscles, [which] is what we call them, they will all stop functioning, and the patient will be unable to move."

"Are you aware that it can be administered intramuscularly?" Hicks, the prosecutor, asked.

"It can," Mailander said. "Most of the anesthesia books, and most of your anesthesia instructors, will tell you that in a pinch, if you have to get someone paralyzed and there is no IV access, you can give them a shot in a muscle. And, it will take a little longer to act, but it will act, and the patient will be paralyzed, and you have to move accordingly."

Mailander said he'd never seen an intramuscular injection of succinylcholine. It was only used in an emergency and is considered a risky maneuver because there is no guarantee that the doctors will be able to get a breathing device properly inserted into the patient. If a patient needs to be put to sleep immediately without an IV line, there are other anesthetic medications, sleeping medications, like hypnotics, that work as quickly, and they put the patient to sleep without paralyzing them.

Mailander testified that succinylcholine administered through an IV takes less than a minute to go to work on a patient. If it is injected through the muscle, it would take about three minutes. Mailander said he knew of no good reason for any medical professional to have etomidate in their home.

"It is a hypnotic medication," Mailander said. "Putting someone from essentially awake to asleep. Etomidate is another medication we have to inject in someone which will put them in a state of sleep. It creates amnesia, which is a good thing . . . [because] it means you're unable to respond to stimulus. [But] it does not relieve any pain."

Mailander then directly contradicted defense attorney David Houston and his defense experts by opining that an intramuscular injection of succinylcholine in the buttock would not necessarily be a bad place to inject the drug if an IV wasn't available.

"It should work very well," he said. "It's a large muscle. One of the reasons the buttock is the general muscle of choice for shots is that it's a very large muscle mass, so the odds of hitting the muscle are very, very good without going too deep into the bone or going too superficially. And, it has a very, very good, strong blood supply for rapid uptake."

Houston immediately challenged Mailander on that contention, even engaging in a mock exercise whereby saline was injected through a needle. Houston demonstrated that, according to the defense experts, the injection would have had to take place "times four" to inject Kathy with the necessary amount of succinylcholine to kill her.

"Guess what? Times that by four," Houston said. "That's

really what you are dealing with when dealing with [the] injection site, and the [prosecution's medical experts] agreed with it."

The defense opened its attempt to clear Chaz Higgs of murder with Dr. Anton Sohn. Sohn is a pathologist and chairman of the Department of Pathology at the University of Nevada School of Medicine. Sohn has performed more than three thousand autopsies, and most of those were forensic cases for Washoe County—the same county Dr. Ellen Clark was now representing. He reviewed Clark's records from Kathy's autopsy and expressed concerns about at least one oversight. Specifically, he said Kathy had a heart condition known as hypertrophy, which is enlargement of the heart or muscle fibers within the heart. This fact was not mentioned in Clark's autopsy report.

"It's very similar to an athlete who lifts a lot of weights, and his arms get bigger," Sohn said. "Muscles get bigger. That's known as hypertrophy. The heart also gets hypertrophy under increased workload. [Kathy's] muscle fibers and the nuclei in the fibers were larger than normal."

There are a number of causes of hypertrophy. They include congestive heart failure and hardening of the arteries. The presence of the condition in Kathy, Sohn said, "indicates to me that something is going wrong that's causing her heart to work harder than normal."

"Did Dr. Clark make any mention whatsoever in her autopsy of this cardiac hypertrophy?" Baum asked.

"No, she did not," Sohn said.

"Do you consider that an omission?" Baum asked.

"Yes, I do," Sohn said.

The pathologist confirmed Clark's finding that Kathy had the defect with her heart valve, called "mitral valve prolapse."

"Mitral valve prolapse means that the fibers or the elastic tissues in the valve are weak so that when the heart beats, the blood is squeezed out. But that mitral valve flops up and prevents the blood from coming back," Sohn told jurors. "When you have prolapse or regurgitation, that mechanism doesn't work so good. The blood goes out, and then the valve draws back so blood comes back into the heart, and that's the reason you get hypertrophy, to push the blood out. It has to work more.

"So in a situation of a floppy valve or mitral valve prolapse, usually these are very insignificant," Sohn said. "But, they can be quite significant. They can cause heart failure. They can cause . . . arrhythmia, an irregular heartbeat. And they can cause sudden death. So, she has a condition that, in rare situations, can cause sudden death."

Sohn pushed the issue even further, though, by raising questions about whether the mark on Kathy's buttock had even been present before she was brought into the hospital. Sohn said he thought the mark could have only been up to forty-eight hours old when the photo was taken at autopsy on July 12. Chaz, prosecutors said, had injected Kathy on the morning of July 8. Sohn said it was "very highly unlikely that it could have been" an injection site that was created on July 8.

It was powerful testimony that the defense attorneys believed held the potential to raise a reasonable doubt as to Kathy's cause of death. They also believed that their best witness was yet to come, and his name was Chaz Higgs.

23 ... DIRECT

The first witness with the last name of Higgs to take the stand in the murder trial of Chaz Higgs was actually Chaz's twin brother, Michael. Michael Higgs is an organized, professional-looking man with dark hair who looks very much like his brother. Michael Higgs lives in Virginia and is a member of the National Guard. He served his country as a platoon leader for a maintenance company, and he was deployed in Iraq for all of 2004. He has supported Chaz from the beginning of his brother's legal ordeal.

Michael Higgs told jurors that he learned about his brother's marriage to Kathy shortly after the wedding in Hawaii, and he was concerned about the rapid pace of the relationship.

"I thought it was fairly quick," Michael Higgs said. "I didn't think they had enough time to learn about each other [but] they . . . seemed like they were very happy to be together. They were bubbly. They were like schoolkids.

They . . . looked like they were in love. I figured they were two adults, and they knew what they were doing."

Michael Higgs exchanged e-mails regularly with both his brother and his new bride. He learned of stresses in the relationship around 2004. The husband and wife were bickering. This was also around the time that Nancy Vinik had claimed that Kathy told her Chaz was cheating on her. Michael Higgs said Kathy's impeachment put her "under a lot of stress." Michael Higgs turned into sort of a marriage counselor via e-mail, and he got numerous questions from Kathy asking what she should do about her crumbling marriage.

"I told her, just stick with it," Michael Higgs said. "It will all work out. You guys haven't been together that long."

Nevertheless, Chaz Higgs told his brother he wanted out of the marriage, and by 2005, the state of the marriage had gotten worse. Michael Higgs said Kathy bossed his brother around, and it seemed Chaz was subservient to his wife, but Michael added that his brother would never be capable of killing Kathy. He just wasn't that type of person.

"Did you suspect your brother had murdered her?" Baum asked.

"No. Never," Michael Higgs said.

Defense attorneys David Houston and Alan Baum called Dr. Earl Nielsen, a clinical psychologist, next. The attorneys knew that Ramirez's testimony about the e-mails Chaz had sent her was damaging. The e-mails made Chaz look like an insensitive, uncaring louse. Making matters worse were the days of testimony from nurses who said Chaz seemed to care little about the condition of his unconscious wife. Dr. Nielsen had met with Chaz on four occasions, and he testified that the kind of stoic reaction Chaz exhibited to his wife's fate was not unheard of. Everyone's grief is individualized, he said. Some people experience initial grief

and are disabled. Others experience grief with some numbness and act as if they don't respond at all. In fact, they may
act as if they don't even know what is happening.

"There are many, many possible responses to grief,"
Nielsen said, adding he thought Chaz's reaction was "consistent with fifteen years of emergency medical training."

Nielsen also offered an explanation for all the flirty
e-mails Chaz had sent: Chaz, he said, is a hopeless romantic who has a problem with monogamous relationships.

"He's a man who enters relationships with great romantic fantasy and great hope," Nielsen said. "He basically
enters personal, intimate relationships wanting the perfect
life. But the weakness that I observed in Mr. Higgs is that
he does have some trouble with the concept of commitment with no back doors. He's been married four times,
he's been divorced three, and [he] had intended to divorce
a fourth. Each of those marriages was very short really."
The clinical psychologist went on to say that what each
of those marriages had in common for Chaz was that "he
started out wanting [the relationship] to be perfect, and as
he discovered it wasn't going to be perfect . . . he looked
for ways out."

On Monday, June 25, 2007, Houston and Baum called
their most important witness. Chaz Higgs, wearing a dark
suit, blue shirt, and shiny blue tie, and sporting a closely
cropped haircut of brown hair, stood up from the defense
table and walked down the maroon carpeting of the courtroom. He stepped up into a jury box of reddish mahogany
wood and swore under oath to tell the truth. He escorted
the jury through his professional life and the details of how
he became a nurse. He looked straight ahead at his attorney
for most of his testimony, but he would occasionally turn
to his left and look directly at jurors as he fought for his
freedom.

Speaking in a deep, velvety voice, he told jurors about the first time he met Kathy, when her husband, Chuck, was ill at Sunrise Hospital in Las Vegas in 2003.

"I was working in a cardiac Intensive Care Unit at Sunrise, and when I came back to work after being off for a couple of days, I was given a couple of patients," Chaz said. "One of those patients was Charles Augustine, which was Kathy's estranged husband at the time. And I walked into the room . . . [and] saw Kathy sitting in a corner reading the newspaper, and we started talking. I introduced myself. [We] talked to her about the plan of care, said what was going on, what we had found, that sort of thing, and what we were going to do in the future. She left after about an hour. That was our first meeting."

Houston asked when he'd next seen Kathy, and Chaz explained how she'd returned to the hospital after her husband's death with thank-you cards for all the nurses in the ICU. She'd forgotten Chaz's card, so she asked if she could buy Chaz a cup of coffee instead.

"I said, 'OK, sure, it sounds great,'" Chaz recalled, adding that the romance between them was almost "instantaneous."

"I guess the best way to describe it was, when you meet somebody and you just feel chemistry," Chaz said. "That's what we had. We started talking while we were having coffee, and we just hit it off. We didn't talk about politics or nursing. We just talked about life. Our views were aligned. And, I'll tell you, the first time, it was fantastic. It was different. You've heard my history and all that sort of thing, and I do jump into things. But it was just different in the way we felt in our hearts."

Chuck Augustine died on August 19, 2003. Chaz and Kathy traveled to Hawaii two weeks later, and they married within the week.

"We were having such a great time," Chaz said. "We were in Hawaii, and it was beautiful. We were talking a lot more about just being happy. Both of us had had a lot of life experiences. And, we just relegated everything down to we just want to be happy. That's all we looked at. It kind of came up with both of us talking, 'Hey, why don't we just get married?' We didn't want to get married in Vegas, because everyone gets married in Vegas, so it was, 'Let's just get married here.' And we did."

"Had it been less than a month after her husband died?" Houston asked.

"Yes," Chaz said.

"Did she kill her husband?" the defense attorney asked.

"No. No," Chaz said.

When the newlyweds returned to Nevada, Chaz said they were uniformly greeted with responses of "What, are you crazy? Do you even know each other? It's so quick!" He and Kathy assured everyone they loved one another, but he soon found that everyone viewed him as Kathy's "arm candy" at political functions. Others thought he was after Kathy's money, but Chaz said he made about $71,000 per year and could not care less about her money. He wasn't interested in politics and was miserable at the Republican fund-raisers and party functions.

"I always felt like a fish out of water [at the functions]," Chaz told jurors. "They're talking bonds and issues which I never even followed, so I couldn't even get in the conversation except for, 'Hey, nice suit, nice shoes,' or something. I never felt comfortable."

According to Chaz, Kathy was actually offered the job as U.S. treasurer, but it slipped away when the Commission on Ethics investigation became public.

"In D.C., they get word of this, and they say, 'Well, we

don't need you anymore,'" Chaz said. "'We're going to go in a different direction,' and [Kathy] was devastated."

Chaz said the impeachment changed his wife.

"Before that, she had been really loving and open," Chaz said. "Like I said, we had this little world we created, and it was fantastic. Then after [the impeachment] started, it was like she just closed off."

Chaz recounted how his wife was cold and defensive. He told of how the entire Republican Party in Nevada had abandoned Kathy after the impeachment. He recalled how people ignored her at political events and that this was terribly painful for Kathy. Acceptance in Republican circles was everything for Kathy, and Chaz recalled how, after the events, "We'd get back in the car, and she'd be crying, she'd be hurt, she'd say, 'Oh my God, I can't believe this is happening to me.'"

Chaz said he asked her to quit politics because he couldn't watch Kathy "destroy herself." He said that she agreed, but then in 2006, she surprised him by telling him she was going to run for state treasurer. Chaz was upset. The marriage went even further south when he got caught e-mailing Ramirez, and Kathy injected herself into the matter by trying to get Ramirez fired from the hospital. Chaz said he regretted sending the love letters.

"Ashamed," Chaz said of the e-mails. "Not proud of it at all."

Even so, Chaz said he thought Kathy's actions had been uncalled for, and his wife's meddling in his professional life embarrassed him.

"I was hurt," Chaz said. "I was mad. I was venting all of this frustration I had from her. She was calling people, trying to have my friends fired. And . . . I would tell my friends . . . 'I'm really sorry she's acting like a bitch.'"

Chaz claimed he didn't even know succinylcholine was

undetectable until "this case." He told jurors Kim Ramey was the one who brought up succinylcholine, and he was just going along with the conversation.

"She seemed pretty angry to me when she started talking about her divorce," Chaz said. "I was a little put off by it."

Chaz recalled the morning in which Kathy was found unconscious. He woke early, made coffee, and returned into their bedroom.

"I walked into the bedroom, and I sat down at the edge of the bed, put my hand on her arm," Chaz said. "Her arm was cold. She's never cold. I used to call her my little heater, and when I felt her arm, it was cold, so I just kind of leaned over and listened. When she sleeps, she doesn't snore. But she breathes really loudly.

"It was dark, so I just wanted to take a look," Chaz said. "So, I walked up to the sliding glass doors and open the blinds to let some light in. Kathy just didn't look right. She looked pale, and her lips were a little blue. And, instantly, what came into my mind was all the people I had taken care of in the past, and I thought, this doesn't look right. . . . She didn't have a pulse, and she wasn't breathing."

Chaz said he didn't even think about putting Kathy on the floor while doing CPR. He conceded he may have seemed detached in the following days. He said he loved Kathy, and on the inside he was full of "turmoil. I was torn apart."

"I asked the [doctors], 'What's going on?'" Chaz said. "They said, 'It looks like she had a heart attack. . . . She's still alive,' so I was hoping everything was going to get better."

Chaz said he, too, was suspicious at the time that someone might have done something to Kathy. He said she'd received "death threats," although he didn't elaborate on the claim. Houston closed Chaz's testimony by asking him why the jury should believe that he didn't kill his wife.

"Because I didn't do it," Chaz said. "I wouldn't do that. I wouldn't do that."

Ed Vogel, the veteran reporter for the *Las Vegas Review-Journal*, had been sitting in the trial for more than a week, and he was watching carefully as Chaz testified. He thought Chaz did well as a witness, and he thought the defense was doing well overall. The testimony indicating it was possible Kathy had a heart attack was mildly convincing. He was especially impressed with Houston and Baum's lawyering, and he thought it was possible that Chaz was going to walk out of the courtroom a free man, but Vogel would change his opinion the very next morning when the bombshell dropped.

Chaz had tried to kill himself.

Again.

24 ... BOMBSHELL

At 3 a.m. the next morning, Chaz Higgs's mother found him on the bathroom floor of the Reno apartment they were renting for the trial. His wrists were bleeding. He'd slashed himself with a kitchen knife. Shirley Higgs ran to the phone and called 911. Chaz was rushed to the hospital by ambulance for his second suicide attempt in less than a year, and the news raced through the Washoe County Courthouse faster than a twenty-dollar bill through a Reno slot machine. *Las Vegas Review-Journal* reporter Ed Vogel heard the news shortly after walking through the security gates at the downtown building, and he was overcome with a certain sense of déjà vu.

"The [witnesses] were saying [Kathy's death] supposedly could have been from heart problems, and then Chaz goes out and does another phony suicide," the reporter said. "I think it disheartened [his] lawyers. I thought, *Oh geez, what a fool.* It was another attempt for sympathy."

Chaz's first suicide attempt had been three days after

his wife had died, and that attempt had prompted a flood
of public suspicion to wash over him. But if that timing
was bad, the timing of his second suicide attempt was even
worse. This time, he'd apparently tried to kill himself on
the day he was to be cross-examined by Washoe County
Chief Deputy District Attorney Thomas Barb. Furthermore, the wrist slitting took place just as his defense team
was convinced they were gaining the momentum necessary to allow Chaz to walk out of court a free man.

District Attorney Barb stood outside the Washoe
County Courthouse in downtown Reno the morning of the
attempted suicide and commented on the development.

"Every time he is under pressure, he does something
strange," Barb said of Chaz.

The Alfano family had been in attendance at the trial every
day, but unlike Vogel, they thought Chaz Higgs was getting
his ass kicked in court, and they perceived the attempted
suicide as yet another failed attempt on his part to draw
sympathy.

Kathy's brother Phil Alfano Jr. learned of the suicide
attempt from a Washoe County victim's witness advocate,
and he was stunned at Chaz's amazing recklessness at such
a critical time of the trial.

" 'There's been a development,' " Phil Jr. said he was
told by the victim's witness advocate. " 'Tom Barb will be
in to talk to you in a few minutes.' . . . I didn't think [Chaz]
would do it a second time. I guess I underestimated his
stupidity."

Kathy's daughter, Dallas Augustine, told reporters that
she, too, felt Chaz was attempting to garner sympathy from
the jury.

"I was hoping this would be over and done with soon,

and it is just going to drag on," Dallas told Las Vegas television station KLAS–Channel 8. "I think he's just trying to get sympathy and trying to draw this out as long as possible."

Chaz Higgs's defense attorneys, David Houston and Alan Baum, awoke that morning thinking they were in for a tense day of cross-examination of their client by District Attorney Thomas Barb. With their client's attempted suicide, however, the day got much worse. They were left trying to spin the suicide attempt as an act of an innocent man who didn't care about the outcome of the trial. Chaz, they said, had only cared about getting his side of the story out. Houston offered reporters a snippet of the brief suicide note Chaz had apparently left to prove his point.

" 'I waited a year to tell my story,' " Houston said, quoting from the note. " 'My destiny is fulfilled. Now I can go and be with my wife.' "

Houston did not explain the obvious contradiction in the contents of the note: that Higgs, who had told multiple people he hated his wife, now wanted to be with her in heaven. Houston acknowledged that the suicide attempt was a problem for him and Baum, as attorneys, and that it "certainly didn't help" Chaz's defense, but he did not believe it was a death knell for a possible acquittal.

"I saw [Chaz] in the hospital," Houston said. "The sheriff's deputies were all around him, and he looked up and said, 'I'm sorry. I know we are winning. I just don't care. I just wanted to tell my side of the story and go back with Kathy.' "

Chaz survived the wrist-slitting episode. The attorneys on both sides appeared in front of Judge Kosach that morning to sort through how the trial should proceed. Kosach immediately revoked Chaz's $250,000 bail, and he was taken into custody. He was put on suicide watch at the county jail. Kosach told jurors that the trial would be suspended indefinitely, and he instructed them to return to their places of work, but he ordered them not to read any news accounts of what had happened. The next day the defense attorneys said that their client wanted the trial to resume.

Chaz's cross-examination by Barb was rescheduled for Thursday, June 27, 2007. Chaz arrived in court, and everyone in the packed courtroom gallery gawked at him. He was becoming a spectacle. People were wondering what meltdown would be next and if they would get to witness it firsthand.

Judge Kosach informed jurors that Chaz had wounded himself on Tuesday morning. Chaz then walked up to the jury box again. When he raised his hand to swear to tell the truth, two large, white bandages on his wrists were plainly evident to everyone in the courtroom.

District Attorney Thomas Barb immediately let loose on Chaz with a barrage of questions about his seemingly careless attitude toward his wife and his second attempted suicide.

"Where did you leave the note?" Barb asked.

"In the bathroom where I was," Chaz said. "From what I remember, on top of the vanity."

"And, was it because you believed you'd told your story and that was all you needed to do?" Barb asked.

"Yes sir. That's what I have waited for the last year to do. I wanted to tell my story," Chaz said.

"OK, would you or could you understand that some people might think that this was just a ploy for sympathy?" the prosecutor said.

"Yes sir, I completely understand that," Chaz said. "But I have to tell you it didn't matter."

"Why didn't you just get a divorce?" Barb said.

"Because Kathy kept making promises to me that things were going to get better, and I believed her," Chaz said.

Barb then attacked Chaz on his e-mails to Linda Ramirez as well as his e-mail to an engaged female friend of his named "Ericka," two months after Kathy's death. Chaz seemed to be hitting on the woman in the e-mail. He wrote to Ericka that he was always there for her if her engagement or marriage faltered.

"If at any time you get hitched and it does not work, just know that I will be there to run away with," Chaz wrote the woman.

What Chaz wrote next was extremely cold and telling: he referenced the fact that he was single, but he said nothing about his dead wife or the suspicions that he'd killed her.

"Oh, by the way, did I tell you that I am single now? We can send Jeremy postcards from where we go. I think you are totally hot, sexy, smart, cool, caring and did I say hot? Jeremy is a lucky man. I wish you the best, but if you change your mind I will be here. I miss you."

"What's the date of that e-mail?" Barb asked.

"September third, 2006," Chaz said.

"Almost two months after Kathy died?" Barb asked.

"Yes, sir," Chaz said.

"You didn't mention to Ericka that your wife died; you just said, oh, I am single again?" the prosecutor asked.

"No," Chaz said.

The prosecutor drove home his point that Chaz didn't love his wife by making Chaz read from yet another document in which he was out trolling for ladies. Chaz had placed a singles ad in the newspaper shortly after Kathy's death, and the prosecutor made the accused read every word of it aloud to the court:

"I'm a happy, healthy, forty-two-year-old male who

likes to have fun doing almost anything," an embarrassed Chaz read from the advertisement. "[I] laugh a lot, and just enjoy life. I look like I am in my late twenties. Long brown hair, blue eyes, very athletic, and an RN with a very good bedside manner in and out of bed. I am completely single, unattached, looking for fun or whatever else, and I am very good to who I am with. . . . I am intelligent, mature, and will travel. As far as sex is concerned, I like to please my woman. I like to see her happy. I love giving oral sex. I love to do just about anything you can think of as far as sex. I have tried a lot and will try more. I'm open to new ideas and [am] completely adventurous."

When Barb questioned where Chaz's supposed love for Kathy was reflected in that ad, Chaz's only defense was "Sir, at that time I was in a fog. . . . I was reaching out for somebody . . . it was after her death."

On June 27, 2007, during the trial, Dallas Augustine had a second interview with *Las Vegas Review-Journal* columnist John L. Smith. Smith is a tall, reserved man and a hard-hitting journalist, about as tough as they come. He is not afraid to take on anyone. He is also a reporter with a great ability to humanize stories by telling the personal details of the events he covers.

Smith described Dallas's presence at the trial as a search for justice. The odyssey she'd been on, from originally suspecting Chaz was innocent to being convinced of his guilt, Smith described as a "learning experience akin to a waking nightmare, but one she hopes will result in justice for her mother, Kathy Augustine, and bring closure. No matter how long it takes."

"Overall, . . . I'm just here to make sure justice is done," Dallas told Smith.

Smith asked Dallas about Chaz's believability on the witness stand in the testimony offered before his bomb-shell suicide attempt (his second wrist slashing). Dallas had been the one who discovered him after his first sui-cide attempt. Dallas said Chaz's testimony was simply not believable.

"I was pretty much convinced by the time he took the stand because the prosecution has done a great job laying out their case and calling the right people to support their evidence," Dallas said. "It's pretty cut-and-dried."

Smith recounted how Dallas had asked the public to be fair to Higgs shortly after Kathy's death.

"I'm sure he saw me [in court], but I haven't had any contact with him or his family since right before he got arrested back in September," Dallas said.

"The only thing I ever heard about their relationship is that my mom was happy," Dallas said in the interview. "I don't know if that was her way of protecting her only child. I was the one at the start standing there saying show me some evidence."

Barb gave the state's closing argument to the jury. He urged a conviction for murder, saying the scientific proof of a homicide was overwhelming.

"The real evidence is nobody testified that there wasn't succinylcholine in Kathy Augustine's urine," Barb told jurors. "Nobody. The succinylcholine was there, and it's toxic if it's not administered therapeutically. Without Kim Ramey and her statement to Dr. Seher, this case [would have never been investigated as a homicide]. You decide what her motive to lie would be. What are the odds of her picking the actual drug that is in Kathy Augustine's urine, from all the drugs in the whole world?"

The prosecutor told jurors that Chaz's account of what happened on the night prior to Kathy's death just didn't make sense. He had testified that he'd told Kathy he wanted a divorce the previous night, and yet the next morning, he was up making coffee for the wife he claimed to love.

"Now you rely on your common sense and you tell me," Barb said. " 'Honey, I want a divorce.' 'You do? OK. Would you please wake me up at 6:45 a.m.?' Come on. The defendant is the only one at the house. Nobody else is there. He has the other drug, [etomidate], that's a companion of succinylcholine in his house. He knows how to get drugs out of the hospital."

The prosecutor told jurors that even if Kathy was the controlling bitch Chaz had described, that didn't mean he had the right to kill her.

"You've heard that Kathy wasn't nice," the prosecutor said. "You heard her painted in very unpleasant terms. And I didn't know her [so] I couldn't help you with that discussion. But let me just say to you [that] even if she wasn't nice, the penalty for [being a] bitch isn't death. You don't get to kill her because she's not nice to you."

Defense attorney David Houston gave an elegant closing argument in which he focused on what he said were blatant flaws in the scientific evidence. He again said that Kim Ramey was the one who brought up succinylcholine and that Chaz had told the jury the truth when he pleaded his innocence.

"If you evaluate Mr. Higgs and his history, there is only one true answer as to who he is and has been," Houston said. "He is a person that has respected the law and has respected the right of other people to be free from violence."

The jury took just seven hours to return with the verdict: guilty of first-degree murder. The Alfanos were inundated with feelings of relief; Kathy, they knew, could finally rest in peace. Phil Jr. talked to his sister in his thoughts in the moments after the verdict was returned.

I told you we'd fight for you, Kathy. He wasn't going to get away with it.

Chaz Higgs hung his head as the jury foreman read the verdict. David Houston, meanwhile, was outraged. He'd been sure that he and Alan Baum had won the trial.

"Stunned," Houston said of his reaction to the verdict. "I couldn't believe it. [The state] lacked a motive, an agency, and cause of death. They lacked any eyewitness testimony. How do you make a case for an injection of succinylcholine with half baked testimony from an FBI toxicologist who admits she did it on the fly? They had nothing to base any sort of criminal homicide on."

There was little time to soak in the verdict after the guilty finding was announced. Judge Kosach ordered the lawyers to immediately head into a sentencing hearing in which the jury would pick from three possible sentences: life without the possibility of parole, fifty years in prison, or life with the possibility of parole after twenty years served.

District attorney Thomas Barb and prosecutor Christopher Hicks began the sentencing hearing by calling anesthesiologist Pamela Russell. Russell told of the impact succinylcholine and its natural parent drug, curare, have on the human body. The testimony reminded jurors of the pure horror Kathy must have experienced after being injected with succinylcholine. Her muscles would have been completely paralyzed, and she would have known that her husband was killing her, but there was nothing she could do about it.

"It was developed in the poison of arrow darts in South

American Indians," Russell told jurors. "[The] muscles go into a massive, taut spasm. We have no other drug in our armamentarium that does that. So, they go into these big spasms that look like probably the worst seizure that you would ever see. And, it lasts approximately thirty to sixty seconds, at which time all those receptors [in the muscles] then have been loaded [with the drug], and the muscles are paralyzed.

"If you think about [it], you're an Amazon Indian and you're trying to get birds, you don't care whether the bird remembers that you killed him," Russell said.

Russell said patients in a medical setting are always sedated before being given succinylcholine, although there have been people who were accidentally administered succinylcholine without any other drugs and survived to tell about it.

"They said, 'I could hear everything, and I could smell everything in the room, and I wanted to scream, but I couldn't open my mouth,'" Russell said. "'I wanted to breathe, but I couldn't.'"

Kathy Augustine's daughter, Dallas, took the witness stand next. She lashed out at Chaz for taking her mother away from her. She made no mention of how she had previously been friendly with Chaz prior to his arrest. Given her words on the stand, it was perfectly clear she now believed that Chaz was a murderer.

"To Chaz, I just want to say that I pity you," she said. "After hearing your indifference toward my mom's suffering, I understand you could never know what it's like to be a human being. My mother was the most influential person in my family. She wasn't perfect, but she worked very hard to truly make something special of her life. She could be here right now. And you, in the span of a morning, took away not only her life, but everything I knew as family. She was my only family. Now, after a year of hell, I will finally be able to move on with my life. And I hope you will spend the rest of your life in a cell. I miss her everyday and will miss her [for] the rest of my life. Nothing will ever take away the pain, but I can find some solace in the fact that you will pay."

Nancy Vinik offered the jury a "definition" of Kathy.

"Daughter, mother, aunt, neighbor, diva, politician, volunteer, the biggest raffle ticket winner ever, airline attendant, teacher, mentor, and my very best friend," Vinik said.

Kay Alfano offered the most heartbreaking testimony of all. Through tears, she summed up her daughter's glorious, roller-coaster ride of an existence.

The jury, however, showed Higgs mercy and sentenced him to life in prison with parole eligibility after twenty years.

Jurors said afterward that they chose that sentence because Chaz appeared to be an intelligent, talented man, and they believed it was possible that he might still be able to contribute to society if they gave him hope that he would one day be released on parole.

Chaz Higgs was ordered housed at the High Desert State Prison for a minimum of twenty years, and it's entirely possible he'll die there.

Chaz Higgs's attorney David Houston continues to protest his client's conviction.

"There is no way I will sit back and let this conviction stand," Houston said. "I'll take every step necessary. This is a bullshit conviction not based on sound evidence. It's not even close. It troubles me greatly, and it's not right."

Others, however, are convinced that justice has been served. Detective Dave Jenkins marvels over the importance of Kim Ramey coming forward. If she hadn't, Jenkins said, Chaz would have gotten away with murder because authorities would never have even known to test for succinylcholine or to preserve Kathy's urine for analysis by the FBI.

"I'm very, very grateful that Kim Ramey came forward," Jenkins said. "I'm not kidding when I say that if not for her, this would have been an unsolved murder. It would have never even been classified as a murder.

"I'm glad justice was done," Jenkins said. "I believe wholeheartedly, from the very core of my being, that Chaz murdered her, and he murdered her in a very cold way. That is a horrible, horrific way to die. You are aware of everything going on around you. You are aware of the sensations, you are aware of the pain, and you are slowly dying, and there is nothing you can do about it. You can't move a finger, and you can't draw a breath. Her last few moments, conscious, must have truly been horrific. After doing this a long time, I still can't fathom the cruelty some people have. To be able to stand there and watch your wife languish.

"No one knows what was said," Jenkins said. "It's only conjecture, but in my mind I think it's likely that he probably talked to her and probably was not very nice. My guess would be it was something to the effect of, 'You fucking bitch. Ha ha.'

"I think he was a bitter, hate-filled man who hated his wife, he wanted to be rid of her, and he thought this was easier than a divorce," the detective said. "It was easier than him being left with no resources. Even though he wouldn't get much, I think he came to hate her, and he wanted the easy way out, and it was just that simple."

25 ... EPILOGUE

I've been to the High Desert State Prison, and I can tell you it's no picnic. The prison is about a forty-minute drive from Vegas, and in 2004, I took a tour of the overcrowded prison with the facility's warden. I was frightened and depressed the whole time I was there. The security is intense. The prison is a modern one, but it is still a prison. It is a world of cold, seemingly endless stretches of gray concrete and bars, and the only people who end up inside the prison's walls are men with long felony rap sheets or individuals convicted of major, violent felony crimes. I actually walked the massive prison yard during my tour, and convicted killers, dope dealers, and rapists milled around us the entire time. I was with the warden and surrounded by an armada of corrections officers, and I was still terrified.

I couldn't wait to leave.

This is the world Chaz Higgs will be living in for the coming two decades. He has a chance at parole, but anyone who has covered the Nevada criminal justice system and its parole hearings knows that it is very difficult to get paroled in the state without first admitting your crime and expressing remorse. Chaz's attorney, David Houston, told me that will never happen.

"If that's the case, I think he'll die in there," Houston said. "He'll never say he did this."

In November 2008, Chaz and his attorneys were granted a full appeals hearing by the Nevada Supreme Court. The entire court wanted to hear about the case, and Houston again made his argument that the science in Chaz's previous trial had not been sound. Prosecutors, of course, disagreed, and so did the State's highest court. Chaz's conviction was upheld.

Kathy's daughter, Dallas, has tried to move on from the murder of her mother and her association with Chaz. In May 2008, Dallas launched a failed bid to win the state assembly seat in District 12 that was once held by her mother. She said on her website she was seeking to create a "New Legacy" for District 12 by addressing crime, graffiti, and vandalism problems.

"I'll work my butt off to make it happen," Dallas said of the New Legacy. "The New Legacy will be our legacy."

She told the *Las Vegas Review-Journal* that her foray into politics was because she wanted to improve the district her mother previously represented.

"The past couple years have been extremely difficult," Dallas said. "I had time to process what happened with my mom and to come back to the district and notice things that need help.

"I never anticipated seeking her old seat, but I think she would be proud of what I am doing," Dallas told the paper.

The Alfano family has no doubt that Chaz Higgs is right

where he should be. Phil Alfano Jr.—a man I've gotten to know well and whom I greatly respect—said he mulls over what Kathy might have accomplished if she'd had a chance to make her comeback. Her longtime political enemy, former Nevada treasurer Brian Krolicki, has since been indicted in Las Vegas on charges of mismanaging an education fund that Kathy had supposedly been asking questions about prior to her death. Krolicki has pleaded not guilty and has vowed to clear his name.

Phil Jr. promises that if he is alive when Chaz comes up for parole, he'll be at the hearing. If he's no longer living, then his daughters will be there.

There is no way, he said, that Chaz should ever be released.

"He's got his mortal body, and his eternal soul is now on the line," Phil Jr. said.

Crying, Phil Jr. told me that the rumors and insinuations that Kathy could have somehow been involved in the death of her third husband, Chuck Augustine, were almost too painful to endure. He knew Kathy, and he knew her well.

"No way," Phil Jr. said.

His sister, he said, deserved better than to be portrayed publicly as a mean-spirited woman who cared only about her political ambitions. Phil Jr. knows that just wasn't the case.

"Seeing Chaz convicted took away some of the anger and the hurt," Phil said through tears. "It's not going to bring her back or change things.

"I want people to know Kathy wasn't just a politician who gave sound bites," he said. "She was a caring human being. She could be demanding, and she could be tough, but I wouldn't still be torn up two years later if she wasn't a special person."

ABOUT THE AUTHOR

Glenn Puit is an investigative journalist and policy specialist for the Michigan Land Use Institute in Traverse City, Michigan. He performs investigative journalism that seeks to protect Michigan's natural environment.

Puit was born and raised in Lansing, in Upstate New York, and he graduated from Indiana State University with a bachelor's degree in journalism communications. He covered the Las Vegas criminal justice system and violent crime in Las Vegas for twelve years in his work as an investigative reporter for the *Las Vegas Review-Journal* newspaper. While at the *Florence Morning News* newspaper in Florence, South Carolina, Puit was the first reporter in the nation to document the identity of John Doe number two in the Oklahoma City bombing. The accomplishment was featured in *American Journalism Review.*

His first book, *Witch: The True Story of Las Vegas's Most Notorious Female Killer*, about the bizarre and gruesome case of matriarchal Vegas killer Brookey Lee West, was released by Berkley to national acclaim in 2005. The book was recently the subject of a literary section cover feature story in the *San Jose Mercury News*. His second book, *Fire in the Desert* (Stephens Press, 2007), is considered the evidentiary handbook for the Las Vegas homicide case of national bodybuilder Craig Titus and his fitness champion wife, Kelly Ryan. His third book, *Father of the Year* (Berkley, 2008), earned Puit recognition as perhaps the nation's most compelling true crime author.

Puit lives in northern Michigan. He communicates regularly with readers on his website, www.kingoftruecrime .com, and he also maintains pages on Facebook and MySpace.